MICROSOFT

# Publisher 2000

## Complete Concepts and Techniques

MICROSOFT

# Publisher 2000

## Complete Concepts and Techniques

**Gary B. Shelly**
**Thomas J. Cashman**
**Joy L. Starks**

**COURSE TECHNOLOGY**
**ONE MAIN STREET**
**CAMBRIDGE MA 02142**

Thomson Learning™

SHELLY
CASHMAN
SERIES®

Australia • Canada • Denmark • Japan • Mexico • New Zealand • Philippines
Puerto Rico • Singapore • South Africa • Spain • United Kingdom • United States

**MICROSOFT**

# Publisher 2000

## Complete Concepts and Techniques

# C O N T E N T S

## ● PROJECT 1

### CREATING AND EDITING A PUBLICATION

| | |
|---|---|
| Objectives | PUB 1.3 |
| What Is Microsoft Publisher 2000? | PUB 1.6 |
| Project One — Advertising Flyer with Tear-Offs | PUB 1.8 |
| Starting Publisher | PUB 1.9 |
| Using Publisher's Flyer Wizard to Create an Advertising Flyer | PUB 1.10 |
| The Publisher Window | PUB 1.14 |
| The Workspace | PUB 1.14 |
| Menu Bar, Standard Toolbar, Formatting Toolbar, and Status Bar | PUB 1.15 |
| Editing Text in a Publication | PUB 1.17 |
| Zooming to Facilitate Editing | PUB 1.20 |
| Adding Text | PUB 1.22 |
| Editing Tear-Offs | PUB 1.23 |
| Saving a Publication | PUB 1.26 |
| Moving and Resizing Objects | PUB 1.29 |
| Moving a Grouped Object Using Snap to Guides | PUB 1.29 |
| Moving and Resizing the Graphic | PUB 1.31 |
| Enhancing a Publication with Formatting and Graphics | PUB 1.33 |
| Editing a Graphic | PUB 1.33 |
| Formatting a Publication | PUB 1.36 |
| Saving an Existing Publication with the Same File Name | PUB 1.39 |
| Printing a Publication | PUB 1.40 |
| Quitting Publisher | PUB 1.41 |
| Opening a Publication | PUB 1.42 |
| Modifying a Publication | PUB 1.45 |
| Types of Changes Made to Publications | PUB 1.45 |
| Adding an Attention Getter to a Publication | PUB 1.46 |
| Deleting an Object from a Publication | PUB 1.49 |
| Creating a Web Site from a Publication | PUB 1.50 |
| Closing the Entire Publication | PUB 1.54 |
| Publisher Help System | PUB 1.55 |
| Using the Office Assistant | PUB 1.55 |
| Quitting Publisher | PUB 1.57 |
| Project Summary | PUB 1.58 |
| What you Should Know | PUB 1.58 |
| Apply Your Knowledge | PUB 1.59 |
| In the Lab | PUB 1.60 |
| Cases and Places | PUB 1.63 |

## ● PROJECT 2

### DESIGNING A NEWSLETTER

| | |
|---|---|
| Objectives | PUB 2.1 |
| Introduction | PUB 2.4 |
| The Newsletter Medium | PUB 2.4 |
| Project Two — Newsletter | PUB 2.5 |
| Starting Publisher | PUB 2.7 |
| Using a Publisher Wizard in the Design Process | PUB 2.7 |
| Creating a Newsletter Template Using a Wizard | PUB 2.8 |
| Editing the Newsletter Template | PUB 2.11 |
| Pagination | PUB 2.11 |
| Editing the Masthead | PUB 2.13 |
| Editing Techniques | PUB 2.14 |
| Importing Files | PUB 2.17 |
| Replacing Default Text Using an Imported File | PUB 2.17 |
| Importing Text for the Secondary Article | PUB 2.20 |
| Importing Text on the Back Page | PUB 2.21 |
| Saving an Intermediate Copy of the Publication | PUB 2.22 |
| Working with Personal Information Sets | PUB 2.23 |
| Editing the Personal Information Components | PUB 2.23 |
| Editing the Design Set | PUB 2.25 |
| Creating Columns within a Text Frame | PUB 2.25 |
| Editing the Attention Getter | PUB 2.28 |
| Deleting the Logo | PUB 2.30 |
| Using Graphics in a Publication | PUB 2.31 |
| Deleting a Graphic | PUB 2.32 |
| Finding a Graphic | PUB 2.32 |
| Adding a Pull Quote | PUB 2.36 |
| Editing the Sidebar | PUB 2.39 |
| Replacing the Graphic | PUB 2.40 |
| Inserting a Line with Arrows | PUB 2.41 |
| WordArt | PUB 2.44 |
| Inserting a WordArt Object | PUB 2.44 |
| Adding Page Numbers to the Background | PUB 2.46 |
| Checking a Publication for Errors | PUB 2.52 |
| Checking the Newsletter for Spelling and Grammar Errors | PUB 2.52 |
| Checking the Newsletter for Design Errors | PUB 2.55 |
| Printing a Two-sided Page | PUB 2.57 |
| Project Summary | PUB 2.59 |
| What You Should Know | PUB 2.59 |
| Apply Your Knowledge | PUB 2.60 |
| In the Lab | PUB 2.61 |
| Cases and Places | PUB 2.64 |

v

## PROJECT 3

### PREPARING A TRI-FOLD BROCHURE FOR OUTSIDE PRINTING

| | |
|---|---|
| **Objectives** | **PUB 3.1** |
| **Introduction** | **PUB 3.4** |
| **Project Three — Tri-Fold Brochure** | **PUB 3.4** |
| The Brochure Medium | PUB 3.6 |
| Starting Publisher | PUB 3.7 |
| **Using a Brochure Wizard to Create a Tri-Fold Brochure** | **PUB 3.7** |
| **Editing Text in the Brochure** | **PUB 3.9** |
| **Deleting Objects** | **PUB 3.13** |
| **Using Photographs and Images in a Brochure** | **PUB 3.14** |
| Inserting a Photograph from a File | PUB 3.15 |
| Inserting Clip Art Using a Keyword Search | PUB 3.17 |
| Saving the Brochure | PUB 3.19 |
| **Creating a Logo from Scratch** | **PUB 3.20** |
| Creating a Shape for the Logo | PUB 3.20 |
| Creating a Symbol Text Frame | PUB 3.22 |
| Creating a Symbol Text Frame Using the Copy Button | PUB 3.27 |
| Grouping and Positioning the Logo Objects | PUB 3.30 |
| **Editing the Front Panel** | **PUB 3.33** |
| Creating a Mirrored Copy of the Heading | PUB 3.33 |
| Editing the Font Color | PUB 3.35 |
| **Brochure Forms** | **PUB 3.37** |
| Editing the Sign-Up Form | PUB 3.37 |
| **Creating a Calendar Using the Design Gallery** | **PUB 3.39** |
| Using a Calendar in Brochures | PUB 3.39 |
| Repositioning Objects to Prevent Overlapping the Calendar | PUB 3.42 |
| Editing the Calendar | PUB 3.43 |
| Checking Spelling and Saving Again | PUB 3.46 |
| **Outside Printing** | **PUB 3.46** |
| Previewing the Brochure Before Printing | PUB 3.46 |
| Printing Considerations | PUB 3.48 |
| Paper Considerations | PUB 3.48 |
| Color Considerations | PUB 3.49 |
| Choosing a Commercial Printing Tool | PUB 3.49 |
| **Packaging the Publication for the Printing Service** | **PUB 3.51** |
| Using the Pack and Go Wizard | PUB 3.51 |
| Using PostScript Files | PUB 3.54 |
| **Working with Multiple Publications** | **PUB 3.54** |
| Opening Multiple Sessions of Publisher | PUB 3.55 |
| Copying Objects between Publications | PUB 3.56 |
| **Project Summary** | **PUB 3.58** |
| **What You Should Know** | **PUB 3.58** |
| **Apply Your Knowledge** | **PUB 3.59** |
| **In the Lab** | **PUB 3.61** |
| **Cases and Places** | **PUB 3.64** |

## WEB FEATURE

### CREATING WEB SITES WITH PUBLISHER 2000

| | |
|---|---|
| **Introduction** | **PUBW 1.1** |
| **Brochure to Web Site Conversion** | **PUBW 1.3** |
| **Web Properties** | **PUBW 1.5** |
| Editing Web Properties | PUBW 1.5 |
| **Editing Web Objects** | **PUBW 1.6** |
| Editing Web Site Text Frames | PUBW 1.6 |
| Inserting Extra Content | PUBW 1.8 |
| Animation | PUBW 1.9 |
| Using Hyperlinks and Command Buttons | PUBW 1.10 |
| **Viewing a Web Site** | **PUBW 1.13** |
| **Saving a Web Site** | **PUBW 1.13** |
| Saving the Publication | PUBW 1.15 |
| **Web Feature Summary** | **PUBW 1.15** |
| **What You Should Know** | **PUBW 1.15** |
| **In the Lab** | **PUBW 1.16** |

## PROJECT 4

### PERSONALIZING AND CUSTOMIZING A PUBLICATION WITH INFORMATION SETS

| | |
|---|---|
| **Objectives** | **PUB 4.1** |
| **Introduction** | **PUB 4.4** |
| **Project Four — Creating Letterhead, Business Cards, and Envelopes** | **PUB 4.4** |
| **Setting Up a Blank Publication Page** | **PUB 4.6** |
| Starting Publisher with a Blank Publication | PUB 4.6 |
| Setting Publication Margins Using Layout and Ruler Guides | PUB 4.7 |
| **Personal Information Sets** | **PUB 4.9** |
| Editing the Personal Information Set | PUB 4.9 |
| **Creating a Company Letterhead** | **PUB 4.12** |
| The Letterhead Background | PUB 4.12 |
| Inserting and Formatting Personal Information Components | PUB 4.16 |
| The CopyCat Creations Logo | PUB 4.20 |
| To Finish Editing the Logo | PUB 4.22 |
| **Using the Measurements Toolbar** | **PUB 4.23** |
| Character Spacing Techniques | PUB 4.24 |
| **Using Styles** | **PUB 4.27** |
| Creating a New Style | PUB 4.28 |
| Saving and Printing the Letterhead | PUB 4.29 |
| **Business Cards** | **PUB 4.30** |
| The Business Card Wizard | PUB 4.30 |
| Editing the Business Card | PUB 4.31 |
| Importing Text Styles | PUB 4.35 |
| Saving and Printing the Business Card | PUB 4.38 |
| **Coupons** | **PUB 4.38** |
| Creating a Custom Size Publication | PUB 4.38 |
| Final Modifications of the Coupon | PUB 4.42 |
| Saving and Printing the Coupon | PUB 4.43 |

| | |
|---|---|
| **Envelopes** | **PUB 4.43** |
| The Envelope Wizard | PUB 4.43 |
| **Using the Mail Merge Feature** | **PUB 4.45** |
| Creating a Publisher Address List | PUB 4.45 |
| Creating a Main Publication Using | |
| a Label Wizard | PUB 4.49 |
| Inserting Field Codes | PUB 4.50 |
| Merging and Printing the Main Publication | |
| with the Address List | PUB 4.54 |
| **Project Summary** | **PUB 4.56** |
| **What You Should Know** | **PUB 4.56** |
| **Apply Your Knowledge** | **PUB 4.57** |
| **In the Lab** | **PUB 4.58** |
| **Cases and Places** | **PUB 4.61** |

### ● PROJECT 5

### CREATING BUSINESS FORMS AND TABLES

| | |
|---|---|
| **Objectives** | **PUB 5.1** |
| **Introduction** | **PUB 5.4** |
| **Project Five — Creating Business Forms** | |
| **and Tables** | **PUB 5.4** |
| Starting Publisher | PUB 5.6 |
| **Creating an Invoice Template** | **PUB 5.6** |
| Creating an Invoice Template | PUB 5.6 |
| **Formatting the Invoice Template** | **PUB 5.11** |
| Using the Nudge Command | PUB 5.11 |
| Using a Drop Cap | PUB 5.13 |
| Working with Tabs and Markers | PUB 5.14 |
| Inserting the System Date | PUB 5.17 |
| Saving and Printing the Invoice Template | PUB 5.19 |
| **Creating a Fax Cover** | **PUB 5.19** |
| Creating a Fax Cover Using the Business | |
| Form Wizard and Pointer Tool | PUB 5.19 |
| Final Modifications of the Fax Cover | PUB 5.21 |
| **Using Tables** | **PUB 5.22** |
| Creating a Work Schedule Table | PUB 5.22 |
| Merging Cells and Inserting a Cell Diagonal | PUB 5.24 |
| Entering Data into the Table | PUB 5.26 |
| Using the Fill Command | PUB 5.27 |
| Inserting a Column | PUB 5.30 |
| Saving the Table | PUB 5.32 |
| **Attaching a Publication to an E-mail** | |
| **Message** | **PUB 5.33** |
| Sending a Publisher File via E-mail | PUB 5.33 |
| **Web Pages with Electronic Forms** | **PUB 5.35** |
| **Creating a Web Page from Scratch** | **PUB 5.36** |
| Inserting a Web Masthead | PUB 5.36 |
| Inserting the Logo and Instruction Text Frames | PUB 5.38 |
| **Hot Spots** | **PUB 5.39** |
| Creating a Hot Spot | PUB 5.40 |
| **Using Form Controls** | **PUB 5.41** |
| Inserting Form Controls on the Web | |
| Reorder Form | PUB 5.42 |

| | |
|---|---|
| Inserting Command Buttons on the Web | |
| Reorder Form | PUB 5.49 |
| **Aligning Objects** | **PUB 5.49** |
| Aligning Objects in the Web Reorder Form | PUB 5.50 |
| **Checking and Saving the Publication** | **PUB 5.53** |
| Running the Design Checker | PUB 5.53 |
| Saving the Web Files | PUB 5.54 |
| Saving and Printing the Publication | PUB 5.54 |
| **Project Summary** | **PUB 5.55** |
| **What You Should Know** | **PUB 5.55** |
| **Apply Your Knowledge** | **PUB 5.56** |
| **In the Lab** | **PUB 5.57** |
| **Cases and Places** | **PUB 5.61** |

### ● INTEGRATION FEATURE

### LINKING A PUBLISHER PUBLICATION TO AN EXCEL WORKSHEET

| | |
|---|---|
| **Introduction** | **PUBI 1.1** |
| **Starting Word and Excel** | **PUBI 1.3** |
| **Linking an Excel Worksheet** | |
| **to a Publisher Publication** | **PUBI 1.4** |
| **Printing and Saving the Publisher Publication** | |
| **with the Linked Worksheet** | **PUBI 1.7** |
| **Editing the Linked Worksheet** | **PUBI 1.8** |
| **Integration Feature Summary** | **PUBI 1.10** |
| **What You Should Know** | **PUBI 1.10** |
| **In the Lab** | **PUBI 1.11** |

### ● APPENDIX A

### MICROSOFT PUBLISHER 2000 HELP SYSTEM

| | |
|---|---|
| | PUB A.1 |
| **Using the Publisher Help System** | **PUB A.1** |
| **The Office Assistant** | **PUB A.2** |
| Showing and Hiding the Office Assistant | PUB A.3 |
| Turning the Office Assistant On and Off | PUB A.3 |
| Using the Office Assistant | PUB A.4 |
| **The Publisher Help Window** | **PUB A.5** |
| Using the Contents Sheet | PUB A.6 |
| Using the Answer Wizard Sheet | PUB A.6 |
| Using the Index Sheet | PUB A.7 |
| **Question Mark Button and the** | |
| **What's This? Button** | **PUB A.8** |
| Question Mark Button | PUB A.8 |
| What's This? Button | PUB A.8 |
| **Microsoft Publisher Web Site Command** | **PUB A.9** |
| **Other Help Commands** | **PUB A.9** |
| Print Troubleshooter Command | PUB A.9 |
| Publisher Tutorials Command | PUB A.10 |
| Detect and Repair Command | PUB A.10 |
| About Microsoft Publisher Command | PUB A.10 |
| **Use Help** | **PUB A.11** |

## ● APPENDIX B

### PUBLISHING OFFICE WEB PAGES TO A WEB SERVER
PUB B.1

## ● APPENDIX C

### RESETTING THE PUBLISHER MENUS AND WIZARDS
PUB C.1

## ● APPENDIX D

### MICROSOFT OFFICE USER SPECIALIST CERTIFICATION PROGRAM
PUB D.1

Why Should You Get Certified?   PUB D.1
The MOUS Exams   PUB D.1
How Can You Prepare for the MOUS Exams?   PUB D.2
How to Find an Authorized Testing Center   PUB D.2
Shelly Cashman Series MOUS Web Page   PUB D.2

Index   I.1

# Preface

The Shelly Cashman Series® offers the finest textbooks in computer education. In our Publisher 2000 books, you will find an educationally sound and easy-to-follow pedagogy that combines a step-by-step approach with corresponding screens. All projects and exercises in this book are designed to take full advantage of the Publisher 2000 enhancements. The popular Other Ways and More About features offer in-depth knowledge of Publisher 2000. The project openers provide a fascinating perspective of the subject covered in the project. The project material is developed carefully to ensure that students will see the importance of learning Publisher 2000 applications for future course work.

## Objectives of This Textbook

*Microsoft Publisher 2000: Complete Concepts and Techniques* is intended for a two-unit course that covers Microsoft Publisher 2000 and desktop publishing. No experience with a computer is assumed, and no mathematics beyond the high school freshman level is required. The objectives of this book are:

- To teach the fundamentals of Microsoft Publisher 2000
- To expose students to practical examples of the computer as a useful desktop publishing tool
- To acquaint students with the proper procedures to create professional quality publications suitable for course work, professional purposes, and personal use
- To develop an exercise-oriented approach that allows learning by example
- To encourage independent study, and help those who are working alone

## The Shelly Cashman Approach

Features of the Shelly Cashman Series Publisher 2000 books include:

- **Project Orientation:** Each project in the book presents a practical problem and complete solution in an easy-to-understand approach.
- **Screen-by-Screen, Step-by-Step Instructions:** Each of the tasks required to complete a project is shown using a step-by-step, screen-by-screen approach. The screens are shown in full color.
- **Thoroughly Tested Projects:** Every screen in the book is correct because it is produced by the author only after performing a step, resulting in unprecedented quality.
- **Other Ways Boxes and Quick Reference Summary:** Publisher 2000 provides a variety of ways to carry out a given task. The Other Ways boxes displayed at the end of most of the step-by-step sequences specify the other ways to do the task completed in the steps. Thus, the steps and the Other Ways box make a comprehensive reference unit. A Quick Reference Summary is available on the Web that summarizes the way specific tasks can be completed.
- **More About Feature:** These marginal annotations provide background information that complements the topics covered, adding depth and perspective.

○ Integration of the World Wide Web: The World Wide Web is integrated into the Publisher 2000 learning experience by (1) More Abouts that send students to Web sites for up-to-date information and alternative approaches to tasks; (2) a Publisher 2000 Quick Reference Summary Web page that summarizes the ways to complete tasks (mouse, menu, shortcut menu, and keyboard); and (3) project reinforcement Web pages in the form of true/false, multiple choice, and short answer questions, and other types of student activities.

*Other Ways*

1. Double-click Horizontal Ruler
2. Right-click text frame, point to Change Text on shortcut menu, click Tabs on Change Text submenu
3. On Format menu click Tabs

**More About**

**Coupons on the Web**

Both large and small companies across the world are publishing coupons on the Web. Customers can download and print the coupons, complete with Universal Product Codes (UPC) on their desktop printers. For more information and to see some examples, visit the Publisher 2000 More About Web page (www.scsite.com/pub2000/more.htm) and click Coupons.

# Organization of This Textbook

*Microsoft Publisher 2000: Complete Concepts and Techniques* provides detailed instruction on how to use Publisher 2000. The material is divided into five projects, a Web Feature, an Integration Feature, and four appendices.

**Project 1 — Creating and Editing a Publication** In Project 1, students are introduced to Publisher terminology and the Publisher screen by preparing an advertising flyer with tear-offs. Topics include starting and quitting Publisher; using a wizard; editing text and repeated design elements; using Publisher's zoom features; moving and resizing graphics; formatting a publication; printing a publication; saving and opening a publication; modifying a publication; adding an attention getter; deleting objects; and creating a Web page from the publication.

**Project 2 — Designing a Newsletter** In Project 2, students create a newsletter using a Publisher Newsletter Wizard. Topics include identifying the advantages of the newsletter medium and the steps in the design process; editing a newsletter template; using the Page Navigation control and pagination; editing a masthead; importing text files; editing personal information components and design sets; creating columns; inserting attention getters, graphics, sidebars, and pull quotes; editing lines and arrows; using WordArt; and moving between foreground and background elements. Finally, students check the publication for spelling and design errors and print it double-sided.

**Project 3 — Preparing a Tri-Fold Brochure for Outside Printing** In Project 3, students use a Brochure Wizard to create a brochure with three panels displaying text, shapes, graphics, a calendar, and a sign-up form. Topics include the use of graphics versus images; inserting a photograph from a file; creating a composite logo using custom shapes; inserting symbols and calendars; grouping, rotating, and overlapping objects; positioning objects precisely; preparing the publication for outside printing by choosing appropriate printing services, paper, and color libraries; and opening multiple sessions of Publisher in order to facilitate copying objects from the brochure to a reply postcard. This project also illustrates Publisher's Pack and Go feature.

**Web Feature — Creating Web Sites with Publisher 2000** In the Web Feature, students are introduced to creating Web sites. Topics include converting the tri-fold brochure created in Project 3 into a four-page Web site; editing Web properties for search engine tags; including background music and animation; editing the navigation bar; inserting Web objects; personalizing the Web site with hyperlinks; editing Web submit buttons; and viewing and saving the Web site.

**Project 4 — Personalizing and Customizing a Publication with Information Sets** In Project 4, students use information sets to create a letterhead and then apply the fields and design scheme to a business card, an envelope, and a coupon. Topics include using layout and ruler guides to assist with design and margins; editing information sets and inserting the components; creating a letterhead with background effects such as tints, shades, patterns, and gradients; inserting and editing a logo; using the Measurements toolbar to format character spacing; and creating, editing, and importing styles. Finally, students create an address list and learn how to merge it using field codes in a main publication.

Project 5 — Creating Business Forms and Tables In Project 5, students learn how to use Publisher to create common business forms including an invoice, a fax cover, a work schedule, and an electronic order form. Topics include creating an invoice template; using the Pointer Tool, Nudge command, and Align command to edit business form components; formatting drop caps, tabs, and margins; inserting a system date; creating and navigating in a table, inserting merged cells and cell diagonals; using the Fill command to insert data; inserting rows and columns in a table; and attaching a publication to an e-mail message. Finally, students create an electronic form for e-commerce including a Web masthead, hot spot, links, and data entry form controls.

Integration Feature — Linking a Publisher Publication to an Excel Worksheet In the Integration Feature, students are introduced to linking a publication to an Excel worksheet. Topics include a discussion of the differences among copying and pasting, copying and embedding, and copying and linking; opening multiple applications; printing and saving a publication with a linked worksheet; and editing a linked worksheet within a publication.

## Appendices

Appendix A presents a detailed step-by-step introduction to the Microsoft Publisher Help system. Students learn how to use the Office Assistant and the Contents, Answer Wizard, and Index sheets in the Publisher Help window. Appendix B describes how to publish Office Web pages to a Web server. Appendix C shows students how to reset the Publisher menus and Wizards. Appendix D introduces students to the Microsoft Office User Specialist (MOUS) Certification program.

# End-of-Project Student Activities

A notable strength of the Shelly Cashman Series Publisher 2000 books is the extensive student activities at the end of each project. Well-structured student activities can make the difference between students merely participating in a class and students retaining the information they learn. The activities in the Shelly Cashman Series Publisher 2000 books include the following.

- What You Should Know A listing of the tasks completed within a project together with the pages where the step-by-step, screen-by-screen explanations appear. This section provides a perfect study review for students.

- Project Reinforcement on the Web Every Publisher project has a Web page accessible from www.scsite.com/off2000/reinforce.htm. The Web page includes true/false, multiple choice, and short answer questions, and additional project-related reinforcement activities that will help students gain confidence in their Publisher 2000 abilities.

- Apply Your Knowledge This exercise requires students to open and manipulate a file on the Data Disk for the Publisher 2000 books. To obtain a copy of the Data Disk, follow the instructions on the inside back cover of this textbook.

- In the Lab Three in-depth assignments per project require students to apply the knowledge gained in the project to solve problems on a computer.

- Cases and Places Up to seven unique case studies that require students to apply their knowledge to real-world situations.

# Shelly Cashman Series Teaching Tools

A comprehensive set of Teaching Tools accompanies this textbook in the form of a CD-ROM. The CD-ROM includes an Instructor's Manual and teaching and testing aids. The CD-ROM (ISBN 0-7895-5624-3) is available through your Course Technology representative or by calling one of the following telephone numbers: Colleges and Universities, 1-800-648-7450; High Schools, 1-800-824-5179; Career Colleges, 1-800-477-3692; Corporations and Government Agencies, 1-800-340-7450; and Canada, 1-800-268-3692. The contents of the CD-ROM are listed below.

- **Instructor's Manual** The Instructor's Manual is made up of Microsoft Word files. The files include lecture notes, solutions to laboratory assignments, and a large test bank. The files allow you to modify the lecture notes or generate quizzes and exams from the test bank using your own word processing software. Where appropriate, solutions to laboratory assignments are embedded as icons in the files. When an icon appears, double-click it and the application will start and the solution will display on the screen. The Instructor's Manual includes the following for each project: project objectives; project overview; detailed lesson plans with page number references; teacher notes and activities; answers to the end-of-project exercises; test bank of 110 questions for every project (25 multiple-choice, 50 true/false, and 35 fill-in-the-blank) with page number references; and transparency references. The transparencies are available through the Figures in the Book. The test bank questions are numbered the same as in Course Test Manager. Thus, you can print a copy of the project test bank and use the printout to select your questions in Course Test Manager.

- **Figures in the Book** Figures and tables in the textbook are available in Figures in the Book.

- **Course Test Manager** Course Test Manager is a powerful testing and assessment package that enables instructors to create and print tests from the large test bank. Instructors with access to a networked computer lab (LAN) can administer, grade, and track tests online. Students also can take online practice tests, which generate customized study guides.

- **Course Syllabus** Any instructor who has been assigned a course at the last minute knows how difficult it is to come up with a course syllabus. For this reason, sample syllabi are included for each of the Office 2000 products that can be customized easily to a course.

- **Lecture Success System** Lecture Success System files are for use with the application software, a personal computer, and a projection device to explain and illustrate the step-by-step, screen-by-screen development of a project in the textbook without entering large amounts of data.

- **Instructor's Lab Solutions** Solutions and required files for all the In the Lab assignments at the end of each project are available.

- **Project Reinforcement** True/false, multiple choice, and short answer questions help students gain confidence in their Publisher 2000 abilities.

- **Student Files** All the files that are required by students to complete the Apply Your Knowledge exercises are included.

- **Interactive Labs** Eighteen hands-on interactive labs that take students from ten to fifteen minutes each to step through help solidify and reinforce mouse and keyboard usage and computer concepts. Student assessment is available.

# Shelly Cashman Online

Shelly Cashman Online is a World Wide Web service available to instructors and students of computer education. Visit Shelly Cashman Online at www.scseries.com. Shelly Cashman Online is divided into four areas:

- Series Information History of the Shelly Cashman Series, technology news, and more
- Teaching Resources Product catalog, Teaching Tools, companion products, and electronic aids
- Community Pressbox, Summer Institute, and more
- Student Resources Data Disk downloads, careers, and links to the Shelly Cashman Series instructional Web sites

# Acknowledgments

The Shelly Cashman Series would not be the leading computer education series without the contributions of outstanding publishing professionals. First, and foremost, among them is Becky Herrington, director of production and designer. She is the heart and soul of the Shelly Cashman Series, and it is only through her leadership, dedication, and tireless efforts that superior products are made possible. Becky created and produced the award-winning Windows series of books.

Under Becky's direction, the following individuals made significant contributions to these books: Doug Cowley, production manager; Ginny Harvey, series specialist and developmental editor; Ken Russo, senior Web designer; Mike Bodnar, associate production manager; Mark Norton, Web designer; Stephanie Nance, graphic artist and cover designer; Meena Mohtadi, production editor; Marlo Mitchem, Chris Schneider, and Hector Arvizu, graphic artists; Jeanne Black and Betty Hopkins, Quark experts; Nancy Lamm, proofreader; Lyn Markowicz and Adrienne Delismon, technical reviewers; Cristina Haley, indexer; Sarah Evertson of Image Quest, photo researcher; and Susan Sebok and Ginny Harvey, contributing writers.

Special thanks go to Richard Keaveny, managing editor; Jim Quasney, series consultant; Lora Wade, product manager; Meagan Walsh, associate product manager; Francis Schurgot, Web product manager; Scott Wiseman, online developer; Rajika Gupta, marketing manager; and Erin Bennett, editorial assistant.

Gary B. Shelly
Thomas J. Cashman
Joy L. Starks

# Shelly Cashman Series – Traditionally Bound Textbooks

The Shelly Cashman Series presents the following computer subjects in a variety of traditionally bound textbooks. For more information, see your Course Technology representative or call 1-800-648-7450. For Shelly Cashman Series information, visit Shelly Cashman Online at **www.scseries.com**

| COMPUTERS | |
|---|---|
| Computers | Discovering Computers 2000: Concepts for a Connected World, Web and CNN Enhanced |
| | Discovering Computers 2000: Concepts for a Connected World, Web and CNN Enhanced Brief Edition |
| | Teachers Discovering Computers: A Link to the Future, Web and CNN Enhanced |
| | Discovering Computers 98: A Link to the Future, World Wide Web Enhanced |
| | Discovering Computers 98: A Link to the Future, World Wide Web Enhanced Brief Edition |
| | Exploring Computers: A Record of Discovery 3e with CD-ROM |
| | Study Guide for Discovering Computers 2000: Concepts for a Connected World, Web and CNN Enhanced |
| | Essential Introduction to Computers 3e (32-page) |

| WINDOWS APPLICATIONS | |
|---|---|
| Microsoft Office | Microsoft Office 2000: Essential Concepts and Techniques (5 projects) |
| | Microsoft Office 2000: Brief Concepts and Techniques (9 projects) |
| | Microsoft Office 2000: Introductory Concepts and Techniques (15 projects) |
| | Microsoft Office 2000: Advanced Concepts and Techniques (11 projects) |
| | Microsoft Office 2000: Post Advanced Concepts and Techniques (11 projects) |
| | Microsoft Office 97: Introductory Concepts and Techniques, Brief Edition (6 projects) |
| | Microsoft Office 97: Introductory Concepts and Techniques, Essentials Edition (10 projects) |
| | Microsoft Office 97: Introductory Concepts and Techniques, Enhanced Edition (15 projects) |
| | Microsoft Office 97: Advanced Concepts and Techniques |
| Microsoft Works | Microsoft Works 4.5[1] • Microsoft Works 3.0[1] |
| Windows | Microsoft Windows 98: Essential Concepts and Techniques (2 projects) |
| | Microsoft Windows 98: Introductory Concepts and Techniques (3 projects) |
| | Microsoft Windows 98: Introductory Concepts and Techniques Web Style Edition (3 projects) |
| | Microsoft Windows 98: Complete Concepts and Techniques (6 projects) |
| | Microsoft Windows 98: Comprehensive Concepts and Techniques (9 projects) |
| | Introduction to Microsoft Windows NT Workstation 4 |
| | Microsoft Windows 95: Introductory Concepts and Techniques (2 projects) |
| | Introduction to Microsoft Windows 95 (3 projects) |
| | Microsoft Windows 95: Complete Concepts and Techniques |
| Word Processing | Microsoft Word 2000[2] • Microsoft Word 97[1] • Microsoft Word 7[1] |
| | Corel WordPerfect 8 • Corel WordPerfect 7 • WordPerfect 6.1[1] |
| Spreadsheets | Microsoft Excel 2000[2] • Microsoft Excel 97[1] • Microsoft Excel 7[1] • Microsoft Excel 5[1] • Lotus 1-2-3 97[1] |
| Database | Microsoft Access 2000[2] • Microsoft Access 97[1] • Microsoft Access 7[1] |
| Presentation Graphics | Microsoft PowerPoint 2000[2] • Microsoft PowerPoint 97[1] • Microsoft PowerPoint 7[1] |
| Desktop Publishing | Microsoft Publisher 2000[1] |

| PROGRAMMING | |
|---|---|
| Programming | Microsoft Visual Basic 6: Complete Concepts and Techniques[1] |
| | Microsoft Visual Basic 5: Complete Concepts and Techniques[1] |
| | QBasic • QBasic: An Introduction to Programming • Microsoft BASIC |
| | Structured COBOL Programming |

| INTERNET | |
|---|---|
| Browser | Microsoft Internet Explorer 5: An Introduction • Microsoft Internet Explorer 4: An Introduction |
| | Netscape Navigator 4: An Introduction |
| Web Page Creation | HTML: Complete Concepts and Techniques[1] • Microsoft FrontPage 2000: Complete Concepts and Techniques[1] • Microsoft FrontPage 98: Complete Concepts and Techniques[1] • Netscape Composer • JavaScript: Complete Concepts and Techniques[1] |

| SYSTEMS ANALYSIS | |
|---|---|
| Systems Analysis | Systems Analysis and Design, Third Edition |

| DATA COMMUNICATIONS | |
|---|---|
| Data Communications | Business Data Communications: Introductory Concepts and Techniques, Second Edition |

[1]Also available as an Introductory Edition, which is a shortened version of the complete book

[2]Also available as an Introductory Edition, which is a shortened version of the complete book and also as a Comprehensive Edition, which is an extended version of the complete book

# Shelly Cashman Series – Custom Edition® Program

If you do not find a Shelly Cashman Series traditionally bound textbook to fit your needs, the Shelly Cashman Series unique **Custom Edition** program allows you to choose from a number of options and create a textbook perfectly suited to your course. Features of the **Custom Edition** program are:

- Textbooks that match the content of your course

- Windows- and DOS-based materials for the latest versions of personal computer applications software

- Shelly Cashman Series quality, with the same full-color materials and Shelly Cashman Series pedagogy found in the traditionally bound books

- Affordable pricing so your students receive the **Custom Edition** at a cost similar to that of traditionally bound books

The table on the right summarizes the available materials.

For more information, see your Course Technology representative or call one of the following telephone numbers: Colleges and Universities, 1-800-648-7450; High Schools, 1-800-824-5179; Career Colleges, 1-800-477-3692; Corporations and Government Agencies, 1-800-340-7450; and Canada, 1-800-268-3692.

For Shelly Cashman Series information, visit Shelly Cashman Online at **www.scseries.com**

| | COMPUTERS |
|---|---|
| Computers | Discovering Computers 2000: Concepts for a Connected World, Web and CNN Enhanced |
| | Discovering Computers 2000: Concepts for a Connected World, Web and CNN Enhanced Brief Edition |
| | Discovering Computers 98: A Link to the Future, World Wide Web Enhanced |
| | Discovering Computers 98: A Link to the Future, World Wide Web Enhanced Brief Edition |
| | A Record of Discovery for Exploring Computers 3e (available with CD-ROM) |
| | Study Guide for Discovering Computers 2000: Concepts for a Connected World, Web and CNN Enhanced |
| | Essential Introduction to Computers 3e (32-page) |
| | **OPERATING SYSTEMS** |
| Windows | Microsoft Windows 98: Essential Concepts and Techniques (2 projects) |
| | Microsoft Windows 98: Introductory Concepts and Techniques (3 projects) |
| | Microsoft Windows 98: Introductory Concepts and Techniques Web Style Edition (3-project) |
| | Microsoft Windows 98: Complete Concepts and Techniques (6 projects) |
| | Microsoft Windows 98: Comprehensive Concepts and Techniques (9 projects) |
| | Microsoft Windows 95: Introductory Concepts and Techniques (2 projects) |
| | Introduction to Microsoft Windows NT Workstation 4 |
| | Introduction to Microsoft Windows 95 (3 projects) |
| | Microsoft Windows 95: Complete Concepts and Techniques |
| DOS | Introduction to DOS 6 (using DOS prompt) |
| | **WINDOWS APPLICATIONS** |
| Microsoft Office | Microsoft Office 2000: Brief Concepts and Techniques (5 projects) |
| | Microsoft Office 97: Introductory Concepts and Techniques, Brief Edition (396-pages) |
| | Microsoft Office 97: Introductory Concepts and Techniques, Essentials Edition (672-pages) |
| | Object Linking and Embedding (OLE) (32-page) |
| | Microsoft Outlook 97 • Microsoft Schedule+ 7 |
| | Using Microsoft Office 97 (16-page) |
| | Using Microsoft Office 95 (16-page) |
| | Introduction to Integrating Office 97 Applications (48-page) |
| | Introduction to Integrating Office 95 Applications (80-page) |
| Word Processing | Microsoft Word 2000* • Microsoft Word 97* • Microsoft Word 7* Corel WordPerfect 8 • Corel WordPerfect 7 |
| Spreadsheets | Microsoft Excel 2000* • Microsoft Excel 97* • Microsoft Excel 7* Lotus 1-2-3 97* • Quattro Pro 6 |
| Database | Microsoft Access 2000* • Microsoft Access 97* • Microsoft Access 7* |
| Presentation Graphics | Microsoft PowerPoint 2000* • Microsoft PowerPoint 97* Microsoft PowerPoint 7* |
| | **INTERNET** |
| Internet | The Internet: Introductory Concepts and Techniques (UNIX) |
| Browser | Netscape Navigator 4 • Netscape Navigator 3 |
| | Microsoft Internet Explorer 5 • Microsoft Internet Explorer 4 |
| | Microsoft Internet Explorer 3 |
| Web Page Creation | Netscape Composer |

*Also available as a mini-module

# Publisher 2000

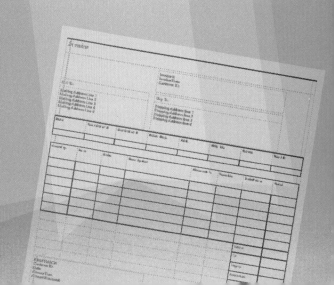

Microsoft **Publisher 2000**

Microsoft Publisher 2000

PROJECT

# Creating and
# Editing a Publication

You will have mastered the material in this project
when you can:

- Define desktop publishing
- Start Publisher
- Use a wizard
- Identify elements of the Publisher window
- Edit text in a publication
- Use the zoom buttons to edit
- Edit repeated design elements
- Save a publication
- Move and resize objects
- Edit a graphic using the Clip Gallery
- Format a publication
- Save a publication with the same file name
- Print a publication
- Quit Publisher
- Open a publication
- Modify a publication
- Add attention getters
- Delete objects
- Create a Web site from a publication
- Use Microsoft Publisher Help

# Just My Type

## The Business of Text and Graphics

If you know your ABCs, then you can distinguish between Copperplate Gothic and Century Gothic. Or Berlin and Georgia. Or Vivaldi and Matisse. These are the names of unique styles of letters, commonly called fonts or typefaces. Thousands of fonts exist, from the elegant French Script font on wedding invitations to the funky Ravie font on advertisements for soft drinks and rock concerts.

The Western system of written communication began with pictograms, which are shapes that portray objects in a language. For example, a stick figure symbolizes man, and a simple building represents shelter.

Next, ideograms evolved, which combine pictograms to represent ideas. For instance, large male and female stick figures combined with a small stick figure could represent a family, and a series of building pictograms could conceptualize a village. Pictograms were followed by phonograms – letters that represent spoken language.

The First Printing Press.

Scribes created the earliest European books, and they painstakingly wrote using a flourishing gothic script. Johannes Gutenberg, a German goldsmith, experimented in the 1400s with molding and casting metal letters to emulate the scribes' handwriting. His first efforts resulted in more than 300 pieces of type consisting of individual and multiple letters. He put the type together to form words on separate lines, then rubbed ink on the letters, and then placed a piece of paper on top of the ink. The last step was to press the paper against the ink to form a good impression of the type. The printing press was born.

Gutenberg's first printing efforts were some small books and a calendar. In 1456, he completed *The Bible of 42 Lines*, which is the oldest printed book in existence in Western society. Historians now credit the publication to him, although during his lifetime he received no credit for his efforts. He also is presumed to have compiled and printed a 748-page encyclopedia by setting type in two columns of 66 lines each.

Printing has come a long way since Gutenberg's day, but some small print shops still prefer to set type by hand as an art form for limited-edition books. In the late 1800s, the Linotype and Monotype machines replaced the painstaking work of setting type manually. Today, designers create digital type with computers, and new fonts are copyrighted daily.

Microsoft features information on many of the latest fonts, including the font of the day, at its Web site (www.microsoft.com/typography/default.asp).

The fonts you choose for your flyer, your brochure, your correspondence, or your wedding invitations reveal much about your personality and image. You can choose to be formal, fancy, or whimsical, and using an appropriate typeface may determine if your reader actually reads your message. Like a fine piece of jewelry, the type should complement your message, not overpower it by being distracting.

Using Publisher 2000 in this book provides you with the latest features of desktop publishing, such as the Design Gallery, that can help you create a variety of high-impact, professional looking publications for your business, organization, school, or home. You can print your publications or publish them to the Web. Wizards, styles, and content are available to help you achieve your desired results. Ultimately, it is as simple as A-B-C.

Microsoft Publisher 2000

Microsoft **Publisher 2000**

# Creating and Editing a Publication

PROJECT 1

Joy Elliot, a close friend of yours, is a sophomore in the Information Systems Department at Central College, a commuter college with 8,000 students, offering a variety of degree programs. Joy is majoring in object-oriented programming with an emphasis in Web page design. She is working part-time at home typing for students and local businesses. She also maintains mailing lists and publishes newsletters for several non-profit agencies, organizations, and churches. She wants to increase her market by posting advertising flyers at school, in the public library, and in area stores.

Because of your experience with HTML and Web page design, Joy has asked for your help in advertising so she can reach the greatest number of people. You have agreed to help Joy prepare a flyer with tear-offs at the bottom promoting her services and special rates to students. Together, you decide to use a Microsoft Publisher Sales Flyer template with strong, bold headings, descriptive text, and sharp graphics to give the flyer a professional look and attract attention. With your assistance, Joy wants to publish a Web version of the flyer on Central's electronic bulletin board.

# What Is Microsoft Publisher 2000?

**Microsoft Publisher** is a powerful **desktop publishing (DTP)** program that assists you in designing and producing professional quality documents that combine text, graphics, illustrations, and photographs. DTP software provides additional tools over and above those typically found in word processing packages, including design templates, graphic manipulation tools, color schemes or libraries, and multiple page wizards and templates. For large jobs, businesses use DTP software to design publications that are **camera ready**, which means the files are suitable for outside commercial printing.

The publishing industry has undergone tremendous change in the past few years due to advancements in hardware and software technology. Books, magazines, and brochures used to be created by slower, more expensive methods such as typesetting — a process that had not changed fundamentally since the days of Guttenburg and his *Bible*. With desktop publishing software, you can create professional looking documents on your own computer and produce work that previously could be achieved only by graphic artists. Both cost and time are significantly decreased. Microsoft Publisher is becoming the choice of people who regularly produce high-quality color publications such as newsletters, flyers, logos, signs, and forms. Saving publications as Web pages or complete Web sites is a powerful feature in Publisher. All publications can be saved in a format that can be easily viewed and manipulated using a browser. Some examples of these publications are shown in Figure 1-1.

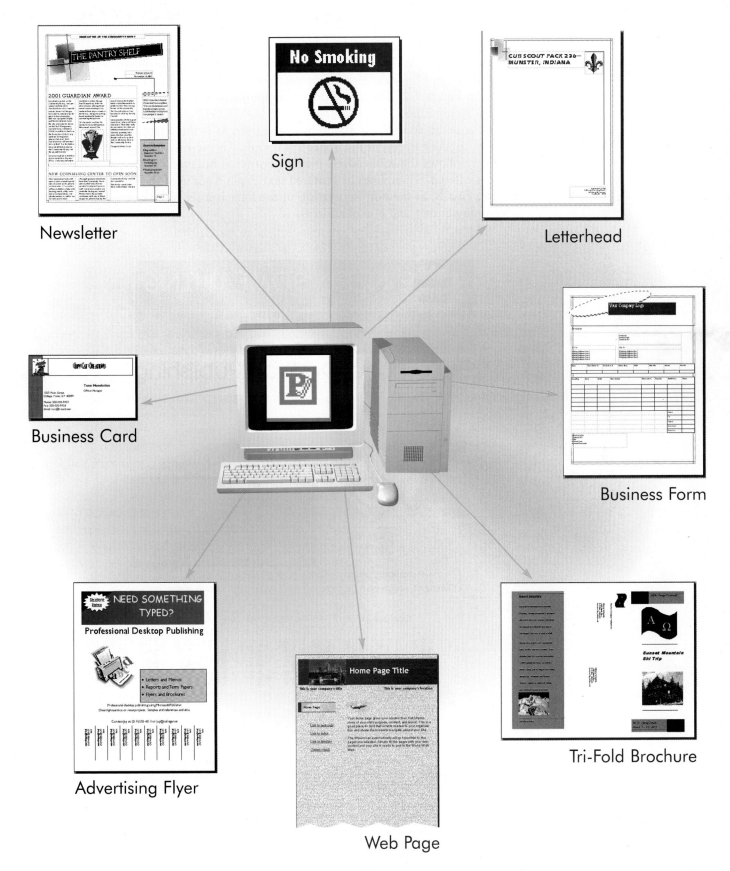

Newsletter

Sign

Letterhead

Business Card

Business Form

Advertising Flyer

Web Page

Tri-Fold Brochure

**FIGURE 1-1**

# Project One — Advertising Flyer with Tear-Offs

To illustrate the features of Microsoft Publisher, this book presents a series of projects that use Publisher to create publications similar to those you will encounter in academic and business environments. Project 1 uses Publisher to produce the flyer shown in Figure 1-2. The flyer informs the public about a desktop publishing service offered by Joy Elliott. The heading, NEED SOMETHING TYPED?, on a blue background is designed to draw attention to the flyer, as is the attention getter containing the text, Student Rates, in the upper-left corner. An eye-catching clip art drawing of a printer follows the subheading. Next, a bordered bulleted list identifies the types of services offered. Three lines of centered text explain some of the details of the typing service. Finally, at the bottom portion of the flyer is a set of tear-offs with Joy's telephone number and e-mail address.

**FIGURE 1-2**

# Starting Publisher

To start Publisher, perform the following steps, or ask your instructor how to start Publisher for your system.

 **To Start Publisher**

**① Click the Start button on the taskbar. Point to Programs on the Start menu and then point to Microsoft Publisher on the Programs submenu.**

*The Start menu and Programs submenu display (Figure 1-3). Microsoft Publisher is highlighted on the Programs submenu. The Programs submenu lists the programs installed on your computer. Your list may differ from Figure 1-3.*

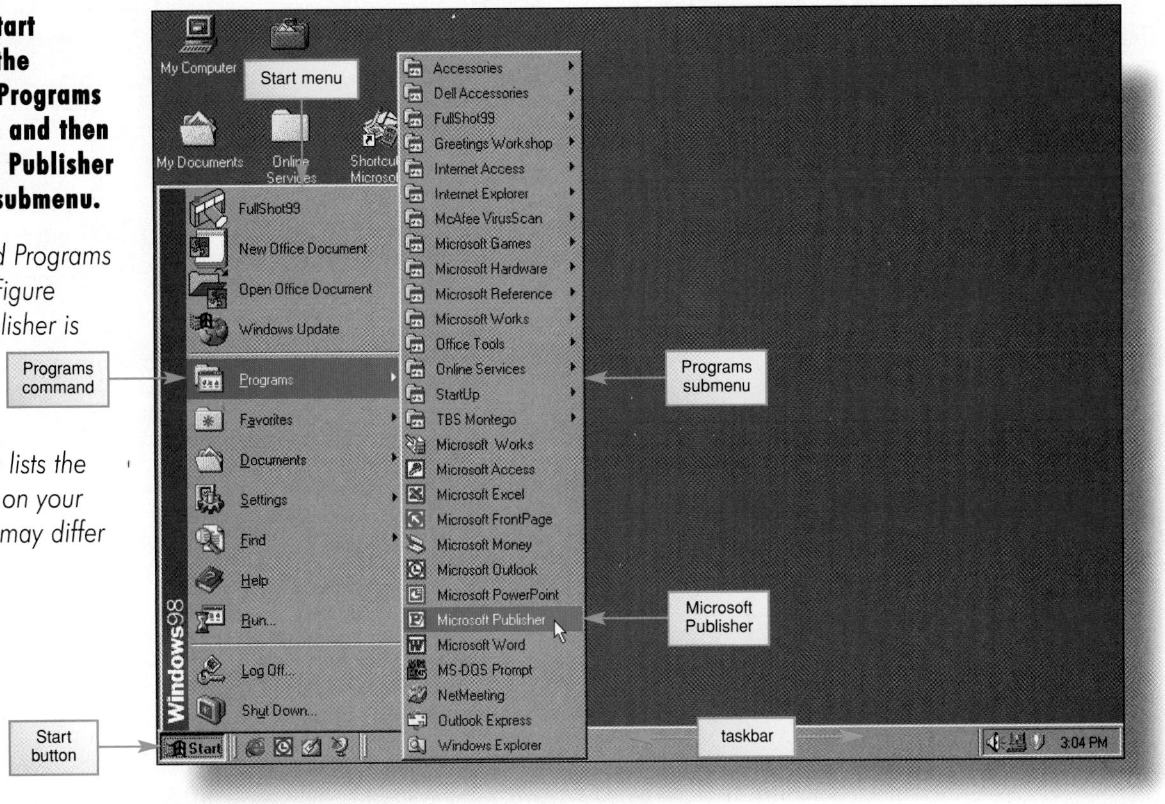

My Computer

Start menu

My Documents

Online Services

Shortcut Microso

FullShot99

New Office Document

Open Office Document

Windows Update

Programs command

Programs

Favorites

Documents

Settings

Find

Help

Run...

Log Off...

Shut Down...

Windows 98

Start button

Start

Accessories

Dell Accessories

FullShot99

Greetings Workshop

Internet Access

Internet Explorer

McAfee VirusScan

Microsoft Games

Microsoft Hardware

Microsoft Reference

Microsoft Works

Office Tools

Online Services

StartUp

TBS Montego

Microsoft Works

Microsoft Access

Microsoft Excel

Microsoft FrontPage

Microsoft Money

Microsoft Outlook

Microsoft PowerPoint

Microsoft Publisher

Microsoft Word

MS-DOS Prompt

NetMeeting

Outlook Express

Windows Explorer

Programs submenu

Microsoft Publisher

taskbar

3:04 PM

**FIGURE 1-3**

**Click Microsoft Publisher. If the Microsoft Publisher Catalog dialog box does not display upon startup, click File on the menu bar and then click New. If necessary, click the Publications by Wizard tab.**

*The Microsoft Publisher Catalog displays with its three tabs (Figure 1-4). The Wizards pane displays on the left and the previews of the selected wizard display on the right in the Quick Publications pane.*

**FIGURE 1-4**

## Other Ways

1. Right-click Windows desktop, click New on shortcut menu, click Microsoft Publisher Publication

### The Publisher Catalog

The Catalog displays publications in four different ways. The Publications by Wizard sheet displays publications by their specific purpose. The Publications by Design sheet displays publications in design sets. The Blank Publications sheet displays blank publication types, such as a Web page, business card, or postcard. The Existing Files button and Templates button make available previously saved publications and templates.

# Using Publisher's Flyer Wizard to Create an Advertising Flyer

Because composing and designing from scratch is a difficult process for many people, Publisher provides wizards and templates to assist in publication preparation. Publisher has more than 1,600 wizards and templates to create professionally designed and unique publications. A **wizard** is a tool that steps you through the design process by asking you questions and changing your publication accordingly. Once Publisher creates a publication from a wizard, you then fill in the blanks, replace prewritten text as necessary, and change the art to fit your needs. You also can use the wizard to design a **template,** which is similar to a blueprint you can use over and over. Once saved, you can edit the elements of the template, just as you do with wizards, to customize them to your situation.

## Steps  To Create a Publication Using a Wizard

**1** **Click Flyers in the Wizards pane. Point to Sale in the Flyers list.**

The Flyers pane replaces the Quick Publications pane (Figure 1-5). The Wizards pane lists seven types of flyers.

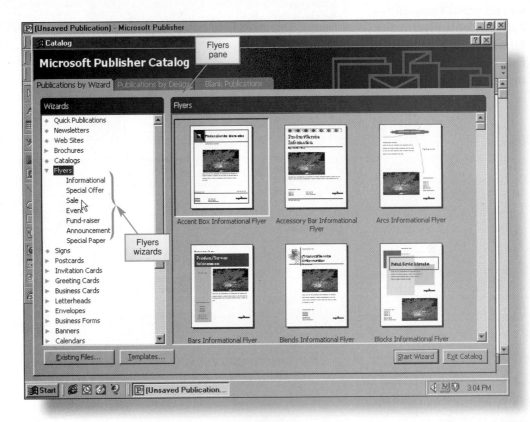

**FIGURE 1-5**

**2** **Click Sale in the Wizards pane. Point to the down scroll arrow in the Sale Flyers pane.**

The Sale Flyers pane displays (Figure 1-6).

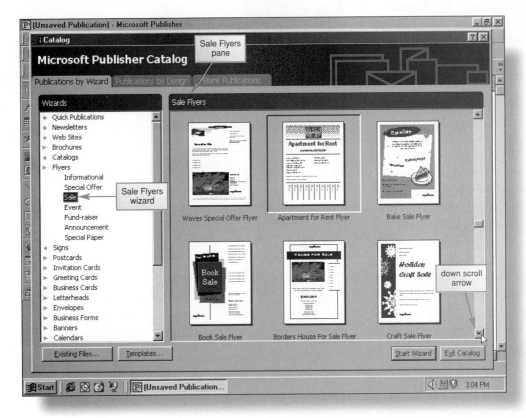

**FIGURE 1-6**

Microsoft **Publisher 2000**

**3** Click the down scroll arrow in the vertical scroll bar until the Pets Available Flyer displays, and then click the Pets Available Flyer. Point to the Start Wizard button.

*The Pets Available Flyer preview displays recessed or selected in the Sale Flyers pane (Figure 1-7).*

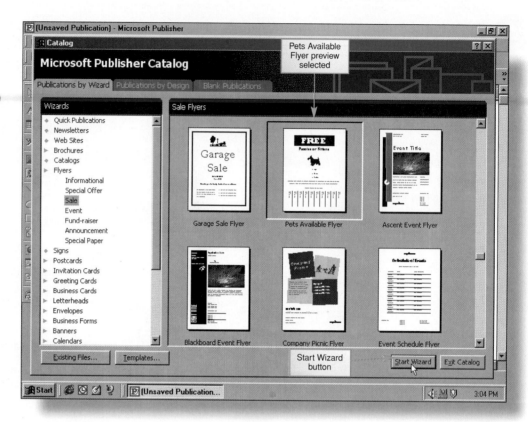

**FIGURE 1-7**

**4** Click the Start Wizard button. When the Flyer Wizard Introduction pane and the Pets Available Flyer display, point to the Next button.

*The Flyer Wizard Introduction and preview panes display (Figure 1-8). A Changing Your Publication working time bar also may display when the Flyer Wizard first starts. The step-by-step wizard displays on the left and the publication on the right. Clicking the Back button allows you to go back a step, and clicking the Finish button allows you to bypass any additional step-by-step wizard panes.*

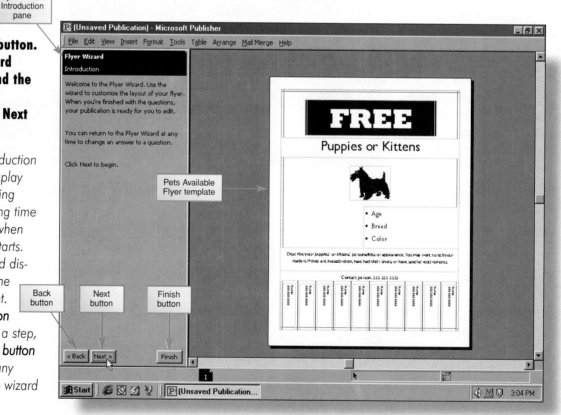

**FIGURE 1-8**

**5** **Click the Next button and then click Marine in the list. Point to the Finish button.**

*The Flyer Wizard Color Scheme pane displays. The Black & White color scheme is replaced with the Marine color scheme (Figure 1-9). The most obvious change to the flyer is the blue background in the heading. Each color scheme uses colors that complement one another.*

FIGURE 1-9

**6** **Click the Finish button. Point to the Hide Wizard button.**

*The Flyer Wizard makes the appropriate changes to the publication and replaces the remaining step-by-step questions with the layout options and Color Scheme pane (Figure 1-10). The publication, ready to edit, displays in the Publisher workspace.*

**7** **Click the Hide Wizard button. If necessary, maximize the Publisher window by clicking the Maximize button. If the Office Assistant displays, click Help on the menu bar, and then click Hide the Office Assistant.**

FIGURE 1-10

Microsoft Publisher 2000

## More About

### Desktop Publishing

Desktop publishing or electronic publishing is an extremely marketable skill in today's information-intensive workplace. For more information on desktop publishing software, visit the Discovering Computers 2000 Chapter 2 WEB INFO Web page (www.scsite.com/dc2000/ch2/webinfo.htm) and then click Desktop Publishing Software.

Publication wizards can be revisited at any time during the design process by clicking the **Show/Hide Wizard button** located at the bottom of the window (Figure 1-10 on the previous page).

# The Publisher Window

The **Publisher window** (Figure 1-11) includes a variety of features to make your work more efficient and the results more professional. Because Publisher is part of the Microsoft Office 2000 suite, the window display is similar to other members of the suite and other Windows-based programs. The main elements of the Publisher window are the workspace, the menu bar, toolbars, rulers, and status bar.

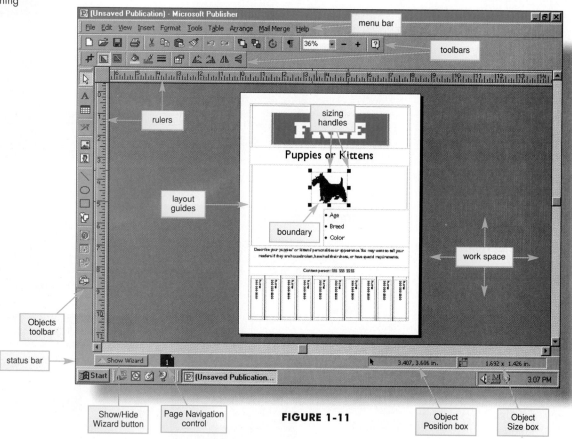

**FIGURE 1-11**

## The Workspace

The **workspace** contains several elements similar to the document windows in other applications, as well as some elements unique to Publisher. As you create a publication, the page layout, rulers, guides and boundaries, text, and objects display in the gray workspace.

**PAGE LAYOUT** The **page layout** contains a view of the entire page, all the objects contained therein, plus the guides and boundaries for the page and its objects. The page layout can be changed to accommodate multi-page spreads. You also can use the Special Paper command to view your page layout as it will be printed on special paper, or see the final copy after preparing your publication for a printing service.

**RULERS**  Two **rulers** outline the workspace. A ruler is used to measure and place objects on the page. Although the vertical and horizontal rulers display at the left and top of the workspace, they can be moved and placed anywhere you need them. You use the rulers to measure and align objects on the page, set tab stops, adjust text frames, and change margins. Additionally, the rulers can be hidden to show more of the workspace. You will learn more about rulers in a later project.

**GUIDES AND BOUNDARIES**  Publisher's page layout displays the guides and boundaries of the page and its objects. Aligning design elements in relation to each other, both vertically and horizontally, is a tedious task. **Layout guides** create a grid that repeats on each page of a publication. They define sections of the page and help you align elements with precision. They also assist you in organizing text pictures and objects into columns and rows to give a consistent look to your publication. Represented by blue and pink dotted lines, layout guides exist on the background of every page.

    **Boundaries** are the gray lines surrounding an object. Boundaries are useful when you want to move or resize objects on the page. Guides and boundaries can be turned on and off using the View menu.

**OBJECTS**  **Objects** include anything you want to place in your publication, such as text, WordArt, tear-offs, graphics, pictures, bullets, lines, and Web tools. You can choose objects from a wizard, from the Design Gallery, or insert them from original material. You click an object on the page to **select** it; selected objects display with small squares, called **sizing handles**, at each corner and middle location of the object boundary. A selected object can be resized, moved, deleted, or grouped as necessary.

## Menu Bar, Standard Toolbar, Formatting Toolbar, and Status Bar

    The menu bar, Standard toolbar, and Formatting toolbar display at the top of the window just below the title bar (Figure 1-12a on the next page). The Objects toolbar (Figure 1-11) displays on the left of the window. The status bar (Figure 1-11) displays at the bottom of the window, above the Windows taskbar.

**MENU BAR**  The **menu bar** is a special toolbar that includes the Publisher menu names. Each menu name represents a menu of commands you can use to retrieve, store, print and format data in your publication and perform other tasks. When you point to a menu name on the menu bar, it changes to a button. When you click a menu name a **short menu** displays, listing the most recently used commands (Figure 1-12b on the next page). If you wait a few seconds or click the arrows at the bottom of the short menu, the full menu displays (Figure 1-12c on the next page). The **full menu** lists all the commands associated with a menu. As you use Publisher, it automatically personalizes the menus for you, based on how often you use commands. You can reset the menus to their original configuration by clicking Options on the Tools menu, and then clicking the Reset My Usage Data button in the General sheet. The process is described in greater detail in Appendix C. In this book, when you display a menu, you should wait a few seconds or click the arrows at the bottom of the menu so that the full menu displays. Many of these commands have pictures beside them to help you quickly identify them. For example, the Save command on the File menu has a picture of a floppy disk beside it. If you point to a command with an arrow on its right, a submenu displays from which you may choose a command. Some menu commands display a check mark that means the command has been chosen previously and is a current setting. The hidden commands that display on the full menu are recessed. **Dimmed** (or grayed) commands indicate that they are not available for the current selection.

### Objects

The Design Gallery Object, available on the Objects toolbar, contains a tab for user-defined objects and objects created with other applications. For more information on the use of objects, visit the Publisher 2000 More About Web page (www.scsite.com/pub2000/more.htm) and click Object Embedding.

### Displaying Toolbars

If two toolbars are positioned on the same row, a More Buttons button displays. Publisher demotes less frequently used buttons to the More Buttons menu. You access these hidden buttons by clicking a toolbar's More Buttons button to display its More Buttons menu or by dragging the toolbar to a new row.

Microsoft **Publisher 2000**

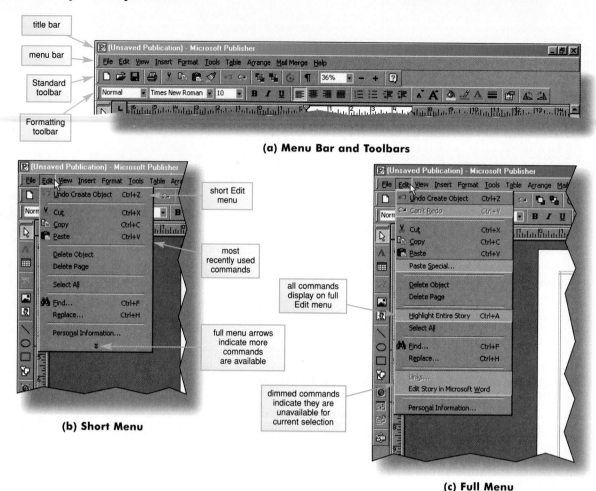

(a) **Menu Bar and Toolbars**

(b) **Short Menu**

(c) **Full Menu**

**FIGURE 1-12**

**STANDARD TOOLBAR AND FORMATTING TOOLBAR** **Toolbars** contain buttons and boxes that allow you to perform tasks more quickly than when using the menu bar. For example, to print a publication, you would click the Print button on the Standard toolbar. The menu bar actually is the first toolbar in the Publisher window. When turned on, the **Standard toolbar** displays just below the menu bar. Immediately below the Standard toolbar, the **Formatting toolbar** displays. Each type of object in Publisher displays its own Formatting toolbar when selected. The toolbars change when you click the object. For instance, a text frame will display a Formatting toolbar with font options, whereas a rectangle shape will not. The **Objects toolbar** displays on the left edge of the Publisher window. If you do not see a toolbar in the window, click Toolbars on the View menu and then click the name of the toolbar you want to display.

Each button on a toolbar has a picture on its face that helps you remember its function. Figure 1-13 illustrates the Standard toolbar and identifies its buttons and boxes. Figure 1-14 illustrates the Formatting toolbar, which is used for text entries. In addition, when you move the mouse pointer over a button or box, the name of the button or box displays below it in a **ScreenTip**. Each button and box is explained in detail as it is used in the projects.

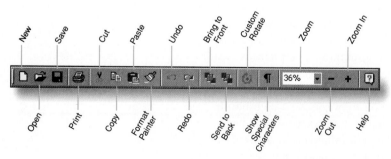

**FIGURE 1-13**

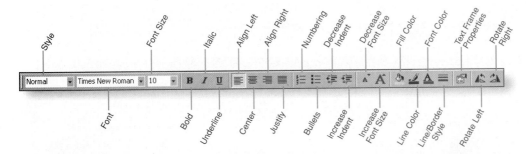

**FIGURE 1-14**

The toolbars initially display **docked**, or attached, to the edge of the Publisher window. Additional toolbars may display automatically in the Publisher window, depending on the task you are performing. These additional toolbars display either stacked below the Formatting toolbar or floating in the Publisher window. A **floating toolbar** is not attached to an edge of the Publisher window. You can rearrange the order of **docked toolbars** and can move floating toolbars anywhere in the Publisher window by dragging them to the desired location.

**STATUS BAR**  Immediately above the Windows taskbar at the bottom of the window is the status bar. The **status bar** contains the Show/Hide Wizard button, the Page Navigation control, the Object Position box, and the Object Size box (Figure 1-11 on page PUB 1.14). The **Show/Hide Wizard button** toggles, or alternates, between showing and hiding the Publisher wizard when clicked. The **Page Navigation control** displays a button for each page of your publication. The current page displays in black. You may click any page to display it in the workspace. The **Object Position** and **Object Size** boxes are used as an alternative to using the rulers as guidelines for lining up objects from the left and top margins. The exact position and size of a selected object is displayed in inches as you create or move it. You may choose to have the measurement displayed in pica, points, or centimeters. If no object is selected, the Object Position box displays the location of the mouse pointer.

# Editing Text in a Publication

Editing the flyer involves making changes to the text to fit your needs. Most of Publisher's Wizards come with text inserted into text frames. A **text frame** is an object in a publication designed to hold text in a specific shape, size, and style. Text frames can be placed by a wizard or can be drawn on the page using the Text Frame Tool on the Objects toolbar. Text frames can be formatted from the Standard toolbar or on the shortcut menu displayed by right-clicking the text frame.

A text frame has changeable properties. A **property** is an attribute or characteristic of an object. Within text frames you can make changes to the following properties: font, spacing, alignment, line/border style, fill color, and margins, among others. Perform the steps on the next page to edit the text of the flyer.

Microsoft **Publisher 2000**

 **To Edit Text in a Publication**

**1** **Click FREE in the heading of the flyer, and then point to the Font box arrow.**

*The text frame displays with sizing handles indicating the object can be resized (Figure 1-15). Publisher displays a ScreenTip immediately below the object. The ScreenTip in this figure is Text Frame. The Group/Ungroup Objects button will be discussed later.*

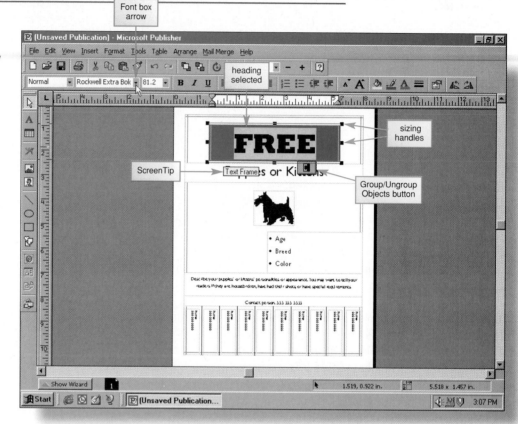

**FIGURE 1-15**

**2** **Click the Font box arrow. Scroll through the Font list until Comic Sans MS displays, and then point to Comic Sans MS.**

*A list of available fonts displays in alphabetical order (Figure 1-16). Comic Sans MS is highlighted. Your list of available fonts may differ, depending on the type of printer you are using. Unlike many word processing programs, Publisher displays the font names in the type style of the font itself.*

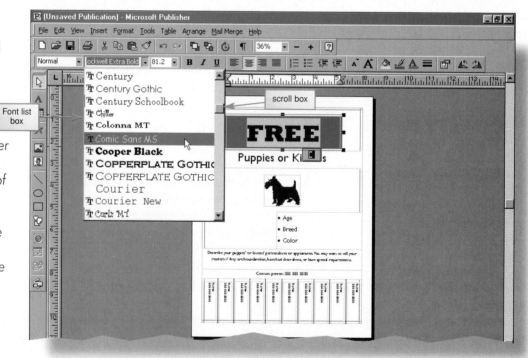

**FIGURE 1-16**

**3** **Click Comic Sans MS.**

*The selected text displays in the Comic Sans MS font (Figure 1-17).*

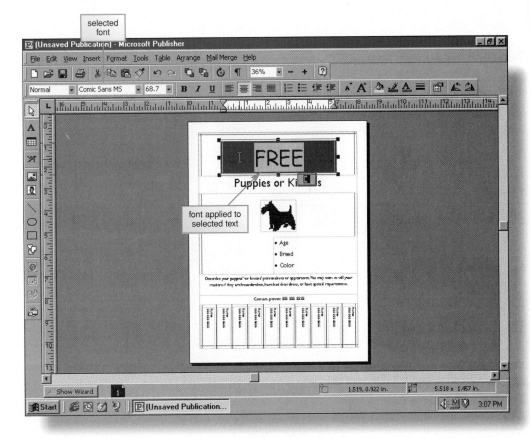

**FIGURE 1-17**

**4** **While the text still is selected, type** NEED SOMETHING TYPED? **in the text frame. Position the mouse pointer in the Puppies or Kittens text frame.**

*The selected text is deleted automatically and the new text displays (Figure 1-18). Publisher uses **wordwrap**, which allows you to type words continually without pressing the ENTER key. Publisher also uses **AutoFit Text** to resize the text so it fits into the allotted amount of space. The font size has been reduced to accommodate the new, longer phrase.*

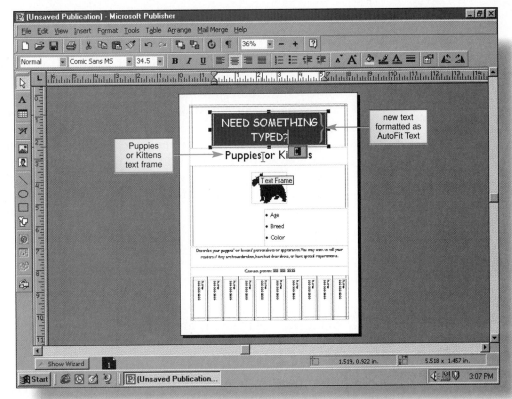

**FIGURE 1-18**

**Click the text, Puppies or Kittens, and then type** Professional Desktop Publishing **in the text frame.**

*The new text displays (Figure 1-19).*

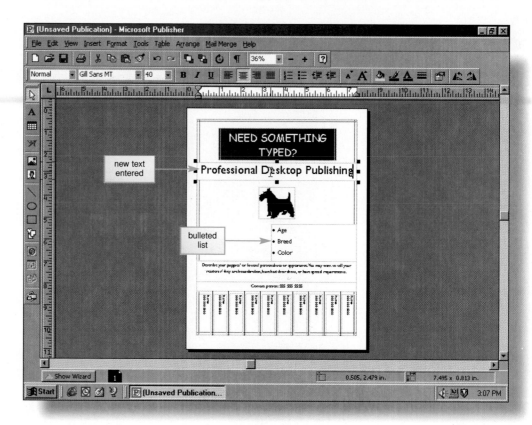

**FIGURE 1-19**

### Other Ways

1. Right-click text, click Change Text on shortcut menu, click Font
2. On Format menu click Font

If the text does not fit in a text frame, or it seems to run over, it is possible that AutoFit Text has been turned off. The AutoFit Text command, available on the Format menu, has three ways to fit text in the text frame: None, Best Fit, or Shrink Text On Overflow. **Best Fit** reduces or enlarges text to fill the frame, whereas **Shrink Text On Overflow** reduces text only if you fill the frame. **None** does not adjust the size of the text.

Publisher automatically checks for spelling errors and duplicate words as you enter text. If you type a word that is not in the dictionary (because it is a proper name or misspelled) a red wavy underline displays below the word. You may right-click the underlined word to see Publisher's suggestions or choose Spelling on the Tools menu to check the spelling of the entire publication.

### Zooming to Facilitate Editing

Editing small areas of text is easier if you use the zoom buttons to enlarge the view of the publication. If you click the object before zooming in, Publisher displays the selected object in the center of the workspace. The following steps illustrate how to use the zoom buttons to edit the bulleted list.

### Flagged Words

Recall that the commands on a shortcut menu differ depending on the object. If you select and right-click a word you can cut, copy, or paste it from the shortcut menu; however, if the selected word has a red wavy underline below it, you can only spell check it from the shortcut menu.

## To Edit a Bulleted List Using the Zoom Buttons

**1 Click the text in the bulleted list. Point to the Zoom In button.**

The text is highlighted and the frame is selected (Figure 1-20). Publisher displays the sizing handles around the frame.

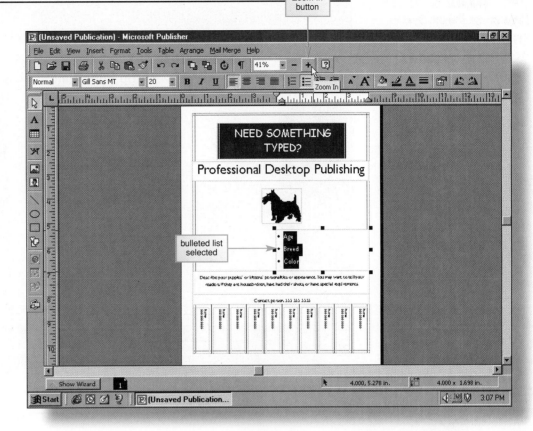

**FIGURE 1-20**

**2 Click the Zoom In button until the Zoom box displays 50%. Type** Letters and Memos **and then press the ENTER key.**

The Zoom box displays 50% (Figure 1-21). Publisher begins to rebuild the bulleted list as you enter text. The insertion point displays at the second bullet.

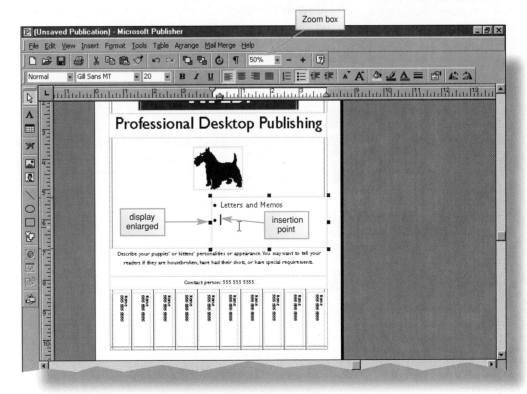

**FIGURE 1-21**

**③ Type** Reports and Term Papers **and then press the ENTER key. Type** Flyers and Brochures **as the last bullet, but do not press the ENTER key.**

*The bulleted list is now complete (Figure 1-22).*

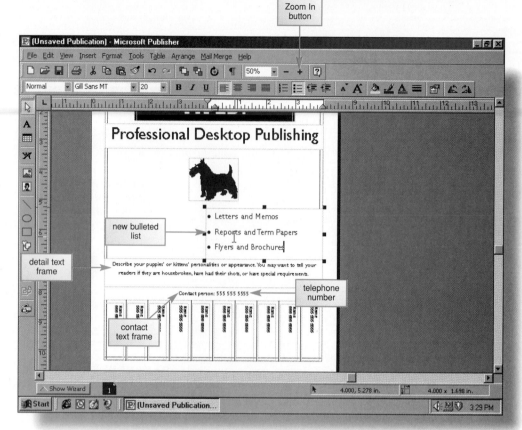

**FIGURE 1-22**

## Adding Text

The next steps finish entering new text in the detail text frame and the contact text frame. Perform the following steps to enter more text.

### TO ADD TEXT

**①** Click the detail text below the bulleted list.

**②** Click the Zoom In button on the Standard toolbar.

**③** Type Professional desktop publishing using Microsoft Publisher. Press the ENTER key and then type Overnight service on most projects. Samples and references available.

**④** Click Contact person: in the contact text frame.

**⑤** Type Contact Joy at: and then press the SPACEBAR.

**⑥** Click the telephone number. Type (219) 555-4313 or joy@college.net in the text frame.

*The two completed text frames display (Figure 1-23).*

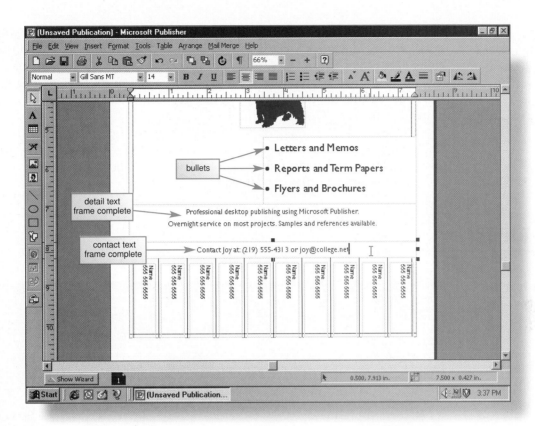

**FIGURE 1-23**

Publisher lists three **page views** in the Zoom list: Whole Page, Page Width, and Selected Objects. **Whole Page** displays a single page publication at approximately 36% of its actual size. **Page Width** resizes the page view to fill the width of the available workspace. **Selected Objects** centers an object and enlarges it to fill the workspace. The **Zoom list** also allows you to choose a percentage of magnification from 10% to 400%. You can type a percentage or choose from the list. Page views and percentages of magnification are available through the **Zoom command** on the View menu.

The bullets displayed in Figure 1-23 are small circles positioned at the beginning of each line. **Bullets** are used to draw attention to specific points in your publication. They show emphasis and make your publication lists look more professional. Toggle bullets on and off using the **Bullets button** on the Formatting toolbar. Indents and Lists on the Formatting menu displays a list of bullet styles from which you may choose.

## Editing Tear-Offs

Publisher provides many design objects such as tear-offs, coupons, and reply forms designed to be perforated or easily torn off from the publication. **Tear-offs** are small tabbed images with some combination of name, telephone, fax, e-mail, or address. Designed for customer use, tear-offs typically are perforated so a person walking by can tear off a tab to keep, rather than having to stop, find a pen and paper, and write down the name and telephone number. Traditionally, small businesses or individuals wanting to advertise something locally used tear-offs; but more recently, large companies are mass-producing advertising flyers with tear-offs to post at shopping centers, display in offices, and advertise on college campuses.

### Zooming

You can adjust the size of the characters on the screen, by typing a percentage increase or decrease into the Zoom box on the Standard toolbar. Zooming a document has no effect on the size of the printed characters. The print size displays in the Font Size box on the Formatting toolbar.

The telephone tear-offs are a repeated design element, **synchronized** to change with editing. This means that when you change the text or format in one tab, Publisher also makes the changes to similar objects so you do not have to change each one manually. Synchronization occurs as soon as you finish editing. It can be cancelled by clicking the Undo button on the Standard toolbar. If needed, you can turn it back on by using Options on the Tools menu.

The tear-offs on a standard 8½-by-11-inch piece of paper include 10 text frames and 9 lines separating them, positioned at the bottom of the page. More repeated design elements and smart objects will be discussed later.

Perform the following steps to edit the tear-offs.

 **To Edit Tear-Offs**

**1** **Click the text in the first tear-off on the left.**

*A solid pink line outlines the individual tear-off (Figure 1-24). The solid gray line with sizing handles is the boundary of the entire tear-off text frame. Each tear-off in the text frame is identical.*

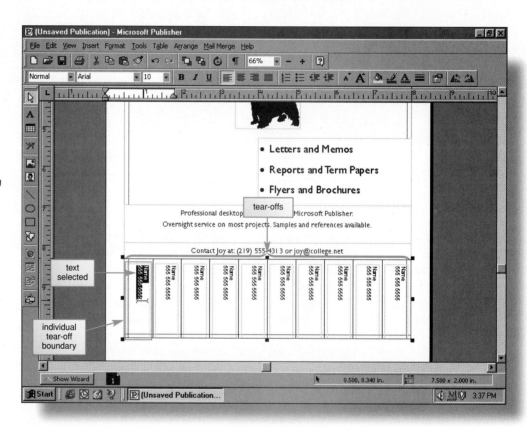

FIGURE 1-24

**2** **Type** Joy **and then press the ENTER key. Type** (219) 555-4313 **and then press the ENTER key. Type** joy@college.net **on the next line.**

*As you begin typing, the insertion point, text, and I-beam mouse pointer display sideways and the text is printed in the flyer (Figure 1-25). If the e-mail address displays with a red wavy underline, right-click it, and then click Ignore All on the shortcut menu.*

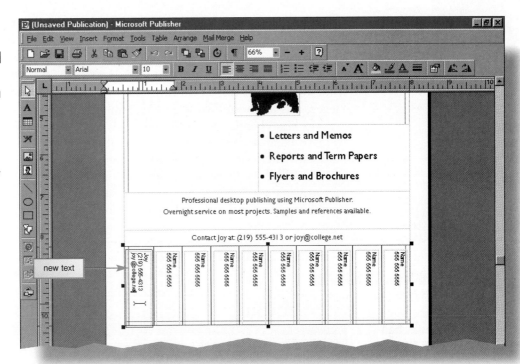

**FIGURE 1-25**

**3** **Click anywhere outside the first tear-off frame.**

*All the tear-offs change to display the new text (Figure 1-26).*

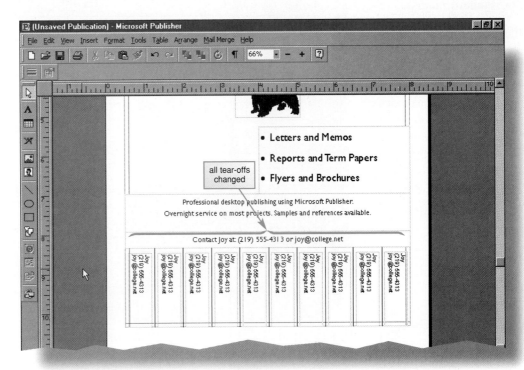

**FIGURE 1-26**

You may want to have forms perforated at the tear-off lines so they tear easily and consistently. When completed in large batches, perforation costs are relatively small. Most print shops, copy shops, and duplicating services have perforation capabilities.

## Saving

When you save a publication, you should create readable and meaningful file names. A file name can include up to 255 characters, including spaces. The only invalid characters are backslash (\), slash (/), colon (:), asterisk (*), question mark (?), quotation mark ("), less than symbol (<), greater than symbol (>), and vertical bar (|).

# Saving a Publication

While you are creating a publication in Publisher, the computer stores it in memory. If the computer is turned off or if you lose electrical power, the publication is lost. Hence, it is important to save on disk any publication that you will use later.

The text changes in your publication now are complete. Because you have made so many changes, now is a good time to save a copy of your work. Publisher's **save reminder feature** may offer you the chance to save your publication at predetermined intervals during your work session. You may click either the Yes button or the No button when Publisher reminds you to save. Perform the next series of steps to save a publication on a floppy disk inserted in drive A using the Save button on the Standard toolbar.

## To Save a New Publication

1 **Insert a formatted floppy disk into drive A on your computer. Click the Save button on the Standard toolbar.**

*The Save As dialog box displays with the insertion point in the File name text box (Figure 1-27). Publisher does not select a preset file name for the publication because most elements on the page are objects. You must enter a file name the first time you save a publication, or when you want to save the file with a different name.*

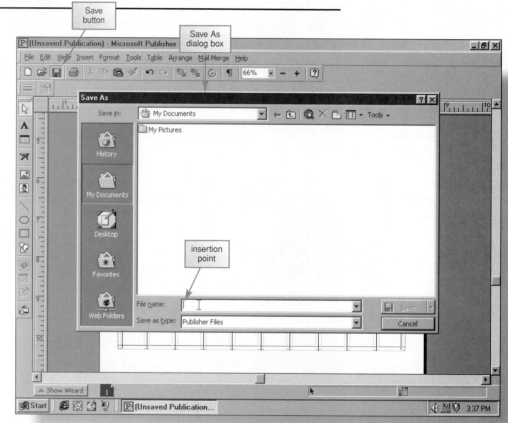

**FIGURE 1-27**

**2** **Type the file name** Need Something Typed **in the File name text box. Do not press the** ENTER **key after typing the file name. Point to the Save in box arrow.**

*The file name, Need Something Typed, displays in the File name box (Figure 1-28). When creating file names, you should make them as meaningful as possible. A **file name** can contain up to 255 characters and can include spaces.*

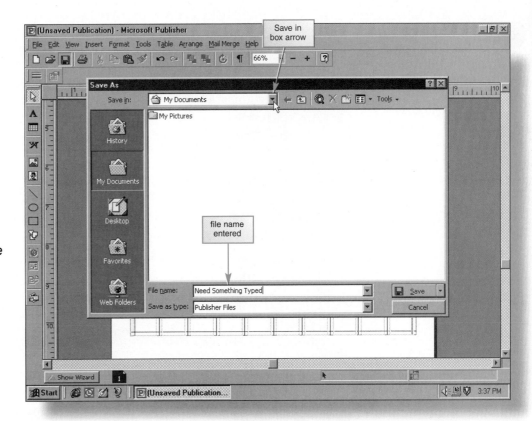

**FIGURE 1-28**

**3** **Click the Save in box arrow and then point to 3½ Floppy (A:).**

*A list of the available drives displays with 3½ Floppy (A:) highlighted (Figure 1-29). Your list may differ depending on your system configuration.*

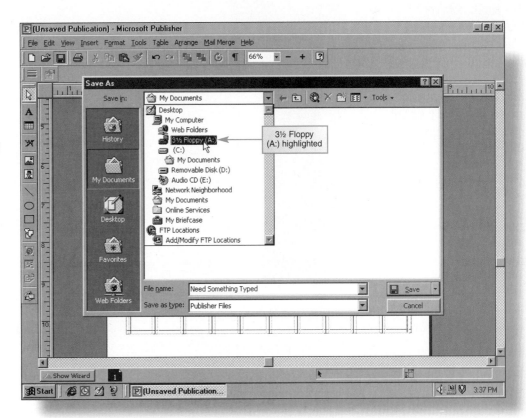

**FIGURE 1-29**

**④ Click 3½ Floppy (A:) and then point to the Save button in the Save As dialog box.**

The 3½ Floppy (A:) drive becomes the selected drive (Figure 1-30). The names of existing files that are stored on the floppy disk in drive A display. In Figure 1-30, no files currently are stored on the floppy disk.

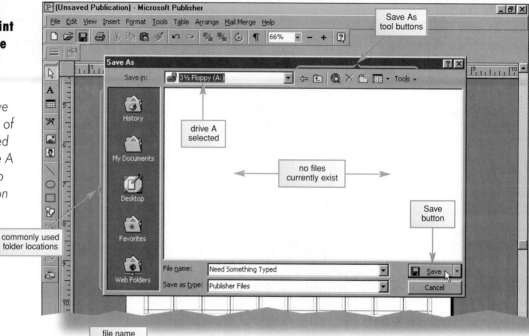

FIGURE 1-30

**⑤ Click the Save button.**

The saved publication displays with the new file name, Need Something Typed, on the title bar and on the taskbar (Figure 1-31). Although the publication is saved on a floppy disk, it also remains in memory and displays in the workspace.

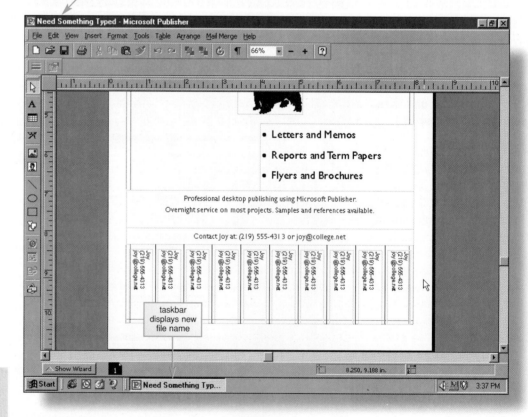

FIGURE 1-31

**Other Ways**

1. On File menu click Save, type file name, select location in Save in list, click Save button in Save As dialog box
2. Press CTRL+S, type file name, select location in Save in list, click Save button in Save As dialog box

The seven buttons at the top and to the right in the Save As dialog box (Figure 1-30) and their functions are summarized in Table 1-1.

The five buttons on the left of the Save As dialog box in Figure 1-30 allow you to select often used folders. The History button displays a list of shortcuts to the most recently used files in a folder titled Recent. You cannot save publications to the Recent folder.

| Table 1-1 | Save As Dialog Box Toolbar Buttons | |
|---|---|---|
| **BUTTON** | **BUTTON NAME** | **FUNCTION** |
| | Default File Location | Displays contents of default file location |
| | Up One Level | Displays contents of next level up folder |
| | Search the Web | Starts browser and displays search engine |
| | Delete | Deletes selected file or folder |
| | Create New Folder | Creates new folder in current location |
| | Views | Changes view of files and folders |
| Tools | Tools | Lists commands to modify file/folder names and locations |

# Moving and Resizing Objects

While creating publications, it sometimes is necessary to move or resize objects, either to better balance the page, to add clarity or emphasis, or for a variety of other reasons. Publisher can accomplish moving and resizing tasks quickly and easily.

## Moving a Grouped Object Using Snap to Guides

Publisher will adjust the placement of an object so it aligns with the page layout guides automatically if you move the object close to the guide. This magnet-like process is called **snapping**. Three variations of snapping are available on the Tools menu: **Snap to Ruler**, **Snap to Guides**, and **Snap to Objects**. All three variations work in a similar manner and apply to both moving and resizing. You will use snapping to modify the heading for a full banner-like effect.

The heading of the publication, NEED SOMETHING TYPED?, is really a combination of two objects: a text frame and a rectangle grouped together.

A **rectangle** is a box on the window used as a geometric graphic to accentuate or provide a background. As a graphic, rectangles with colors, patterns, and borders enhance design and help you create elegant looks for your publications. A rectangle becomes a background when other objects, such as text frames, are **layered** on, or placed on top of, rectangles. Rectangles and text frames can be placed by a wizard or created from scratch using the Objects toolbar. To use the Objects toolbar to create a new shape, just click the desired button, move the mouse pointer to the publication, and drag through the area in which you want the shape to display.

Publisher, like other software packages, allows you to group objects, such as rectangles and text frames, for common resizing and moving. **Grouping** simply means selecting more than one object at a time to create a composite object. Although the text frame and rectangle in this heading have been grouped together already by the wizard, it is easy to group. Simply select an object and then press and hold the SHIFT key while selecting a second object. The **Group/Ungroup Objects button** displays automatically. You also can use the **Pointer Tool** on the Objects toolbar to draw around objects you want to group.

Because the object already is grouped, moving and resizing will take place without having to worry about grouping and ungrouping. The Snap to Guide feature also is automatic. The steps on the next page describe how to move and resize the grouped heading.

More About

### Grouping

An alternate to selecting multiple objects using the SHIFT-click method is simply to drag the mouse around them. A box and the Group/Ungroup button will display. This method is useful especially when objects have been layered or when you want to group more than two or three objects that are close together.

*Steps* **To Move and Resize a Grouped Heading**

**1** **To view the whole page, click the Zoom box arrow, and then click Whole Page. Point to the upper-left corner of the banner heading.**

*The whole page displays (Figure 1-32). When you point to a boundary line, the mouse pointer changes to a moving truck icon called the* **Mover***.*

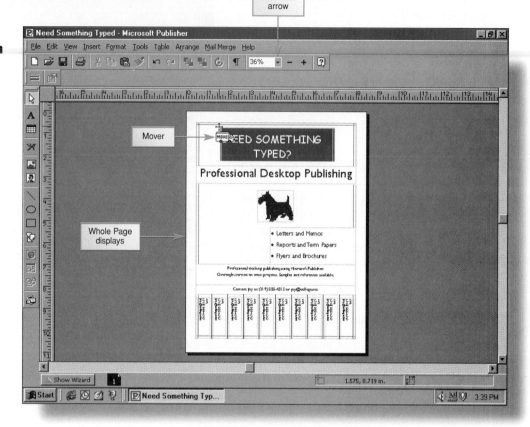

**FIGURE 1-32**

**2** **Drag the heading up and left until it is closely aligned with the top and left guides. After releasing the mouse button, point to the lower-right sizing handle.**

*The grouped heading snaps to the corner (Figure 1-33). When you point to the sizing handle, the mouse pointer changes to a resize icon called the* **Resizer***.*

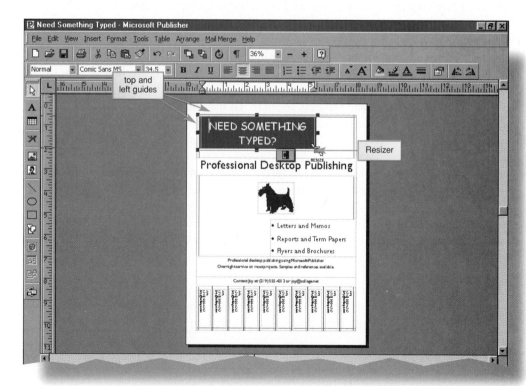

**FIGURE 1-33**

**3** To make the heading fill the area at the top of the page, drag the lower-right sizing handle diagonally to the gray boundary line on the bottom and the blue layout guide on the right.

*The heading fills the top portion of the flyer (Figure 1-34). Publisher uses AutoFit Text to adjust the font size automatically and fill the text frame.*

FIGURE 1-34

The rectangle and the text are in place. In addition to the Rectangle Tool, the Objects toolbar contains ovals, lines, and custom shapes. Any shape or text frame can be moved, resized, or formatted to fit your personal design specifications. Furthermore, shapes created with drawing tools can be flipped, rotated, and mirrored. Additional text editing techniques will be discussed in future projects.

## Moving and Resizing the Graphic

A **graphic** is any object in Publisher other than a text frame. You can move a Publisher graphic by placing the mouse pointer anywhere over the selected graphic. To resize a graphic, however, the mouse pointer must be on one of the sizing handles. **Resizing** simply means changing the size or shape of an element by dragging the sizing handle.

Perform the steps on the next page to move and resize the graphic.

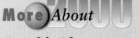

1. On Format menu click Size and Position
2. Press ALT, press arrow key to move selected object

### More About

**Graphic Placement**

The spacing around a graphic should be at least 1/8 inch and should be consistent among the graphics in your publication. You can place the graphic manually or let Publisher maintain the graphic margin and the way text wraps around pictures. The Picture Frame Properties button on the Formatting toolbar allows you to set all four margins as well as text wrapping.

Microsoft **Publisher 2000**

 **To Move and Resize a Graphic**

**①** **Click the picture of the dog. While holding down the SHIFT key, drag the picture until it aligns at the one-inch mark in the upper ruler. Release the SHIFT key and the mouse button.**

*The graphic displays one inch from the left margin (Figure 1-35). Holding down the SHIFT key while dragging keeps the graphic parallel to its original position.*

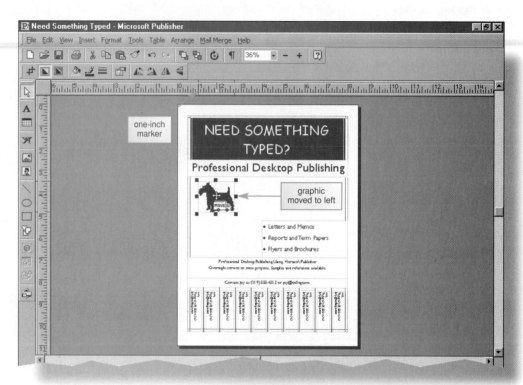

**FIGURE 1-35**

**②** **Drag the lower-right sizing handle of the graphic toward the bulleted list to enlarge it.**

*The graphic displays enlarged (Figure 1-36). It is not important that you match the exact location; however, the status bar displays the position shown. Using a corner sizing handle rather than a side one, maintains the proportions of the graphic.*

*Other* **Ways**

1. On Format menu click Size and Position
2. On Arrange menu click Nudge

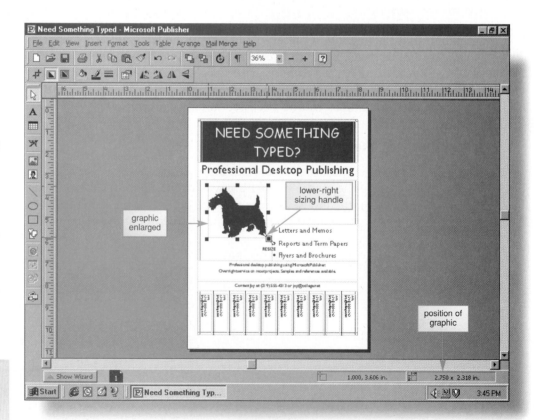

**FIGURE 1-36**

Resizing includes both enlarging and reducing the size of an object. Dragging a corner sizing handle maintains the proportions of the graphic, whereas dragging a middle sizing handle distorts the proportion of the graphic. Proportionally resizing an object other than a picture requires that you hold down the SHIFT key while dragging the corner sizing handle. To keep the center of an object in the same place as you resize it, hold down the CTRL key as you drag.

# Enhancing a Publication with Formatting and Graphics

Once a publication has been created, you can enhance its appearance by editing the color schemes, adding appropriate graphics, using borders, and by formatting text. **Formatting** means changing the look of an object by adjusting the style, font, graphic enhancement, alignment, or color. In this first series of steps, you will choose a graphic that enhances the message of the publication, and then you will format the bulleted list.

## Editing a Graphic

Publisher's CD-ROM comes with thousands of graphics including clip art, pictures, sounds, video clips, and animation. A full installation of Publisher copies these clips to the computer's hard disk. Alternately, the clips may remain on the Publisher CD-ROM for insertion as needed. For network installations, ask your instructor for the location of the graphic files. **Clip art** is an inclusive term given to draw-type images that are created from a set of instructions (also called object-based or vector graphics). **Images** usually are digital photographs, scanned images, or other artwork made from a series of small dots. More information on graphics, animation, and sound is presented in later projects.

Publisher includes a series of graphic files located in the Clip Gallery. The **Clip Gallery** is a tool for previewing and inserting clip art, pictures, sounds, videos, and animated objects. It also contains its own Find and Help systems to assist you in locating an image suited to your application. The Clip Gallery displays in the Insert Clip Art window when you choose to insert or edit a picture.

The steps on the next page illustrate how to edit the graphic and retrieve an appropriate picture from the Clip Gallery. If you cannot access the graphic described, choose a suitable replacement from your system's Clip Gallery.

More About

### Resizing a Graphic

Sometimes you might resize a graphic and realize it is the wrong size. In these cases, you may want to return the graphic to its original size and start over. To return a resized graphic to its original size, click Format on the menu bar and then click Scale Picture. When the Scale Picture dialog box displays, click Original size to add a check mark.

More About

### Graphics on the Web

Microsoft has graphic files you may download from its Web site. To do this, click Clips Online on the Insert Clip Art dialog box toolbar. The Microsoft Clip Gallery Online will display. Follow the instructions to import a graphic or picture.

**Steps** To Edit a Graphic

**1** **Double-click the graphic of the dog.** **If necessary, when the Insert Clip Art window displays, click the Pictures Tab, and then click the Search for clips box.**

*The Insert Clip Art window displays (Figure 1-37).*

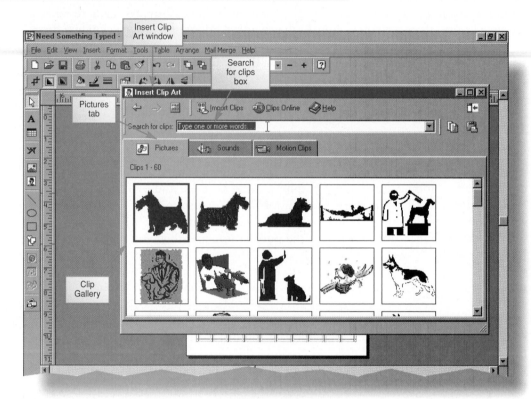

**FIGURE 1-37**

**2** **Type** printer **and then press the ENTER key. When the pictures display, point to the Pictures sheet down scroll arrow.**

*The Pictures sheet displays clip art associated with printer topics from the Clip Gallery (Figure 1-38). Your pictures may vary depending on the installation of Publisher or the files on your network.*

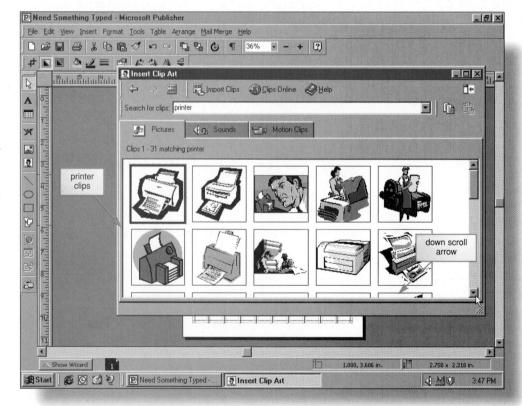

**FIGURE 1-38**

**3** Scroll down until you see the graphic of the printer producing colored letters a, b, c, d. Click the picture and then point to the Insert clip button on the pop-up menu.

*The selected graphic displays with a box around it (Figure 1-39). If this specific graphic is not available, choose any suitable picture in the Clip Gallery. The associated key-words, size, and type of file display in a ScreenTip.*

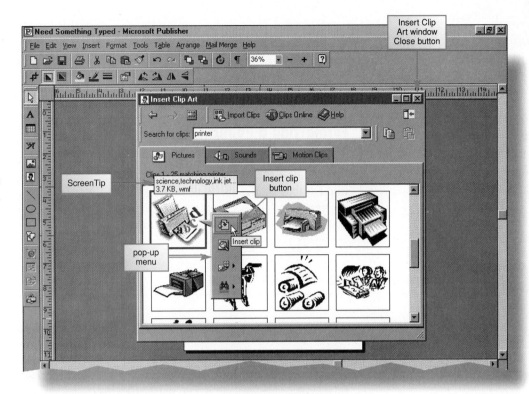

FIGURE 1-39

**4** Click the Insert clip button. If necessary, click the Insert Clip Art window Close button.

*Publisher closes the Insert Clip Art window, returns to the workspace, and replaces the picture of the dog with the picture of the printer (Figure 1-40).*

FIGURE 1-40

Graphic files are available from a variety of sources. If you have a scanner attached to your system, Publisher can insert the scanned photograph directly from the scanner, or you can scan the picture into a file and then insert the scanned file into the publication at a later time. Instead of scanning your own pictures, you can purchase photographs from a local software retailer, usually on a CD-ROM, or you can locate a picture on the Web.

*Other Ways*

1. On Objects toolbar click Picture Frame Tool
2. Right-click graphic, click Change Object on shortcut menu
3. On Insert menu click Picture

You also can use the Clip Gallery to organize your clips by category or keyword so that finding the one you want is made easier. Some graphics are more suitable for display on the Web, while others print better on color printers. Future projects discuss the various types of graphics files in detail, including their advantages and disadvantages.

## Formatting a Publication

To format the publication, you need to add color and a border to the bulleted list. Because the list is a single text frame, once it is selected, you can use the Formatting toolbar or the shortcut menu to complete the formatting. The following steps illustrate how to accomplish the formatting, first by adding color and then by adding a border to the bulleted list text frame.

 **To Add Color and a Border to a Text Frame**

**1** **Click the bulleted list to select it. Point to the Fill Color button on the Formatting toolbar.**

*The bulleted list is selected (Figure 1-41). The ScreenTip displays for the Fill Color button.*

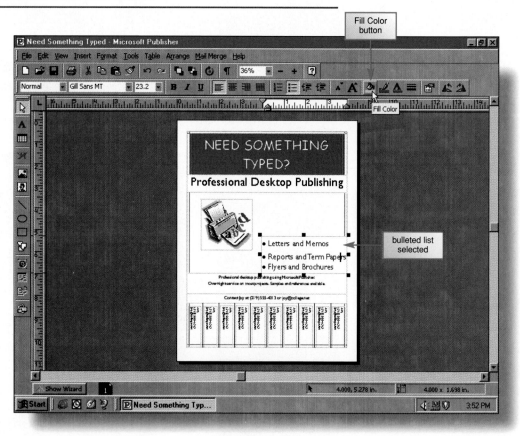

**FIGURE 1-41**

**2** **Click the Fill Color button. Point to the Accent 2 button under Scheme colors.**

The Marine color scheme colors chosen in the wizard at the beginning of the project display (Figure 1-42). Color schemes include colors that complement each other, as well as shades and tints of those colors.

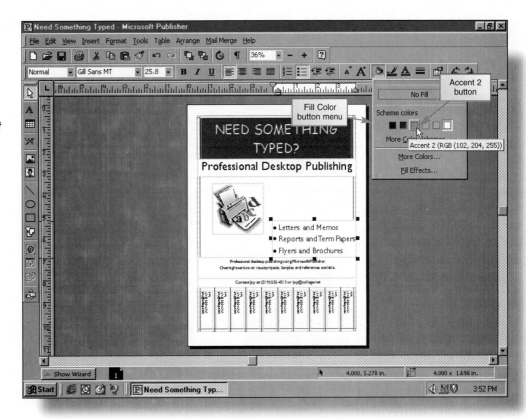

**FIGURE 1-42**

**3** **Click the Accent 2 button.**

The bulleted list displays with a medium blue background (Figure 1-43).

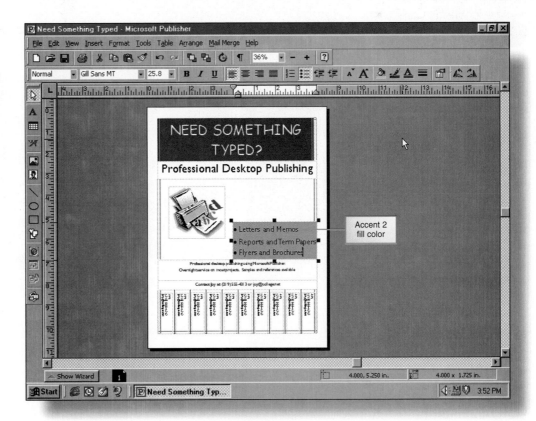

**FIGURE 1-43**

**4** **Right-click the bulleted list. Point to Change Frame on the shortcut menu.**

*The shortcut menu and the Change Frame submenu display (Figure 1-44). Shortcut menus are available on most objects in Publisher. Commands specific to the object display on the shortcut menu.*

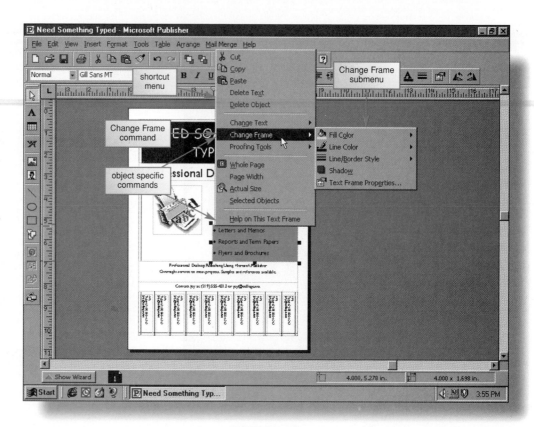

**FIGURE 1-44**

**5** **Point to Line/ Border Style.**

*The Line/Border Style submenu displays with variously sized lines and a More Styles command (Figure 1-45).*

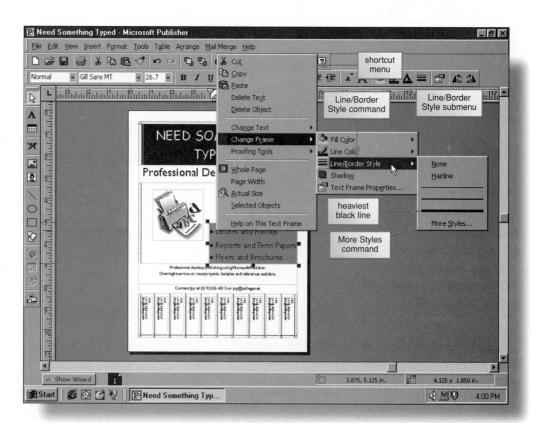

**FIGURE 1-45**

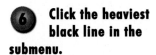

**6** **Click the heaviest black line in the submenu.**

*Publisher displays a heavy black border around the text frame (Figure 1-46).*

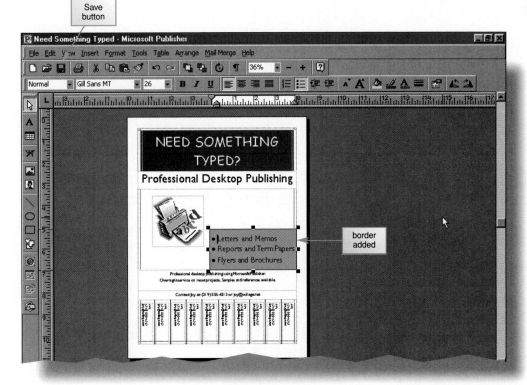

**FIGURE 1-46**

Publisher has hundreds of color schemes and border styles available. The Fill Color and Line/Border Style features contain many additional colors and effects from which you may choose. Publisher suggests certain color schemes and styles designed to make your publication look as consistent and professional as possible. For Web publishing, it is best to use one of the standard borders, rather than a customized or fancy border. Fancy borders, or **Border Art** as Publisher calls it, generates an extra graphic on Web pages, significantly increasing the time it takes for the Web page to load.

## Saving an Existing Publication with the Same File Name

The publication for Project 1 now is complete. To transfer the formatting changes and imported graphic to your floppy disk in drive A, you must save the publication again. When you saved the publication the first time, you assigned the file name, Need Something Typed. Publisher assigns this same file name automatically to the publication each time you subsequently save it, if you use the following procedure. Perform the following step to save the publication using the same file name.

### TO SAVE AN EXISTING PUBLICATION WITH THE SAME FILE NAME

 Click the Save button on the Standard toolbar.

*Publisher saves the publication on a floppy disk inserted in drive A using the current file name, Need Something Typed? The publication remains in memory and displays on the screen.*

If for some reason, you want to save an existing publication with a different file name, click Save As on the File menu to display the Save As dialog box. Then, fill in the Save As dialog box as discussed in Steps 2 through 5 on pages PUB 1.27 and PUB 1.28 using a different file name in the File name text box.

# Printing a Publication

The next step is to print the publication you created. A printed version of the publication is called a **hard copy** or **printout**. Perform the following steps to print the publication created in Project 1.

## To Print a Publication

**1** **Ready the printer according to the printer instructions. Click the Print button on the Standard toolbar.**

*A dialog box briefly displays indicating it is preparing to print the publication. A few moments later, the publication begins printing on the printer. The tray status area displays a printer icon while the publication is printing (Figure 1-47).*

**2** **When the printer stops, retrieve the printout.**

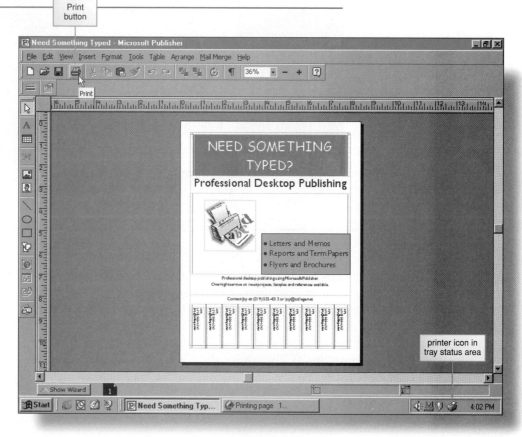

**FIGURE 1-47**

### Other Ways

1. On File menu click Print, click OK button
2. Press CTRL+P, press ENTER

### Printing

To print multiple copies of the same publication, click File on the menu bar and then click Print. When the Print dialog box displays, type the desired number of copies in the Number of copies text box and then click the OK button.

When you use the Print button to print a publication, Publisher prints the entire publication automatically. You then may distribute the hard copy or keep it as a permanent record of the publication.

If you want to cancel a job that is printing or waiting to be printed, double-click the printer icon in the tray status area (Figure 1-47). In the Print dialog box, right-click the job to be canceled and then click Cancel Printing on the shortcut menu.

# Quitting Publisher

After you create, save, and print the publication, you are ready to quit Publisher and return control to Windows. Perform the following steps to quit Publisher.

 **To Quit Publisher**

Close button

**1** **Point to the Close button in the upper-right corner on the title bar (Figure 1-48).**

**FIGURE 1-48**

**2** **Click the Close button.**

*If you made changes to the publication since the last save, Publisher displays a dialog box asking if you want to save the changes (Figure 1-49). Clicking the Yes button saves changes; clicking the No button ignores the changes; and clicking the Cancel button returns to the publication. If you did not make any changes since you saved the publication, this dialog box does not display.*

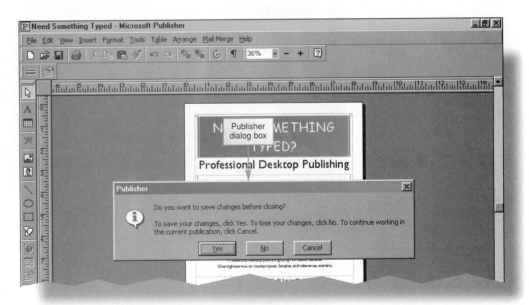

**FIGURE 1-49**

1. On File menu click Exit
2. Press ALT+F4

Project 1 now is complete. You created and formatted the publication, inserted a picture from the Clip Gallery, printed it, and saved it. You might decide, however, to change the publication at a later date. To do this, you must start Publisher again and then retrieve your publication from the floppy disk in drive A.

# Opening a Publication

Earlier, you saved the Publisher publication built in Project 1 on a floppy disk using the file name, Need Something Typed. Once you have created and saved a publication, you often will have reason to retrieve it from the disk. For example, you might want to revise the publication, correct errors, or save the publication as an HTML file for posting to the Web. Perform the following steps to open the publication, Need Something Typed.

 **To Open an Existing Publication**

**1** **With the floppy disk containing the publication, Need Something Typed, in drive A, click the Start button on the taskbar and then point to Programs on the Start menu. Point to Microsoft Publisher (Figure 1-50).**

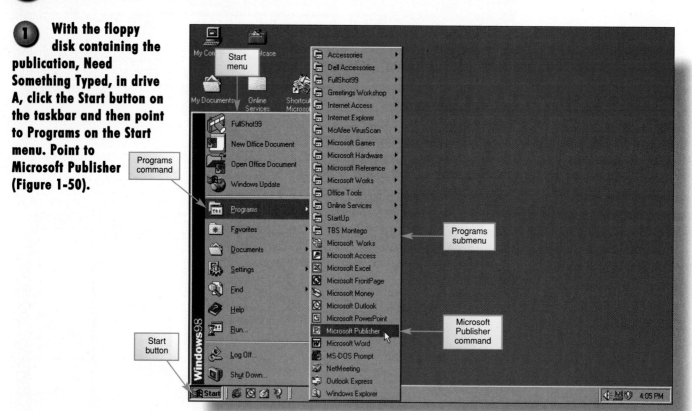

FIGURE 1-50

## 2 Click Microsoft Publisher on the Programs submenu. When the Catalog dialog box displays, point to the Existing Files button.

*The Catalog dialog box displays (Figure 1-51). If Publisher does not display the Catalog dialog box, click New on the File menu.*

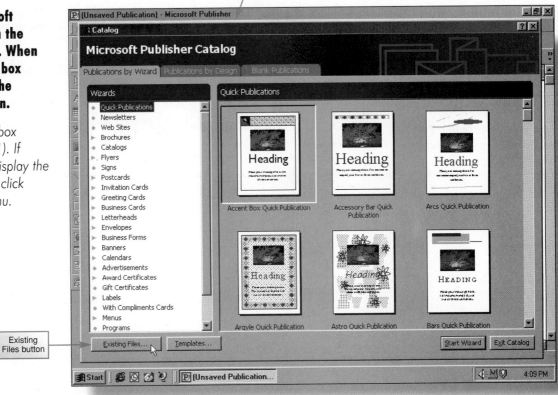

**FIGURE 1-51**

## 3 Click the Existing Files button. When the Open Publication dialog box displays, point to the Look in box arrow.

*Publisher displays the Open Publication dialog box with the insertion point in the File name box (Figure 1-52). Your file list may vary. Make sure the appropriate floppy disk is located in drive A.*

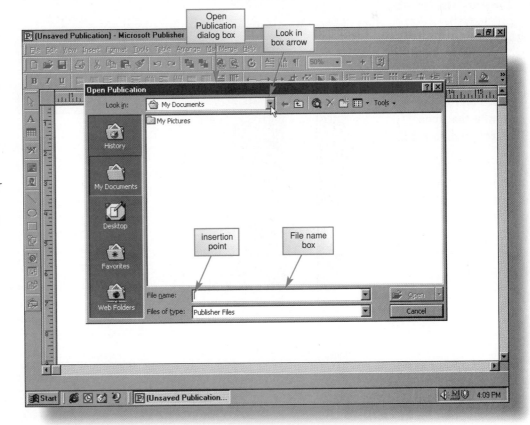

**FIGURE 1-52**

Microsoft **Publisher 2000**

**4** Click the Look in box arrow and then point to 3½ Floppy (A:).

A list of the available drives displays with 3½ Floppy (A:) highlighted (Figure 1-53). Your list may differ depending on your system configuration.

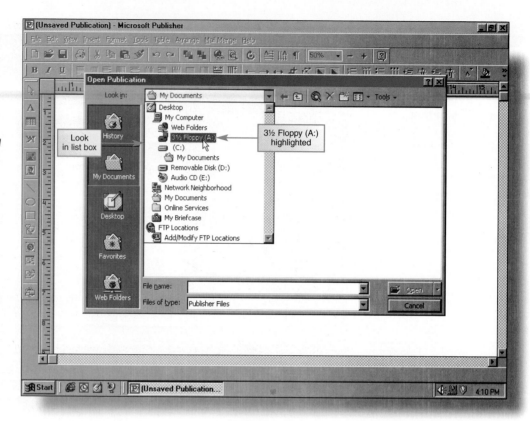

**FIGURE 1-53**

**5** Click 3½ Floppy (A:). If it is not already selected, click the file name, Need Something Typed. Point to the Open button in the Open Publication dialog box.

The 3½ Floppy (A:) drive becomes the selected drive (Figure 1-54). The names of existing files stored on the floppy disk in drive A display.

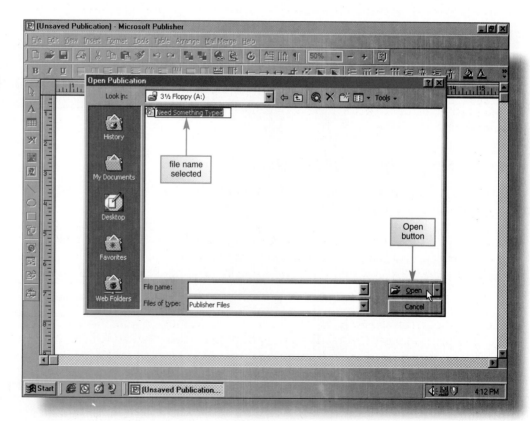

**FIGURE 1-54**

**Click the Open button.**

*Publisher opens the publication on the floppy disk in drive A with the file name, Need Something Typed, and displays the publication (Figure 1-55). A copy of the publication remains on the floppy disk as well.*

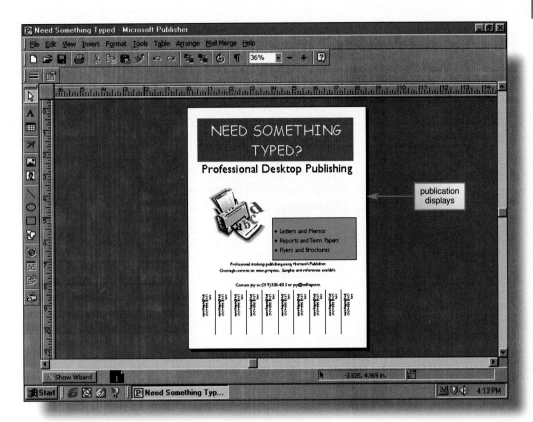

**FIGURE 1-55**

# Modifying a Publication

After creating a publication, you often will find that you must make changes to it. Changes can be required because the document contains an error or because of new circumstances.

## Types of Changes Made to Publications

The types of changes made to publications normally fall into one of the three following categories: additions, deletions, or modifications.

**ADDITIONS**   Additional text, objects, or formatting may be required in the publication. **Additions** occur when you are required to add items to a publication. For example, in Project 1 you would like to add something about special rates to attract students to the typing service.

**DELETIONS**   Sometimes **deletions** are necessary in a publication because objects are incorrect or are no longer needed. For example, to place this advertising flyer on the electronic bulletin board at the college, the tear-offs are no longer needed. In that case, you would delete them from the page layout and then save the publication as an HTML file.

**MODIFICATIONS**   If you make an error in a document or want to make other **modifications**, normal combinations of inserting and deleting techniques for text and graphics apply.

**Other Ways**

1. Double-click My Computer icon on desktop, double-click 3½ Floppy (A:), double-click file name
2. Click Open button on Standard toolbar, select file name, click Open button in Open dialog box
3. On File menu click Open, select file name, click Open button in Open dialog box
4. Press CTRL+O, select file name, press ENTER

Publisher provides several methods for correcting errors in a document. For each of the error correction techniques, you first must move the insertion point to the error.

## Adding an Attention Getter to a Publication

Drawing attention to a flyer such as this one is important. You want the customer to notice your flyer over others posted in the same area. The bright blue heading is a start, but adding a graphic to the upper-left corner will help draw attention to the top of the flyer. Publisher has a **Design Gallery** of objects intended to add flair and style to your publications. The Design Gallery has three tabs: **Objects by Category, Objects by Design,** and **Your Objects**. A fourth tab called **Extra Content** displays if you switch design wizards in the middle of creating a publication and some elements in the first design are not included in the new design. The Extra Content tab holds elements that you no longer need.

The **Attention Getters** display in the Objects by Category sheet. They contain graphic boxes, text frames, geometric designs, and colors intended to draw attention to your publication.

To assist you in making new objects fit your design, Publisher associates a **smart object wizard** with many of its Design Gallery objects. A small wizard button displays when the object is selected. When you click it, the smart object wizard asks you one or more questions to change these special publication elements. Perform the following steps to add an attention getter to the publication.

*Steps* **To Add an Attention Getter to a Publication**

**1** **Click the Design Gallery Object button on the Objects toolbar. If necessary, when the Design Gallery dialog box displays, click the Objects by Category tab, and then point to Attention Getters in the Categories pane.**

*The Design Gallery dialog box consisting of three tabbed sheets displays (Figure 1-56).*

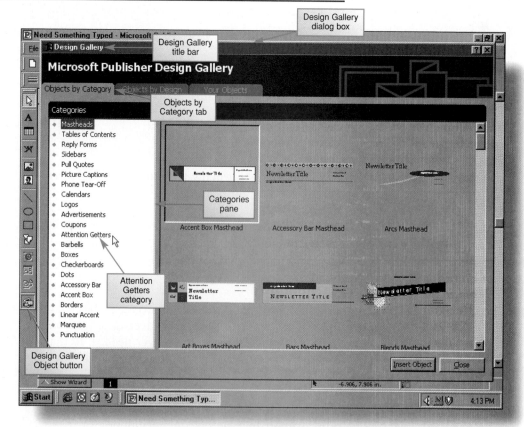

**FIGURE 1-56**

**2** Click Attention Getters. When the Attention Getters pane displays on the right, click the down scroll arrow until the Corner Starburst Attention Getter displays. Click the Corner Starburst Attention Getter and then point to the Insert Object button.

The Attention Getters previews pane displays (Figure 1-57). The Corner Starburst Attention Getter is selected.

**FIGURE 1-57**

**3** Click the Insert Object button.

The attention getter displays in the publication (Figure 1-58). The smart object wizard button displays below the attention getter.

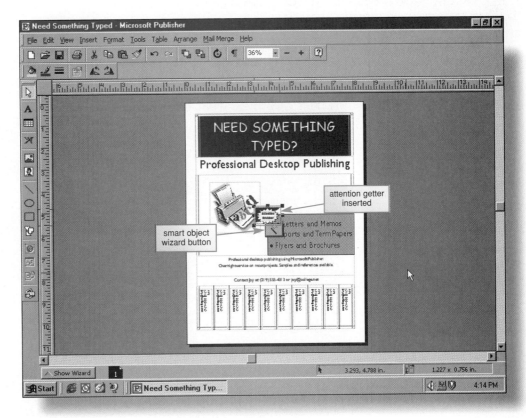

**FIGURE 1-58**

**④** **Position the mouse pointer over the boundary of the attention getter. When the mouse pointer changes to the Mover, drag the attention getter to the upper-left corner of the publication. Point to the Zoom In button.**

*The object displays snapped to the guide (Figure 1-59).*

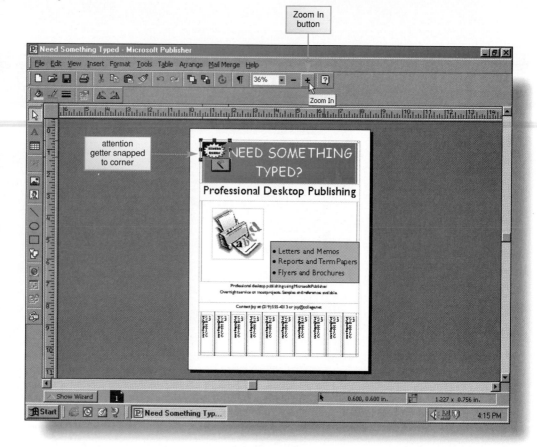

FIGURE 1-59

**⑤** **Click the Zoom In button twice.**

*The object displays centered and enlarged, making it easier to edit (Figure 1-60).*

FIGURE 1-60

**6** **Click the text, Attention Grabber. Type** Student Rates **in the text frame.**

*The new text replaces the old (Figure 1-61). The AutoFit Text feature adjusts the font size.*

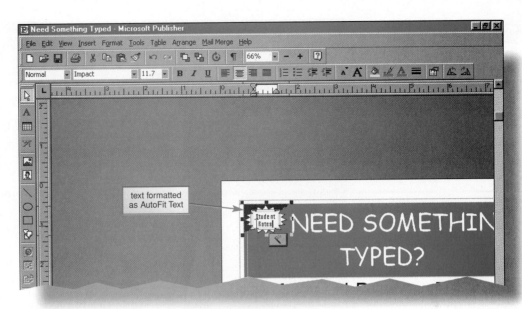

**FIGURE 1-61**

## Deleting an Object from a Publication

It is not unusual to type incorrect characters or words in a text frame, or to change your mind about including an object. If this flyer displays on an electronic bulletin board, the tear-offs are unnecessary. Perform the following steps to delete the tear-offs from the publication.

 **To Delete an Object**

**1** **Right-click the workspace. Point to Whole Page.**

*The shortcut menu displays (Figure 1-62). It contains some of the same view choices as the Zoom list box.*

**FIGURE 1-62**

**2** Click Whole Page. Right-click any of the tear-offs, and then point to Delete Object on the shortcut menu.

*The publication displays in Whole Page view and the text frame shortcut menu displays (Figure 1-63).*

**3** Click Delete Object.

*The tear-offs are deleted (see Figure 1-64).*

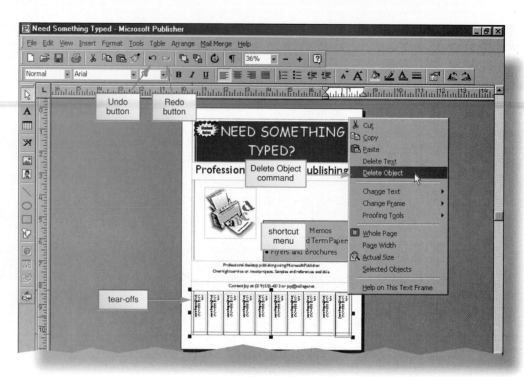

**FIGURE 1-63**

Publisher provides an **Undo button** on the Standard toolbar that you can use to cancel your recent command(s) or action(s). For instance, if you delete an object accidentally, you can bring it back. If you want to cancel your undo, you can use the **Redo button**. Some actions, such as saving or printing a document, cannot be undone or redone.

# Creating a Web Site from a Publication

Publisher can create a Web site from your publication. It is a two-step process. First, Publisher uses a **Design Checker** to look for potential problems if the publication were transferred to the Web. If your publication contains a layout that is not appropriate, such as overlapping objects, the Design Checker will alert you. If you use links or hot spots to other Web pages within your publication, Design Checker will verify the addresses.

The second step is to save the verified Web publication. Normally, Publisher saves a file with the three-letter extension, .pub. The **.pub extension** allows Publisher easily to open your formatted file and assign a recognizable icon to the shortcut on your disk. Files intended for use on the Web, however, need a different format. A **Hypertext markup language (HTML) file** is a file capable of being stored and transferred electronically on a file server in order to display on the Web. Publisher can save your file in the HTML format.

Publisher suggests creating a folder to hold each separate publication intended for the Web. A **folder** is a logical portion of a disk created to group and store similar documents. Inside this folder, Publisher will include the main HTML file, called the **index**, and copies of the associated graphics. Once created, your publication can be viewed by a Web browser, such as Microsoft Internet Explorer.

The concept of a Web folder facilitates integration of Publisher with other members of the Microsoft Office Suite and Windows 98. With Windows 98, you can

**HTML**

For more information on HTML including code fragments and Web design issues, visit the HTML More About Web page (www.scsite.com/html/more.htm).

choose to use Web style folders on your desktop, which means that the desktop is interactive and all your folders look like Web pages. Publisher also will take care of **uploading**, or transferring, your files to the Web, if you are connected to an Internet service provider or host. See Appendix B for more information on Web folders. Perform the following steps to create a Web site from your publication.

 **To Create a Web Site from a Publication**

**1** **Click File on the menu bar. After a few seconds, when the full File menu displays, point to Create Web Site from Current Publication.**

*The full File menu displays (Figure 1-64).*

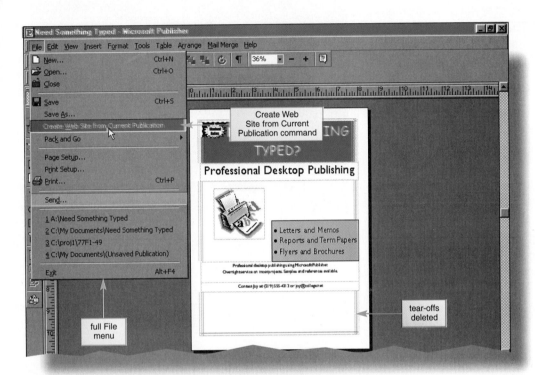

FIGURE 1-64

**2** **Click Create Web Site from Current Publication. If you are asked to save changes, click the No button. When the Publisher dialog box displays, asking if you would like to run the Design Checker, point to the Yes button.**

*The Publisher dialog box displays (Figure 1-65).*

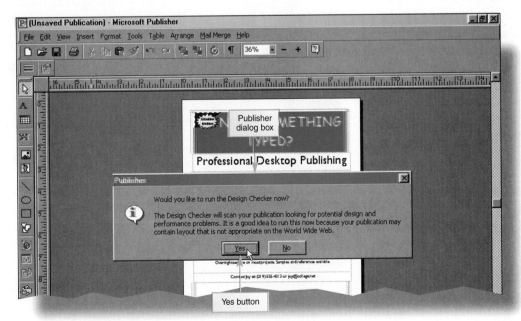

FIGURE 1-65

**3** **Click the Yes button. The Design Checker dialog box asks if you want to check all pages in the publication. Point to the OK button.**

*The Design Checker dialog displays (Figure 1-66). Because the publication only has one page, the Pages option button is not available.*

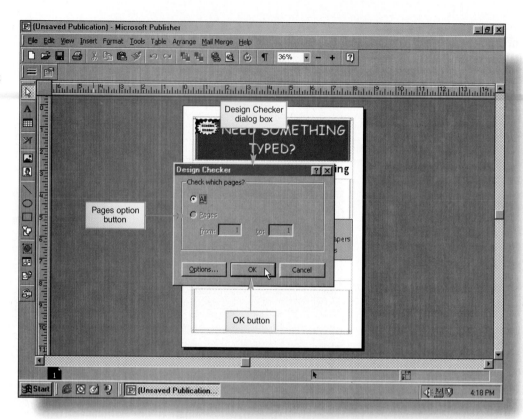

**FIGURE 1-66**

**4** **Click the OK button. Point to the Yes button in the Publisher dialog box.**

*A Publisher dialog box and a Design Checker dialog box display (Figure 1-67). The Design Checker wants to check the publication for its ability to **download**, or display, quickly. Certain types of large graphics slow the display process on the Web, as do a large number of fonts and borders.*

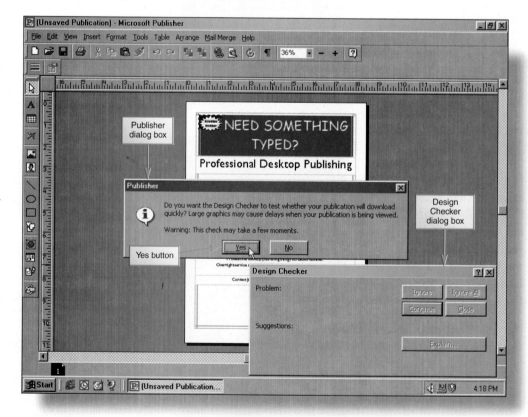

**FIGURE 1-67**

**5** **Click the Yes button. After a few moments, Publisher's Design Checker indicates that the Design Check is complete. Click the OK button. Click File on the menu bar and then point to Save As Web Page.**

*The Design Checker is complete and the project displays (Figure 1-68). If there were problems with your publication, you would have been given the option to ignore, continue, or obtain more information about the problems.*

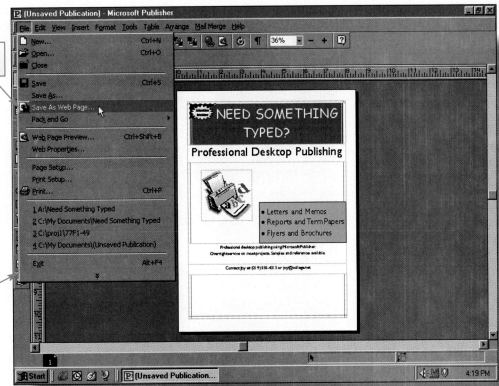

**FIGURE 1-68**

**6** **Make sure a floppy disk is inserted in drive A. Click Save As Web Page. Click 3½ Floppy (A:) in the Look in list. Point to the Create New Folder button.**

*The Save as Web Page dialog box displays (Figure 1-69). The graphics, text, and links, if any, will save on the floppy disk in drive A.*

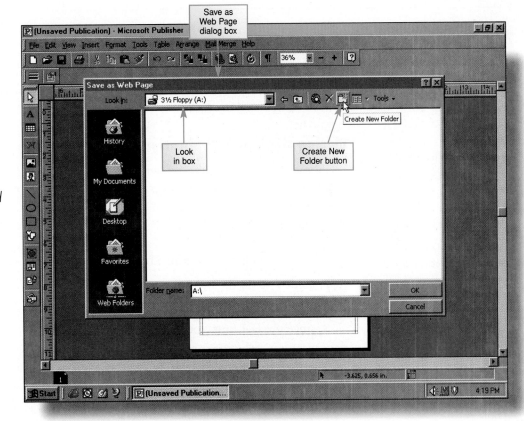

**FIGURE 1-69**

 **7** Click the Create New Folder button. When the New Folder dialog box displays, type `flyer` in the Name box. Point to the OK button.

*The new folder name displays in the Name box (Figure 1-70).*

**8** Click the OK button in the New Folder dialog box, and then click the OK button in the Save as Web Page dialog box.

*The saved files are ready to send to the Web.*

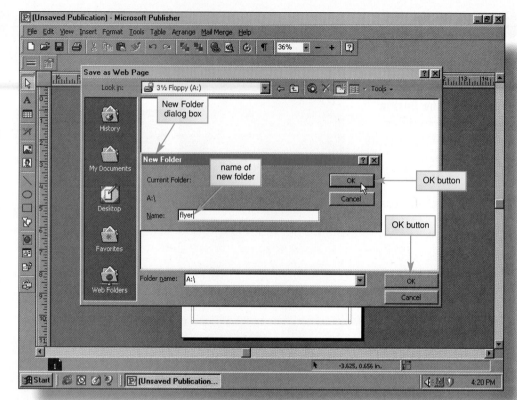

**FIGURE 1-70**

---

The Design Checker looks for appropriate layouts. If text overlaps an object, the Design Checker converts the text to a graphic so it will display properly. The Design Checker looks at all graphics and may display suggestions on those that load slowly. Types of graphics will be covered in future projects.

## Closing the Entire Publication

Sometimes, everything goes wrong. If this happens, you may want to close the publication entirely and start over. You also may want to close a publication when you are finished with it so you can begin a new one. To close the publication, perform the following steps.

### TO CLOSE THE PUBLICATION AND START OVER

**1** Click File on the menu bar and then click Close.

**2** If Publisher displays a dialog box, click the No button to ignore the changes since the last time you saved the publication.

**3** If you want to start a publication from the Catalog, click the New button on the Standard toolbar. Otherwise, a clear page layout begins your next publication with the Quick Publications Wizard.

# Publisher Help System

At any time while you are working in Publisher, you can get answers to your questions by using the **Publisher Help system**. Used properly, this form of online assistance can increase your productivity and reduce your frustrations by minimizing the time you spend learning how to use Publisher.

The following section shows how to get answers to your questions using the Office Assistant. For additional information on using the Publisher Help system, see Appendix A and Table 1-2 on page PUB 1.57.

## Using the Office Assistant

The **Office Assistant** answers your questions and suggests more efficient ways to complete a task. With the Office Assistant active, for example, you can type a question, word, or phrase in a text box and the Office Assistant provides immediate help on the subject. Also, as you create a publication, the Office Assistant accumulates tips that suggest more efficient ways to complete the tasks performed while building a publication, such as formatting, printing, and saving. This tip feature is part of the IntelliSense™ technology that is built into Publisher, which understands what you are trying to do and suggests better ways to do it. When the light bulb displays above the Office Assistant, click it to see a tip.

The following steps show how to use the Office Assistant to obtain information on running Publisher tutorials.

### More About

#### Quick Reference

For a table that lists how to complete the tasks covered in this book using the mouse, menu, shortcut menu, and keyboard, visit the Shelly Cashman Series Office Web page (www.scite.com/off2000/qr.htm) and then click Microsoft Publisher 2000.

### More About

#### Microsoft Certification

The Microsoft Office User Specialist (MOUS) Certification program provides an opportunity for you to obtain a valuable industry credential - proof that you have the Office 2000 skills required by employers. For more information see Appendix D or visit the Shelly Cashman Series MOUS Web page at www.scite.com/off2000/cert.htm.

### Steps  To Obtain Help Using the Office Assistant

**1** If the Office Assistant is not on the screen, click Help on the menu bar and then click Show the Office Assistant. With the Office Assistant on the screen, click it. **Type** Does Publisher have any tutorials **in the What would you like to do? text box in the Office Assistant balloon. Point to the Search button.**

*The question displays in the Office Assistant balloon (Figure 1-71).*

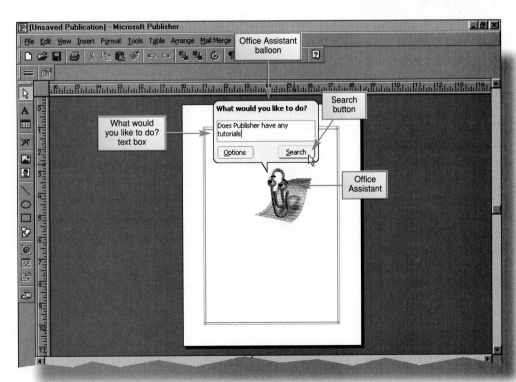

**FIGURE 1-71**

**2** **Click the Search button. Point to the topic, Tutorial Table of Contents, in the Office Assistant balloon.**

*The Office Assistant displays a list of topics relating to the question, Does Publisher have any tutorials (Figure 1-72).*

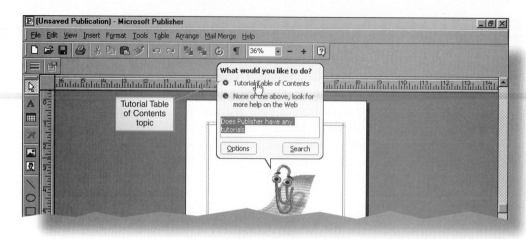

**FIGURE 1-72**

**3** **Click Tutorial Table of Contents.**

*The Microsoft Publisher - Tutorial window displays (Figure 1-73). The Publisher tutorial list contains a variety of links. When you point to a link, the mouse pointer shape changes to a pointing hand.*

**4** **Click a link to run any tutorial of your choosing. Use the Page Navigation control at the bottom of the window to advance through the tutorial. When finished, click the Close button on the Tutorial title bar.**

*The Microsoft Publisher – Tutorial window closes and the publication again is active.*

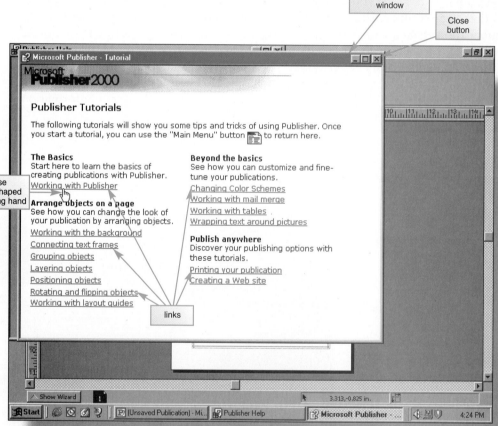

**FIGURE 1-73**

1. If Office Assistant is turned on, click Help button on Standard toolbar, or on Help menu click Microsoft Publisher Help

You can use the Office Assistant to search for Help on any topic concerning Publisher.

Table 1-2 summarizes the nine categories of Help available to you. Because of the way the Publisher Help system works, please review the rightmost column of Table 1-2 if you have difficulties activating the desired category of Help. For additional information on using the Publisher Help system, see Appendix A.

## Table 1-2  Publisher Help System

| TYPE | DESCRIPTION | HOW TO ACTIVATE | TURNING THE OFFICE ASSISTANT ON AND OFF |
|---|---|---|---|
| Answer Wizard | Similar to the Office Assistant in that it answers questions that you type in your own words. It displays when the Office Assistant is turned off or when you click the Show button on the Publisher Help toolbar. | Click the Microsoft Publisher Help button on the Standard toolbar. If necessary, maximize the Help window by double-clicking its title bar. Click the Answer Wizard tab. | If the Office Assistant displays, right-click it, and then click Options. Click Use the Office Assistant to remove the check mark. Click the OK button. |
| Contents sheet | Groups Help topics by general categories. Use when you know only the general category of the topic in question. It displays when the Office Assistant is turned off or when you click the Show button on the Publisher Help toolbar. | Click the Microsoft Publisher Help button on the Standard toolbar. If necessary, maximize the Help window by double-clicking its title bar. Click the Contents tab. | If the Office Assistant displays, right-click it, and then click Options. Click Use the Office Assistant to remove the check mark. Click the OK button. |
| Detect and Repair | Automatically finds and fixes errors in the application. | Click Detect and Repair on the Help menu. | |
| Hardware and Software Information | Shows Product ID and allows access to system information and technical support information. | Click About Microsoft Publisher on the Help menu and then click the appropriate button. | |
| Index sheet | Similar to an index in a book; use when you know exactly what you want. It displays when the Office Assistant is turned off or when you click the Show button on the Publisher Help toolbar. | Click the Microsoft Publisher Help button on the Standard toolbar. If necessary, maximize the Help window by double-clicking its title bar. Click the Index tab. | If the Office Assistant displays, right-click it, and then click Options. Click Use the Office Assistant to remove the check mark. Click the OK button. |
| Microsoft Publisher Web Site | Used to access technical resources and download free product enhancements on the Web. | Click Microsoft Publisher Web Site on the Help menu. | |
| Object-specific Help | Used to access Help topics on manipulating specific objects. | Right-click the object and then click a Help link. | |
| Office Assistant | Answers questions that you type in your own words, offers tips, and provides Help for a variety of Publisher features. | Click the Microsoft Publisher Help button on the Standard toolbar or double-click the Office Assistant icon. Some dialog boxes also include the Microsoft Publisher Help button. | If the Office Assistant does not display, click Show the Office Assistant on the Help menu. |
| Question Mark button and What's This? button | Displays as a question mark (?) character or What's This? button. Used to identify unfamiliar items on the screen. | In a dialog box, click the Question Mark button and then click an item in the dialog box. Right-click an item and then click the What's This? button when it displays. | |

## Quitting Publisher

To quit Publisher, complete the following steps.

### TO QUIT PUBLISHER

1. Click the Close button on the title bar.
2. If the Microsoft Publisher dialog box displays, click the No button.

## CASE PERSPECTIVE SUMMARY

Joy Elliot's flyer is complete. With your help, she now has a full-color flyer with tear-offs that she can post at the school, the library, and stores in the area. The flyer consists of a graphic illustrating the purpose of the flyer, a bulleted list identifying her services, and perforated tear-offs for potential customers to take with them. The attention getter and banner heading should attract people to the flyer.

An added enhancement will be the Web page version of the flyer. Joy can publish the Web folder you created on Central College's electronic bulletin board, thus widening her advertising scope. Students with electronic mail access can reach Joy quickly at her e-mail address.

## Project Summary

Project 1 introduced you to starting Publisher and creating an advertising flyer. You learned how to choose and run a wizard to design a template for editing. After choosing a color scheme, you learned how to edit text frames, bulleted lists, and repeating elements such as tear-offs. You also learned how to use the zoom buttons to assist you in editing. Once you saved the publication, you learned how to change a graphic, change a background color, and move and resize elements on the window. In anticipation of posting your publication to the Web, you learned how to delete and insert objects. You then saved the publication as a Web page in a Web folder, and quit Publisher. Finally, you learned to use Publisher's Help system.

## What You Should Know

Having completed this project, you now should be able to perform the following tasks:

- Add an Attention Getter to a Publication *(PUB 1.46)*
- Add Color and a Border to a Text Frame *(PUB 1.36)*
- Add Text *(PUB 1.22)*
- Close the Publication and Start Over *(PUB 1.54)*
- Create a Publication Using a Wizard *(PUB 1.11)*
- Create a Web Site from a Publication *(PUB 1.51)*
- Delete an Object *(PUB 1.49)*
- Edit a Bulleted List Using the Zoom Buttons *(PUB 1.21)*
- Edit a Graphic *(PUB 1.34)*

- Edit Tear-Offs *(PUB 1.24)*
- Edit Text in a Publication *(PUB 1.18)*
- Move and Resize a Grouped Heading *(PUB 1.30)*
- Move and Resize a Graphic *(PUB 1.32)*
- Obtain Help Using the Office Assistant *(PUB 1.55)*
- Open an Existing Publication *(PUB 1.42)*
- Print a Publication *(PUB 1.40)*
  Quit Publisher *(PUB 1.41, PUB 1.57)*
- Save a New Publication *(PUB 1.26)*
- Save an Existing Publication with the Same File Name *(PUB 1.39)*
- Start Publisher *(PUB 1.9)*

# *Apply Your Knowledge*

Project Reinforcement at www.scsite.com/off2000/reinforce.htm

## 1 Editing a Publication

**Instructions:** Start Publisher. Open the publication, apply-1 from the Data Disk. See the inside back cover of this book for instructions on downloading the Data Disk or see your instructor for information on accessing the files required in this book. The publication is shown in Figure 1-74.

Perform the following tasks.

1. Highlight the text, Home for Sale. Type Cape Cod for Sale in the text frame.
2. Highlight the text, $139,900, and then delete it.
3. Select the bulleted list text frame. Delete the text, New Carpeting. Type 4-Star Schools as the new bullet.
4. Select the picture of the home. Make the picture a little smaller by dragging the corner Resizer toward the center.
5. Select the bulleted list. Make the bulleted list larger by dragging the left side Resizer toward the center of the page.
6. Click the orange rectangle close to the corner attention getter, to select only the rectangle. Click the Fill Color button on the Formatting toolbar. Choose a different color from the Scheme colors.
7. Click any tear-off. Click the Zoom In button until the tear-off is easy to read.
8. In the tear-off text frame, click after the telephone number. Press the ENTER key and then type Fax: (317) 555-1065 in the text frame. Click outside the text frame.
9. Click File on the menu bar and then click Save As. Use the file name, Cape Cod for Sale, and then save the publication on a floppy disk.
10. Print the revised publication.

**FIGURE 1-74**

*In the Lab*

# 1 Creating a Sign

**Problem:** The video store you work for has asked you to make a sign for the front door that lists company business hours. Using the Business Hours Sign Wizard, create a sign listing the days and business hours from Table 1-3.

**Instructions:** Perform the following tasks to create a sign using the data in Table 1-3.

| Table 1-3 | Video Store Hours | | |
|---|---|---|---|
| Monday | 10:00 | To | 10:00 |
| Tuesday | 10:00 | To | 10:00 |
| Wednesday | 10:00 | To | 10:00 |
| Thursday | 10:00 | To | 10:00 |
| Friday | 10:00 | To | 12:00 |
| Saturday | 10:00 | To | 12:00 |
| Sunday | 1:00 | To | 10:00 |

1. Start Publisher. In the Catalog dialog box, click Signs.
2. In the Quick Publications pane, click Business Hours Sign. Click the Start Wizard button.
3. Because this sign will be posted in the window of the video store, it needs to be clear and easy to read from the sidewalk. Choose the Black and White color scheme. Click the Finish button, and then hide the wizard.
4. Each cell in the timetable is a text frame. Change the hours in each frame to match Table 1-3.
5. Click the text frame below the table. Type Telephone (303) 555-5800 in the bottom text frame.
6. Save the publication on a floppy disk with the file name, Business Hours Sign.
7. Print a copy of the sign.

# 2 Creating an Event Flyer

**Problem:** You are a junior student at a university. In addition to carrying a full class load this semester, you are on a student council committee to organize a fall food drive for the community food pantry. People bringing a canned food item will receive $1.00 off the admission to Friday night's football game. Using Publisher's Flyers Wizard, create an announcement for the food drive.

**Instructions:** Perform the following tasks.

1. Start Publisher. If the Catalog dialog box does not display, click File on the menu bar and the click New.
2. In the Flyers list, click Fund-raiser. Click Even Break Fund-raiser Flyer, and then click the Start Wizard button.
3. When asked for a color scheme, choose Vineyard and then click the Finish button to accept the preset value for all other wizard choices.
4. Make the following changes to the personal information set. For each text frame, select the template text, and then type in the new text.
    a. Type Student Council in the Organization Name Text Frame on the right side of the flyer. The vertical Organization Name Text Frame in the masthead will synchronize automatically.
    b. Type Room 334 Student Union Building in the Address Text Frame.
    c. Type Phone: 816-555-9320 in the Phone/Fax/E-mail Text Frame.
    d. Type Receive $1.00 off your admission to the football game. in the Tag Line Text Frame.
    e. Type 10/12/01 as the date.
    f. Type 7:00 P.M. as the time.

# In the Lab

5. Delete the contact place holding text frame by right-clicking the Text Frame, and then clicking Delete Object on the shortcut menu.

6. For the remaining text frames, drag through the text and then type the new text as shown in Figure 1-75.

7. To adjust the font size of the large text frame, click Format on the menu bar and then click AutoFit Text. If necessary, click Best Fit on the AutoFit Text submenu.

8. Double-click the picture to display the Insert Clip Art window. Type jars in the Search for clips text box and then press the ENTER key. Choose an appropriate graphic from those available in the Clip Gallery, and then close the Insert Clip Art window.

9. Keep Publisher's standard logo in the lower-right corner, and then type Student Council as the name of the organization.

10. Save the publication on a floppy disk using the file name, Food Drive Flyer. If prompted to keep the changes to the Organization Logo, click the No button.

11. Print a copy of the flyer.

**FIGURE 1-75**

## 3 Composing an Event Flyer from Scratch

**Problem:** You are the publicity chairperson for the Fall Concert Series in the School of Music. The conservatory is sponsoring a violin recital of its senior music majors. You want to prepare an event flyer to post around campus.

**Instructions:** Create the event flyer in Figure 1-76 on the next page. Using the techniques presented in this project, start Publisher and then click the Blank Publications tab. Select the Full Page preview. Click the Create button and then hide the wizard. Below are some general guidelines. *Hint:* Use the ScreenTips on the Objects toolbar and Help to solve this problem.

1. Create the rectangles and graphics before the text frames.

*(continued)*

## *In the Lab*

**Composing an Event Flyer from Scratch** *(continued)*

2. Click the Rectangle Tool on the Objects toolbar. On the blank publication, drag the mouse pointer in the shape desired to create the vertical stripe and the lower rectangle. Use the Fill Color button to add color.

3. Choose the Oval Attention Getter from the Design Gallery. Edit the attention getter as necessary.

4. Use the Clip Gallery to insert the picture (or another appropriate graphic). Move and resize it as necessary.

5. Use the Text Frame Tool on the Objects toolbar to create all other text. After drawing the frame, insert the text. Drag each text area and add formatting to make the publication closely resemble the figure. *Hint:* You may need to use the Bold, Italics, and Increase Font Size buttons on the Formatting toolbar.

6. Save the publication on a floppy disk with the file name, Violin Recital Flyer.

7. Print a copy of the flyer.

**FIGURE 1-76**

# Cases and Places

The difficulty of these case studies varies:
▶ are the least difficult; ▶▶ are more difficult; and ▶▶▶ are the most difficult.

**1** ▶ Use the Flyers Wizard titled Car Wash Fund-raiser Flyer to create a flyer for your sorority's upcoming car wash. The car wash is Saturday, September 18 from 10:00 A.M. to 2:00 P.M. Use the name of your own school and address in the appropriate areas. The location is the College Library parking lot.

**2** ▶ Start the Play Announcement Flyer Wizard to create a flyer for a local dramatic production. When the wizard asks you, use the Burgundy color scheme. Use the techniques in Project 1 to edit the text as follows: The name of the play is *The Taming of the Shrew*. The author is William Shakespeare. The dates are October 8, 9, and 10. The time is 8:00 P.M. at the Performing Arts Center. The ticket price is $7.00. Choose an appropriate graphic in the Clip Gallery in the Insert Clip Art window by searching for the word, entertainment. Add an attention grabber in the lower-right corner. You may delete the sponsor logos, or edit them as you desire.

**3** ▶▶ Create an advertising flyer to look for a new roommate. Use a wizard that includes tear-offs and a graphic, such as the Pets Available Flyer in Project 1. Decide where you might place such a flyer and think about how you could attract the most attention as you plan your publication. Describe your apartment. Include the features in the bulleted list. Include a picture of your apartment, room, or house. Use tear-offs with your name and telephone number.

**4** ▶▶ You are the secretary for a university academic office. Part of your job is to let students know the advising hours during registration periods. Using the Business Hours Sign Wizard, create a sign listing the professors and their hours. Professor Abrams has hours on Monday, Wednesday, and Friday from 12:00 P.M. to 3:30 P.M. Professor Brent is in from 8:00 A.M. to 10:00 A.M. on Monday, Tuesday, and Wednesday. Professor Collier is in on Tuesday and Thursday from 12:00 P.M. to 4:00 P.M. Professor Diaz is in on Tuesday and Thursday from 8:00 A.M. to 11:30 A.M. Professor Ezral is available every Monday and Tuesday from 5:00 P.M. to 8:00 P.M.

**5** ▶▶▶ Many communities offer free Web page hosting for religious organizations. Using a one-page design wizard, such as a flyer or sign, create a Web page for a local house of worship. Include the name, address, telephone, worship and education hours, as well as the name of a contact person. If possible, include a photo or line drawing of the building. Use the Create Web Site from Current Publication feature and let Publisher run through its Design Checker.

## Cases and Places

**6**  ▶▶▶  Your Internet service provider maintains an electronic bulletin board where customers may post one-page business announcements. Create an advertising flyer for the place where you work or want to work. You may use one of Publisher's wizards, or design the flyer from scratch. Use color and graphics to attract attention. Use a bulleted list to describe your company's services. Use words in your text frames that will produce many hits during Web searches.

**7**  ▶▶▶  Your Aunt Pearl has sent you the note shown in Figure 1-77 asking you to help her create a flyer for her class reunion. Use the concepts and techniques presented in this project to create the flyer. Be sure to include at least two bulleted items in a list, an attention getter, and insert an appropriate graphic from the Clip Gallery or the Web.

Hi there,

We are having our 25-year class reunion. I know you are "into" computers, so I was wondering if you could print up something I could use as a flyer to announce the reunion?

The reunion is Saturday, November 17, at 6:00 p.m. We are planning dinner at Violet's Restaurant, live entertainment by The Montgomery Band, and a special guest appearance by Shorty Cooper, a local comedian/magician. Have you seen his audience participation card tricks? He really is good!

Hopefully, we will have the opportunity to reminisce about old times, catch up on current projects, and share future plans. We would like everyone to take part in the food and fun.

Call Joyce Lyle - you remember her - if you need more information at (576) 555-2223.

Thanks a lot,

Aunt Pearl

**FIGURE 1-77**

Microsoft Publisher 2000

PROJECT

2

# Designing a Newsletter

## OBJECTIVES

You will have mastered the material in this project when you can:

- Describe the advantages of using a newsletter medium
- Identify the steps in the design process
- Create a newsletter using Publisher's Newsletter Wizard
- Edit a newsletter template
- Change pages using the Page Navigation control
- Insert and delete pages in a publication
- Select and edit text
- Edit a masthead
- Import text files
- Toggle publication views
- Save a newsletter
- Edit personal information components
- Edit a design set
- Create columns in a text frame
- Edit an attention getter
- Edit graphics
- Add a pull quote
- Edit sidebars
- Insert and modify lines and arrows
- Insert a WordArt object
- Add page numbers to the background
- Identify foreground and background elements
- Check a publication for errors
- Print a two-sided publication

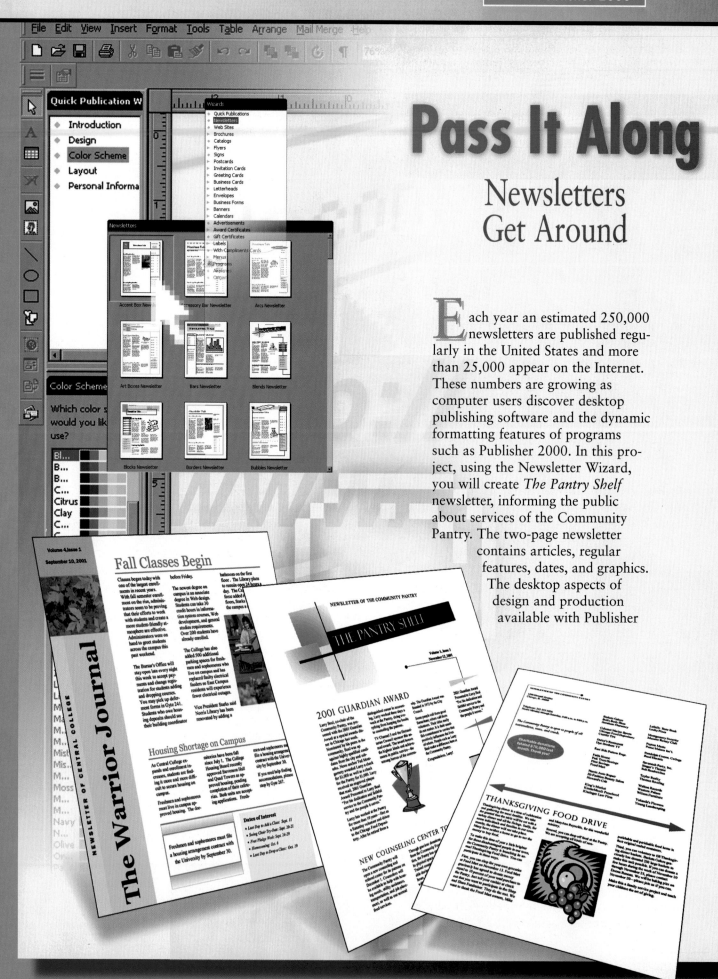

# Pass It Along

## Newsletters Get Around

ach year an estimated 250,000 newsletters are published regularly in the United States and more than 25,000 appear on the Internet. These numbers are growing as computer users discover desktop publishing software and the dynamic formatting features of programs such as Publisher 2000. In this project, using the Newsletter Wizard, you will create *The Pantry Shelf* newsletter, informing the public about services of the Community Pantry. The two-page newsletter contains articles, regular features, dates, and graphics. The desktop aspects of design and production available with Publisher

make it easy and inexpensive to produce printed publications such as newsletters. In addition, newsletters provide a forum for entertainment, education, and advertisement of dated information. They are more focused in scope than newspapers and include a myriad of design possibilities and appeal.

Newsletters are inexpensive, effortlessly passed along, and they make good reading material in reception and waiting areas.

From the church bulletin to the homeowners association, a newsletter exists to suit every interest. The *At-Home Dad* newsletter, in an online edition and a print version, is devoted to providing connections and resources for fathers who stay home with their children. *The Nutrition Connection* is a newsletter dedicated to helping you feel your best. *Stormtrack* is a publication to which weather buffs can subscribe that features storm chasers in pursuit of cumulonimbus clouds, severe storms, and tornadoes.

Other specialty newsletters have been created, such as *Catnip* for feline lovers, published by Tufts University School of Veterinary Medicine, *Childfree Network* for individuals without children who desire equity in the corporate world, and *Naturally Well* for health-conscious individuals interested in homeopathic remedies.

Baby boomers' interests account for an increase in specialized publications. For example, *Homeground*, a quarterly newsletter started

by a former gardening columnist, and *Virtual Garden*, on the Internet, are among the newsletters filling the gardening niche. Health and nutrition newsletters have become very popular in the last ten years; among the titles are *Health After 50*, *Nutrition Advocate*, and *Health Wisdom for Women*.

Internet users can find an abundance of online publications, some of which are available in printed versions, as well. Investors might surf to the Merrill Lynch site that features a weekly newsletter devoted to developments in Washington and an online forum or the *Wilson Financial Report*, an online financial newsletter for the new investor. Sports lovers will find *International Tennis Weekly*, the official newsletter of the ATP Tour or the *Penn State Sports Medicine Newsletter*. Scientists can discover the *NATO Review*, the *Electronic Zoo*, and *Science Online*.

Newsletters.com was founded on the premise that the new wave of sophisticated Internet users should have access to the wisdom of newsletters written by experts in their respective fields. This site groups more than 350 titles into a variety of categories with more than 800 affiliates. Newletters.com captures the attention of millions of eyes and directs them to newsletters of their choice.

With Americans reading print and online newsletters in record numbers, it is easy to understand the increase in their popularity and circulation. Be sure to pass them along.

Microsoft Publisher 2000

# Designing a Newsletter

P R O J E C T

**2**

**CASE PERSPECTIVE**

The Community Pantry has asked you to prepare the November issue of their monthly newsletter, *The Pantry Shelf*. The Community Pantry is a not-for-profit community organization that supports needy individuals and families with food and services that they otherwise could not afford. November is a busy time for the Pantry, as it prepares for the holiday season.

The Pantry mails *The Pantry Shelf* to its patrons, donors, and interested community members. The newsletter includes articles of interest and a monthly feature called "Donor Declaration" — a list of individuals and businesses who have contributed goods, services, and financial assistance to the Pantry. In addition, *The Pantry Shelf* newsletter contains the usual volume, date, and organizational information.

Donna Reneau, secretary of the Community Pantry Foundation, has written and word-processed several articles to include in the November issue. Donna has asked you to prepare the newsletter using bright, attractive colors, boxes, and graphics. You will use Microsoft Publisher's Newsletter Wizard to publish the two-page, three-column newsletter.

# Introduction

As discussed in Project 1, desktop publishing is becoming the most popular way for businesses of all sizes to produce their printed publications. The desktop aspects of design and production make it easy and inexpensive to produce high-quality documents in a short amount of time. Desktop implies doing everything from a desk, including the planning, designing, writing, layout, cutting and pasting, as well as printing, collating, and distributing. With a PC and a software program like Microsoft Publisher, you can create a professional document from your computer without the cost and time of sending it to a professional publisher.

## The Newsletter Medium

Newsletters are a popular way for offices, businesses, and other organizations to distribute information to their clientele. A **newsletter** is usually a multi-page publication, double-sided, with newspaper features like columns and a masthead, and the added eye appeal of sidebars, pictures, and other graphics.

Newsletters have several advantages over other publication media. They are easy to produce. Brochures, designed to be in circulation for longer periods of time as a type of advertising, usually are published in greater quantities and on more expensive paper than newsletters and are, therefore, more costly. Additionally, newsletters differ from brochures in that they commonly have a shorter shelf life, making newsletters a perfect forum for dated information.

Newsletters are more narrow and focused in scope than newspapers; their eye appeal is more distinctive. Many organizations and companies distribute newsletters inexpensively to interested audiences, although that is beginning to change. Newsletters are becoming an integral part of many marketing plans because they offer a legitimate medium by which to communicate services, successes, and issues. Table 2-1 lists some benefits and advantages of using the newsletter medium.

| Table 2-1 Benefits and Advantages of Using a Newsletter Medium | |
| --- | --- |
| AREA | BENEFITS AND ADVANTAGES |
| Exposure | • An easily distributed publication — office mail, bulk mail, electronically<br>• A pass-along document for other interested parties<br>• A coffee table reading item in reception areas |
| Education | • An opportunity to inform in a nonrestrictive environment<br>• A directed education forum for clientele<br>• An increased, focused feedback — unavailable in most advertising |
| Contacts | • A form of legitimized contact<br>• A source of free information to build credibility<br>• An easier way to expand a contact database than other marketing tools |
| Communication | • An effective medium to highlight the inner workings of a company<br>• A way to create a discussion forum<br>• A method to disseminate more information than a brochure |
| Cost | • An easily designed medium using desktop publishing software<br>• An inexpensive method of mass production<br>• A reusable design |

# Project Two — Newsletter

Project 2 uses a Publisher Newsletter Wizard to produce *The Pantry Shelf* newsletter shown in Figures 2-1a and 2-1b on the next page. This monthly publication informs the public about services offered by the Community Pantry. The Pantry's two-page newsletter contains articles, monthly features, dates, and graphics.

### More About 2000

### Newsletters

Many newsletters are published regularly on the Web. To look at some samples and for more information on newsletter content, visit the Publisher 2000 More About Web page (www.scsite.com/pub2000/more.htm) and click Newsletters.

Microsoft Publisher 2000

NEWSLETTER OF THE COMMUNITY PANTRY

THE PANTRY SHELF

**Volume 1, Issue 3**
**November 12, 2001**

## 2001 GUARDIAN AWARD

Larry Beal, co-chair of the Community Pantry, was presented with the 2001 Guardian Award at a special awards dinner in Chicago last week. Nominated by his peers in the community, Beal was up against highly qualified candidates from the city and suburbs. News anchor Ted Montgomery awarded Larry a check for $1,000 as well as a check for the Pantry for $1,000. Larry received an engraved plaque that read, 2001 Guardian Award Presented to Larry Beal "For his dedication and faithful service to the Community Pantry and the people it serves."

Larry has worked at the Pantry for more than 10 years—first as a Saturday volunteer and driver to the Chicago Food Depository. After he retired from a

distinguished career in accounting, Larry worked three days a week at the Pantry, doing everything from keeping the books to counseling the patrons.

TV Channel 5 and the Humanitarian Council sponsor this annual award. The award honors the highest ideals and achievements in public service—the unsung heroes of the commu-

nity. The Guardian Award was founded in 1972 by the City Council.

Some people call them good Samaritans; others call them volunteers. Their titles really do not matter. It is their unselfish commitment to service that positively influences the lives of others. People such as Larry Beal make a difference here at the Community Pantry.

Congratulations, Larry!

2001 Guardian Award Presented to Larry Beal "For his dedication and faithful service to the Community Pantry and the people it serves."

## NEW COUNSELING CENTER TO OPEN SOO

The Community Pantry will open a new counseling and referral center for its patrons on December 1. Counselors will be available to help with housing needs, utility assistance, transportation, and job placement, as well as our normal food services.

Through gracious donations from the Community Foundation, the Pantry has expanded its physical space as well. Trained counselors are available during our normal Pantry hours. If you need assistance with any of these programs, please stop by the Community

Pantry and talk to a couns

The Pantry wants to be th when help is needed.

**(a)**

**(b)**

NEWSLETTER OF THE COMMUNITY PANTRY

1248 Howard Avenue
Chicago, IL 60609

Telephone: 312-555-9876
Hours: Monday through Saturday, 8:00 a.m. to 8:00 p.m.

*The Community Pantry is open to people of all nationalities, races, and creeds.*

**Charitable donations totaled $70,000 last month. Thank you!**

# DONOR DECLARATION

Baskets Galore
Bob's Body Shop
Burnham Pharmacy

Calumet Marine Sports
Chicago Food Depository
Ciastko Tire

Dulce's Restaurant
Dye Brothers TV

East Side Pattern Engr.

Faith House
Fed. Trust/Savings
First Savings
Food Mart

Harris Auto Repair
Hi-Fashion Beauty Salon
Howard's Cab

King's Market
KinderMusik Preschool
Kissinger Law Firm

LaSalle State Bank
Lucky Pizza

Montgomery Security
Munster Rotary Club

Payton Music
Peace Makers Int'l.

Randolph Comm. College
Reed Electric

Savannah Party, Inc.
Singer's Theater
Sub Sandwiches

Taylor Realty
Thomas Roofing

Walton Records
Western Palace
Wilson Furniture

Yolanda's Flowers
Young Landscaping

## THANKSGIVING FOOD DRIVE

Thanksgiving dinner is a time of celebration and gathering for most families. We take for granted that the table will be set with a turkey dinner and all the fixings. Sadly, for some individuals and families in our community, the dinner will not take place. Many have neither a home to go to nor the money to buy food.

To make this time of year a little brighter for those disadvantaged people in our town, the Community Pantry is launching its annual Thanksgiving Food Drive. You can participate in three ways.

First, you can shop for your own groceries at Food Mart on November 13. Food Mart graciously has agreed to donate money equal to 10 percent of your total purchase to the Pantry. Just tell your cashier at check out that you want to participate in the Shop and Share Fundraiser. They do the rest. We want to thank the Food Mart owners, Mike

and MaryAnn Reynolds, for this wonderful ministry.

Second, you can drop off food at the Pantry. We are accepting all kinds of non-

perishable and perishable food items in their original sealed containers.

Third, you can volunteer to fill Thanksgiving dinner baskets. Baskets Galore graciously has donated 250 large baskets to make this task possible. If you can donate a few hours during the week of November 20 through November 25, please contact Donna Reneau. We will be baking pies on November 20—please join us if you can.

Make this a family service project and teach your children the art of giving.

Page 2

**FIGURE 2-1**

## Starting Publisher

To start Publisher, Windows 95 or Windows 98 must be running. Perform the following steps to start Publisher.

### TO START PUBLISHER

1. Click the Start button on the taskbar and then point to Programs on the Start menu.
2. Click Microsoft Publisher on the Programs submenu.
3. If the Catalog does not display, click File on the menu bar and then click New.
4. Click the Publications by Wizard tab in the Catalog window.

Publisher's **Catalog** is a visual directory of publication designs. The three tabs display publication choices in different ways. Each tab contains two panes: the **Wizards pane** that lists the different types of publications, and the **previews pane** that displays the publication layouts available. These are shown in Figure 2-2 on the next page.

The **Publications by Wizard tab** categorizes publications by their purpose. For instance, Publisher displays all the Newsletter Wizards grouped together. The **Publications by Design tab,** displays design sets. A **design set** is a collection of related publication types that share a consistent design or look. For example, all the types of publications that use a marquee logo display together as a master set.

The **Blank Publications tab,** displays previews of formats, rather than a complete template or wizard. The previews have preset page dimensions, margins, and orientations, but do not have placeholders for text or graphics like the previous two tabs. The Blank Publications tab allows you to start from scratch.

The **Existing Files button** provides access to previously saved publications. The **Templates button** provides access to saved or downloaded templates.

# Using a Publisher Wizard in the Design Process

Designing an effective newsletter involves a great deal of planning. A good newsletter, or any publication, must deliver a message in the clearest, most attractive, and effective way possible. You must clarify your purpose and know your target audience. You need to gather ideas and plan ahead for the printing of the newsletter. Finally, you must determine the best layout for eye appeal and reliable dissemination of content. Table 2-2 outlines the issues to consider during the design process and their application to newsletters.

**More About**

## Design Issues

The steps in good design and attractive layout are similar to the steps in designing any new product, program, or presentation. For more information on design, visit the Publisher 2000 More About Web page (www.scsite.com/pub2000/more.htm) and click Design Issues.

| Table 2-2 Design Process Issues | |
|---|---|
| **DESIGN ISSUE** | **NEWSLETTER APPLICATION** |
| Purpose | to communicate and to educate readers about the organization |
| Audience | local interested clientele or patrons, both present and future |
| Gather data | articles, pictures, dates, figures, tables, discussion threads |
| Plan for printing | usually mass-produced, collated, and stapled |
| Layout | consistent look and feel; simple, eye-catching graphics |
| Synthesis | edit, proofread, and publish |

### Creating a Newsletter Template Using a Wizard

You can type a newsletter from scratch by choosing a blank publication from the Blank Publications tab, or you can use a wizard and let Publisher format the newsletter with appropriate headings, graphics, and spacing. You can customize the resulting newsletter by filling in the blanks and selecting and replacing objects.

Microsoft Publisher has many of the design planning features built into the software. Publisher has 25 different kinds of publications from which you may choose, each with its own set of design wizards and templates, more than 1,600 in all. As you may remember from Project 1, a wizard is a tool that guides you through the design process by asking questions and changing the publication accordingly. Once Publisher creates a publication from a wizard, you then can use it as a template to fill in the blanks, replace prewritten text as necessary, and change the art to fit your needs. Along the way, Publisher may periodically remind you to save your work. As you work through the project, you will save the newsletter on page PUB 2.6; however, you may save any time you wish. Perform the following steps to create a newsletter template using the Newsletter Wizard.

 **To Create a Newsletter Template Using Publisher's Newsletter Wizard**

**1** **Click Newsletters in the Wizards pane. If necessary, click the down scroll arrow until the Blends Newsletter preview is visible. Point to the Blends Newsletter preview.**

*On the Publications by Wizard tab, Publisher displays the Wizards pane on the left and the previews of the selected Wizard on the right in the Catalog window (Figure 2-2). The list of previews may display differently on your computer.*

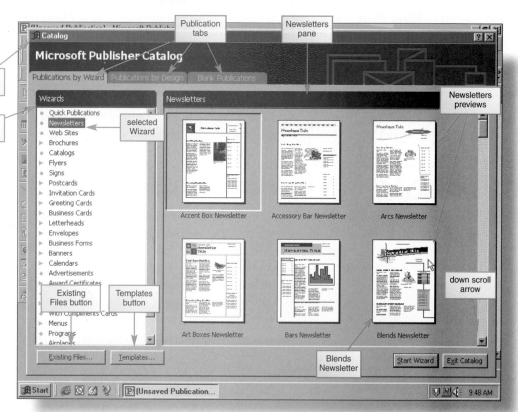

**FIGURE 2-2**

**2** Click the Blends Newsletter. Point to the Start Wizard button.

The selected preview displays with a box around it (Figure 2-3).

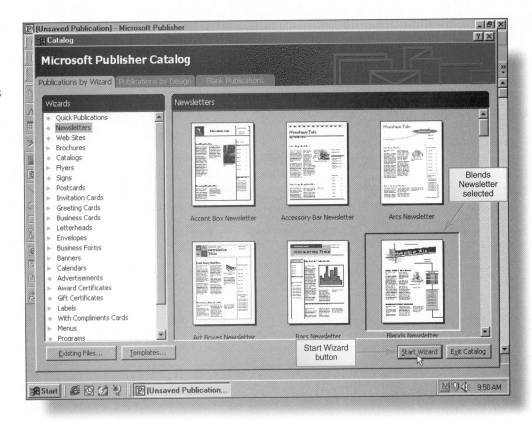

**FIGURE 2-3**

**3** Click the Start Wizard button. When Publisher finishes changing the publication, point to the Finish button in the Newsletter Wizard Introduction pane.

The Newsletter Wizard displays the Introduction pane on the left (Figure 2-4). In the workspace, page 1 of the Blends Newsletter displays. The Wizard pane includes command buttons to progress back and forth through the Wizard's questions, as well as a Finish button.

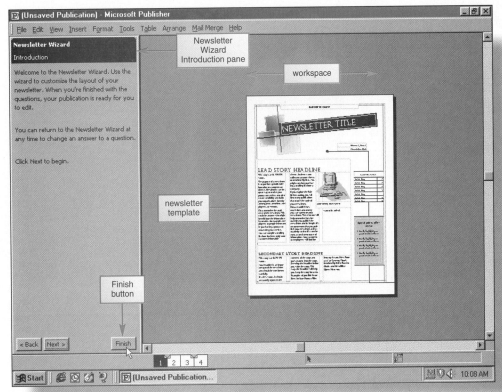

**FIGURE 2-4**

**4** **Click the Finish button to accept the default values of the Newsletter Wizard. Point to the Show/Hide Wizard button.**

*Publisher displays the finished template in the workspace (Figure 2-5). The Newsletter Wizard pane displays on the left with the Wizard's choices. The Show/Hide Wizard button currently displays, Hide Wizard.*

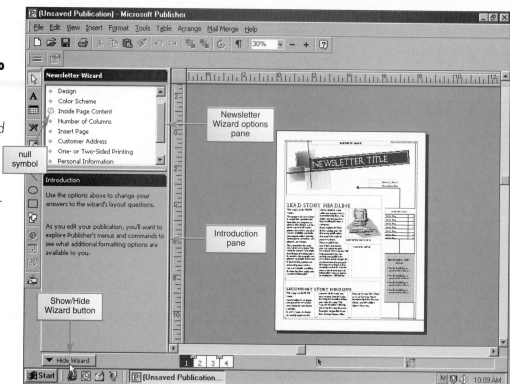

FIGURE 2-5

**5** **Click the Hide Wizard button. Maximize the screen, if necessary, and hide the Office Assistant if it displays.**

*The publication displays centered in the workspace (Figure 2-6). The Show/Hide Wizard button now displays, Show Wizard.*

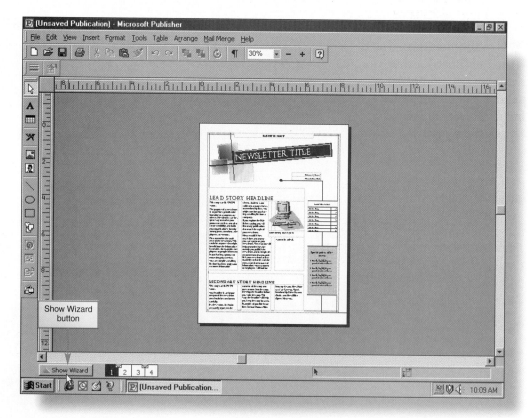

FIGURE 2-6

Clicking the Finish button bypasses the individual questions about design, color schemes, columns, pages, and printing options. Table 2-3 lists design options and default values provided by the Newsletter Wizard. The term **default** means any preset feature or data provided as part of the initial setup. Publisher's text and graphics use the default values provided by the Newsletter Wizard. Publisher applies the most popular formats to the newsletter. In Figure 2-5, options with the **null symbol** (ø) are not available in that particular wizard. You can revisit these options to make changes by clicking the Show/Hide Wizard button on the status bar.

| Table 2-3 | Newsletter Wizard Design Options and Default Values |
|---|---|
| *DESIGN* | *VALUES FOR THE BLENDS NEWSLETTER* |
| Color Scheme | Wildflower |
| Number of Columns | 3 |
| Customer Address | No |
| Printing Style | Double-sided |
| Number of Pages | 4 |

**Design Sets**

Each Newsletter Wizard is part of a design set, which is a collection of related publication types that share a consistent color scheme, design, and look. For example, a master set includes a business card, a company letterhead, and a company brochure, each with a matching design.

Any publication you choose from the Publications Wizard tab or the Design Wizards tab is a **Publisher-designed Publication**. You may use these publications, of course, as part of Publisher's licensing agreement. Using proven design strategies, Publisher places text and graphics in the publication at appropriate places for a professional looking newsletter.

# Editing the Newsletter Template

As the first step in the design process, the purpose of a newsletter is to communicate and educate its readers. Publisher places the lead story in a prominent position on the page, and uses a discussion of purpose and audience as the default text.

The following pages discuss how to edit various articles and objects in the newsletter.

## Pagination

Publisher's Newsletter Wizard creates four pages of text and graphics. This template is appropriate for some applications, but the Community Pantry wants to print a single sheet, two-sided newsletter. Page 4 of the newsletter contains objects typically used on the back page, so you will delete pages 2 and 3. Follow the steps on the next page to change and delete pages.

Microsoft Publisher 2000

 **To Change and Delete Pages in a Newsletter**

### 1 Click the page 2 icon on the Page Navigation control.

*Pages 2 and 3 display (Figure 2-7). The Page Navigation control displays the selected pages in black.*

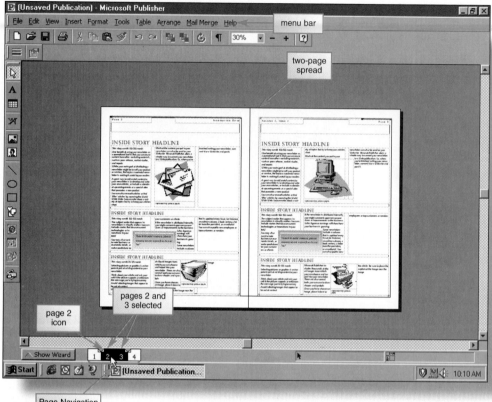

**FIGURE 2-7**

### 2 Click Edit on the menu bar and then click Delete Page. When the Delete Page dialog box displays, if the Both pages option is not selected, click it. Point to the OK button.

*Publisher displays a dialog box with options for deleting either or both pages (Figure 2-8).*

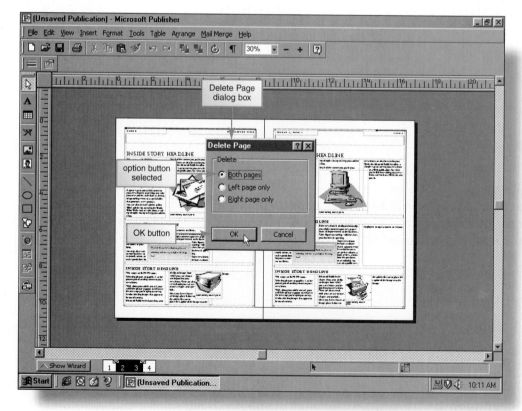

**FIGURE 2-8**

**3** **Click the OK button.**

*Publisher deletes pages 2 and 3 and displays the back page as the new page 2 (Figure 2-9).*

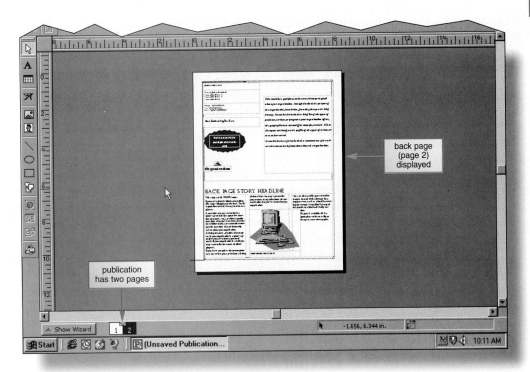

back page (page 2) displayed

publication has two pages

**FIGURE 2-9**

**Other Ways**

1. On View menu click Go to Page
2. Press CTRL+G
3. Press F5

Inserting pages in a newsletter is just as easy as deleting them. The Page command on the Insert menu provides the option of inserting a left- or right-hand page, as well as choices in the types of objects to display on the page. If you are on the first or last page when you choose to insert or delete, Publisher will warn you of pagination problems and offer you a confirmation button.

Now that the newsletter contains two pages, you are ready to edit the graphics and articles.

# Editing the Masthead

Most newsletters and brochures contain a masthead like the ones used in newspapers. A **masthead** is a box or section printed in each issue displaying information like the name, publisher, location, volume, and date. The Publisher-designed masthead, included in the Blends design set, contains several text frames, rectangles, and lines (Figure 2-10). The colored rectangles and lines create an attractive, eye-catching graphic that complements the Blends design set. You need to edit the text frames, however, to convey appropriate messages.

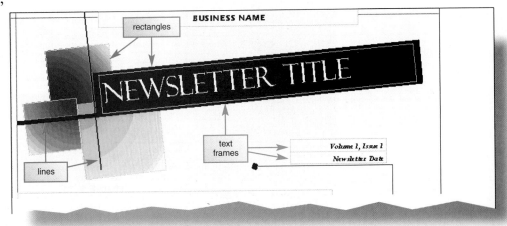

rectangles

BUSINESS NAME

NEWSLETTER TITLE

text frames

Volume 1, Issue 1

Newsletter Date

lines

**FIGURE 2-10**

Publisher incorporates four text frames in the Blends Newsletter masthead. The Newsletter Title displays in a text frame layered on top of a black rectangle. Two text frames display in the lower-right corner of the masthead for the volume and date. Across the top of the newsletter is a special text frame for the business name. You will edit the business name later in this project.

### Editing Techniques

Publisher uses text-editing techniques similar to most word processing programs. To insert text, position the insertion point and type the new text. Publisher always inserts the text to the left of the insertion point. The text to the right of the insertion point moves to the right and downward to accommodate the new text.

The BACKSPACE key deletes text to the left of the insertion point. However, to delete or change more than a few characters, you should select the text. Publisher handles selecting text in a slightly different manner than word processors. Publisher selects unedited default text, like placeholder titles and articles in the newsletters with a single click. To select large amounts of text, click the text and press CTRL+A, or drag through the text. To select individual words, double-click the word, as you would in word processing.

Perform the following steps to practice some of these techniques as you select and edit text.

### More About

### Deleting

Whether to delete using the BACKSPACE key or the DELETE key is debated hotly in word processing circles. It really depends on the location of the insertion point in your publication. If the insertion point already is positioned left of the character you want to delete, it makes more sense to press the DELETE key rather than reposition the insertion point just to use the BACKSPACE key.

 **Steps** **To Edit the Masthead**

**1** **Click the page 1 icon on the Page Navigation control. Point to the text, Newsletter Title.**

*Page 1 displays (Figure 2-11).*

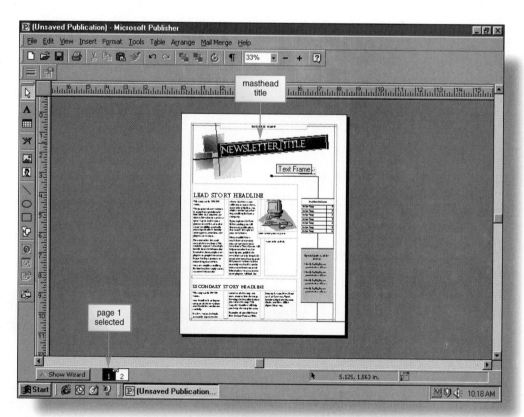

**FIGURE 2-11**

**2** Click Newsletter Title. Press F9 to view the masthead more closely.

Publisher enlarges the masthead and selects the entire text because it is placeholder text (Figure 2-12). Because the text frame is a layered object on top of a black rectangle, the highlight color is white.

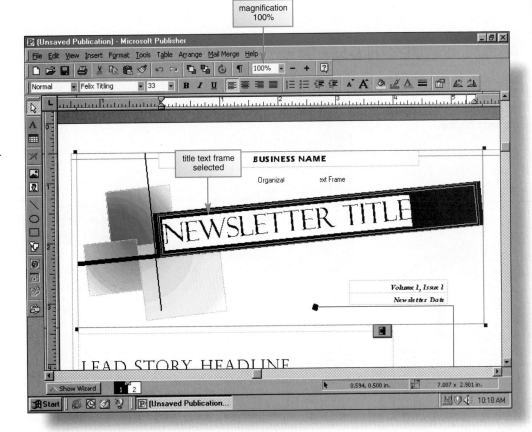

**FIGURE 2-12**

**3** Type THE PANTRY SHELF in the text frame. Point to the text frame containing the volume information.

Publisher replaces the text using the font from the design set (Figure 2-13). Because fonts are sometimes printer-dependent, your font may differ from the one shown.

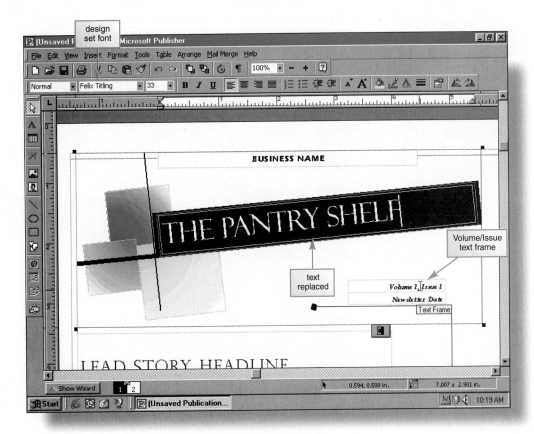

**FIGURE 2-13**

**4** Carefully double-click the numeral 1 in the Issue number, and then type 3 to replace it. Point to the Newsletter Date text frame.

*The number 1 changes to the number 3 (Figure 2-14).*

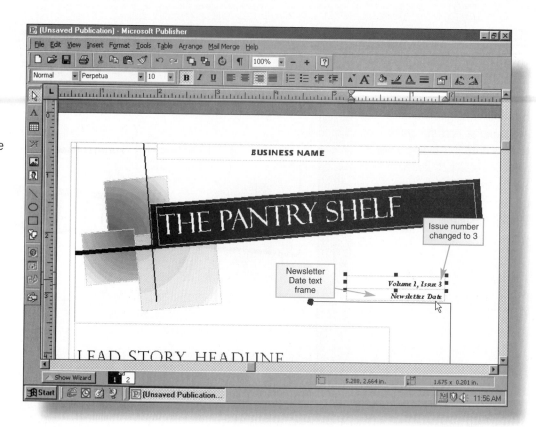

**FIGURE 2-14**

**5** Click the Newsletter Date text frame.

*Publisher selects the entire date because it is place-holder text, designed to be replaced (Figure 2-15).*

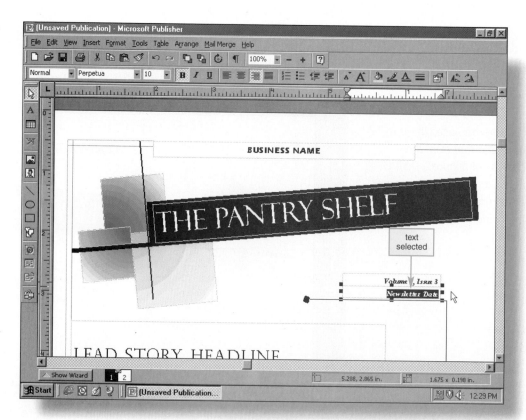

**FIGURE 2-15**

**6** **Type** November 12, 2001 **in the text frame.**

*The masthead edits are complete (Figure 2-16).*

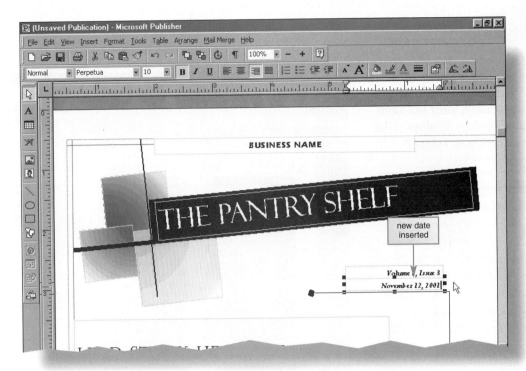

**BUSINESS NAME**

THE PANTRY SHELF

new date inserted

*Volume 1, Issue 3*
*November 12, 2001*

**FIGURE 2-16**

# Importing Files

Publisher allows users to import text and graphics from many sources into its publications. Publisher accepts imported objects from a variety of different programs and in many different file formats. Gathering data of interest to the readers is an important phase in the design process. The stories for the newsletter are provided on the data disk associated with this text. See the inside back cover for instructions for downloading the Publisher Data Disk or see your instructor for information on accessing the files required in this book. **Downloading** means moving data or programs from a larger computer system to a smaller one. Publisher uses the term **importing** to describe inserting text or objects from any other source into the Publisher workspace.

## Replacing Default Text Using an Imported File

Publisher suggests that 175 to 225 words will fit in the space allocated for the lead story. This Publisher-designed newsletter uses a three-column text format, **wrapping** or connecting the running text from one column to the next. Perform the steps on the next page to import a text file from a floppy disk to replace the Publisher supplied default text.

### Steps: To Replace Default Text

**1** **With the Publisher Data Disk in drive A, scroll down until the Lead Story article displays. Click the article to select it.**

*Publisher selects the entire article (Figure 2-17). Clicking Publisher-supplied default text automatically selects the entire text. At 100% view, the Lead Story article can be edited easily. Read the article. It contains valuable suggestions about the design process of newsletter publications.*

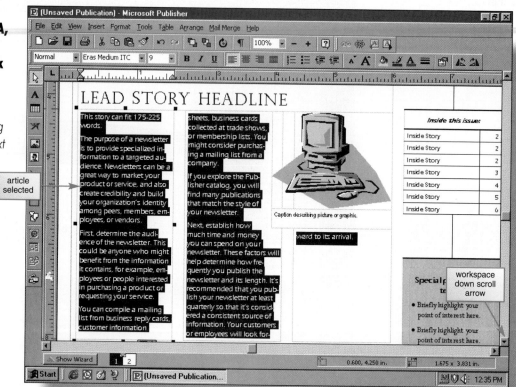

**FIGURE 2-17**

**2** **Click Insert on the menu bar, and then click Text File. Point to the Look in box arrow.**

*Publisher displays the Insert Text dialog box (Figure 2-18).*

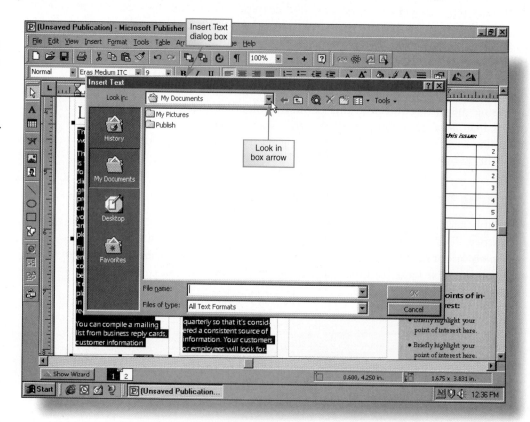

**FIGURE 2-18**

**3** **Click the Look in box arrow, and then click 3½ Floppy (A:). Point to the Guardian Award Article file name.**

*The data files on the floppy disk display below the Look in box (Figure 2-19).*

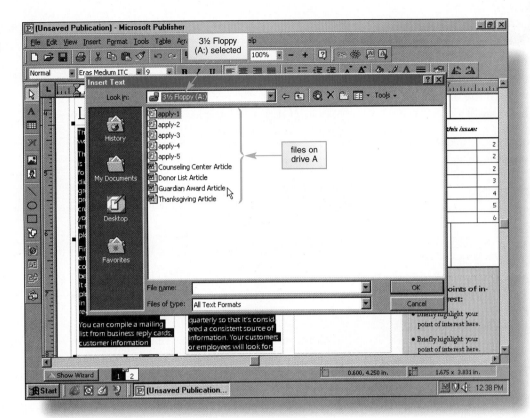

**FIGURE 2-19**

**4** **Double-click Guardian Award Article. When the article displays, point to LEAD STORY HEADLINE above the article.**

*Publisher replaces the selected default text with the Guardian Award Article (Figure 2-20). The article wraps, or connects, across the columns. The Go to Previous Frame button displays above the last column.*

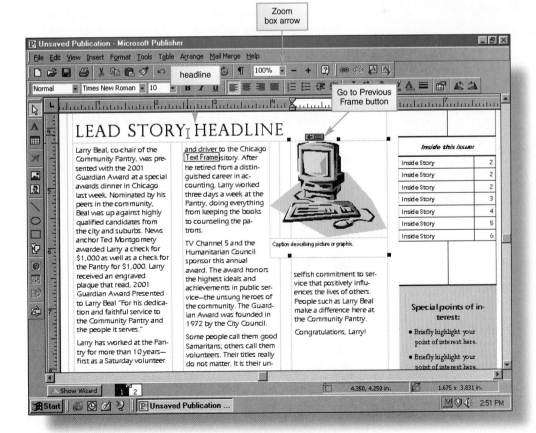

**FIGURE 2-20**

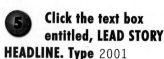

**5** **Click the text box entitled, LEAD STORY HEADLINE. Type** 2001 GUARDIAN AWARD **to replace the default headline.**

*Publisher displays the new headline (Figure 2-21).*

**FIGURE 2-21**

**Other Ways**

1. Right-click default text, click Change Text on shortcut menu, click Text File
2. Press ALT+I, type E

**Zooming**

To adjust the size of the characters on the screen, you can click the Zoom In or Zoom Out button; click the Zoom box arrow and then select the desired percentage or magnification style, or type a percentage of your choice in the Zoom box. To have the screen redraw even faster during zooming, you can reduce the quality of the picture display on the View menu.

Continuing a story across columns or text frames is one of the features that Publisher performs for you. If the story contains more text than will fit in the frame, Publisher displays a message to warn you. You then have the option of connecting to another frame or continuing the story on another page. Publisher will add the *continued* notices, or **jump lines,** to guide readers through the story.

The F9 function key toggles between the current page view and 100% magnification. **Toggle** means the same key will alternate views, or turn a feature on and off. Editing text is much easier if you view the text frame at 100% magnification or even larger. Page editing techniques, such as moving graphics, inserting new frames, and aligning objects, more easily are performed in Whole Page view. Toggling back and forth with the F9 function key works well. You also may choose different magnifications and views from the Zoom list on the Standard toolbar.

## Importing Text for the Secondary Article

The next step is to import the text for the secondary article in the lower portion of page 1 of the newsletter as explained in the steps below.

### TO IMPORT MORE TEXT

**1** If necessary, press F9 to view the whole page, and then click the Secondary Story article to select it.

**2** Click Insert on the menu bar and then click Text File.

**3** If not already selected, click 3½ Floppy (A:) in the Look in list.

**4** Double-click the Counseling Center Article file name.

**5** Click the headline, SECONDARY STORY HEADLINE, to select it.

**6** Type NEW COUNSELING CENTER TO OPEN SOON to replace the headline of the article.

*Figure 2-22 shows the completed article at 50% magnification. Your screen may differ slightly, depending on the fonts your system uses.*

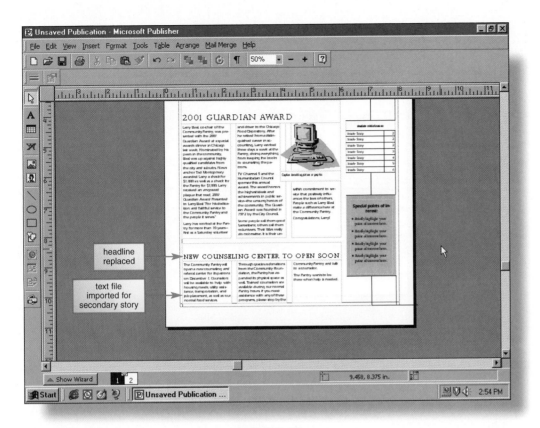

**FIGURE 2-22**

## Importing Text on the Back Page

The final steps to finish the articles in the newsletter involve importing text for the Thanksgiving Story.

### TO IMPORT THE BACK PAGE STORY

**1** Click the page 2 icon on the Page Navigation control.

**2** Click the Back Page Story article.

**3** Click Insert on the menu bar and then click Text File.

**4** If not already selected, click 3½ Floppy (A:) in the Look in list.

**5** Double-click the Thanksgiving Article file name.

**6** Click the BACK PAGE STORY HEADLINE text frame.

**7** Type THANKSGIVING FOOD DRIVE to replace the headline.

*The Thanksgiving article and headline display (Figure 2-23 on the next page).*

### Text Columns

Publisher provides two ways to create text in columns: connected text frames and columns. The Newsletter Wizard creates separate text frames and connects them. You also can use multiple columns within one text frame. Either way, the text will flow automatically, and jump lines will guide the reader. If you want separate stories in adjacent columns on the same page, or if you want your story to have unequal column widths, use separate text frames.

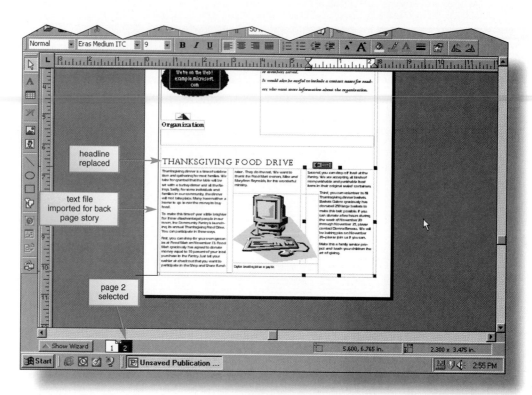

**FIGURE 2-23**

All the articles for the newsletter now are complete. Importing the articles instead of typing them saves time and adds the convenience of using a word processor. Publisher accepts most file formats from popular word processors and text editors. Once imported, Publisher lets you edit the articles using Microsoft Word by choosing Change Text on the shortcut menu. Editing your articles with Word allows you to manipulate the text using the full capabilities of a word processor.

**More About 2000**

**Importing Files**

Publisher accepts many types of files including plain text, spreadsheet data, and files from the many versions of the popular text editing and word processing programs. Publisher will not import HTML as text. To see a listing of the types of files Publisher accepts, click the Files of Type box arrow in the Insert Text dialog box.

# Saving an Intermediate Copy of the Publication

A good practice is to save intermediate copies of your work. That way, if your computer loses power or you make a serious mistake, you always can retrieve the latest copy from disk. Use the Save button on the Standard toolbar often, because you can save time later if the unexpected happens.

Because the masthead has been edited and the text files imported, it is now a good time to save the entire newsletter before continuing. For a detailed description of the procedure summarized below, refer to pages PUB 1.26 through PUB 1.28 in Project 1. For the following steps, it is assumed you have a floppy disk in drive A.

### TO SAVE AN INTERMEDIATE COPY OF THE PUBLICATION

**1** Click the Save button on the Standard toolbar.

**2** Type Pantry Newsletter in the File name text box. If necessary, select 3½ Floppy (A:) in the Save in list.

**3** Click the Save button in the Save As dialog box.

*Publisher saves the publication on a floppy disk in drive A using the file name, Pantry Newsletter (Figure 2-24).*

# Working with Personal Information Sets

Publisher permits you to store four unique sets of personal information for use at work and home. The name of the organization, the address, the telephone number, and other pieces of information like tag lines and logos are stored in **personal information sets**. Publisher can keep track of data about you, your business, an organization affiliation, or other personal information that you might use to create publications. In this newsletter, you will edit the text frames for the Organization Name, Address, Phone/Fax/E-mail, and Tag Line. You will learn more about permanently changing personal information components in a future project.

## Editing the Personal Information Components

Both pages of the newsletter contain an Organization Name Text Frame. Editing one of these text frames automatically changes the other. Additionally, after typing the name of your organization, Publisher can reuse the text in other publications, if it is saved as a personal information component. A **personal information component** is a text frame that contains information about the organization from the personal information set. This information can carry over from one publication to the next. For example, the name of the company might display at the top of the newsletter, on the business cards, and on the letterhead stationery.

Perform the following steps to edit personal information components for this publication only.

**Personal Information Sets**

Publisher maintains four Personal Information Sets: Primary Business, Secondary Business, Other Organization, and Home/Family. Every new publication has the Primary Business personal information set selected by default. You can apply another personal information set to the publication, however.

*Steps* **To Edit Personal Information Components**

**1** **With page 2 still displayed, click the Organization Name Text Frame in the upper-left corner. If necessary, press F9 to display the frame at 100% magnification.**

*The text frame displays at 100% magnification (Figure 2-24). Your personal information set may display a different organization name in the text frame.*

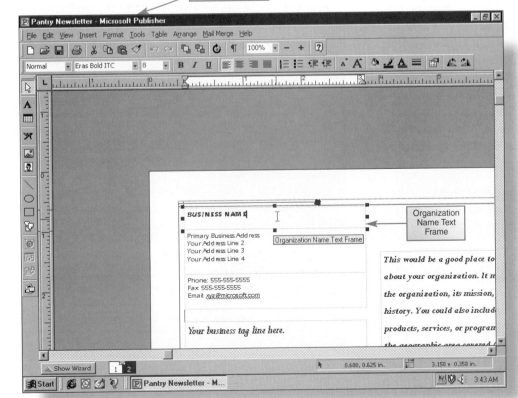

FIGURE 2-24

**Microsoft Publisher 2000**

**2** **Drag through the text in the Organization Name Text Frame, and then type** NEWSLETTER OF THE COMMUNITY PANTRY **in the text frame.**

*NEWSLETTER OF THE COMMUNITY PANTRY replaces the previous organization name (Figure 2-25). Because it is part of the personal information set, Publisher changed the Organization Name Text Frame on both pages.*

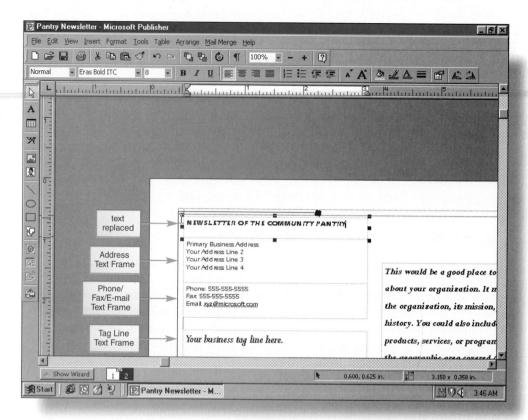

**FIGURE 2-25**

**3** **Repeat Step 2 to edit the text frames for Address, Phone/Fax/ E-mail, and Tag Line as shown in Figure 2-26. As you type, press the ENTER key for new lines of text inside the Address and Phone/Fax/E-mail text frames. Allow the text in the Tag Line text frame to wrap.**

*The edited personal information components display in the newsletter (Figure 2-26).*

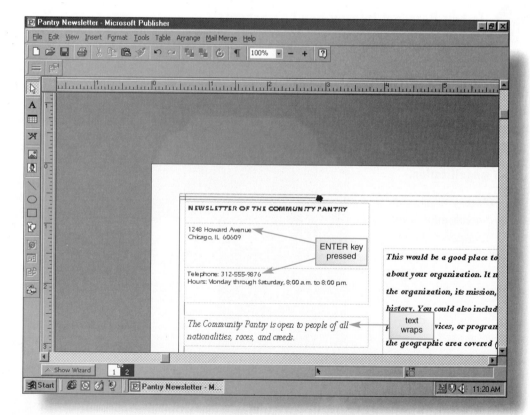

**FIGURE 2-26**

Each personal information component has its own preset font, font size, and text alignment. If desired, you can make changes to the formatting for individual publications. If you want to keep Publisher from **synchronizing**, or repeating, the changed component on other pages, click Undo on the Edit menu.

# Editing the Design Set

Page 2 of *The Pantry Newsletter* contains several objects that are part of the newsletter publication design set. A design set is specific to the type of publication and chosen design scheme. Recall that an object in Publisher is any text frame, shape, border, image, or table inserted in the publication. The Blends Newsletter design contains a text frame and an attention getter on the back page, among other objects.

## Creating Columns within a Text Frame

The text frame in the upper-right corner of page 2 is not large enough to hold the list of people donating to the Community Pantry. Wrapping the text to another frame makes it more difficult for the reader to follow. Reducing the font size decreases readability, and there is not enough room to make the frame larger on the page. One solution is to create columns within the frame itself, so the list can flow downward and then to the right.

Follow these steps to import the text and format the columns.

### More About

## Fitting Text in Frames

When you cannot fit all the required text into a text frame, you might try one of these alternatives. Create columns within the frame, turn on automatic copyfitting, increase the size of the text frame, decrease the size of the text characters, reduce the margins within the text frame, tighten character spacing, reduce line spacing, delete some text, or choose a different font.

 ## To Import the Donor List and Create Columns

**1** **Press F9 to view the whole page. Click the text in the upper-right text frame to select it.**

*Remember that clicking placeholder text automatically selects the entire text (Figure 2-27). You also may display the whole page by clicking the Zoom box arrow, and then clicking Whole Page in the Zoom list.*

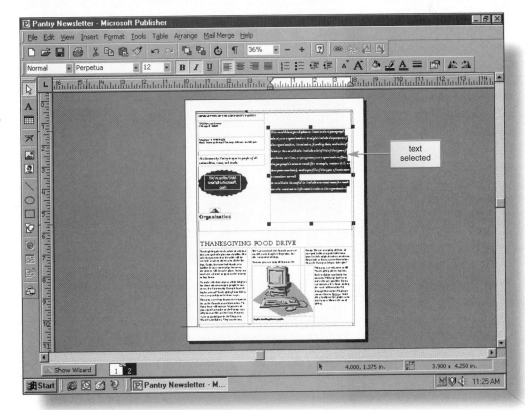

**FIGURE 2-27**

**2** Click Insert on the menu bar, and then click Text File. If not already selected, click 3½ Floppy (A:) in the Look in list. Double-click Donor List Article. When the dialog box displays, point to the No button.

*A Publisher dialog box displays because the Donor List Article is too large to fit in the frame (Figure 2-28). Clicking No allows you to connect the frames for yourself or format the text differently.*

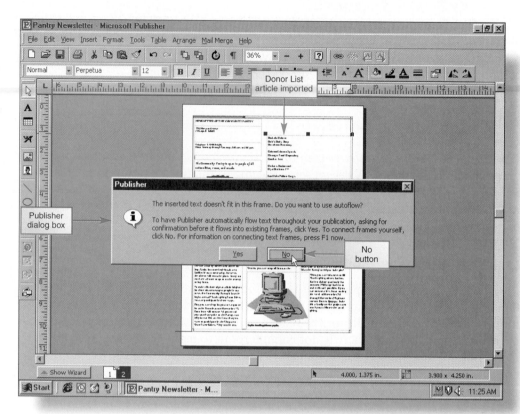

FIGURE 2-28

**3** Click the No button.

*A Text in Overflow indicator displays (Figure 2-29). The rest of the Donor List Article is stored in an overflow area, similar to the Clipboard, waiting to be edited or moved to another text frame.*

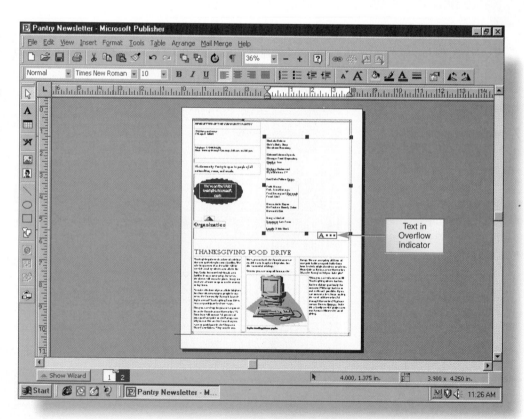

FIGURE 2-29

**4** **Click Format on the menu bar and then click Text Frame Properties. Point to the Number text box in the Columns frame.**

*The Text Frame Properties dialog box displays (Figure 2-30). Notice the mouse pointer changes to an insertion point when positioned on text boxes. The Text Frame Properties dialog box includes options for margins, columns, and wrapping.*

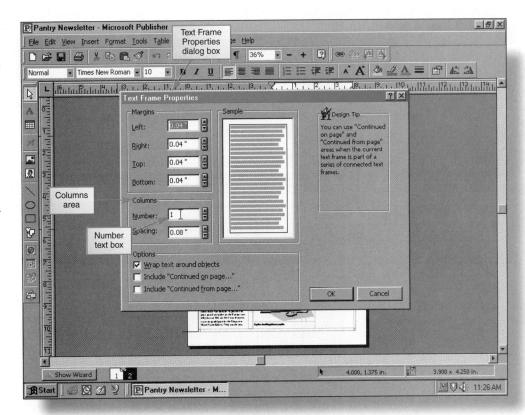

**FIGURE 2-30**

**5** **Double-click the number 1. Type 2 in the Number text box. Point to the OK button.**

*The Number text box now displays 2 as the number of columns for the donor list, instead of 1 (Figure 2-31). As in most Windows-based applications, double-clicking a text box selects the text and allows you to enter new information.*

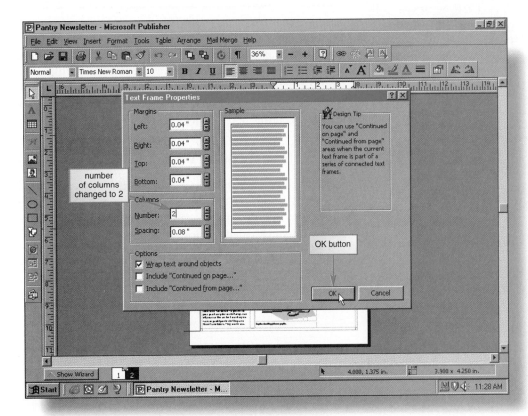

**FIGURE 2-31**

**6** **Click the OK button.**

*The list displays in a two-column format (Figure 2-32).*

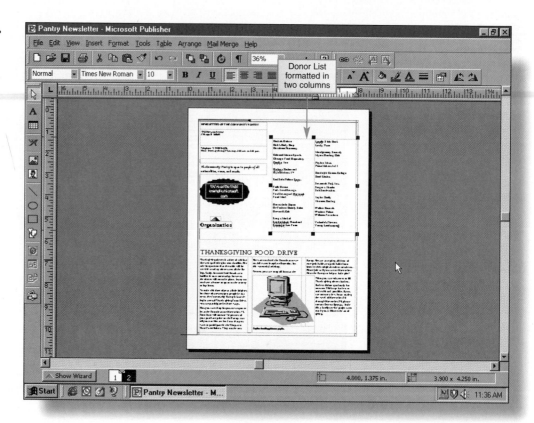

**FIGURE 2-32**

With an imported list, it is easier to create columns within one text frame than wrap the list to the next frame. All columns within a single text frame are the same width; however, you can adjust the space between columns and the location in the text where the second column begins. Separate stories in adjacent columns would require separate text frames, as would stories across pages.

## Editing the Attention Getter

As discussed in Project 1, attention getters are eye-catching graphics and text that draw attention to a location on the page. The Blends Newsletter set uses an oval and a text box grouped together as an attention getter on the back page. Perform the following steps to add color and change the text in the attention getter.

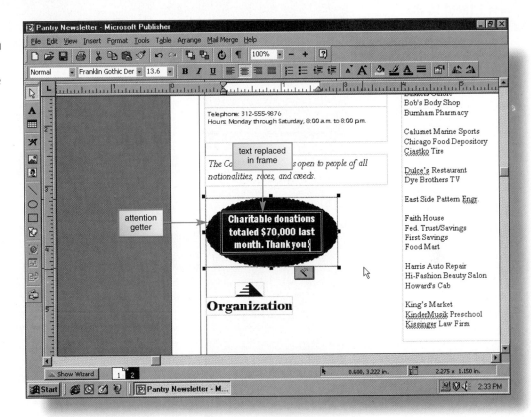

## To Edit the Attention Getter

**1** **Click the Attention Getter text frame on the back page, and then press F9. Type** Charitable donations totaled $70,000 last month. Thank you! **in the text frame.**

*The new text displays in Actual Size view (Figure 2-33). Publisher resizes the text as you type using the best fit option and wraps the text as necessary.*

FIGURE 2-33

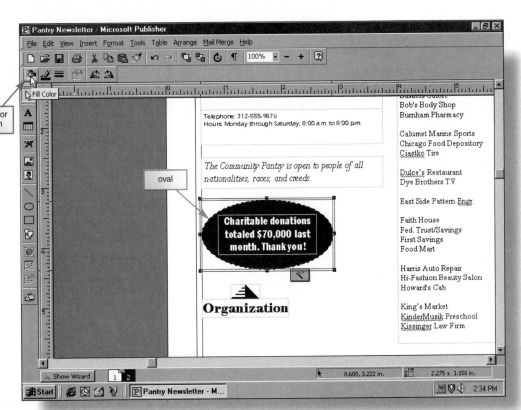

**2** **Click the oval outside the Attention Getter text frame. Point to the Fill Color button on the Formatting toolbar.**

*The oval is selected, but the text frame is not (Figure 2-34).*

FIGURE 2-34

**3** **Click the Fill Color button. Point to Accent 1 (Red) in the Scheme colors area.**

*The Blends Newsletter color scheme displays in the Fill Color button menu (Figure 2-35). Your colors may vary.*

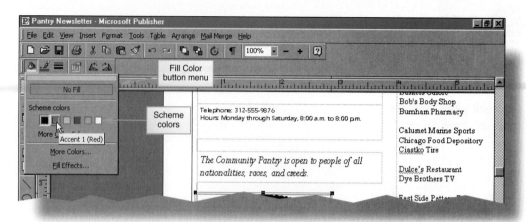

**FIGURE 2-35**

**4** **Click Accent 1 (Red).**

*The Attention Getter oval color changes to red (Figure 2-36). The attention getter now is complete.*

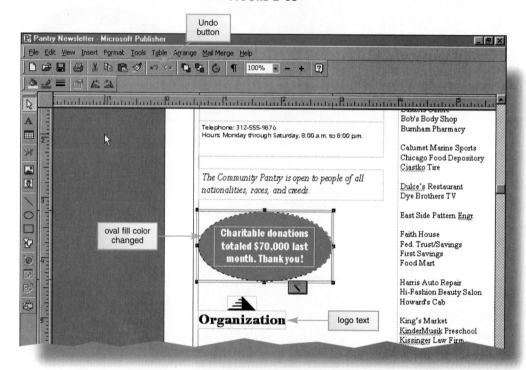

**FIGURE 2-36**

*Other Ways*

1. Right-click oval, point to Change Oval on shortcut menu, point to Fill Color, click desired color
2. On Format menu click Fill Color

You can edit the text, text color, fill color, borders, and shadows of attention getters. Publisher's Design Gallery has other styles and shapes from which you may choose, as well.

## Deleting the Logo

The Blends Newsletter design set displays an organization logo on the back page (Figure 2-36). A **logo** is a personal information component that varies with each personal information set. Because the Community Pantry has no logo, perform the following steps to delete the logo.

### TO DELETE THE LOGO

**1** Right-click the logo on the back page.

**2** Click Delete Object on the shortcut menu.

If you delete an object by accident, click the Undo button on the Standard toolbar. The Edit menu also contains a Delete Object and an Undo option.

# Using Graphics in a Publication

Most graphic designers employ an easy technique for deciding how many graphics are too many. They hold the publication at arm's length and glance at it. Then, closing their eyes, they count the number of things they remember. Remembering more than five graphics indicates too many, two or less indicates too few. There is no question that graphics can make or break a publication. The world has come to expect them. Used correctly, graphics enhance the text, attract the eye, and brighten the look of the publication.

You can use Publisher's clip art images in any publication you create, including newsletters. Publisher also accepts graphics and pictures created by other programs, as well as scanned photographs and electronic images. In newsletters, you should use photographs as true-to-life representations, such as pictures of employees and products. Graphics, on the other hand, can explain, draw, instruct, entertain, or represent images for which you have no picture. The careful use of graphics can add flair and distinction to your publication.

Graphics do not have to be images and pictures. They also can include tables, charts, shapes, lines, boxes, borders, pull quotes, and sidebars. A **sidebar** is a small piece of text, set off with a box or graphic, and placed beside an article. It contains text that is not vital to understanding the main text; it usually adds interest or additional information. Tables of contents and bulleted points of interest are examples of sidebars. A **pull quote** is an excerpt from the main article to highlight the ideas or to attract readers. As with other graphics, it adds interest to the page. Pull quotes, like sidebars, can be set off with a box or graphic (Figure 2-37).

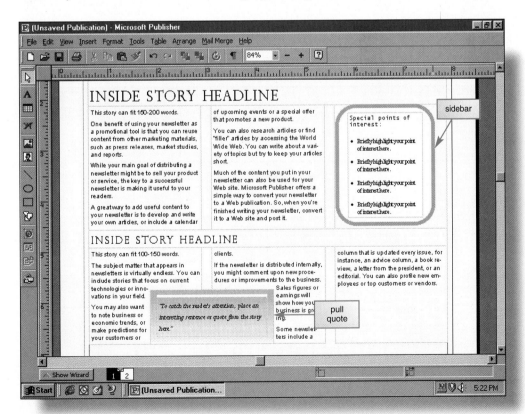

**FIGURE 2-37**

### Deleting a Graphic

The sidebar in the Blends Newsletter is a table of contents. Because the newsletter now has only two pages, a table of contents is not necessary. Perform the following steps to delete the sidebar.

**More About**

#### Sidebars

This More About is an example of a sidebar. The Shelly Cashman Series textbooks use sidebars to offer more information about subjects in the text, as well as to direct readers to Web pages about the topic. The Other Ways feature in this book also is a sidebar.

#### TO DELETE THE SIDEBAR

**1** Click the page 1 icon on the Page Navigation control. If the whole page is not in view, press F9 to display it.

**2** Right-click the table of contents sidebar table located to the right of the lead story.

**3** Click Delete Object on the shortcut menu.

This table was an index used to locate articles in longer newsletters. Many newsletters have a table of contents, not only to reference and locate, but also to break up a long text page and attract readers to inside pages. Tables can be used for purposes other than displaying contents and page numbers. You will learn more about tables in a later project.

### Finding a Graphic

As you may remember from Project 1, the clip art provided with Publisher has assigned **keywords** to make finding clips easier. Rather than searching through thousands of graphics for just the right picture, you may type in a keyword or words and Publisher will display only the graphics related to those keywords. You may add additional keywords to stored clips or assign keywords to new and imported clips. Perform the next steps to find an appropriate graphic for the lead story.

*Steps* **To Find a Graphic**

**1** **Double-click the lead story graphic. When the Insert Clip Art window displays, click the Search for clips text box.**

*The Insert Clip Art window displays (Figure 2-38). Images on the Pictures tab on your screen may vary.*

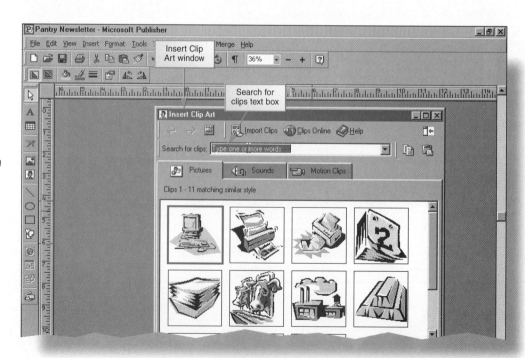

**FIGURE 2-38**

**2** Type awards **in the Search for clips text box and then press the ENTER key. Point to the down scroll arrow on the Pictures tab.**

*The clips associated with the keyword, awards, display (Figure 2-39).*

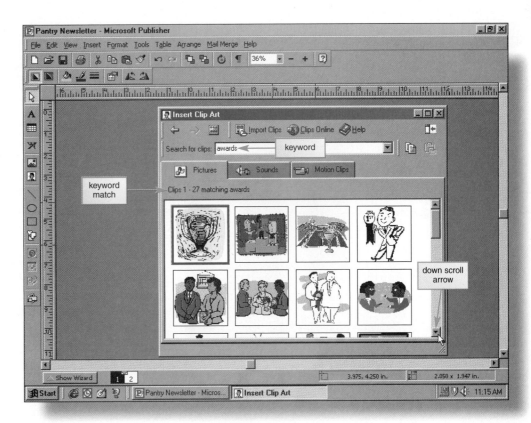

**FIGURE 2-39**

**3** Scroll through the **available awards clips and then click an appropriate image. When the Pop-up menu displays, point to the Insert clip button.**

*The image selected in Figure 2-40 is located on the Publisher CD-ROM. Your clips may vary. If your clip art is limited, the graphics toward the top of preview panes usually are included as part of the installation on your hard disk.*

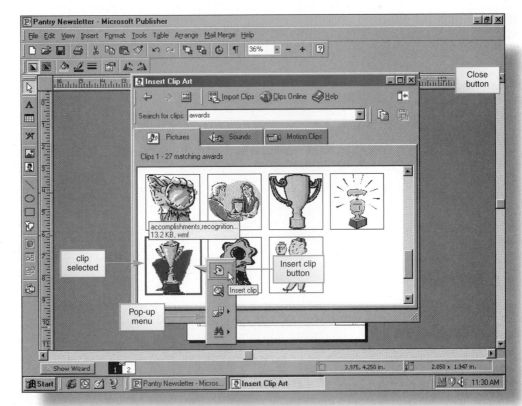

**FIGURE 2-40**

**4** Click the Insert clip button. If you get a message to insert the CD-ROM, and it is unavailable, click the Cancel button and then insert another graphic. Click the Close button in the Insert Clip Art window.

*The graphic displays in the newsletter (Figure 2-41).*

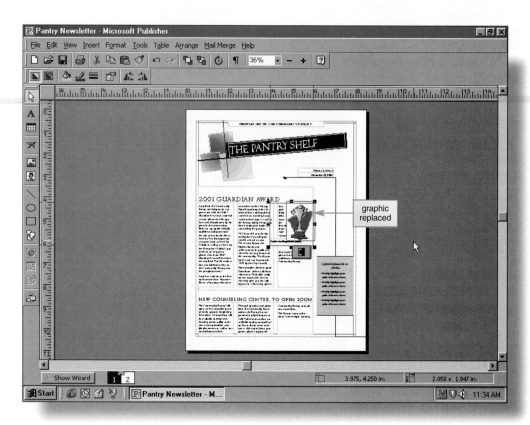

**FIGURE 2-41**

**5** Position the mouse pointer over the edge of the graphic until the pointer changes to the Mover. Drag the graphic to the lower half of the middle column of the Guardian Award Article.

*The text automatically wraps around the graphic and its caption (Figure 2-42). The Group/Ungroup Objects button displays.*

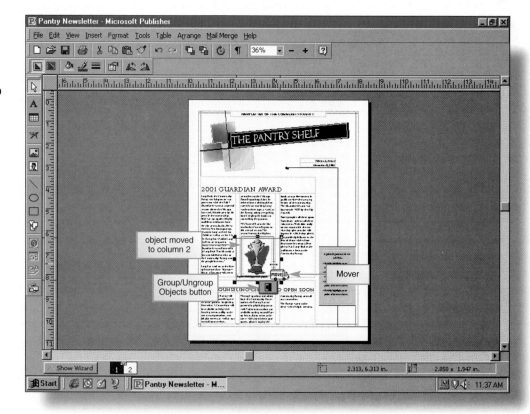

**FIGURE 2-42**

**6** **Press F9 to view the graphic in Actual Size view. Click the Group/Ungroup Objects button. Point to the caption.**

*The Group/Ungroup Objects button displays (Figure 2-43). The caption and image are ready for individual editing.*

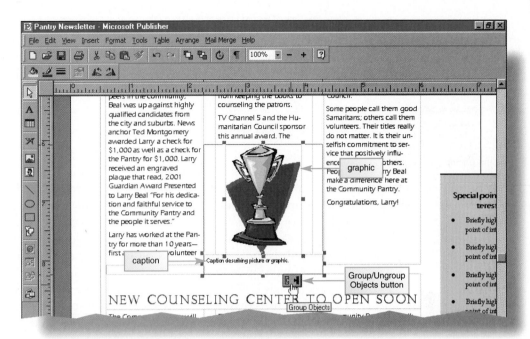

FIGURE 2-43

**7** **Click the caption. Click Edit on the menu bar and then click Delete Object.**

*The caption is deleted (Figure 2-44). After you view the image alone, in Actual Size, you may need to reposition it at the bottom of the middle column.*

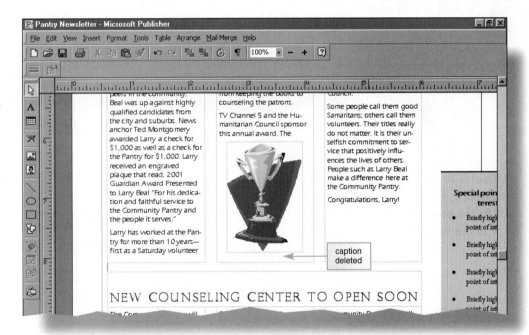

FIGURE 2-44

Graphics in the Clip Gallery are not all the same size. Some of the images and clip art are **portrait** oriented, which means they are taller than they are wide. The opposite graphic orientation is **landscape**. When you change graphics, your choice may alter both the way the columns look and where the columns break. You may want to experiment with dragging the picture in small increments to make the columns symmetrical. The text automatically wraps around the graphic in the newsletter wizard. The column breaks do not have to match the project newsletter exactly.

**More About**

## Portrait and Landscape

The terms portrait and landscape are used to refer to more than just graphic orientation. Portrait also refers to printing a document so the short edge of the paper is the top of the page. Landscape printing assumes the long edge to be the top of the page.

Microsoft Publisher 2000

## More About

### Pull Quotes

When you create a pull quote, use a large, bold font to make it really stand out from the rest of the text. You also can add shading behind the text, add a decorative border above or below the text, or create hanging quotation marks around the text.

Graphics in the Clip Gallery are **proportional**, which means the height and width have been set in relation to each other, so as not to distort the picture. If you resize the graphic, be sure to hold down the SHIFT key while dragging the corner sizing handle as described in Project 1. Shift-dragging maintains the graphic's proportional height and width.

### Adding a Pull Quote

Desktop publishers use pull quotes for reasons other than merely adding visual interest. People often make reading decisions based on the size of the text. Bringing a small portion of the text to their attention, through the use of a pull quote, invites readership. **Pull quotes** are especially useful for breaking the monotony of long columns of text. Finally, pull quotes and sidebars are good multiple entry devices, offering readers many ways to digest the article. Layout specialists say the title of the article and the pull quote should outline the intended message.

The final step to complete the Lead Story is to create a pull quote using Publisher's Design Gallery. The pull quote graphic will contain some text from the article, and be placed appropriately on the page so as to draw the reader's attention to the article. Follow these steps to add a pull quote to the publication.

### Steps To Add a Pull Quote

1. Press F9 to view all of page 1, and then click the Design Gallery Object button on the Objects toolbar. When the Design Gallery dialog box displays, click Pull Quotes in the Categories pane. Point to the down scroll arrow in the Pull Quotes pane.

*Previews of pull quotes display in the Pull Quotes pane on the right (Figure 2-45).*

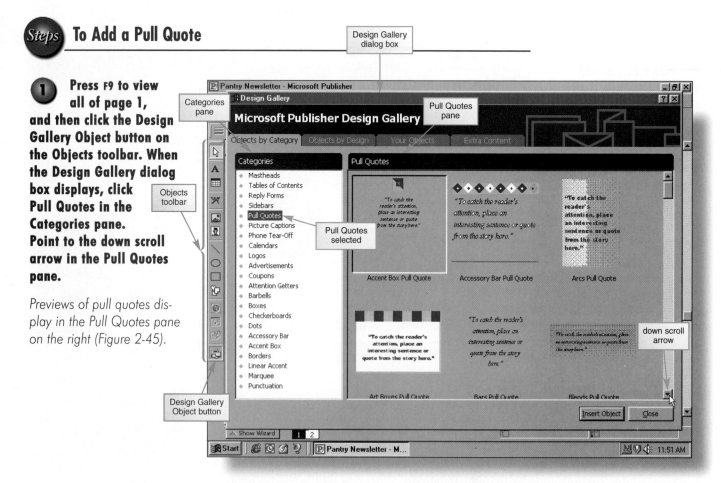

**FIGURE 2-45**

**2** Click the Pull
Quotes down scroll
arrow until the Tilt Pull
Quote displays. Click the
Tilt Pull Quote preview.
Point to the Insert Object
button.

*The previews display in
alphabetical order in the
previews pane (Figure 2-46).
Tilt Pull Quote is selected.*

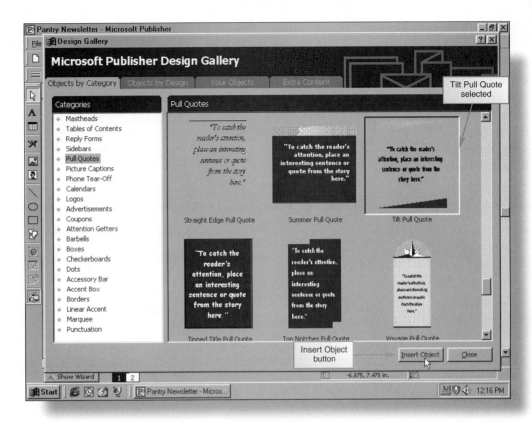

FIGURE 2-46

**3** Click the Insert
Object button. When
the newsletter displays,
drag the pull quote to the
right side, above the
Special points of interest
sidebar. Point to the
Guardian Award Article.

*The pull quote displays
above the sidebar (Figure
2-47).*

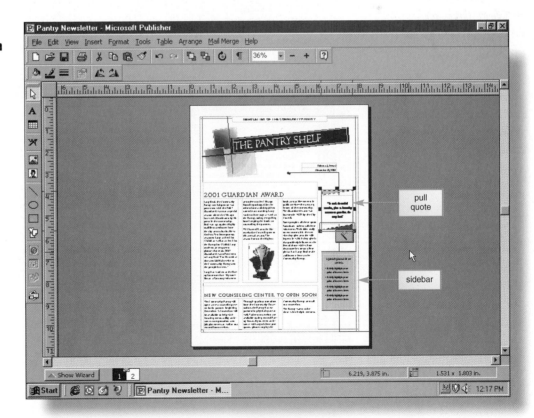

FIGURE 2-47

**4** **Click the Guardian Award Article, and then press F9 to facilitate editing. Drag through the text shown in Figure 2-48 for a quotation to use in the pull quote. Point to the Copy button on the Standard toolbar.**

*The text is selected (Figure 2-48). Drag carefully to include the quotation mark at the end of the paragraph.*

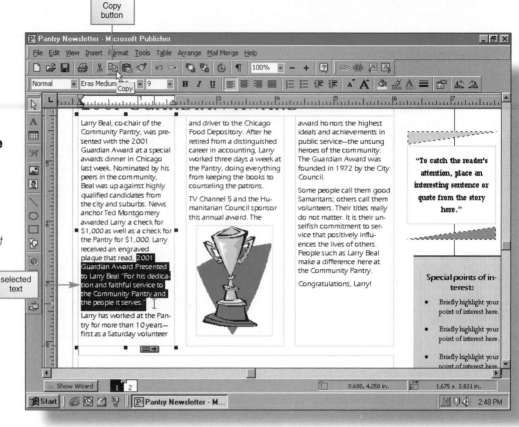

FIGURE 2-48

**5** **Click the Copy button on the Standard toolbar and then click the text in the pull quote. Point to the Paste button on the Standard toolbar.**

*The Copy button copies the quotation from the article to the Clipboard. Clicking the text in the pull quote selects the text (Figure 2-49).*

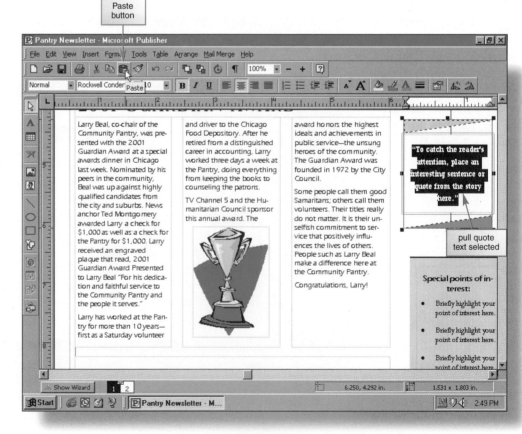

FIGURE 2-49

**6** **Click the Paste button.**

*Pasting transfers text from the Clipboard to the selected area (Figure 2-50).*

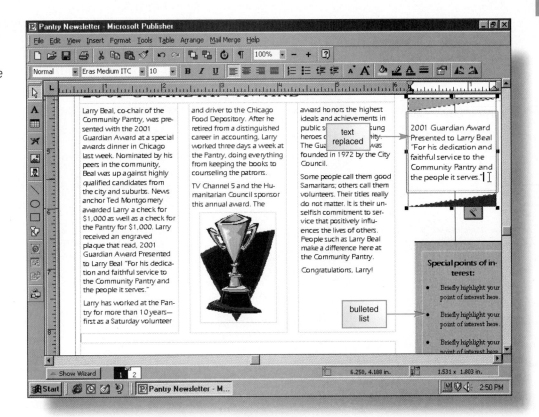

**FIGURE 2-50**

**Other Ways**

1. On Insert menu click Design Gallery Object
2. Create text frame with shading and border

The pull quote fills the gap left by the table of contents sidebar. The proportion and balance of two graphics beside the text enhance the layout.

## Editing the Sidebar

The sidebar of the newsletter contains a list of dates to remember. **Sidebars** should be placed close to their related text or in a prominent place. Although the sidebar is not vital to understanding the main text, it is important and adds interest.

The yellow text frame below the pull quote is a sidebar containing a text frame, a rectangle, and two lines. Using the editing techniques you learned in Project 1, edit the text and bullets to create the object as shown in Figure 2-51 on the next page.

### TO EDIT THE BULLETED TEXT FRAME SIDEBAR

**1** Click the yellow text frame below the pull quote and then press F9.

**2** Click the heading, and then type `Dates to Remember` to replace the selected text.

**3** Click the bulleted list and then type the text shown in Figure 2-51. Press SHIFT+ENTER at the end of lines within the bullets. Press the ENTER key after each bulleted item is entered.

*The edited sidebar displays as shown in Figure 2-51.*

**Lines**

The lines at the top and bottom of the sidebar can be formatted to be a different color, a different thickness, a different style of dash or line, or shadowed. To format a line, right-click it and then click Change Line on the shortcut menu.

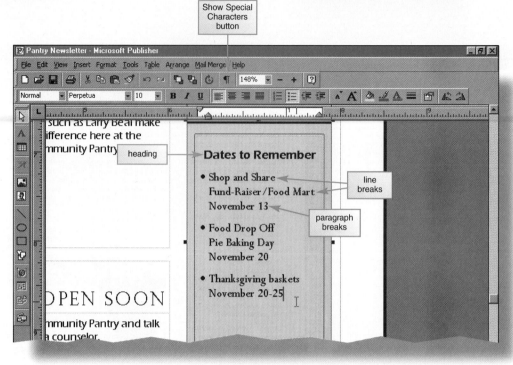

**FIGURE 2-51**

If you have any word processing experience, you may know that SHIFT+ENTER is called a line break. Use a **line break** when you have short lines or want to advance the insertion point to a new line without new paragraph formatting. The line break is especially useful when wordwrap creates ragged lines or poor hyphenations. Press ENTER when you want a **paragraph break** between each line. Normal formatting, or bullets, apply when you use a paragraph break. If you want the special characters for line and paragraph breaks to display on the screen, click the Show Special Characters button on the Standard toolbar (Figure 2-51).

## Replacing the Graphic

The graphic on page 2 does not have anything to do with the article about Thanksgiving. Graphics placed by the wizard are meant to be changed. The clip art in Publisher contains numerous graphics relating to holidays. Perform the following steps to replace the graphic provided by the wizard on page 2 with an article-specific graphic.

### TO REPLACE THE GRAPHIC ON THE BACK PAGE

1. Click the page 2 icon on the Page Navigation control. Click the Zoom box arrow on the Standard toolbar and then click Whole Page in the Zoom list.

2. Double-click the graphic. Type Thanksgiving in the Search for Clips text box, and then press the ENTER key.

3. Select an appropriate Thanksgiving graphic, and then click the Insert clip button on the Pop-up menu.

4. Close the Insert Clip Art window and then use the Group/Ungroup Objects button to ungroup the graphic.

5. Click the caption. Click Edit on the menu bar and then click Delete Object.

*Your graphic may be a different size than the one shown in Figure 2-52.*

## Typing

Publisher tries to help you as you type. This AutoFormat feature, similar to the same feature in word processing applications, will format text for you as you type. For instance if you type 2nd, Publisher will convert it to 2nd. If you type teh and then press the SPACEBAR key, Publisher will convert it to the word, the.

## The Clip Art Pop-up Menu

The Pop-up menu that displays when you click a clip art category button in the Insert Clip Art window contains four unique buttons: Insert clip, Preview clip, Add clips to Favorites, and Find similar clips.

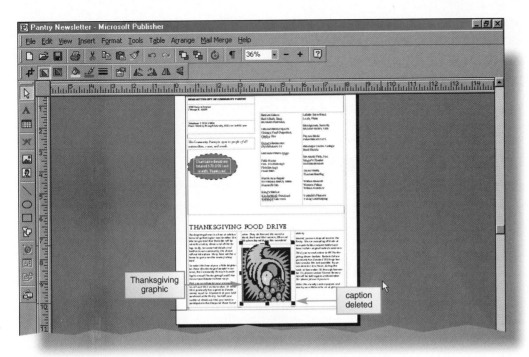

Thanksgiving graphic

caption deleted

**FIGURE 2-52**

## Inserting a Line with Arrows

**Lines** have dual purposes in desktop publishing. On one hand, lines simply separate groups of objects, either by giving the reader a visual break from text only, or by separating ideas or content. On the other hand, lines can add color, flair, and a border to complement the newsletter style. Many of the design sets in Publisher include lines for both purposes.

To separate the article from the rest of the objects on page 2, and to add color to the page, perform the following steps to insert a line with arrows.

### Lines and Text

If you want to use lines simply to create borders or ruling lines above and below text, click the Line/Border Style button on the Formatting toolbar. The Line Border tab allows you to choose any or all of the four sides of a text frame.

*Steps* **To Insert a Line with Arrows**

**1** **Click the Line Tool button on the Objects toolbar. Point to the middle of the page at the left margin.**

*The mouse pointer changes to a crosshair (Figure 2-53).*

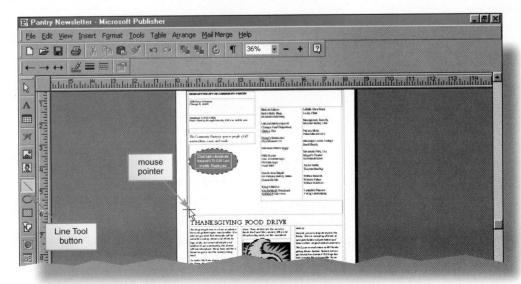

mouse pointer

Line Tool button

**FIGURE 2-53**

**2** While holding down the SHIFT key, drag through the newsletter to the right margin. Release both the SHIFT key and the mouse button. Point to the Line/Border Style button on the Formatting toolbar.

*A horizontal line displays in the publication (Figure 2-54). Publisher uses the combination of SHIFT and drag to create a perfectly straight line, horizontally or vertically.*

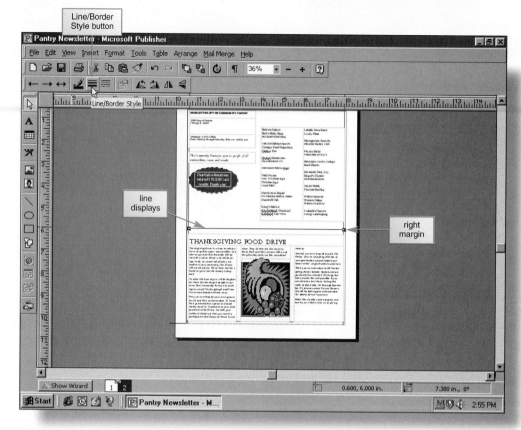

**FIGURE 2-54**

**3** Click the Line/Border Style button, and then click More Styles on the Line/Border Style button menu. Point to the 10 pt line thickness on the right side of the Line thickness area.

*The Line dialog box displays (Figure 2-55).*

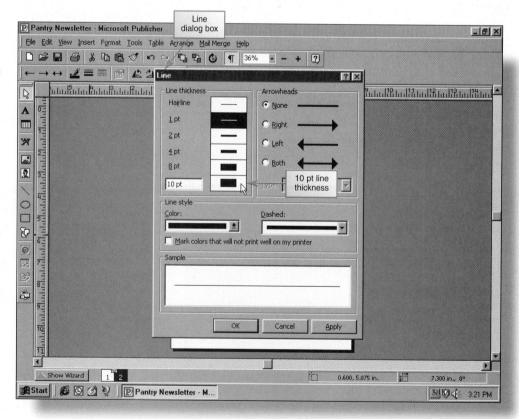

**FIGURE 2-55**

**Click the 10 pt example. Click Both in the Arrowheads area. Click the Color box arrow and then click Accent 3 (Blue) on the Scheme colors palette. Point to the OK button.**

*The Sample frame changes to reflect the selections (Figure 2-56). Your colors may vary.*

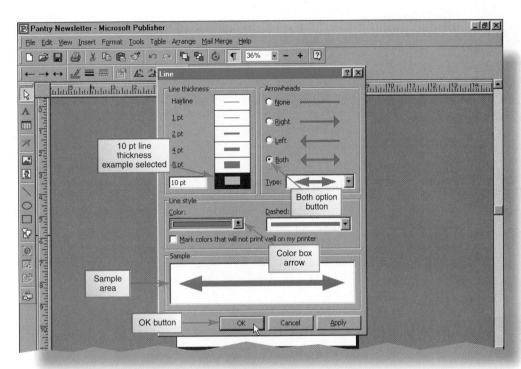

**FIGURE 2-56**

**5** **Click the OK button.**

*Publisher displays a blue, 10 pt, double-headed arrow across the middle of the page (Figure 2-57).*

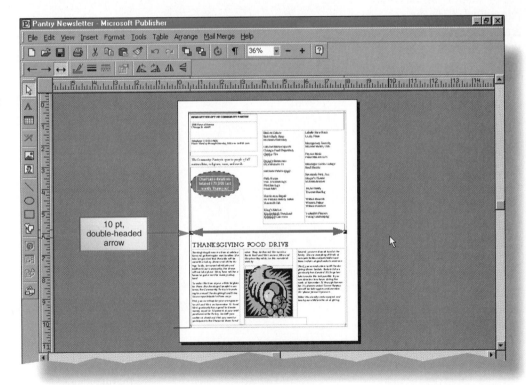

**FIGURE 2-57**

If you use a line or arrow to point to an object in a publication, it is a good idea to group the arrow with the object. Then, if you decide to move the object, the arrow moves as well. The careful use of lines and arrows can enhance a publication's readability.

**Other Ways**

1. Select line, click Line/Border Style button
2. Select line, click Add/Remove Both Arrows button

## More About

### WordArt Objects

Keep in mind that WordArt objects are drawing objects and are not treated as Publisher text. Thus, if you misspell the contents of a WordArt object and then spell check the publication, Publisher will not catch the misspelled word(s) in the WordArt text.

# WordArt

**WordArt** is a program that works with Publisher to create fancy text effects. A WordArt object, created in a frame, is actually a graphic and not text at all. Publication designers typically use WordArt to catch the reader's eye with fancy headlines, banners, and other attention grabbers. WordArt uses its own toolbar to add effects to the graphic.

## Inserting a WordArt Object

The final graphic to add to the newsletter is a headline for the Donor List. Headlines can be text, formatted to draw attention, but using WordArt increases the number of special effect possibilities and options.

Perform the following steps to add a WordArt object as the headline for the Donor List Article in the newsletter.

**Steps** **To Add WordArt to the Newsletter**

**1** With page 2 displaying in Whole Page view, click the WordArt Frame Tool button on the Objects toolbar. Point to the area above the Donor List article.

*The mouse pointer changes to a crosshair (Figure 2-58).*

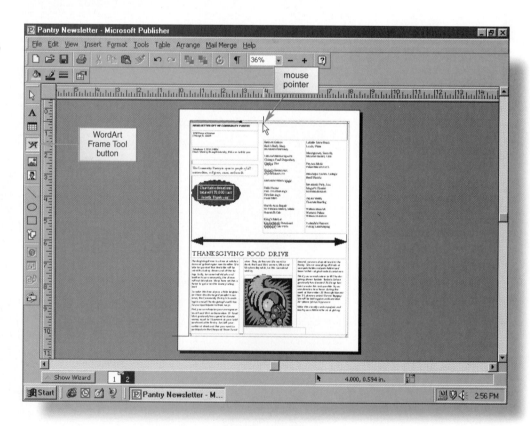

**FIGURE 2-58**

**2**  **Drag from the top margin of the page, just above the Donor List article, to the top right corner of the article itself, creating a rectangle to fill the blank area above the Donor List article. Release the mouse button.**

*The rectangle snaps to the page margin. The WordArt toolbar and Enter Your Text Here dialog box display (Figure 2-59). The words, YOUR TEXT HERE, are selected.*

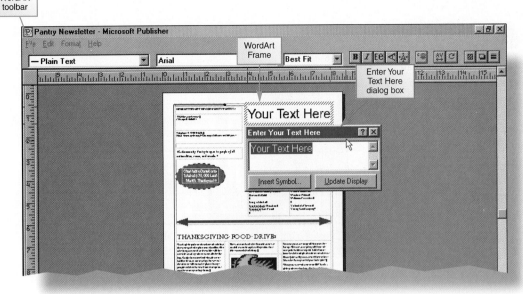

**FIGURE 2-59**

**3**  **Type** DONOR DECLARATION **to replace the selected text, and then point to the Shape box arrow on the WordArt toolbar.**

*DONOR DECLARATION replaces the text in the Enter Your Text Here dialog box (Figure 2-60). Various formatting buttons and boxes on the WordArt toolbar are shown.*

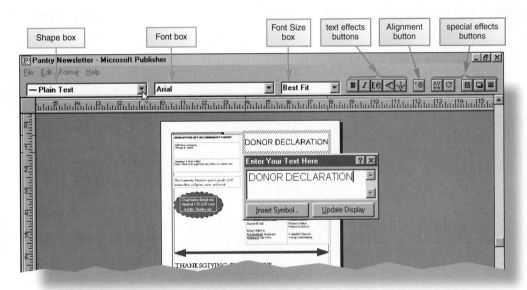

**FIGURE 2-60**

**4**  **Click the Shape box arrow. Point to the Deflate shape in the second column.**

*WordArt displays a list of shapes from which you may choose (Figure 2-61). As the mouse pointer moves over a shape in the list, WordArt highlights the shape. The shape's name does not display until you click it.*

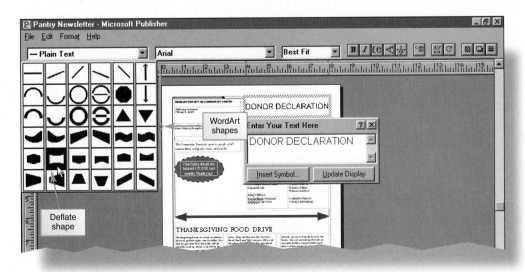

**FIGURE 2-61**

**5** Click the Deflate shape, and then point to the Stretch to Frame button on the WordArt toolbar.

*The text shape changes as shown in Figure 2-62. Deflate now displays as the caption for the Shape box on the WordArt toolbar.*

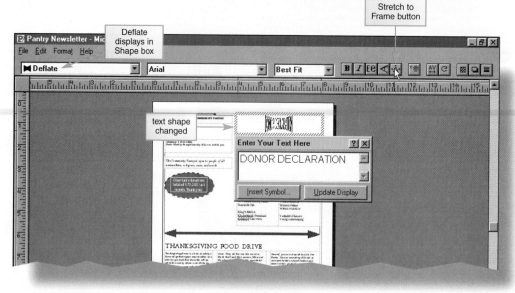

**FIGURE 2-62**

**6** Click the Stretch to Frame button, and then click the newsletter anywhere outside the WordArt Frame.

*The publication with the WordArt object displays (Figure 2-63). Publisher's toolbars display.*

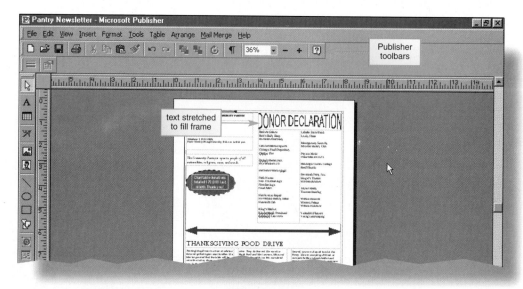

**FIGURE 2-63**

WordArt includes options for spacing, rotating, shadows, and borders, as well as many of the same features Publisher provides on its Formatting toolbar, such as alignment, bold, italics, underline, and fonts.

# Adding Page Numbers to the Background

Page numbering on a two-page newsletter is probably not as important as it is for longer publications. Many readers, however, reference articles and points by page numbers. Part of the design process is to provide a consistent look and feel to the layout, so page numbers can furnish a reference for the organization in designing future, perhaps longer, newsletters. Additionally, certain features always may appear, for example, on page 2. Placing page numbers in prominent locations, or using fancy fonts and colors, can make numbering a design element in and of itself.

The next steps in this project describe how to add page numbers to the lower-right corner of each page of the newsletter by creating a text frame and adding it to the publication background. The **background** is a blank sheet located behind your publication where you place objects that will display on every page, such as headers and footers, page numbers, and logos. Most publication objects, like text and graphics, actually lie in front of the background, allowing the format to display from behind. You can insert and edit these recurring objects in two ways. If you want an object to display on every page, you can move it to the background. Alternatively, you can go to the background view, and create the object there.

Publisher requires automatic page numbers to be located in their own text frame. You should be familiar with text frames, having used them in both this project and Project 1; however, some special features are worth noting. You cannot type directly on the page or into the workspace, so Publisher creates an area to hold text and keep it within certain boundaries. A **text frame,** created by clicking a button on the Objects toolbar and then drawing a rectangle, keeps the text together so it is easier to move and edit. Options such as **copyfit** and **connect across columns** automatically reformat your text after editing. You can cut and paste large amounts of text without changing the shape or size. It is easy to add additional formatting, such as borders, alignment, and text rotation, to the entire text frame.

You will create the text frame, insert the automatic page number, and then send it to the background so it will display on all pages. For the page number to be as close to the corner as possible and yet remain within the margins, you will verify the selection of the snap options. Snapping, as you may remember from Project 1, is Publisher's way of aligning objects created very close to other objects, guides, or boundaries. Perform the following steps to create and insert a page number on every page.

**More** *About*

### Objects on the Background

Text frames for page numbers and headers/footers are not the only objects that appear in backgrounds. A watermark is a lightly shaded object appearing behind everything else on the page. For example, you can place a gray graphic, or a gray WordArt object such as, Confidential, on the background of a publication, so it appears behind text on the foreground.

 ## To Insert Page Numbering

**Click Tools on the menu bar. If any of the three Snap options do not have a check mark next to them, click them.**

*In Figure 2-64, all three Snap options display with a check mark to the left of the option, which means they currently are turned on or available.*

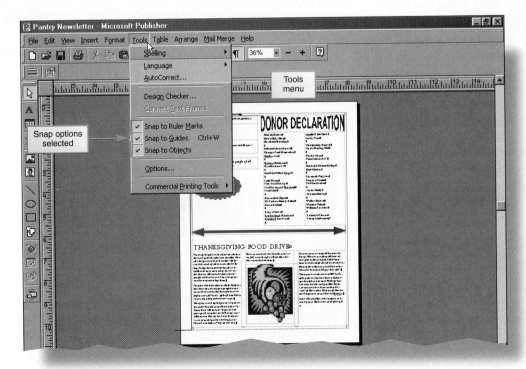

**FIGURE 2-64**

**Step 2**

**Click the third column of the Thanksgiving article, and then press F9 to view the article more closely. Point to the Text Frame Tool button on the Objects toolbar.**

*The text frame displays (Figure 2-65). Enlarging the lower-right corner of the newsletter makes it easier to add a page number.*

FIGURE 2-65

**Step 3**

**Click the Text Frame Tool button. Point to the lower-right portion of the newsletter. The Object Position box on the status bar will read approximately 7 by 10 inches.**

*The mouse pointer changes to a crosshair (Figure 2-66). You need not place the crosshair at the exact numeric location in the Object Position indicator.*

FIGURE 2-66

**4** Drag the mouse diagonally downward and to the right until it touches the corner guide, and then release the mouse button.

*The object snaps to the corner (Figure 2-67). Publisher displays a selected, rectangular text frame with an insertion point.*

**FIGURE 2-67**

**5** Type the word Page in the text frame and then press the SPACEBAR to add a blank space.

*The word, Page, displays in the text frame (Figure 2-68).*

**FIGURE 2-68**

Microsoft **Publisher 2000**

**6** **Click Insert on the menu bar and then click Page Numbers.**

The page number displays in the text frame (Figure 2-69). Publisher automatically reflects the current page number.

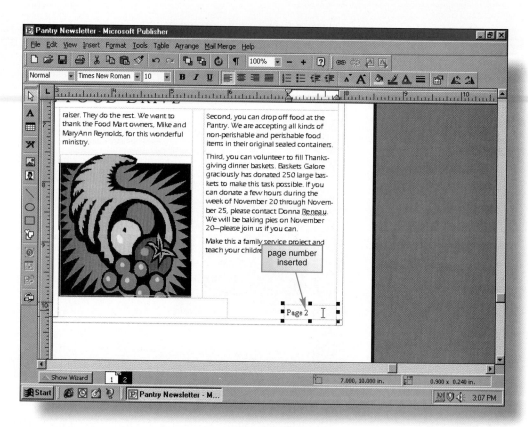

**FIGURE 2-69**

**7** **Click Arrange on the menu bar. When the long menu displays, click Send to Background. When the dialog box displays, point to the OK button.**

A Publisher dialog box displays, informing you that the text frame was moved to the background (Figure 2-70).

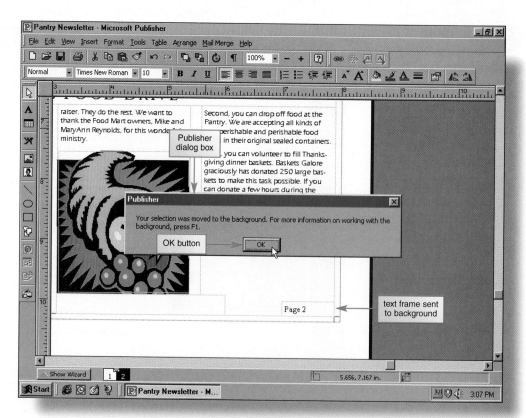

**FIGURE 2-70**

**8** **Click the OK button.**

*The page displays without the page number (Figure 2-71). The page number text frame is behind the column of text in the article.*

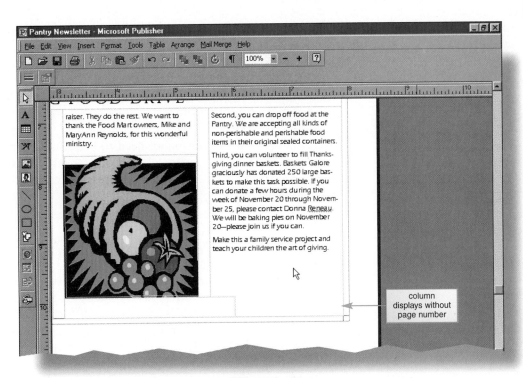

FIGURE 2-71

**9** **Click the right column text frame again, and then press CTRL+T.**

*The text frame becomes transparent so the page number shows through (Figure 2-72). Both the word, Page, and the page number will display on each page of the printed publication.*

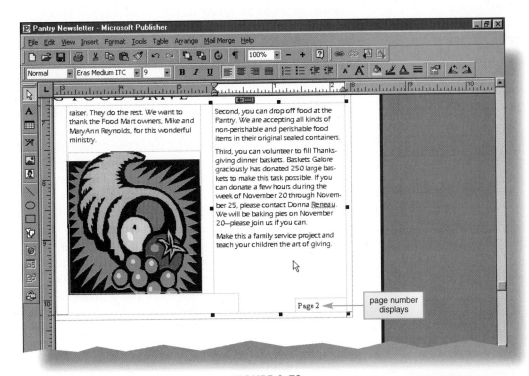

FIGURE 2-72

Logical choices for a text frame on a background might include personal information, dates, times, headers and footers, and page numbers. Options on the Insert menu allow you to insert dates and times derived from the operating system that will update automatically when the publication is edited or printed.

**Other Ways**

1. On View menu click Go To Background, create recurring text
2. Press CTRL+M, type recurring text

## Backgrounds

If you want the background not to display on a given page, click Ignore Background on the View menu.

Many newsletters have a background texture or pattern on each page. As with watermarks, a background pattern can provide additional interest and contrast. By creating a text box on the background, you can use fill colors or gradient patterns from the color scheme to add singularity to your newsletter.

In Figure 2-72 on the previous page, the text frame becomes **transparent**. This does not mean that it becomes invisible; rather, any object behind the frame will show through. Typically, items in the **foreground**, or in the front, which partially cover an item in the background, need to be transparent. The combination keystrokes of CTRL+T will convert selected objects into transparent ones. Should you change your mind, CTRL+T is a toggle; press it again to turn transparency off and make the object opaque again.

# Checking a Publication for Errors

The final phase of the design process is a synthesis involving editing, proofreading, and publishing. Publisher offers several methods to check for errors in your publication. None of these methods is a replacement for careful reading and proofreading. Similar to the spell checking programs in word processing applications, Publisher looks for misspelled words, grammatically incorrect sentences, punctuation problems, and mechanical errors in text frames.

As you type text into a text frame, Publisher checks your typing for possible spelling and grammar errors. If a typed word is not in the dictionary, a red wavy underline displays below it. Likewise, if typed text contains possible grammar errors, a green wavy underline displays below the text. You can check the entire publication for spelling and grammar errors at once or as you are typing.

When a word is flagged with a red wavy underline, it is not in Publisher's dictionary. A flagged word is not necessarily misspelled. For example, many names, abbreviations, and specialized terms are not in Publisher's main dictionary. In these cases, tell Publisher to ignore the flagged word. To display a list of suggested corrections for a flagged word, right-click it.

When using imported text, as in the newsletter, it may be easier to check all the spelling at once. Publisher's **Check Spelling feature** looks through the selected text frame for errors. Once errors are found, Publisher offers suggestions and provides the choice of correcting or ignoring the flagged word. If you are creating this project on a personal computer, your text frames may contain different misspelled words, depending on the accuracy of your typing.

A second way Publisher checks a publication for errors is with the Design Checker. The **Design Checker** looks for errors related to design issues and object interaction, providing comments and correction choices. Design errors are the most common type of problem when submitting a publication to a professional printer. In a later project, you will learn that, in addition to the interactive Design Checker, Publisher's Pack and Go Wizard checks for errors related to embedded fonts and graphics. Table 2-4 lists errors detected by the Design Checker.

## Spelling Options

On the Tools menu, the Spell command allows you to access certain options for checking the spelling of your publication. Included in the Spelling Options dialog box are check boxes for checking the spelling as you type, flagging repeated words, and ignoring words in uppercase.

| Table 2-4   Design Checker Options |
| --- |
| Empty frames |
| Covered objects |
| Text in overflow area |
| Objects in nonprinting region |
| Disproportional pictures |
| Spacing between sentences |

### Checking the Newsletter for Spelling and Grammar Errors

The Spelling command displays on the Tools menu. As you perform the following steps to check your publication for spelling and grammar errors, you may encounter spelling mistakes you have made while typing. Choose to correct those errors as necessary. Perform the following steps to check the publication for spelling and grammar errors.

## To Check the Newsletter for Spelling and Grammar Errors

**1** **With the Thanksgiving article still selected, click Tools on the menu bar. Point to Spelling.**

*The Spelling submenu displays (Figure 2-73).*

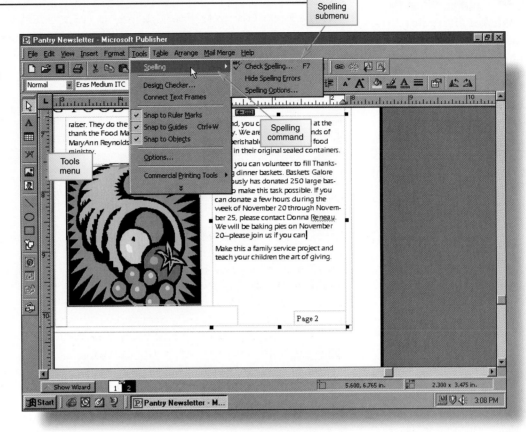

**FIGURE 2-73**

**2** **Click Check Spelling. When the Check Spelling dialog box displays, point to the Ignore button.**

*Publisher flags the name, Reneau, as shown in Figure 2-74. Because this is a personal name and spelled correctly, you will ignore this flag.*

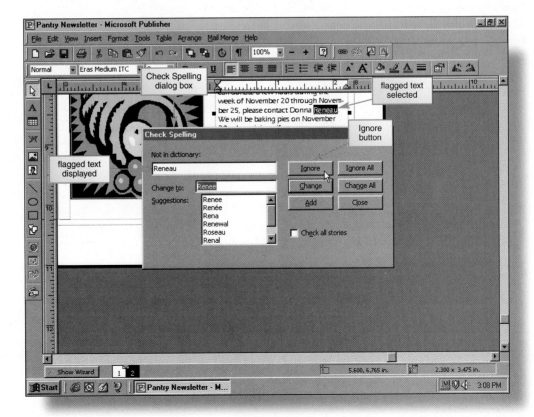

**FIGURE 2-74**

**3** **Click the Ignore button. When the Publisher dialog box displays, point to the Yes button.**

*Publisher did not find any more errors in the Thanksgiving article. It displays a dialog box that asks if you want to check the rest of the publication (Figure 2-75).*

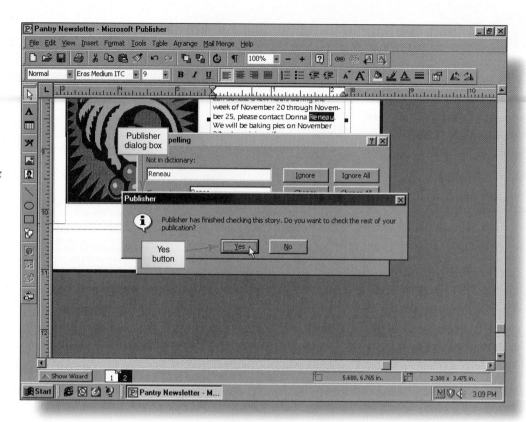

**FIGURE 2-75**

**4** **Click the Yes button. When the Check Spelling dialog box again displays, point to the Ignore button.**

*Publisher flags the name, Ciastko (Figure 2-76). The Check all stories check box now displays with a check mark.*

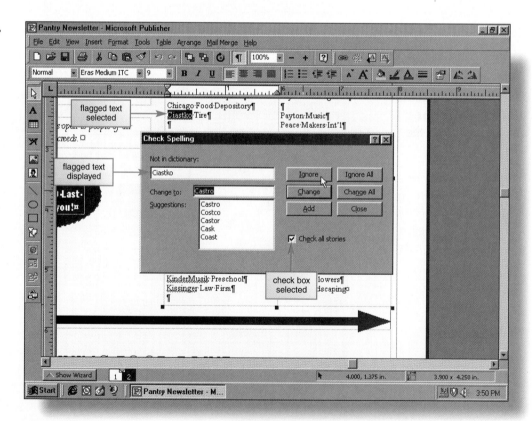

**FIGURE 2-76**

**Click the Ignore button. As Publisher displays other personal names in the Donor List, click the Ignore button for each. When the Check Spelling process is complete, point to the OK button.**

*Publisher displays a dialog box informing you that the process is complete (Figure 2-77).*

 **Click the OK button.**

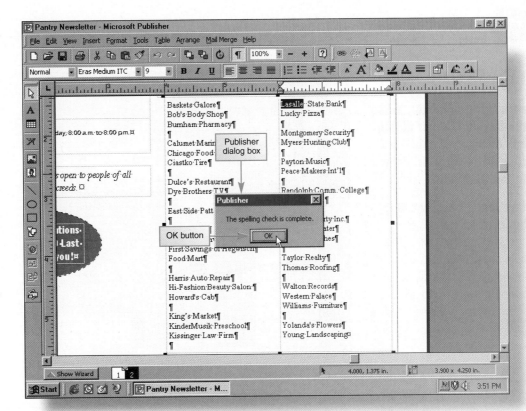

**FIGURE 2-77**

Even if text is checked for spelling before it is imported, Publisher flags words, phrases, and punctuation not found in its dictionary. The process is worth the time it takes, but again, there is no substitute for proofreading the text yourself.

## Checking the Newsletter for Design Errors

You now are ready to check the publication for design errors. The **Design Checker** can check single pages or entire publications, for a specific type of error or all types of errors. Perform the steps on the next page to have Publisher check for all kinds of design errors throughout the publication.

*Other Ways*

1. Right-click text, click Proofing Tools, click Check Spelling
2. Press F7

*More About*

**Web Design**

For more information on the design problems associated with loading Web pages quickly, visit the Publisher 2000 More About Web page (www.scsite.com/pub2000/more.htm) and click Web Design.

**Steps** To Check the Newsletter for Design Errors

**1** **Click Tools on the menu bar and then click Design Checker. When the Design Checker dialog box displays, if necessary click All to select it. Point to the OK button.**

The *Design Checker dialog box* contains options for checking parts or all of the publication (Figure 2-78). When clicked, the Options button allows you to check specific design issues listed in Table 2-4 on page PUB 2.52.

**2** **Click the OK button to start the Design Checker. When the Design Checker terminates, click the OK button.**

If you have made errors in typing, you may have to accept or ignore other Design Checker recommendations.

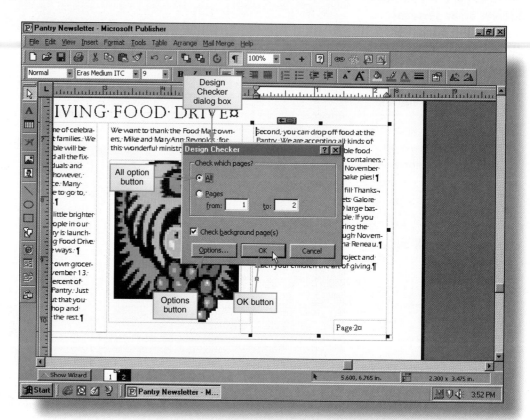

**FIGURE 2-78**

If you resized any graphic in the newsletter, Publisher's Design Checker will warn you that the graphic may not be proportionally correct. At that time, you may choose to resize the graphic or ignore the change.

The newsletter is complete, and should be saved again before printing. Follow this step to save the publication using the same file name.

### TO SAVE AN EXISTING PUBLICATION USING THE SAME FILE NAME

**1** With your floppy disk in drive A, click the Save button on the Standard toolbar.

*Publisher saves the publication using the same file name, Pantry Newsletter, on the floppy disk in drive A.*

# Printing a Two-Sided Page

Printing the two pages of the newsletter back to back is a process that is highly dependent upon the printer. Some printers can perform **duplex printing**, which prints both sides before ejecting the paper, while other printers require the user to reload the paper manually. If you are attached to a single-user printer, you must check the printer's documentation to see if it supports double-sided printing. If you are connected to a network printer, you probably will need to feed the paper through a second time manually.

The following steps illustrate how to print the first page and then manually feed the page through a second time. Adjust the steps as necessary for your printer.

 **To Print a Two-Sided Page**

**1** If necessary, click the page 1 icon on the Page Navigation control. Ready the printer according to the printer instructions. Click File on the menu bar and then click Print. When the Print dialog box displays, point to Current page in the Print range area.

*The Print dialog box displays (Figure 2-79).*

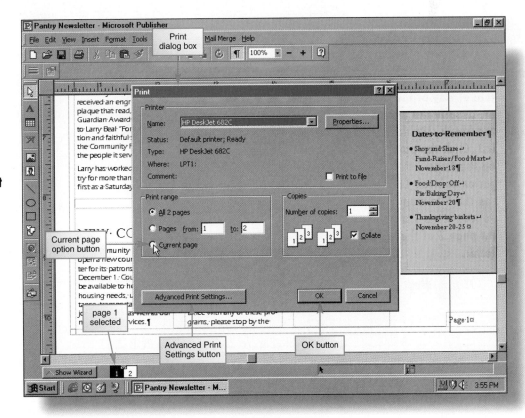

**FIGURE 2-79**

**2** **Click Current page and then click the OK button. When printing is complete, retrieve the printout.**

*Publisher displays a printer icon in the tray status area on the taskbar while printing (Figure 2-80). Publications with many graphics and fonts take longer to print than plain text documents. The printed publication is shown in Figures 2-1a and 2-1b on page PUB 2.6.*

**3** **After retrieving the printout, wait a few seconds for it to dry. Reinsert the printout in the manual tray of the printer. Usually the page is inserted blank side down, top first. Click the page 2 icon on the Page Navigation control. Click Print on the File menu and then repeat Steps 1 and 2 to print page 2 of the newsletter.**

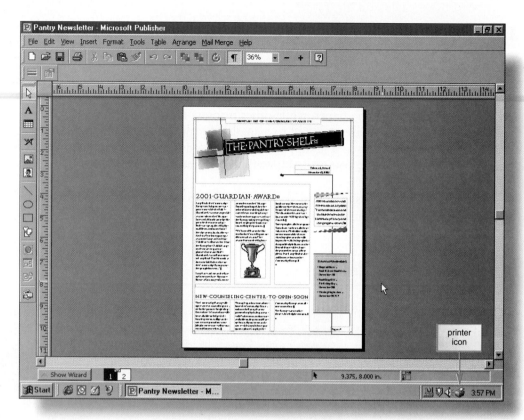

FIGURE 2-80

*Other* Ways

1. Click Print button on Standard toolbar
2. Press CTRL+P

If you have an Option button or an Advanced Print Settings button in your Print dialog box (Figure 2-79 on page PUB 2.57), you may be able to duplex print. Check your printer documentation, or click the button for more information.

If you are unsure how to load the paper, you can run a test page through the printer. Mark an X in the upper-right corner of a blank sheet, and then insert the sheet into the printer, noting where the X is. If your printer has a manual feed button or paper source list box, be sure to click manual. Print the first page. Note where the X is in relation to the printed page and turn the paper over to print the other side accordingly.

In a later project, you will learn more about types of paper best suited for printing on both sides, as well as how to prepare a publication for a printing service.

The newsletter is now complete. Perform the following step to quit Publisher.

### TO QUIT PUBLISHER

**1** Click the Close button in the Publisher window.

*Publisher closes and the Windows desktop displays.*

## CASE PERSPECTIVE SUMMARY

The Community Pantry's newsletter is complete. The Pantry's information is located in the masthead and in the personal information sets. You imported two articles, written by Donna Reneau, for the front page of the newsletter. Donna likes the graphics you chose.

On the back page, you inserted WordArt for the Donor List heading, and formatted the list in two columns. Donna's article on the Thanksgiving food drive is complemented by an appropriate graphic. The Pantry's motto displays prominently, as do last month's donations in an attention getter.

The Community Pantry is pleased with the effect, the quick turn around, and the professional look of its new newsletter. It is equally pleased that future newsletters will be easy to create using this template.

# Project Summary

Project 2 introduced you to the design process and the newsletter medium. You used the newsletter wizard to design a template for editing. Using the Blends Newsletter style, you learned how to edit a masthead, import text from other sources, and add appropriate graphics. You also learned how to insert and delete pages in a publication and incorporate personal information components. With WordArt, you inserted a fancy headline with special text effects. You added page numbers to the background and used the Spell Check feature to identify spelling, grammar, and design errors. Finally, you printed the publication double-sided and saved it on a floppy disk.

# What You Should Know

Having completed this project, you now should be able to perform the following tasks:

▶ Add a Pull Quote *(PUB 2.36)*
▶ Add WordArt to the Newsletter *(PUB 2.44)*
▶ Change and Delete Pages in a Newsletter *(PUB 2.12)*
▶ Check the Newsletter for Design Errors *(PUB 2.56)*
▶ Check the Newsletter for Spelling and Grammar Errors *(PUB 2.53)*
▶ Create a Newsletter Template Using Publisher's Newsletter Wizard *(PUB 2.8)*
▶ Delete the Logo *(PUB 2.30)*
▶ Delete the Sidebar *(PUB 2.32)*
▶ Edit Personal Information Components *(PUB 2.23)*
▶ Edit the Attention Getter *(PUB 2.29)*
▶ Edit the Bulleted Text Frame Sidebar *(PUB 2.39)*
▶ Edit the Masthead *(PUB 2.14)*

▶ Find a Graphic *(PUB 2.32)*
▶ Import More Text *(PUB 2.20)*
▶ Import the Back Page Story *(PUB 2.21)*
▶ Import the Donor List and Create Columns *(PUB 2.25)*
▶ Insert a Line with Arrows *(PUB 2.41)*
▶ Insert Page Numbering *(PUB 2.47)*
▶ Print a Two-Sided Page *(PUB 2.57)*
▶ Quit Publisher *(PUB 2.58)*
▶ Replace Default Text *(PUB 2.18)*
▶ Replace the Graphic on the Back Page *(PUB 2.40)*
▶ Save an Intermediate Copy of the Publication *(PUB 2.22)*
▶ Save an Existing Publication Using the Same File Name *(PUB 2.56)*
▶ Start Publisher *(PUB 2.7)*

# *Apply Your Knowledge*

➕ **Project Reinforcement at www.scsite.com/off2000/reinforce.htm**

## 1 Editing a Publication

**Instructions:** Start Publisher. Open the publication, apply-2, from the Publisher Data Disk. See the inside back cover for instructions on downloading the Publisher Data Disk or see your instructor for information on accessing the files required in this book. The publication is shown in Figure 2-81.

Perform the following tasks.

1. On page 1, highlight the text `The Weekly Warrior` in the vertical masthead. Type `The Warrior Journal` to replace the text.

2. In the lower center of the page, right-click the sidebar table entitled, Inside this Issue. Click Delete Object.

3. Click the Design Gallery Object button on the Objects toolbar and then click the Pull Quotes Category. Insert the Nature Pull Quote. Drag it to the empty space left by the deleted sidebar.

4. Select and copy the next to the last sentence of the article entitled, Housing Shortage on Campus. Click the pull quote text. Paste the sentence into the pull quote.

5. Delete the picture of the student. Use Insert Clip Art to find a different picture of students. Drag the picture to the end of the article.

6. Drag a corner sizing handle to resize the picture proportionally until it fits in the third column.

7. Click the Organization Name Text Frame on the left side of the masthead. Click the Fill Color button and choose a color from the Scheme colors.

8. Click page 2 in the Page Navigation control. Use the Edit menu to delete pages 2 and 3.

9. On the back page, click the colored rectangle in the upper-left portion of the page. Zoom as necessary. Replace the text with information from your college or business. Use your school or business Web page address (URL) in the attention getter.

10. Click File on the menu bar and then click Save As. Save the publication using Warrior Journal Newsletter, as the file name. Print the revised publication, double-sided.

Volume 4, Issue 1

September 10, 2001

NEWSLETTER OF CENTRAL COLLEGE

# The Warrior Journal

## Fall Classes Begin

Classes began today with one of the largest enrollments in recent years. With fall semester enrollment on the rise, administrators seem to be proving that their efforts to work with students and create a more student-friendly atmosphere are effective. Administrators were on hand to greet students across the campus this past weekend.

The Bursar's Office will stay open late every night this week to accept payments and change registration for students adding and dropping courses. You may pick up deferment forms in Gyte 241. Students who owe housing deposits should see their building coordinator

before Friday.

The newest degree on campus is an associate degree in Web design. Students can take 30 credit hours in information system courses, Web development, and general studies requirements. Over 200 students have already enrolled.

The College has also added 500 additional parking spaces for freshmen and sophomores who live on campus and has replaced faulty electrical feeders so East Campus residents will experience fewer electrical outages.

Vice President Starks said Norris Library has been renovated by adding a

bathroom on the first floor . The Library plans to remain open 24 hours a day. The Campus police force added two new officers, Starks said, making the campus a safer place.

## Housing Shortage on Campus

As Central College expands and enrollment increases, students are finding it more and more difficult to secure housing on campus.

Freshmen and sophomores must live in campus approved housing. The dor-

mitories have been full since July 1. The College Housing Board recently approved Stevenson Hall and Quad Towers as approved housing, pending completion of their cafeterias. Both units are accepting applications. Fresh-

men and sophomores must file a housing arrangement contract with the University by September 30.

If you need help finding accommodations, please stop by Gyte 267.

Freshmen and sophomores must file a housing arrangement contract with the University by September 30.

**Dates of Interest**
- *Last Day to Add a Class: Sept. 15*
- *Swing Choir Try-Outs: Sept. 20-21*
- *Frat Pledge Week: Sept. 24-29*
- *Homecoming: Oct. 6*
- *Last Day to Drop a Class: Oct. 19*

**FIGURE 2-81**

*In the Lab*

# 1 Creating a Masthead from Scratch

**Problem:** The accounting firm of A. W. Wright and Associates has asked you to create a masthead for its newsletter. Mr. Wright wants you to incorporate the company logo and colors in the masthead. You decide to use a rectangle, two lines, three text boxes, a graphic, and a WordArt text frame for the newsletter title.

**Instructions:** Perform the following tasks to create the masthead shown in Figure 2-82.

1. Start Publisher. From the Catalog, click the Blank Publications tab. In the previews pane, click Full Page and then click the Create button.
2. Using the Rectangle Tool button on the Objects toolbar, draw a large rectangle across the center of the page, toward the top. Click the Fill Color button, and choose Accent 1 (Blue) in the Scheme colors.

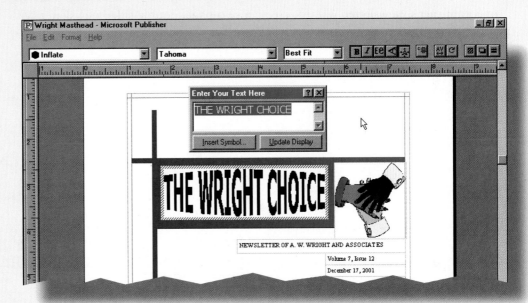

**FIGURE 2-82**

3. Using the Line Tool button on the Objects toolbar, draw a line across the top of the rectangle extending beyond its edges, as shown in Figure 2-82. Draw another line on the left extending down the page. Hold down the SHIFT key while you draw to keep your lines straight. Use the Line/Border Style button on the Formatting toolbar to make both lines 8 pt and blue.
4. Using Insert Clip Art, find a clip related to teamwork. Insert the graphic and move it to the right of the rectangle.
5. For the newsletter title, draw a WordArt text frame just inside the rectangle. Type THE WRIGHT CHOICE in the dialog box. Use the shape and font settings shown in Figure 2-82. Click the Stretch button. Use the Line/Border Style button on the far right of the WordArt toolbar to change the border color to white.
6. Use the Text Frame Tool button on the Objects toolbar to create a text frame to hold the words, NEWSLETTER OF A. W. WRIGHT AND ASSOCIATES. Use a bold font, and place the text frame at the approximate location shown in Figure 2-82.
7. Create two small text frames below the name of the company. Type Volume 7, Issue 12 in the first text frame. Type December 17, 2001 in the second text frame. Using the shortcut menu, change each frames Line/Border Style to a thin line.
8. Use the Design Checker to correct any errors in the publication.
9. Save the publication on your floppy disk using the file name, Wright Masthead.
10. Print a copy of the masthead.

*In the Lab*

# 2 Creating a Special Purpose Newsletter

**Problem:** You are a teacher of fourth grade students at a local elementary school. You thought the students and parents might find a monthly newsletter interesting and informative. Students could write the articles concerning happenings in the school and in your classroom, and you could include dates of future events and projects (Figure 2-83a). In addition, you would like to include a monthly feature called "Caught Being Good," a list of students who have gone out of their way to do something good and caring in the classroom (Figure 2-83b). Using Publisher's Newsletter Wizard, create a two-page, double-sided newsletter with columns.

**Instructions:** Perform the following tasks.

1. Start Publisher.
2. Using Newsletters on the Publications by Wizard tab, select the Kid Stuff Newsletter. Click Start Wizard and then click Finish to accept the default values.
3. Make the following changes on page 1:
   a. Change the Newsletter Title to Fourth Grade News using the default font.
   b. Change the Lead Story Headline to Fourth Grade Goes on Fieldtrip.
   c. Change the Secondary Story Headline to Our Chicks Are Hatching!
   d. Change the Business Name to Lincoln Elementary.
   e. In the bulleted list sidebar, change the title to Specials Each Week and then in the list, type the following: Monday: Music, Tuesday: Gym, Wednesday: Art, Thursday: Computers, Friday: Library, each with a separate bullet.

## Fourth Grade News

### Fourth Grade Goes on Fieldtrip

This story can fit 175-225 words.

The purpose of a newsletter is to provide specialized information to a targeted audience. Newsletters can be a great way to market your product or service, and also create credibility and build your organization's identity among peers, members, employees, or vendors.

First, determine the audience of the newsletter. This could be anyone who might benefit from the information it contains, for example, employees or people interested in purchasing a product or requesting your service.

You can compile a mailing list from business reply cards, customer information sheets, business cards collected at trade shows, or membership lists. You might consider purchasing a mailing list from a company.

If you explore the Publisher catalog, you will find many publications that match the style of your newsletter.

Next, establish how much time and money you can spend on your newsletter. These factors will help determine how frequently you publish the newsletter and its length. It's recommended that you publish your newsletter at least

quarterly so that it's considered a consistent source of information. Your customers or employees will look forward to its arrival.

BIG NEWS

### Our Chicks Are Hatching!

This story can fit 75-125 words.

Your headline is an important part of the newsletter and should be considered carefully.

In a few words, it should accurately represent the

contents of the story and draw readers into the story. Develop the headline before you write the story. This way, the headline will help you keep the story focused.

Examples of possible headlines include Product Wins

Industry Award, New Product Can Save You Time!, Membership Drive Exceeds Goals, and New Office Opens Near You.

**Lincoln Elementary**

Volume 1, Issue 1

Newsletter Date

**Specials Each Week**
☺ Monday: Music
☺ Tuesday: Gym
☺ Wednesday: Art
☺ Thursday. Computers
☺ Friday: Library

First Issue

**FIGURE 2-83a**

# In the Lab

   f.  Delete the table sidebar and insert a WordArt object in its place. Type First Issue as the text. Click the Shape box and choose the top to bottom arrow. Click the shading button (third from the right), and choose a blue foreground color.

4. Use the Page Navigation control to move to page 2. Delete pages 2 and 3.

5. Make the following changes to the back page:
   a.  Change the back page story headline to, This Month's Spelling Words.
   b.  Use a keyword to locate and insert graphics about children.
   c.  Delete the logo on the back page.
   d.  Click the text frame in the upper-right corner. Click Format on the menu bar and then click Text Frame Properties to change the text frame to contain two columns.
       With the text still selected, type the following names on separate lines: Jared Allen, Dara Arslanian, Fredrick Carl, Marsha Louks, Katie Marie. Then, press CTRL+SHIFT+ENTER to create a column break. Continue the list by typing: Michael Montgomery, Hannah Murphy, Jon Reneau, Nathan Thomas, Rebecca Witte, each on a separate line.
   e.  Add a WordArt text frame with the text, Caught Being Good, positioned above the list. Stretch the text to fit the frame. Add an attention getter under the list.

6. Spell Check and Design Check the publication.

7. Save the publication on a floppy disk using the file name, Kids Newsletter, and print a copy.

**FIGURE 2-83b**

## 3  Looking at Publisher's Newsletter Choices

**Problem:**   You work in the public relations department of an architectural firm. Your supervisor wants to publish a weekly newsletter for customers and potential clients, but would like to see some samples first. You decide to use Publisher's Newsletter Wizard to give him a variety from which he may choose.

**Instructions:**   Using the techniques presented in this project, access the Publisher Catalog and choose five different newsletter wizards. Choose wizards you have not used before. Below are some general guidelines for each wizard.

1. Start the wizard and go through each step, reading about the wizard. Make a note of the default values as you choose them.

2. When the wizard finishes, print page 1 of each newsletter.

3. Identify the parts of the newsletter on the printout. Label things such as the masthead, design set, color scheme, personal information components, and all objects.

4. Pick your favorite of the five newsletters. For that one, print all the pages and identify any different components or objects. If possible, print double-sided.

5. Let your instructor look at all the printouts.

Microsoft **Publisher 2000**

# Cases and Places

The difficulty of these case studies varies:
▶ are the least difficult; ▶▶ are more difficult; and ▶▶▶ are the most difficult.

**1** ▶ Use the Newsletter Wizard entitled Checkers Newsletter to create a letterhead for your personal use. Delete all the pages except page 1. Delete all the objects on page 1 except the masthead and the checkers graphic across the bottom. Put your name in the newsletter title and your address and telephone number in the volume and date text frames.

**2** ▶ Use the Newsletter Wizard entitled Voyage Newsletter to create a two-page newsletter for the Seniors Abroad Club. This local club of senior citizens gets together to take group trips. For the newsletter title, use Seniors On the Go, and place today's date in the masthead. Include an article headline for the lead story, which concerns the club's most recent trip to London (you may use the default text), and a secondary article headline that tells how to pack light for the Orient. Add a list of dates for upcoming trips to Quebec, Paris, and Tokyo in the Special points of interest sidebar. Replace the graphics with suitable pictures from Publisher's Clip Gallery.

**3** ▶▶ You are associate editor of *The Weekly Warrior*, a two-page newsletter for students at Central College. Last week's edition is shown in Figure 2-81 on page PUB 2.61. Volume 4, Issue 2 is due out in three weeks. Using the same masthead and design set, your assignment is to decide on a feature article for *The Weekly Warrior* newsletter and develop some announcements. Select a topic about your school that would interest other students, such as extracurricular activities, the fitness center, the day-care center, the bookstore, the Student Government Organization, registration, the student body, a club, a sports team, etc. Obtain information for your article by interviewing a campus employee or student, visiting the school library, or reading brochures published by your school. Use appropriate clip art graphics, sidebars, and pull quotes. Run your final product through the Design Check and Spell Check, making corrections as necessary. Print a double-sided hard copy.

**4** ▶▶▶ Ask a local civic group or scouting organization for a sample of its newsletter. Try to recreate its style and format using a blank publication page in Publisher. Use Publisher's Design Gallery and personal information components to customize the newsletter. Print your final product and compare the two.

**5** ▶▶▶ Many clubs and organizations put their newsletters out on the Web. Browse the Web and look for examples of newsletters. Note how many pages, graphics, and articles they use. Look at their mastheads and logos. Then, using a Publisher Newsletter Wizard, create a newsletter for a club or organization with which you are affiliated. Include at least three articles, one sidebar or pull quote, a masthead, and several graphics. Use the Create Web Site from Current Publication command on the File menu to create a group of files for posting to the Web.

Microsoft Publisher 2000

PROJECT

3

# Preparing a Tri-Fold Brochure for Outside Printing

You will have mastered the material in this project when you can:

O B J E C T I V E S

- Understand the advantages of the brochure medium
- Use the Brochure Wizard
- Describe the use of photographs versus images
- Insert a photograph from a file
- Create a logo from scratch using custom shapes
- Create a composite object in the scratch area
- Insert a symbol
- Group and ungroup objects
- Rotate objects and create mirror copies
- Edit a sign-up form
- Create a calendar using the Design Gallery
- Position objects using the Size and Position command
- Reposition objects to prevent overlapping
- Edit a calendar
- Preview a brochure before printing
- Choose appropriate printing services, paper, and color libraries
- Prepare a publication for outside printing
- Use the Pack and Go Wizard
- Thread multiple sessions of Publisher
- Create a postcard
- Copy objects across publications

# Attention Getters

## Publications That Encourage Second Looks

In 1971 when John Jay Osborn, Jr. wrote *The Paper Chase*, he portrayed the frenzied quest of first-year graduate students at Harvard University for a specific kind of document known as a law degree. Obtaining a law degree or other academic degree is a milestone in a student's life. Seemingly, individuals' lives are defined by a paper trail of documents.

A newborn receives a birth certificate to declare that he or she is indeed a real person. From that point on, a succession of documents tracks his or her progress through life and even beyond. Medical records, diplomas, military orders, marriage certificates, wills, contracts, drivers licenses, and resumes, are among the many publications organized in the personal filing cabinets of the general population.

In addition, a number of other publications such as the *Holy Bible*, the *Koran*, or the *Talmud*, as well as the works of countless great thinkers and authors influence the minds and personalities of people. Yet, the most meaningful and gratifying kinds of publications are those created by the individuals themselves; whether they are works of art, words of poetry, letters, journals, term papers, news-

letters, flyers, personal greetings, business cards, or brochures, whatever the medium, individual creativity provides the most significant sense of accomplishment.

Still, for many people, the mere act of creating any publication ranks high in difficulty. You have a powerful tool, however, with the Publisher Brochure Wizard in this project in which you will create a tri-fold brochure. The brochure medium is intentionally tactile, making it an effective communication tool. Whether you want to advertise an event or service or provide information to a large audience, brochures are a popular type of promotional publication. Brochures can be produced quickly with lots of color and graphics. Strategically placed, they reach a wide audience and can influence and educate.

Publisher allows you to choose from a variety of brochure types and designs in the Microsoft Publisher Catalog. Then, you can edit and delete text to fit your personal, academic, or professional needs. Enhancing your brochure using photographs and images adds a special touch. Publisher also makes it possible to combine numerous shapes to create a logo of your choice. As you examine the Objects by Category in the Design Gallery, you will find a large selection of objects to insert into your brochures and other publications.

Finally, you will learn about packaging the publication for the printing service using the Pack and Go Wizard. With these productivity tools, you are sure to produce publications that encourage a second look.

Microsoft Publisher 2000

# Preparing a Tri-Fold Brochure for Outside Printing

P R O J E C T

**3**

C A S E   P E R S P E C T I V E

Alpha Omega is a coed national service fraternity with a chapter on the campus of Midland University. With more than 100 active members, the fraternity has been looking for ways to further its principles of leadership, friendship, and service. Alpha Omega has participated in many service-related campus events and now is planning a friendship ski trip to Sunset Mountain, Colorado during spring break. They have asked you to design a brochure that advertises the trip, together with a postcard to send to students who respond.

Alpha Omega would like a full-color, tri-fold brochure on glossy paper. The fraternity has budgeted the money to send the final copy to a printing service. The brochure should include pictures of Sunset Mountain, a sign-up form, the Alpha Omega logo, and a calendar showing the dates of the trip.

You decide to use Publisher to set up a tri-fold brochure for outside printing. After printing a proof for the fraternity, you package the publication on a floppy disk containing all of the items the printing service will need to produce mass quantities.

# Introduction

Whether you want to advertise a service, event, or product, or merely want to inform the public about a current topic of interest, brochures are a popular type of promotional publication. A **brochure**, or pamphlet, usually is a high-quality document with lots of color and graphics, created for advertising purposes. Businesses that may not be able to reach potential clientele effectively through traditional advertising such as newspapers and radio can create a long-lasting advertisement with a well-designed brochure.

Brochures come in all shapes and sizes. Colleges and universities produce brochures about their programs. The travel industry uses brochures to entice tourists. Service industries and manufacturers display their products using this very visual, hands-on medium.

# Project Three — Tri-Fold Brochure

Project 3 uses Publisher to illustrate the production of the two-page, tri-fold brochure shown in Figure 3-1. The brochure informs the public about a fraternity-sponsored ski trip. Each side of the brochure has three panels. Page 1 contains the front and back panels, as well as the inside fold. Page 2 contains a three-panel display that, when opened completely, provides the reader with more details about the trip and a sign-up form.

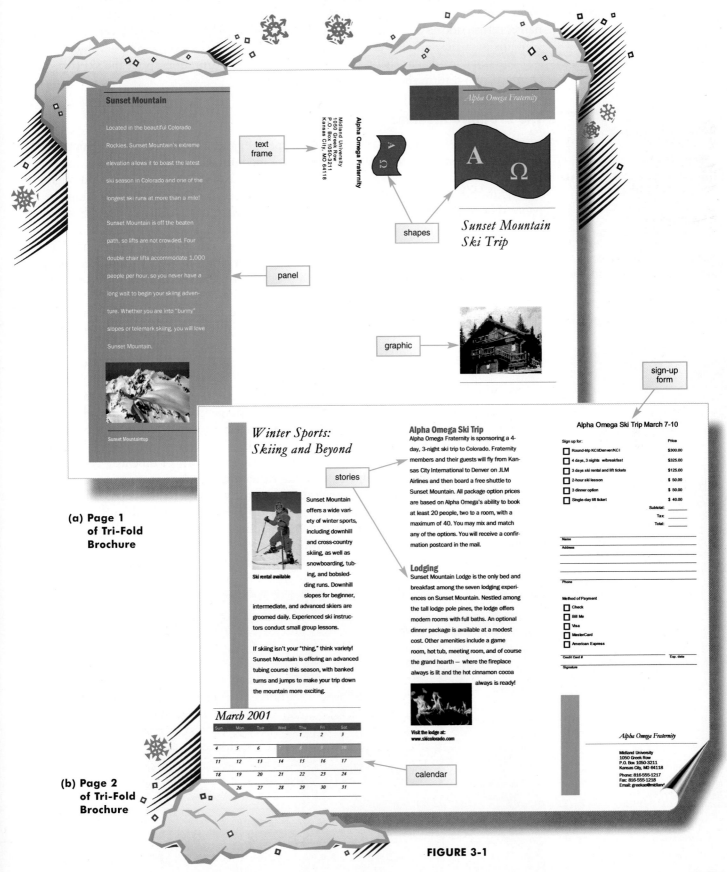

**(a) Page 1 of Tri-Fold Brochure**

**(b) Page 2 of Tri-Fold Brochure**

**FIGURE 3-1**

On page 1, the front panel contains shapes, text frames, and a graphic, designed to draw the reader's attention and inform the reader of the intent of the brochure. The back panel, which displays in the middle of page 1, contains the fraternity's name, return address, and a space for the mailing label. The inside fold, on the left, contains an article about the ski resort, with a colored background and graphic.

The three inside panels on page 2 contain more information about the ski trip, graphics, and a form the reader may use to register.

## The Brochure Medium

**Brochures** are professionally printed on special paper to enhance the graphics and provide long-lasting documents. The brochure medium is intentionally tactile. Brochures are meant to be touched, carried home, passed along, and looked at, again and again. Newspapers and fliers usually are produced for short-term readership on paper that soon will be thrown away or recycled. Brochures frequently use a heavier stock of paper so they can stand better in a display rack.

The content of a brochure needs to last longer too. On occasion, the intent of a brochure is to educate, such as a brochure on health issues in a doctor's office; but more commonly, the intent is to market a product or sell a service. Prices and dated materials that are subject to frequent change affect the usable life of a brochure.

Typically, brochures use a great deal of color, and they include actual photographs instead of drawings or graphic images. Photographs give a sense of realism to a publication, and should be used to show people, places, or things that are real, whereas images or drawings more appropriately are used to convey concepts or ideas.

Many brochures incorporate newspaper features such as columns and a masthead, and the added eye appeal of logos, sidebars, shapes, and graphics. Small brochures are separated into panels and folded. Larger brochures resemble small magazines, with multiple pages and a stapled binding.

Brochures, designed to be in circulation for longer periods of time as a type of advertising, ordinarily are published in greater quantities and on more expensive paper than newsletters, and are, therefore, more costly. The cost, however, is less prohibitive when produced **in-house** using desktop publishing rather than hiring an outside service. The cost per copy is sometimes less than a newsletter, because brochures are produced in mass quantities.

Table 3-1 lists some benefits and advantages of using the brochure medium.

**More** *About*

### Brochures

Many brochures are published regularly on the Web. To look at some samples and for more information on brochure content, visit the Publisher 2000 More About Web page (www.scsite.com/pub2000/more.htm) and click Brochures.

| Table 3-1 | Benefits and Advantages of Using the Brochure Medium |
|---|---|
| *AREA* | *BENEFITS AND ADVANTAGES* |
| Exposure | • An attention getter in displays<br>• A take-along document encouraging second looks<br>• A long-lasting publication due to paper and content<br>• An easily distributed publication — mass mailings, advertising sites |
| Information | • Give readers an in-depth look at a product or service<br>• An opportunity to inform in a nonrestrictive environment<br>• An opportunity for focused feedback using tear-offs and forms |
| Audience | • Interested clientele and retailers<br>• A way to attract a wide, diverse population<br>• A pull to new customers |
| Communication | • An effective medium to highlight products and services<br>• A source of free information to build credibility<br>• An easier method to disseminate information than a magazine |

Besides the intent and content of the brochure, you must consider the shape and size of the page when designing this type of publication. Publisher can incorporate a variety of paper sizes from the standard 8½-by-11-inch paper to 8½-by-24-inch. You also can design smaller brochures, such as those used as liner notes for CD jewel cases or inserts for videotapes. In addition, you need to think about how the brochure or pamphlet will be folded. Publisher's brochure wizard can create three or four panels. Using the page setup options you may create special folds, such as book or card folds.

## Starting Publisher

Follow these steps to start Publisher or ask your instructor how to start Publisher for your system.

### TO START PUBLISHER

1. Click the Start button on the taskbar.

2. Point to Programs on the Start menu.

3. Click Microsoft Publisher on the Programs submenu

4. If the Catalog does not display, click File on the menu bar and then click New.

5. If necessary, click the Publications by Wizard tab in the Catalog dialog box.

*Publisher displays Publications by Wizard in the Catalog dialog box.*

## Using a Brochure Wizard to Create a Tri-Fold Brochure

Publisher wizards use proven design strategies and combinations of objects placed to attract attention and disseminate information effectively. The brochure wizards differ from wizards used in previous projects in that they allow you to choose from special kinds of response forms and panel/page layout options. Like all the wizards, the Brochure Wizard walks you through the creation process by asking you design questions as described in the steps on the next page.

## To Create a Brochure Using a Wizard

**1** **Click Brochures in the Wizards pane. Scroll down and then click the Straight Edge Informational Brochure in the previews pane. Point to the Start Wizard button.**

*The Straight Edge Informational Brochure is selected (Figure 3-2). Depending on your screen size and resolution, the number of previews displayed may vary.*

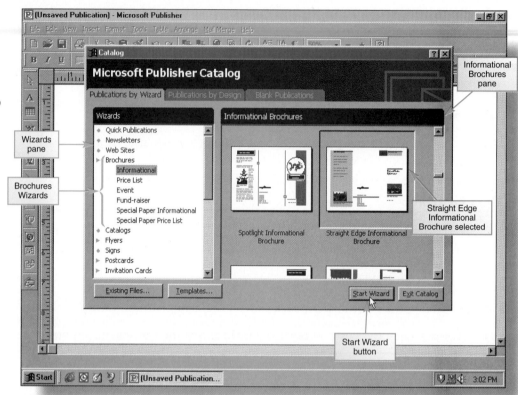

**FIGURE 3-2**

**2** **Click the Start Wizard button. Select the options shown in Table 3-2, clicking the Next button to proceed with each wizard step. When you click Sign-up form, a dialog box will display. Point to the OK button.**

*The Publisher dialog box displays (Figure 3-3). The dialog box indicates that the form displays on page 2. Later, you will look at page 2 to see the results.*

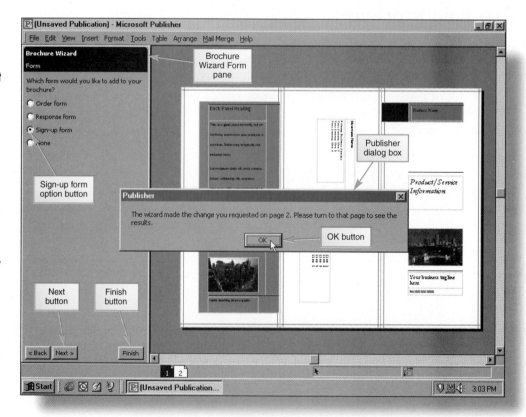

**FIGURE 3-3**

**3** Click the OK button and then click the Finish button. When Publisher completes the changes to the publication, click the Show/Hide Wizard button.

*The Brochure Wizard makes the appropriate changes to the publication (Figure 3-4). Bypassing the other options of the wizard causes Publisher to accept the preset values. The publication, ready to edit, displays in the Publisher workspace.*

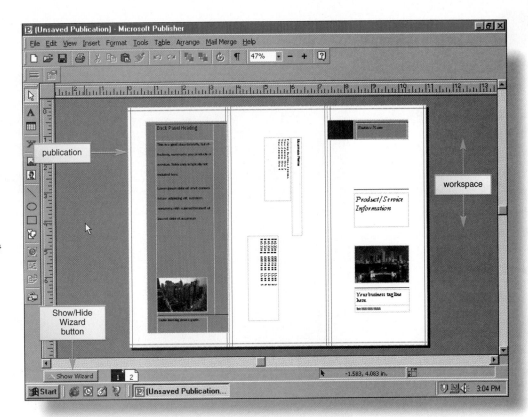

FIGURE 3-4

| Table 3-2 | Wizard Selections |
|-----------|-------------------|
| **BROCHURE WIZARD PANE** | **SELECTION** |
| Introduction | Next button |
| Color Scheme | Clay |
| Paper Size (Panels) | Letter (8.5 by 11 in), 3 panels |
| Customer Address | Yes |
| Form | Sign-up form |

*Other* Ways

1. Click New button on Standard toolbar
2. On File menu click New
3. Press CTRL+N

Publication wizards can be revisited at any time during the design process by clicking the **Show/Hide Wizard button** located at the bottom of the screen (Figure 3-4).

# Editing Text in the Brochure

Editing the brochure involves making changes to the text to fit your needs. The Brochure Wizard has inserted placeholder text in some of the frames and personal information components in others.

Editing the brochure involves selecting the current text and replacing it with new, appropriate text in one of three ways. Placeholder text is selected by a single click. The best way to select small portions of nonplaceholder text is to drag through the text. Entire frames of text are selected quickly by clicking inside the frame and then pressing CTRL+A. Perform the steps on the next page to practice editing the text of the brochure in all three ways.

**To Edit Text in the Brochure**

**① Click Product/ Service Information in the front panel on page 1.**

*The placeholder text is selected with a single click (Figure 3-5). This text is the title of the brochure.*

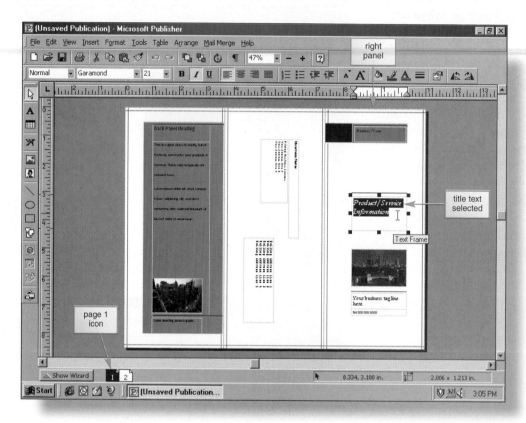

**FIGURE 3-5**

**② Type** Sunset Mountain Ski Trip **to replace the title text. Drag through the text in the Organization Name Text Frame at the top of the front panel.**

*The new title text displays and the text, Business Name, is selected (Figure 3-6).*

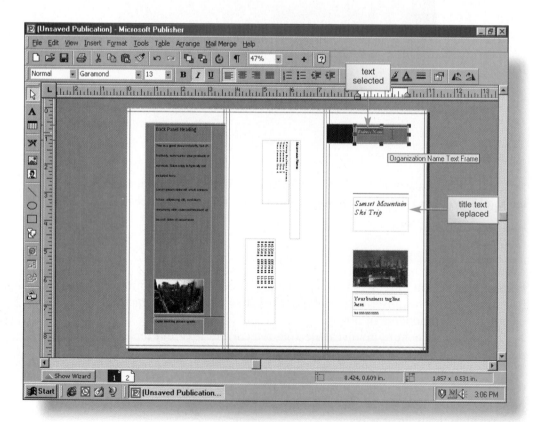

**FIGURE 3-6**

**3** **Type** Alpha Omega Fraternity **in the text frame and then click the return Address Text Frame in the center panel.**

*The new text for the business name displays (Figure 3-7). Notice the Organization Name Text Frame in the center panel changes as well. The return Address Text Frame is selected with sizing handles displayed.*

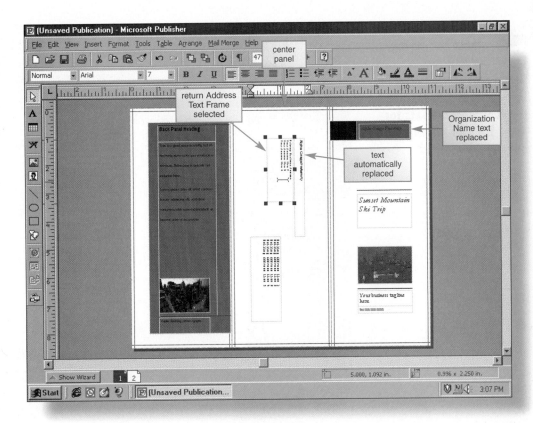

FIGURE 3-7

**4** **If necessary, press** F9 **to increase the magnification of the display and then press** CTRL+A **to select all of the text. Type the return address text as shown in Table 3-3 on the next page, pressing the** ENTER **key after each line except the last. Repeat the process for the remaining text replacements on page 1. Table 3-3 shows the new text for the frames that require editing.**

*The completed text replacements display (Figure 3-8).*

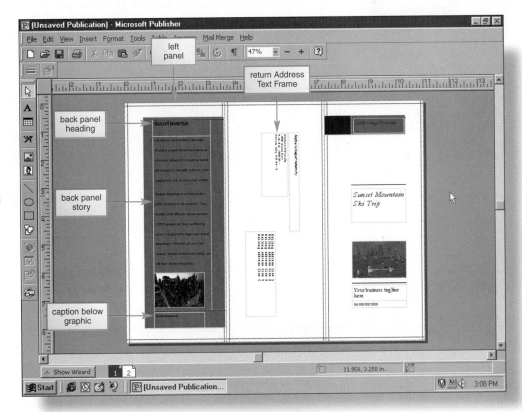

FIGURE 3-8

**5** **Click page 2 on the status bar. Using Table 3-4 and the techniques you learned in the previous steps, make the text replacements for page 2. Press the ENTER key only where marked.**

*The new text displays on page 2 (Figure 3-9).*

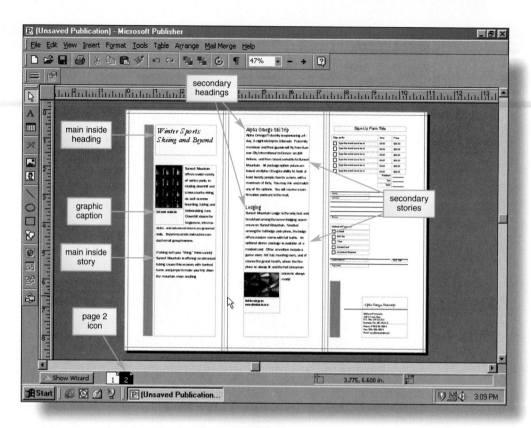

**FIGURE 3-9**

**Other Ways**

1. Right-click default text, click Change Text on shortcut menu, click Text File
2. On Edit menu click Highlight Entire Story, type new text
3. Click beginning of text, SHIFT-click end of text, type new text
4. Press ALT+I, press E

| Table 3-3 New Text for Page 1 | | |
|---|---|---|
| *TEXT FRAME* | *PAGE 1 LOCATION* | *NEW TEXT* |
| Address Text Frame | Center panel | Midland University<br>1050 Greek Row<br>P.O. Box 1050-3211<br>Kansas City, MO 64118 |
| Back Panel Heading | Left panel | Sunset Mountain |
| Back Panel Story | Left panel | Located in the beautiful Colorado Rockies, Sunset Mountain s extreme elevation allows it to boast the latest ski season in Colorado and one of the longest ski runs at more than a mile!<br><br>Sunset Mountain is off the beaten path, so lifts are not crowded. Four double chair lifts accommodate 1,000 people per hour, so you never have a long wait to begin your skiing adventure. Whether you are into bunny slopes or telemark skiing, you will love Sunset Mountain. |
| Caption below graphic | Left panel | Sunset Mountaintop |

You may remember that Publisher automatically checks for spelling errors and duplicate words as text is entered. If you type a word that is not in the dictionary (because it is a proper name or misspelled) a red wavy underline displays below the word. You may right-click the underlined word to see Publisher's suggestions or click Spelling on the Tools menu to check the spelling of the entire publication.

## Table 3-4 New Text for Page 2

| TEXT FRAME | PAGE 2 LOCATION | NEW TEXT |
|---|---|---|
| Main Inside Heading | Left panel | Winter Sports: Skiing and Beyond |
| Main Inside Story | Left panel | Sunset Mountain offers a wide variety of winter sports, including downhill and cross-country skiing, as well as snowboarding, tubing, and bobsledding runs. Downhill slopes for beginner, intermediate, and advanced skiers are groomed daily. Experienced ski instructors conduct small group lessons. <ENTER><br><br>If skiing isn't your "thing," think variety! Sunset Mountain is offering an advanced tubing course this season, with banked turns and jumps to make your trip down the mountain more exciting. |
| Graphic Caption | Left panel | Ski rental available |
| Secondary Heading | Upper portion of center panel | Alpha Omega Ski Trip |
| Secondary Story | Upper portion of center panel | Alpha Omega Fraternity is sponsoring a 4-day, 3-night ski trip to Colorado. Fraternity members and their guests will fly from Kansas City International to Denver on JLM Airlines and then board a shuttle to Sunset Mountain. All package option prices are on Alpha Omega's ability to book at least 20 people, two to a room, with a maximum of 40. You may mix and match any of the options. You will receive a confirmation postcard in the mail. |
| Secondary Heading | Lower portion of center panel | Lodging |
| Secondary Story | Lower portion of center panel | Sunset Mountain Lodge is the only bed and breakfast among the seven lodging experiences on Sunset Mountain. Nestled among the tall lodge pole pines, the lodge offers modern rooms with full baths. An optional dinner package is available at a modest cost. Other amenities include a game room, hot tub, meeting room, and of course the grand hearth, where the fireplace always is lit and the hot cinnamon cocoa always is ready! |
| Graphic Caption | Center panel | Visit the lodge at: <ENTER> www.skicolorado.com |

As you work through the steps in this project, or as you design publications on your own, Publisher may remind you to save your work. You may do so at that prompt, or wait until the project steps instruct you to do so.

# Deleting Objects

Several text frames of the Straight Edge Informational Brochure will not be included in the final product. Simply selecting the text and then cutting or deleting it leaves the frame still on the page. To delete the unnecessary text frames entirely, perform the steps on the next page.

## TO DELETE TEXT FRAMES

1  If necessary, click page 1 on the status bar. Click the Zoom box arrow and then click Whole Page to facilitate editing.

2  Right-click the Tag Line Text Frame in the lower-right portion of the front panel. Click Delete Object on the shortcut menu.

3  Right-click the telephone number on the front panel. Click Delete Object on the shortcut menu.

4  Right-click the mailing address in the center panel of page 1. Click Delete Object on the shortcut menu.

*Other Ways*

1. On Edit menu click Delete Object

*Page 1 displays with the text frames deleted (Figure 3-10). The Whole Page view is approximately 47% magnification.*

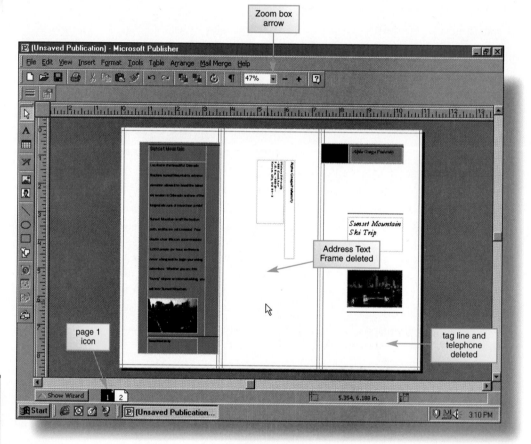

**FIGURE 3-10**

### Inserting a New Drawing

On the Insert menu, the Picture command contains an option to insert a new drawing into your publication. This command actually launches the embedded draw application (formerly known as Msdraw) similarly to launching WordArt. When clicked, the New Drawing command displays a drawing frame, the Drawing toolbar, the Autoshapes toolbar, and new buttons on the Standard and Formatting toolbars to assist you in drawing objects.

# Using Photographs and Images in a Brochure

The advent of inexpensive photo CDs has increased exponentially the possibilities for photographic reproduction in publications. Regular cameras using popular types of film now can take pictures and have them digitized, a process that previously required digital cameras. **Digitizing** means converting colors and lines into digital impulses capable of being read by a computer. Digitized photos and downloaded graphics from the Web, combined with high-resolution production from scanners, create endless possibilities. Small businesses now can afford to include photographs in their brochures and other types of publications.

Publisher can accept photographs and images from a variety of input sources. Each graphic you import has a file name, followed by a dot or period, followed by a three-letter extension. Publisher uses **extensions** to recognize individual file formats. Table 3-5 displays some of the graphic formats Publisher can import.

## Inserting a Photograph from a File

Publisher can insert a photograph into a publication by accessing the Clip Gallery, by externally importing from a file, by directly importing an image from a scanner or camera, or by creating a new drawing. The next sequence of steps illustrate how to insert a previously scanned photograph from a file into the brochure. The photograph for the brochure is provided on the Data Disk. See the inside back cover of this book for instructions for downloading the Data Disk or see your instructor for information on accessing the files required for this book.

| Table 3-5 Supported Graphic Formats | |
|---|---|
| **GRAPHIC FORMAT** | **FILE EXTENSION** |
| Computer Graphics Metafile | .cgm |
| CorelDRAW! | .cdr |
| Encapsulated PostScript | .eps |
| Graphics Interchange Format | .gif |
| Joint Photographic Experts Group | .jpeg or .jpg |
| Kodak Photo CD or Pro Photo CD | .pcd |
| Macintosh PICT | .pct |
| PC Paintbrush | .pcx |
| Portable Network Graphics | .png |
| Tagged Image File Format | .tif |
| Windows Bitmap File | .bmp |
| Windows Enhanced Metafile | .emf |
| Windows Metafile | .wmf |
| WordPerfect Graphics | .wpg |

*Steps* **To Insert a Photograph from a File**

① **Insert the Data Disk in drive A. If necessary, click page 1 on the status bar and then click the picture on the right panel. Click Insert on the menu bar and then point to Picture.**

*The Insert menu and Picture submenu display (Figure 3-11).*

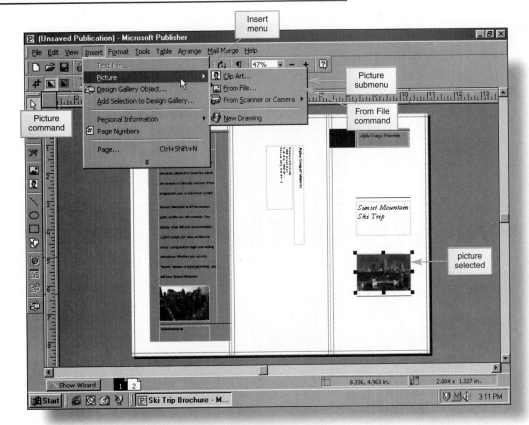

**FIGURE 3-11**

**2** **Click From File.
When the Insert
Picture dialog box displays,
click the Look in box arrow
and then click 3½ Floppy
(A:) in the list. Point to the
file name, lodge.**

*The list of picture format
files on drive A displays
(Figure 3-12). The lodge
picture is stored as a .gif file
(Table 3-5 on the previous
page), scanned from an
actual photograph.*

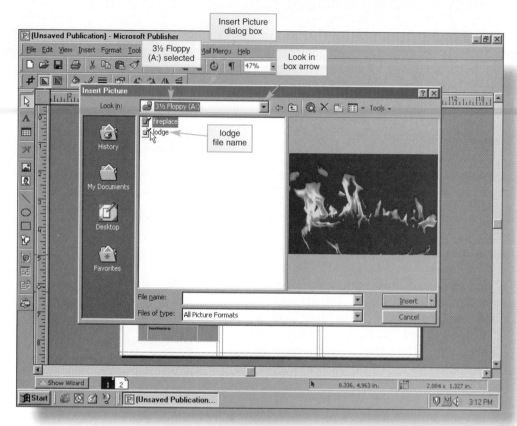

**FIGURE 3-12**

**3** **Double-click the
file name, lodge.**

*The lodge picture replaces
the original picture (Figure
3-13).*

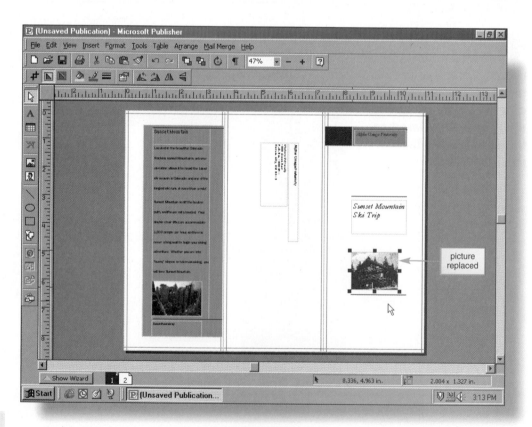

**FIGURE 3-13**

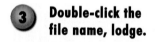

1. Right-click picture, click
   Change Picture, click Picture

Publisher resizes replacement clip art and photographs to match the size and shape of the wizard-placed graphic without distorting the picture. If you import a picture into a spot where no picture was placed previously, you may have to resize it yourself.

Another common method of creating new image files, other than scanning, is to use **illustration software.** Designed for artists, illustration software packages such as CorelDRAW! and Adobe Illustrator create graphics to import into desktop publishing software.

### Inserting Clip Art Using a Keyword Search

Recall from Project 1, the Clip Gallery provided with Publisher saves keywords with each image to facilitate finding suitable clip art. The next sequence of steps uses a keyword search to retrieve and insert pictures associated with skiing and mountains into the brochure.

More *About*

**Clip Art**

For samples of clip art available on the Internet, visit the Discovering Computers 2000 Chapter 2 WEB INFO Web page (www.scsite.com/dc2000/ ch2/webinfo.htm) and click Clip Art.

 **To Insert Clip Art Using a Keyword Search**

**1** **Double-click the picture in the left panel of page 1. When the Insert Clip Art window displays, click the Search for clips text box, type** wilderness **and then press the ENTER key.**

*The pictures and images associated with the keyword, wilderness, display (Figure 3-14). Depending on your installation of Publisher, your previews may vary.*

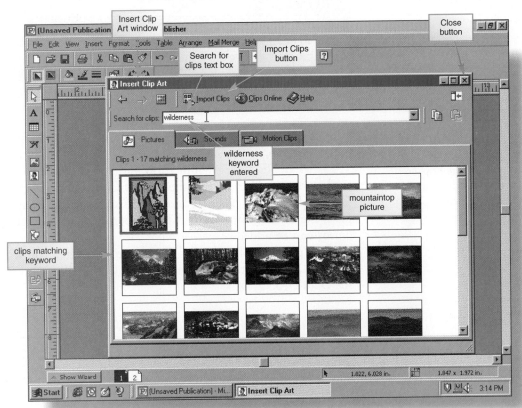

**FIGURE 3-14**

**2** Right-click the picture of the mountaintop (Figure 3-14 on the previous page) and then click Insert on the shortcut menu. If you do not see the exact picture, select an appropriate replacement from the previews available. Close the Insert Clip Art window by clicking its Close button.

*The picture of the mountaintop replaces the original picture in the left panel (Figure 3-15).*

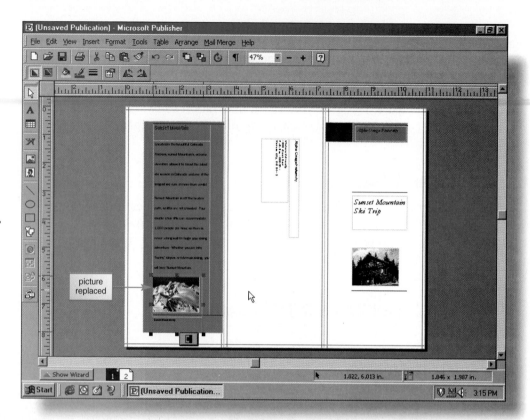

picture replaced

**FIGURE 3-15**

You can add your own pictures and keywords to the Clip Gallery. At the top of the Insert Clip Art window, the Import Clips button displays an Add clip to Clip Gallery dialog box when clicked. Right-clicking any image in the Clip Gallery displays the shortcut option for Clip Properties, where descriptions, categories, and keywords can be added.

The photographs on page 1 now are complete. You will replace one of the pictures on page 2 with a picture from the Clip Gallery and the other with a file from the Data Disk.

### TO FINISH REPLACING THE PHOTOGRAPHS

**1** Click the page 2 icon on the status bar.

**2** Double-click the picture in the left panel. Search for an appropriate picture, using the keyword, ski.

**3** Insert the clip and then close the Insert Clip Art window.

**4** Click the picture in the center panel. Click Insert on the menu bar, point to Picture, and then click From File. On drive A, double-click the file name, fireplace.

*The two pictures display on page 2 (Figure 3-16). Your pictures may vary.*

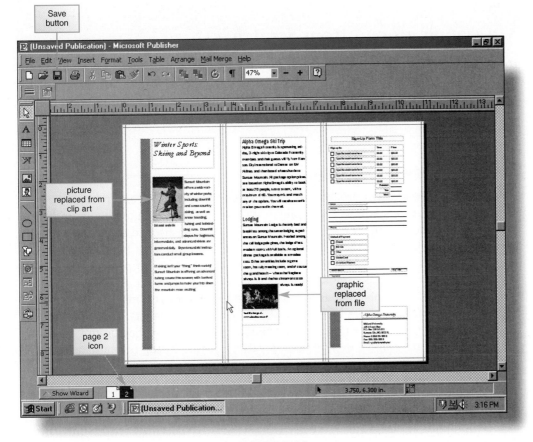

**FIGURE 3-16**

In addition to the clip art images included in the Clip Gallery, other sources for clip art include retailers specializing in computer software, the Internet, bulletin board systems, and online information systems. Some popular online information systems are The Microsoft Network, America Online, CompuServe, and Prodigy. A **bulletin board system** is a computer system that allows users to communicate with each other and share files. Microsoft has created a special page on its Web site where you can add new clips to the Clip Gallery.

## Saving the Brochure

You have learned that it is prudent to save your work on disk at regular intervals. Because you have performed several tasks thus far, you should save your brochure. For a detailed example of the procedure summarized below, refer to pages PUB 1.26 through PUB 1.28 in Project 1.

### TO SAVE A BROCHURE

1. Insert your floppy disk in drive A.

2. Click the Save button on the Standard toolbar.

3. Type Ski Trip Brochure in the File name text box. Do not press the ENTER key after typing the file name.

4. Click the Save in box arrow and then click 3½ Floppy (A:) in the list.

5. Click the Save button in the Save As dialog box.

Microsoft **Publisher** 2000

## More About 2000

### Logo Copyrights

A logo is a recognizable symbol that identifies you or your business. The Design Gallery consists of many logo styles from which you may choose if you do not want to create one from scratch. Although Publisher's logo styles are generic, commercial logos typically are copyrighted. Consult with a legal representative before you commercially use materials bearing clip art, logos, designs, words, or other symbols that could violate third party rights, including trademarks.

# Creating a Logo from Scratch

Many types of publications use logos to identify and distinguish the page makeup. A **logo** is a recognizable symbol that identifies a person, business, or organization. A logo may be composed of a name, a picture, or a combination of symbols and graphics. In a later project, you will learn how to add a permanent logo to an information set for a company.

## Creating a Shape for the Logo

The logo in the ski trip brochure is a combination of a shape and two text frames with the Greek symbols for Alpha and Omega. Created individually in the workspace and then grouped together, the logo easily is positioned and sized to the proper places in the brochure. The logo appears both on the front panel above the brochure title and above the return address on the center panel of page 1.

The background of the logo is from the Custom Shapes menu. Accessed from the Objects toolbar, the **Custom Shapes** menu displays 36 shapes you may use as graphics in a publication. These shapes include polygons, arrows, starbursts, and bubbles, among others. The Custom Shapes differ from WordArt in that they do not contain text; rather, they are graphic designs with a variety of formatting options such as color, border, size, and shadow.

The following steps illustrates creating the logo in Publisher's workspace to the right of the brochure.

 **To Create a Shape for the Logo**

**1** If necessary, click the page 1 icon on the status bar and then increase the magnification to view the whole page. Click to the right of the scroll box on the horizontal scroll bar to view more of the workspace. Point to the Custom Shapes button on the Objects toolbar.

*The brochure moves left as you scroll right, providing more workspace area (Figure 3-17).*

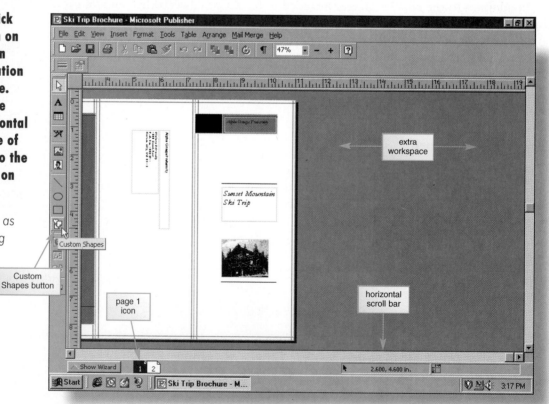

**FIGURE 3-17**

**2** **Click the Custom Shapes button. Point to the wave shape.**

*The Custom Shapes button menu displays (Figure 3-18).*

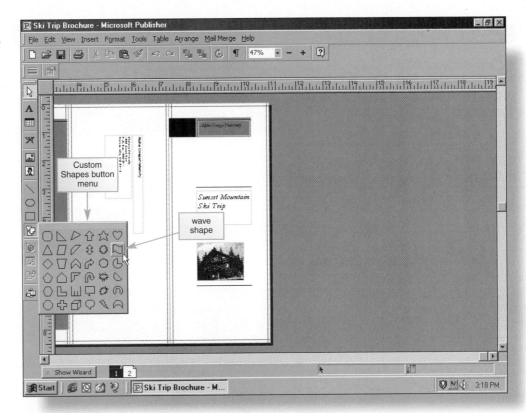

**FIGURE 3-18**

**3** **Click the wave shape and then move the mouse pointer to an open space to the right of the brochure. Drag down and to the right until the shape is approximately 2.000 x 1.500 in. as displayed in the Object Size box on the status bar. Release the mouse button and then point to the Fill Color button on the Formatting toolbar.**

*The workspace displays the wave shape for the logo (Figure 3-19). The Object Size box displays the size of the object.*

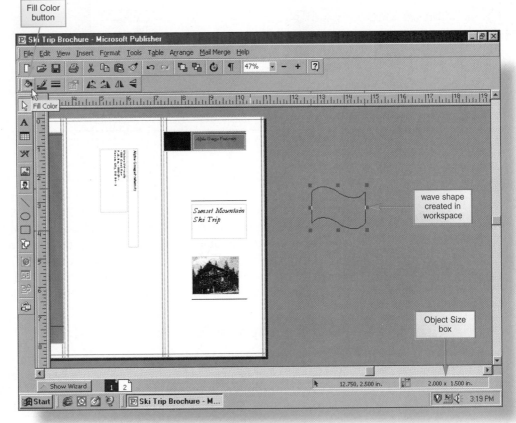

**FIGURE 3-19**

Microsoft **Publisher 2000**

④ **Click the Fill Color button. When the Fill Color button menu displays, point to Accent 1 (Dark Red) in the Scheme colors (Figure 3-20).**

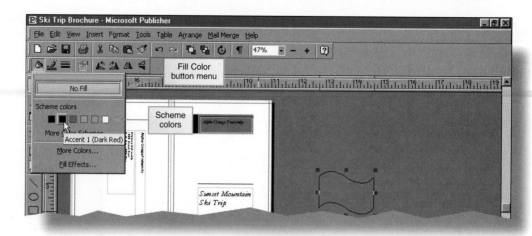

**FIGURE 3-20**

⑤ **Click Accent 1 (Dark Red).**

*The wave shape's fill color changes to dark red to match the brochure's Clay color scheme (Figure 3-21).*

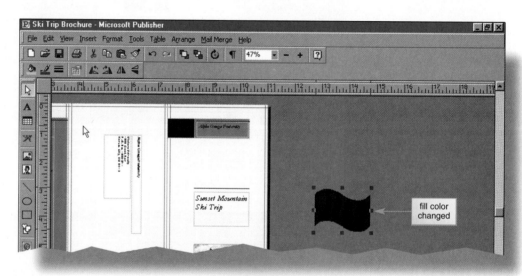

**FIGURE 3-21**

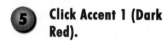 

### The Workspace

Placing objects in the workspace is an easy way to move them from one page to the next. Simply drag them to the workspace, click the appropriate page icon in the Page Navigation control, and then drag the object onto the new page. Publisher allows you to save a publication with objects still in the scratch area or the workspace. Be sure to remove them, however, to avoid confusion before submitting a file to a commercial printer.

The workspace, also called the **scratch area**, can serve as a kind of drawing board to create new objects. Without disturbing any object already on the publications page, you can manipulate and edit objects in the workspace and then move them to the desired location. The rulers and status bar display the exact size of the new object. Moving objects off the page and into the workspace is sometimes advantageous as well. Small objects that are difficult to revise on the publication can be moved into the workspace, magnified and edited, and then moved back. As you place new objects in the workspace, more workspace room is allocated.

### Creating a Symbol Text Frame

The Greek symbols, and many other special symbols not available on standard keyboards, can be accessed easily by using the **Symbol command** on the Insert menu. The types of symbols you can insert depend on the available fonts. Each font has its own extensive subset of special symbols including fractions, international characters, and international monetary symbols. Some subsets even have arrows, bullets, and scientific symbols. You also may have additional symbol fonts, such as Wingdings, which include decorative symbols.

Symbols are inserted as text into text frames. The following steps illustrate creating the text frame, inserting a symbol, and formatting it using the Formatting toolbar.

## Steps To Create a Symbol Text Frame for the Logo

**1** **Click the Zoom In button on the Standard toolbar to magnify the workspace area. Click the Text Frame Tool button on the Objects toolbar and then move the mouse pointer to the workspace below the wave shape. Drag a small text frame approximately 0.600 x 0.700 in. as shown in the Object Size box. Release the mouse button.**

*The text frame displays in the magnified workspace (Figure 3-22).*

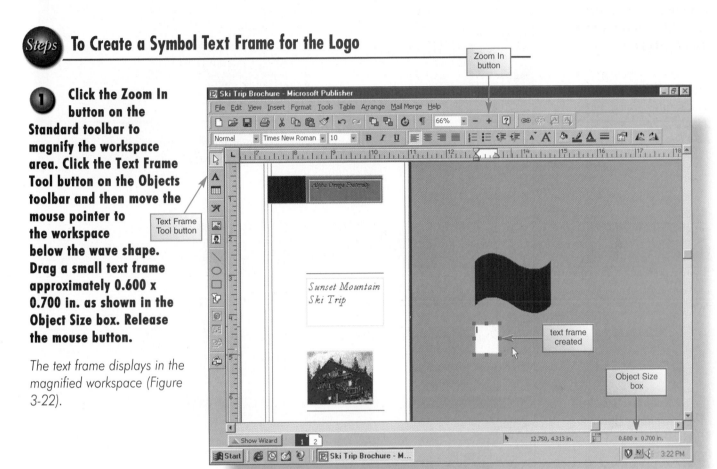

**FIGURE 3-22**

**2** **Click Insert on the menu bar and then click Symbol. If Times New Roman does not display in the Font box, click the Font box arrow and click Times New Roman in the Font list. Point to the Subset box arrow.**

*The Symbol dialog box displays (Figure 3-23). The dialog box contains symbols that are not available on the standard keyboard. Because fonts are printer-dependent, the symbols available to you may be different from those shown.*

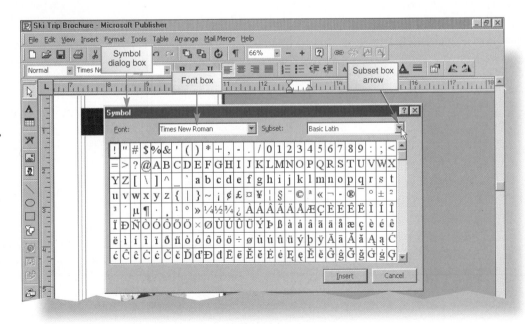

**FIGURE 3-23**

**3** Click the Subset box arrow and then click Basic Greek in the Subset list. Point to the Alpha symbol in the third row of the Symbol grid.

*The Basic Greek portion of the grid displays the symbol for the Greek letter, Alpha (Figure 3-24).*

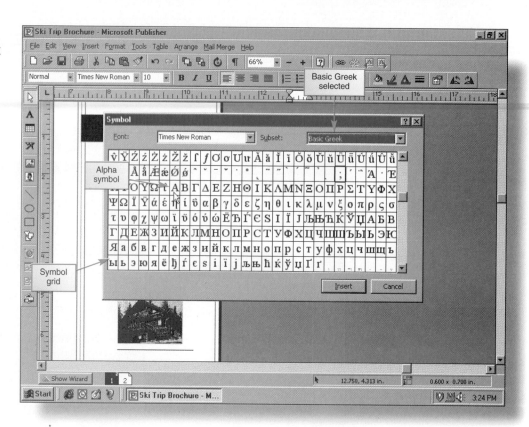

**FIGURE 3-24**

**4** Double-click the Alpha symbol. Right-click the text frame in the workspace.

*The shortcut menu displays (Figure 3-25). The Alpha symbol with a font size of 10 is inserted in the text frame after double-clicking the symbol in the Symbol grid. Fonts and font sizes may vary.*

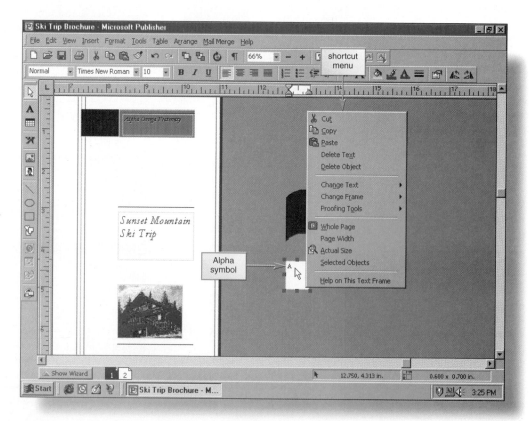

**FIGURE 3-25**

**⑤** **Point to Change Text on the shortcut menu and then point to AutoFit Text (Figure 3-26).**

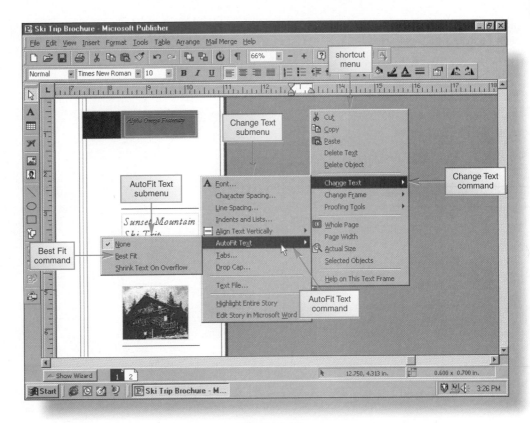

**FIGURE 3-26**

**⑥** **Click Best Fit on the AutoFit Text submenu. Point to the Fill Color button on the Formatting toolbar.**

*The text in the text frame displays in a larger font size (Figure 3-27). With the **Best Fit command** active on the AutoFit Text submenu, the font size is adjusted any time the frame is resized or moved.*

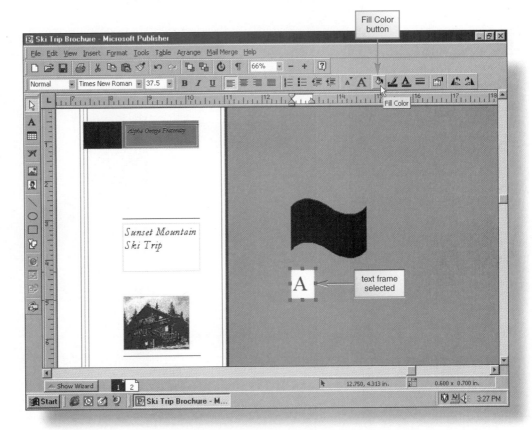

**FIGURE 3-27**

**7** Click the Fill Color button and then click Accent 1 (Dark Red) in Scheme colors. Drag through the Alpha symbol in the text frame and then point to the Font Color button on the Formatting toolbar.

*The color of the text frame changes to dark red (Figure 3-28). The Alpha symbol is highlighted in preparation for additional formatting.*

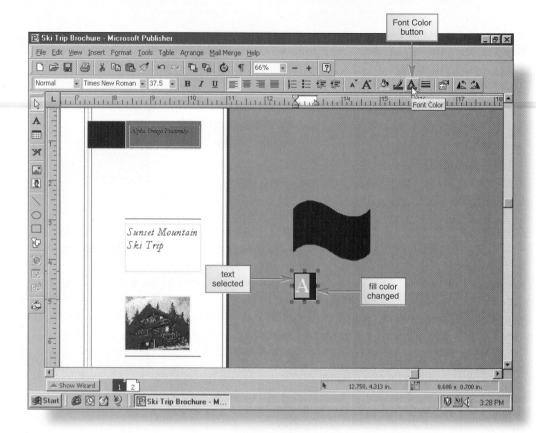

FIGURE 3-28

**8** Click the Font Color button and then click Accent 4 (RGB, (204, 204, 204)) in Scheme colors. Click outside the text.

*The text now displays in gray to match the brochure's color scheme (Figure 3-29). The Alpha text frame is complete.*

### Other Ways

1. To change font, right-click text, click Change Text on shortcut menu
2. Select text, on Format menu point to AutoFit Text, click Best Fit on AutoFit Text submenu

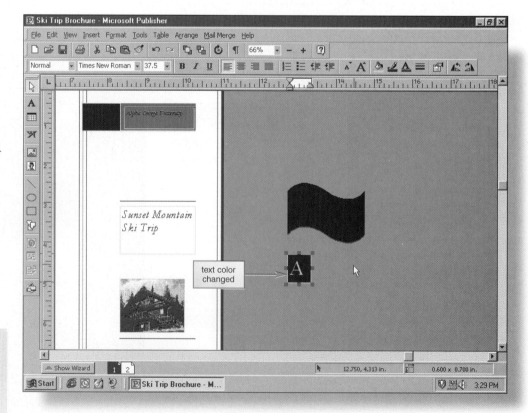

FIGURE 3-29

Not all fonts have a subset list. An **expanded font**, such as Arial or Times New Roman, displays a subset list. Occasionally, the fonts on a specific printer may not contain the special symbol set. Check with your instructor for the best font and printer driver to use.

## Creating a Symbol Text Frame Using the Copy Button

Changing the font, size, and color of each text frame is tedious. If you copy a text frame, you can save some time, because its formatting is copied as well. An alternative is to use the **Format Painter button** on the Standard toolbar. Simply click the formatted text, click the Format Painter button and then click the new text. The formatting will be applied automatically. The Format Painter button does not copy the AutoFit Text formatting, however. You still need to apply Best Fit if your text runs over, or manually change the size of the frame or text. The **Copy button** copies the object, its Font format, and the AutoFit formatting as well.

The second Greek symbol for the brochure logo is the Omega symbol. It is easier to copy the Alpha text frame and change the symbol than to recreate the entire text frame and formatting. Copying the text frame not only copies the formatting for you, but also guarantees the same size frame. The Copy button, on the Formatting toolbar, saves a copy of the selected object on the **Clipboard**, which is a temporary holding area in the memory of the computer. You then use the **Paste button** to bring a copy from the Clipboard back to the workspace of the publication. The Clipboard retains the contents of the copy until it is replaced with another copy, or the electrical power to the computer is turned off.

### More About

### Symbols

Each symbol in the Symbol dialog box includes a keystroke equivalent. For instance, to insert a cent sign, hold down the ALT key and then type 0162 on the numeric keypad. Microsoft Window's Charmap (character map) displays each symbol's keystroke equivalent in its lower right corner.

## Steps To Create a Symbol Text Frame Using Copy and Paste

**1** **If necessary, click to the right of the Alpha symbol to select the text frame and not merely the text. Point to the Copy button on the Standard toolbar.**

*The text frame is selected (Figure 3-30). The Copy button would be **grayed**, or dimmed, if no object were selected.*

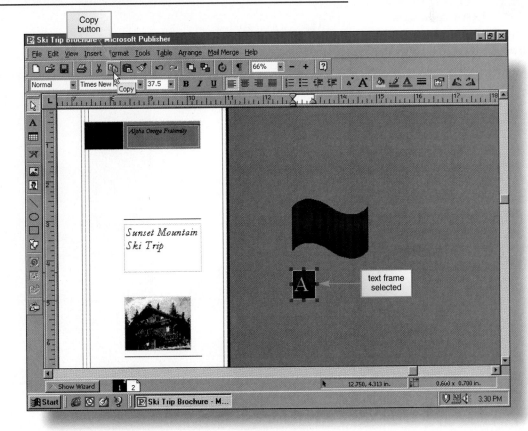

**FIGURE 3-30**

**2** **Click the Copy button. Click the Paste button on the Standard toolbar.**

*A second copy of the Alpha text frame displays on top of the first (Figure 3-31).*

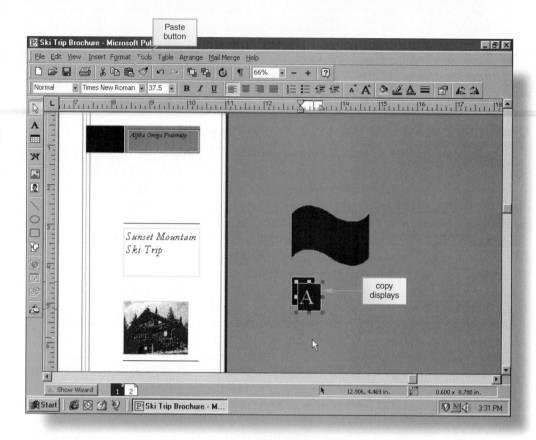

FIGURE 3-31

**3** **Drag the new text frame to an open area in the workspace. Drag through the text to select it.**

*The Alpha symbol is selected (Figure 3-32).*

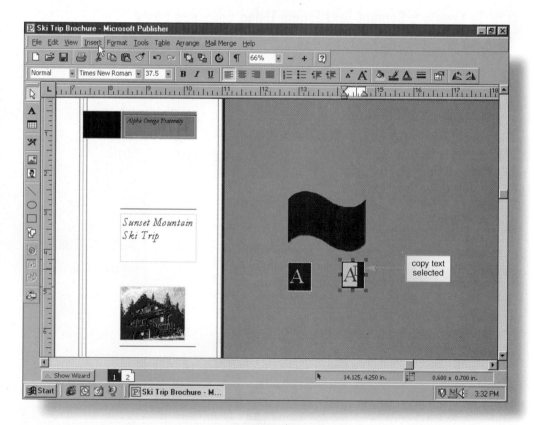

FIGURE 3-32

**④ Click Insert on the menu bar and then click Symbol. When the Symbol dialog box displays, if necessary, click Basic Greek in the Subset list. Point to the Omega symbol in row four (Figure 3-33).**

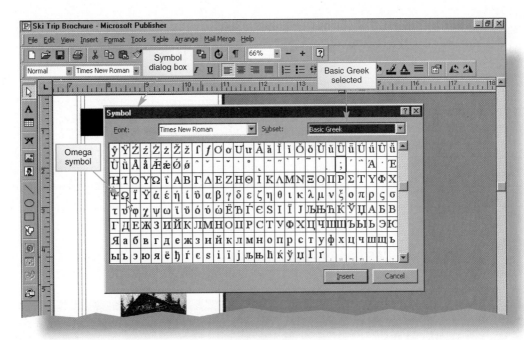

**FIGURE 3-33**

**⑤ Double-click the Omega symbol.**

*The copied text frame displays the Omega symbol (Figure 3-34).*

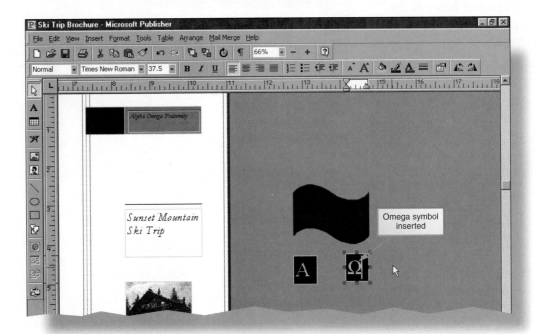

**FIGURE 3-34**

You also can insert ANSI characters into a document. **ANSI,** which stands for **American National Standards Institute,** uses a standardized number to represent a pre-defined set of characters, including both characters on the keyboard and other special characters. For instance, the number 171 represents the symbol for ½, which is not on the keyboard. To enter the ANSI code, make sure the NUM LOCK key is on. Press and hold the ALT key and then type the ANSI code for the character. You must use the numeric keypad to enter the ANSI code. Pressing and holding the ALT key and then typing 171 would display ½ in the text frame. For a complete list of ANSI codes, see your Microsoft Windows documentation.

1. Select object, on Edit menu click Copy, on Edit menu click Paste
2. Select object, press CTRL+C, press CTRL+V

### Grouping and Positioning the Logo Objects

The logo, when complete, is a three-part composite object: two text frames, and a background shape. Repositioning and resizing these objects independently would be tedious and prone to error. Placing objects on top of other objects, known as **layering**, can cause design errors if you are not careful. Moving the front objects first can cause an **order** error with parts of objects obscured behind others. Mixed colors of layered objects create additional challenges for commercial printing.

When these objects are grouped carefully, however, adhering to the scheme colors and paying careful attention to the layering, they can be moved, resized, rotated, and copied quite easily as a group. Perform the following steps to group and position the logo.

## To Group and Position the Logo Objects

**1** **Drag the Alpha text frame to position it on the left portion of the wave shape. Drag the Omega text frame to the right portion of the wave shape.**

*The text frames display in front of the wave shape (Figure 3-35).*

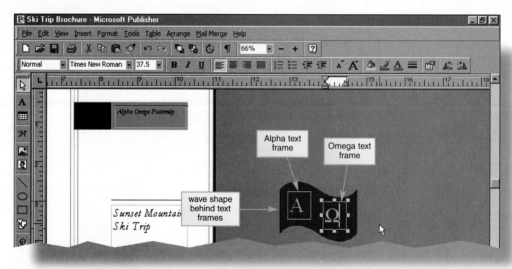

**FIGURE 3-35**

**2** **Click the wave shape, outside of the two text frames. SHIFT-click the Alpha text frame. SHIFT-click the Omega text frame. Point to the Group Objects button.**

*All three objects are selected, each with its own set of sizing handles (Figure 3-36). The Group Objects button displays when multiple objects are selected.*

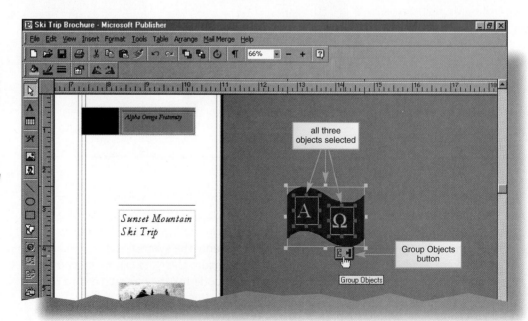

**FIGURE 3-36**

**3** **Click the Group Objects button. Point to the Copy button on the Standard toolbar.**

*The three objects display as a grouped object with a single set of sizing handles (Figure 3-37). The Group Objects button becomes the Ungroup Objects button as indicated by the button's changed icon.*

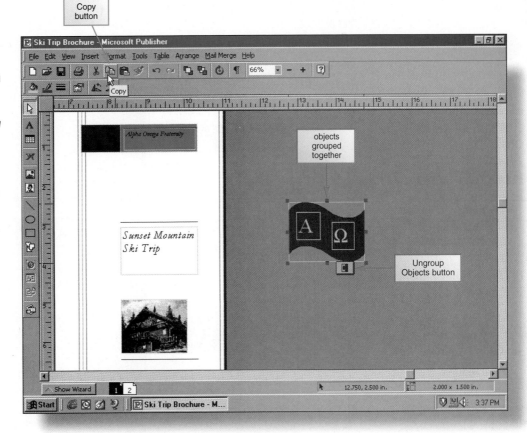

FIGURE 3-37

**4** **Click the Copy button and then click the Paste button. When the copy displays, drag the copy to an open area of the workspace. Point to the corner sizing handle.**

*Both copies display (Figure 3-38). The corner Resizer also displays.*

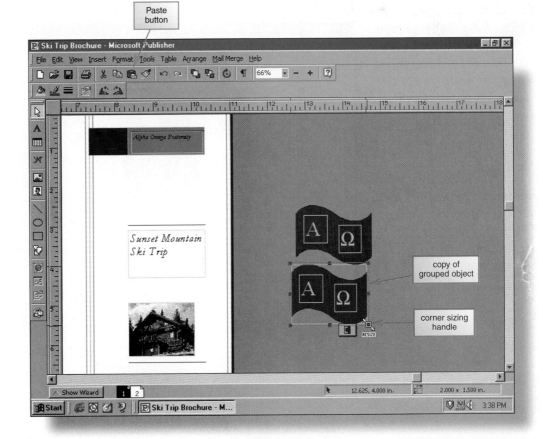

FIGURE 3-38

Microsoft **Publisher 2000**

**5** SHIFT-drag the corner Resizer toward the center of the logo, until the size is approximately 0.700 x 0.800 in. as shown in the Object Size box. Click the Rotate Right button on the Formatting toolbar, so the logo displays on its side.

*The resized logo displays rotated 90 degrees to the right (Figure 3-39). The Object Size box on the status bar reflects the change in size.*

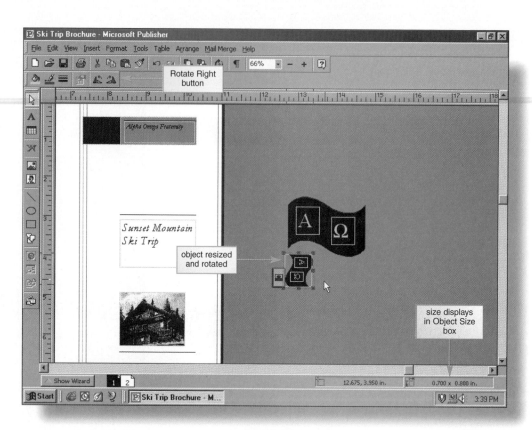

**FIGURE 3-39**

**6** Drag the large logo to the space above the title of the brochure. Drag the small logo to the space above the return address in the center panel. If necessary, scroll left and zoom to facilitate positioning.

*The logos display in the brochure (Figure 3-40).*

**Other Ways**

1. To group, click Group Objects on shortcut menu
2. To position, on Format menu click Size and Position
3. To position, insert locations on Measurements toolbar

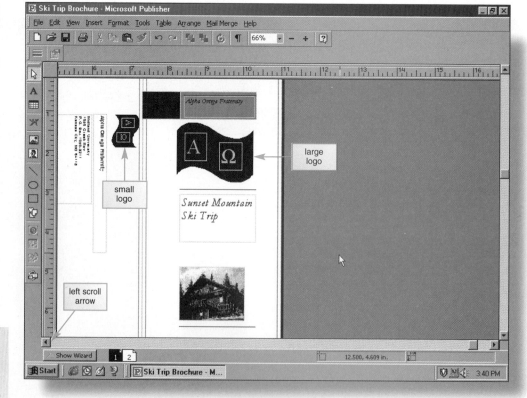

**FIGURE 3-40**

Again, dragging a corner sizing handle maintains the proportions of the graphic, whereas dragging a middle sizing handle distorts the proportion of the graphic. Proportionally resizing an object other than a graphic requires that you hold down the SHIFT key while dragging the corner sizing handle. To keep the center of an object in the same place as you resize it, hold down the CTRL key as you drag. You will see later in this project that the measurements and position of ungrouped objects can be entered even more precisely using the Size and Position command on the Format menu.

# Editing the Front Panel

The final step to complete the front panel of the brochure involves recreating the banner heading for the bottom of the panel. You will use the copy and paste techniques you learned earlier, as well as rotation and text editing.

## Creating a Mirrored Copy of the Heading

The banner heading at the top of the front panel is a group of individual objects positioned next to each other and layered. The heading contains two rectangles, a text frame, and a line. Creating a mirror copy of this heading will involve moving it to the bottom of the panel and then rotating it 180 degrees. Additionally, the text needs to be changed. Follow these steps to create a mirrored copy of the heading.

### More About

**Positioning Objects**

If you increase the magnification of the screen, you can resize and reposition objects precisely. For instance, at 400% magnification in the Zoom box list, you can move an object .003 inch by pressing and holding the ALT key and then pressing an arrow key.

**Steps** **To Create a Mirrored Copy of the Heading**

**1** **If necessary, zoom out to display the entire right panel. Click the dark red portion of the banner heading. Click the Copy button on the Standard toolbar and then click the Paste button on the Standard toolbar. Drag the copy down, below the picture, aligning the left side of the grouped object with the pink layout guide. Point to the Rotate Right button on the Formatting toolbar.**

*The copy of the banner displays aligned with the pink layout guide (Figure 3-41).*

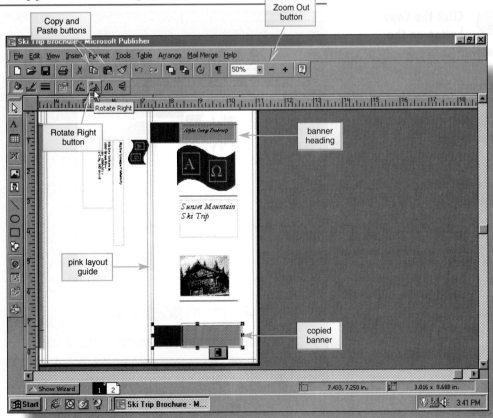

**FIGURE 3-41**

### Repositioning Objects to Prevent Overlapping the Calendar

Whether you are designing a brochure for desktop printing, commercial printing, or publishing to the Web, objects on the brochure should not overlap one another unless you intend to create some type of special effect. Running the Design Checker will point out design problems, but if you can position objects to prevent overlapping as you create them, you avert possible complications. If you overlap objects on a publication intended for the Web, Publisher automatically creates a **graphic region** and adds an image to your Web page, which may prohibit some search and cut-and-paste functionality for individual objects.

Occasionally, you may want objects to overlap for a 3-D effect or to **bleed** the colors or patterns. Commercial printers use bleeds to change the background color of a page, to add a pattern to an entire page, or to add a sidebar or other background element that runs the entire length of the page. You also can create bleeds on desktop printers.

Making room for the calendar will involve resizing some objects so they do not print on top of each other or bleed across the page. Follow these steps to safeguard against overlapping objects.

 **To Prevent Objects from Overlapping**

**1** **Click the blue rectangle shape in the left panel. Point to the lower-middle sizing handle.**

*The rectangle shape displays selected (Figure 3-55). Notice the shape runs behind the calendar and extends slightly below it.*

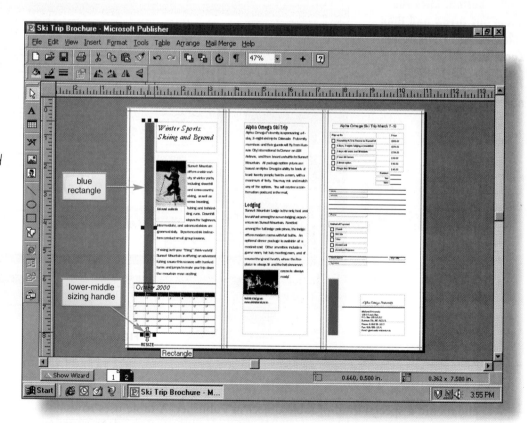

**FIGURE 3-55**

**2**  **Drag the sizing handle directly above the calendar.**

*The rectangle shape snaps to the edge of the calendar so the objects do not overlap (Figure 3-56). If your rectangle does not snap to the calendar's edge, make sure the Snap to Objects command is selected on the Tools menu.*

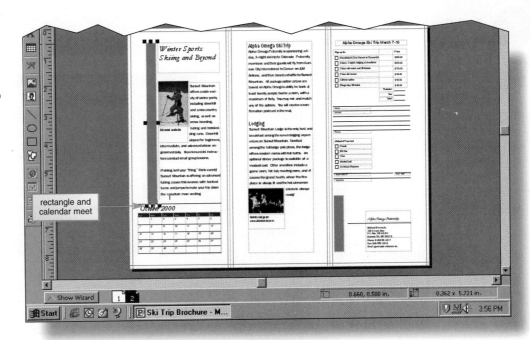

rectangle and calendar meet

**FIGURE 3-56**

**3**  **Repeat Steps 1 and 2 for the text frame located to the right of the blue rectangle shape.**

*The text frame shape snaps to the edge of the calendar so the objects do not overlap (Figure 3-57).*

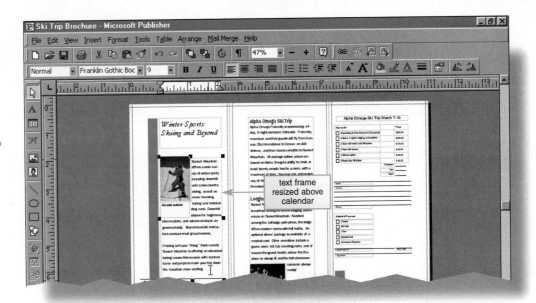

text frame resized above calendar

**FIGURE 3-57**

Sometimes, for a visual effect, you may elect to overlap objects slightly. Professional printers trap objects to eliminate white space in the printed copy. **Trapping** extends the lighter colors of one object into the darker colors of an adjoining object. This color overlaps just enough to fill areas where gaps could appear due to the slight stretching or movement of the paper in the press.

**Other Ways**

1. On Tools menu click Design Checker, respond in Overlap dialog box

## Editing the Calendar

The final steps in customizing the calendar for the brochure involve changing the month and highlighting the specific days of the ski trip. Perform the steps on the next page to edit the calendar.

*Steps* **To Edit the Calendar**

**1** **Click the calendar on page 2. If necessary, press F9 to zoom to 100% magnification. Point to the smart object Wizard button.**

*The calendar is selected (Figure 3-58).*

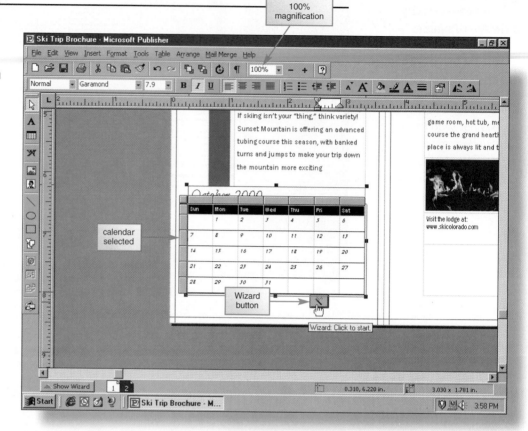

**FIGURE 3-58**

**2** **Click the smart object Wizard button and then click Dates in the Calendar Creation Wizard pane. Point to the Change Dates button.**

*The Calendar Creation Wizard displays two options, Design and Dates (Figure 3-59).*

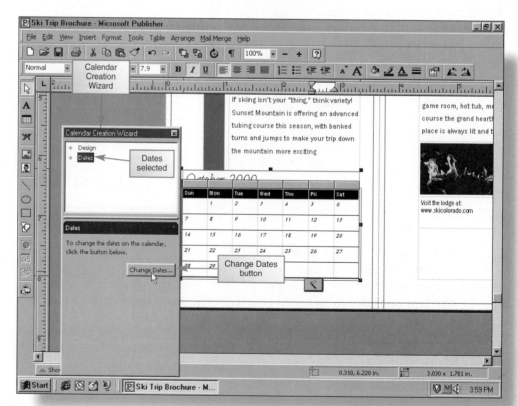

**FIGURE 3-59**

**3** Click the Change Dates button. When the Change Calendar Dates dialog box displays, click the Start date box arrow and then click March. Press the TAB key and then type 2001 in the Start date box (year). Point to the OK button.

*The Change Calendar Dates dialog box reflects the month and year of the ski trip (Figure 3-60).*

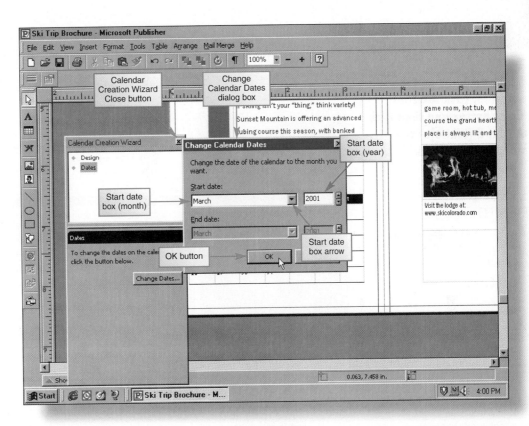

**FIGURE 3-60**

**4** Click the OK button and then click the Close button on the Calendar Creation Wizard pane title bar. Drag through the cells in the calendar table for Wednesday, March 7 through Saturday, March 10. Point to the Fill Color button on the Formatting toolbar.

*The ski trip dates are highlighted (Figure 3-61).*

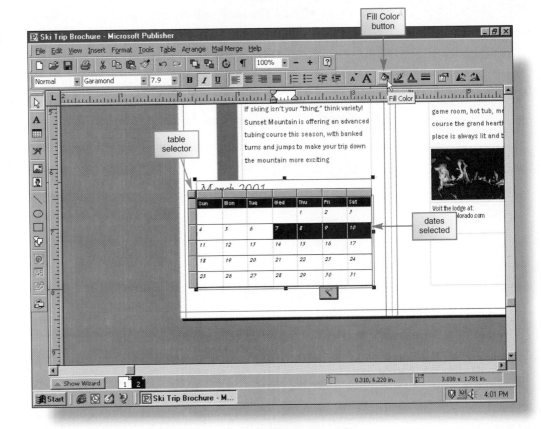

**FIGURE 3-61**

**5** **Click the Fill Color button. Click Accent 2 (RGB (102, 153, 204)). With the dates still selected, click the Font Color button and then click Accent 5 (White). Click outside the calendar.**

*The trip dates display with a fill color of light blue (Figure 3-62). Clicking away from the selected dates removes the highlight so the true fill color displays.*

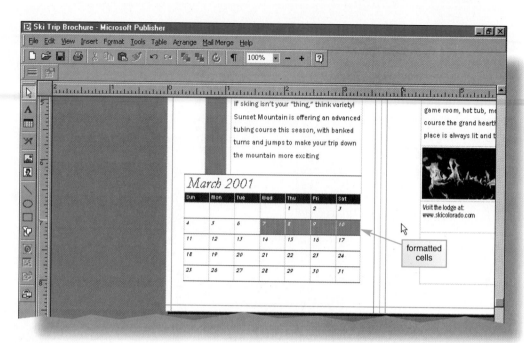

**FIGURE 3-62**

If you want to select an entire row or column for formatting, you can click the gray row or column selector button at the edge of the table. At the upper-left corner of the table is the **table selector** that highlights all the dates in the calendar when clicked. Additionally, you can add graphics, borders, or text to cells in a table.

The Calendar object is not the only type of table Publisher supports. You can import spreadsheet tables from programs such as Microsoft Excel, or use the **Table Frame Tool button** on the Objects toolbar to create custom tables.

## Checking Spelling and Saving Again

The publication now is complete. After completing the publication, you should check the spelling of the document by clicking the Check Spelling command on the Tools menu. Because you have performed several tasks since the last save, you should save the brochure again by clicking the Save button on the Standard toolbar.

# Outside Printing

When they need mass quantities of publications, businesses generally **outsource**, or submit their publications to an outside printer, for duplicating. You must make special considerations when preparing a document for outside printing.

## Previewing the Brochure Before Printing

The first step in getting your publication ready for outside printing may be to look at a printed copy from your desktop. Because Publisher presents the entire printed page, proportionally correct, on the workspace, its does not need a print preview command typically provided with most word processing applications. You can, however, perform a few steps to get the best representation of how your brochure will look.

### TO PREVIEW THE BROCHURE BEFORE PRINTING

**1** Enter 50% in the Zoom box on the Standard toolbar and then, if necessary, scroll to view the whole page.

**2** Click View on the menu bar and then click Hide Boundaries and Guides.

*Page 2 displays without the special characters and guides (Figure 3-63). You also may preview page 1 by clicking the page 1 icon on the status bar.*

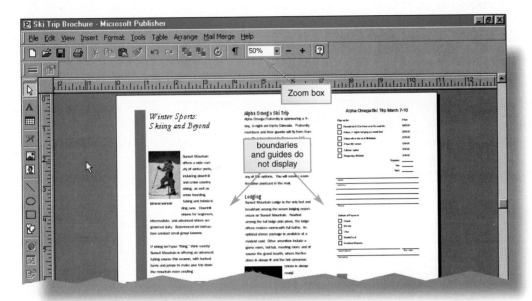

**FIGURE 3-63**

The next sequence of steps recommends publishing this brochure on a high grade of paper to obtain a professional look. A heavier stock paper helps the brochure to stand up better in display racks, although any paper will suffice. If you do use a special paper, be sure to click the Properties or Advanced Settings button in the Print dialog box for your printer, and then specify the paper you are using. For a detailed example of the duplex printing procedure summarized below, refer to pages PUB 2.57 and PUB 2.58 in Project 2. Following your printer's specifications, print one side of the paper, turn it over, then print the reverse side. The completed brochure prints as shown in Figure 3-1 on page PUB 3.5. You then can fold the brochure to display the title panel on the front.

Follow these steps to print a copy of the brochure.

### TO PRINT THE BROCHURE

**1** Ready the printer according to the printer instructions, and insert paper.

**2** With page 1 displaying in the workspace, click File on the menu bar and then click Print. Click Current page. If necessary, click the Properties button to choose a special paper. Click the OK button.

**3** When page 1 finishes printing, turn the page over and reinsert it top first (or as your printer requires) into the paper feed mechanism on your printer.

**4** Click the page 2 icon on the status bar. Click File on the menu bar and then click Print. When the Print dialog box displays, again click Current page and then click the OK button.

*The brochure prints as shown in Figure 3-1 on page PUB 3.5.*

### Laser Printers

For details on laser printers, visit the Discovering Computers 2000 Chapter 4 WEB INFO Web page (www.scsite.colm/dc2000/ch4/webinfo.htm) and click Laser Printer.

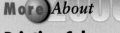

### Printing Color

Some printers do not have enough memory to print a wide variety of images and color. In these cases, the printer prints up to a certain point on a page and then chokes — resulting in only the top portion of the publication printing. Check with your instructor as to whether or not your printer has enough memory to work with colors.

## Printing Considerations

If you start a publication from scratch, it is best to **set up** your publication for the type of printing you want before you place objects on the page. Otherwise you may be forced to make design changes at the last minute. You also may set up an existing publication for a printing service, however. In order to provide you with experience in setting up your publication for outside printing, this project takes you through the preparation steps — even if you are submitting this publication to only your instructor.

Printing options, such as whether or not to use a copy shop or commercial printer, have advantages and limitations. You may have to make some tradeoffs before deciding on the best printing option. Table 3-6 shows some of the questions you can ask yourself about printing.

| Table 3-6 Picking a Printing Option | | | |
|---|---|---|---|
| CONSIDERATION | QUESTIONS TO ASK | DESKTOP OPTION | PROFESSIONAL OPTIONS |
| Color | Is the quality of photographs and color a high priority? | Low- to medium-quality | High quality |
| Convenience | Do I want the easy way? | Very convenient and familiar | Time needed to explore different methods, unfamiliarity |
| Cost | How much do I want to pay? | Printer supplies and personal time | High-resolution color/high quality is expensive. The more you print, the less expensive the per copy price. |
| Quality | How formal is the purpose of my publication? | Local event Narrow, personal audience | Business marketing Professional services |
| Quantity | How many copies do I need? | 1 to 10 copies | 10 to 500 copies: copy shop 500+ copies: commercial printer |
| Turnaround | How soon do I need it? | Immediate | Rush outside printing, probably an extra cost |

## Paper Considerations

Professional brochures are printed on a high grade of paper to enhance the graphics and provide a longer lasting document. Grades of paper are based on weight. Desktop printers commonly use **20 lb. bond paper**, which means they use a lightweight paper intended for writing and printing. A commercial printer might use 60 lb. glossy or linen paper. The finishing options and their costs are important considerations that may take additional time to explore. **Glossy paper** is a coated paper, produced using a heat process with clay and titanium. **Linen paper**, with its mild texture or grain, can support high-quality graphics without the shine and slick feel of glossy paper. Users sometimes pick a special stock of paper such as cover stock, card stock, or text stock. This textbook is printed on 45 lb., blade coated paper. **Blade coated paper** is coated and then skimmed and smoothed to create the pages you see here.

These paper and finishing options may sound burdensome, but they are becoming conveniently available to desktop publishers. Local office supply stores have shelf after shelf of special computer paper especially designed for laser and ink-jet printers. Some of the paper you can purchase has been prescored for special folding.

## Color Considerations

When printing colors, desktop printers commonly use a color scheme called **Composite RGB.** RGB stands for the three colors — red, green, and blue — that are used to print the combined colors of your publication. Professional printers, on the other hand, can print your publication using color scheme processes or **libraries.** These processes include black-and-white, spot-color, and process-color.

In **black-and-white printing**, the printer uses only one color of ink (usually black, but you can choose a different color if you want). You can add accent colors to your publication by using different shades of gray, or printing on colored paper. Your publication can have the same range of subtleties as a black-and-white photo.

A **spot color** is used to accent a black and white publication. Newspapers, for example, may print their masthead in a bright, eye-catching color on page 1 but print the rest of the publication in black and white. In Publisher, you may apply up to two spot colors with a color matching system called **Pantone. Spot-color printing** uses semitransparent, premixed inks typically chosen from standard color-matching guides, such as Pantone. Choosing colors from a **color-matching library** helps ensure high-quality results because printing professionals who license the libraries agree to maintain the specifications, control, and quality.

In a spot-color publication, each spot color is **separated** to its own plate and printed on an offset printing press. The use of spot colors has become more creative in the last few years. Printing services use spot colors of metallic or florescent inks, as well as screen tints to get color variations without increasing the number of color separations and cost. If your publication includes a logo with one or two colors, or if you want to use color to emphasize line art or text, then consider using spot-color printing.

**Process-color printing** means your publication can include color photographs and any color or combination of colors. One of the process-color libraries, called **CMYK**, or **four-color printing**, is named for the four semitransparent process inks — cyan, magenta, yellow, and black. CMYK process-color printing can reproduce a full range of colors on a printed page. The CMYK color model defines color as it is absorbed and reflected on a printed page rather than in its liquid state.

Process-color is the most expensive proposition; black-and-white is the cheapest. Using color increases the cost and time it takes to process the publication. When using either the spot-color or process-color method, the printer first must output the publication to film on an **image setter**, which recreates the publication on film or photographic paper. The film then is used to create color **printing plates.** Each printing plate transfers one of the colors in the publication onto paper in an offset process. Publisher can print a preview of these individual sheets showing how the colors will separate before you take your publication to the printer.

A new printing technology called **digital printing** uses toner instead of ink to reproduce a full range of colors. Digital printing does not require separate printing plates. Although not yet widely available, digital printing promises to become cheaper than offset printing without sacrificing any quality.

Publisher supports all three kinds of printing and provides the tools commercial printing services need to print the publication. You should ask your printing service which color-matching system it uses.

## Choosing a Commercial Printing Tool

After making the decisions about printing services, paper, and color, you must prepare the brochure for outside printing. The first task is to assign a color library from the commercial printing tools, as illustrated in the steps on the next page.

### Spot Color Printing

If you choose black plus one spot color, Publisher converts all colors except for black in your publication to tints of the spot color. If you choose black plus two spot colors, Publisher changes only those objects that exactly match the second spot color to 100 percent of the second spot color, and all other colors to tints of the first spot color. You can apply the second spot color manually, however, to objects in the publication.

### CMYK Process Colors

Publisher converts all colors in text, graphics, and other objects to CMYK values, and then creates four plates, regardless of the color model originally used to create the colors. Some RGB colors, including some of Publisher's standard colors, cannot be matched exactly to a CMYK color. After setting up for process-color printing, be sure to evaluate the publication for color changes. If a color does not match the color you want, you will have to include the new color library when you pack the publication.

### Printing Service Colors

Your printing service may use the initials SWOP, which stand for Standard for Web Offset Printing — a widely accepted set of color standards used in web offset printing. Web offset printing has nothing to do with the World Wide Web. It is merely the name for an offset printing designed to print thousands of pieces in a single run from a giant roll of paper.

**Steps** **To Choose a Commercial Printing Tool**

**1** Click Tools on the menu bar. Point to Commercial Printing Tools and then point to Color Printing on the Commercial Printing Tools submenu.

*The Commercial Printing Tools submenu displays (Figure 3-64).*

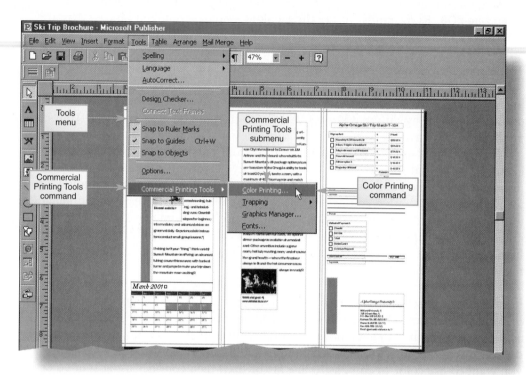

**FIGURE 3-64**

**2** Click Color Printing. When the Color Printing dialog box displays, point to Process colors (CMYK).

*The three color choices display in the Color Printing dialog box (Figure 3-65).*

**3** Click Process-colors (CMYK) and then click the OK button.

*Publisher converts all colors in text, graphics, and other objects to CMYK values and then internally creates four plates, regardless of the color model originally used to create the colors. Depending on your screen colors and resolution, you may or may not see a noticeable difference.*

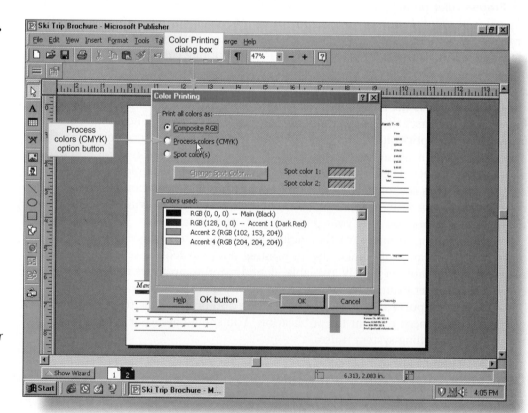

**FIGURE 3-65**

# Packaging the Publication for the Printing Service

The publication file can be packaged for the printing service in two ways. The first way is to give the printing service the Publisher file in Publisher format using the Pack and Go Wizard. The second way is to save the file in a format called Encapsulated PostScript. Both of these methods are discussed in the following sections.

## Using the Pack and Go Wizard

The **Pack and Go Wizard** guides you through the steps to collect and pack all the files the printing service needs and then compress the files to fit on one or more disks. Publisher checks for and embeds the TrueType fonts used in the publication. **Embedding** ensures that the printing service can display and print the publication with the correct fonts. The Pack and Go Wizard adds a program called **Unpack.exe** to the disk that the printing service can use to unpack the files. At the end of Publisher's packing sequence, you are given the option of printing a composite color printout or color separation printouts on your desktop printer.

You need either sufficient space on a floppy disk or another formatted disk readily available when using the Pack and Go Wizard. Graphic files and fonts require a great deal of disk space. The Pack and Go Wizard also creates on disk a **Readme file** intended for the printing service. In the following steps, if you use a disk other than the one on which you previously saved the brochure, save it again on the new disk before beginning the process.

Perform the following steps to use the Pack and Go Wizard to ready the publication for submission to a commercial printing service.

### More About

**The Pack and Go Readme File**

To look at a sample Pack and Go readme file, visit the Publisher 2000 More About Web page (www.scsite.com/pub2000/more.htm) and click Pack and Go.

*Steps* **To Use the Pack and Go Wizard**

① **With a floppy disk in drive A, click File on the menu bar. Point to Pack and Go and then point to Take to a Commercial Printing Service.**

*The File menu and Pack and Go submenu display (Figure 3-66). Publisher also uses a Pack and Go Wizard to transport publications to other computers for printing and viewing purposes only.*

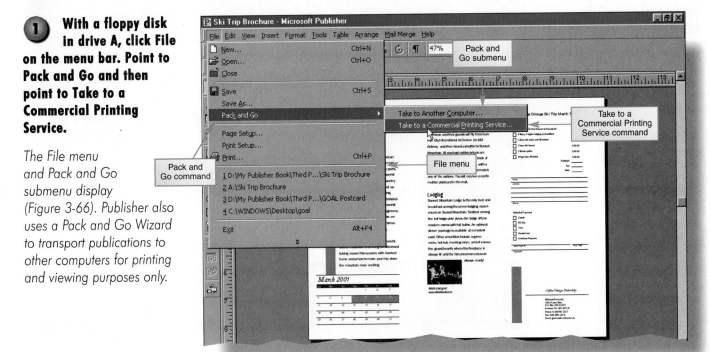

**FIGURE 3-66**

Microsoft **Publisher** 2000

**2** Click Take to a Commercial Printing Service. When the Pack and Go Wizard dialog box displays, point to the Next button.

*The Pack and Go Wizard dialog box displays (Figure 3-67). This wizard guides you through each step of the packing process. Read each individual screen as you progress through the steps.*

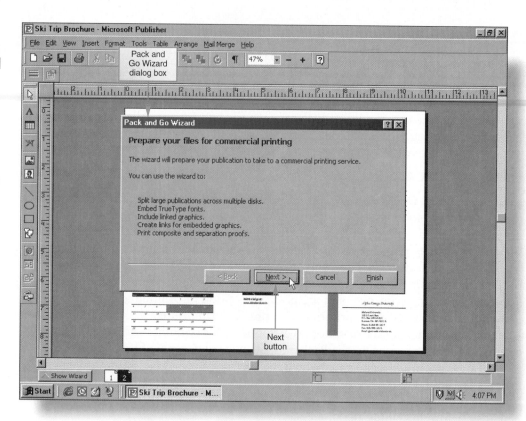

FIGURE 3-67

**3** Click the Next button for each of the wizard steps, accepting the preset options. When the last step, Pack My Publication, displays, point to the Finish button.

*The last dialog box of the Pack and Go Wizard displays (Figure 3-68).*

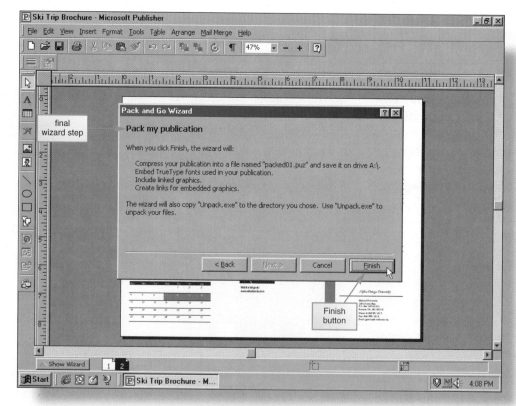

FIGURE 3-68

**4** **Click the Finish button. If you used graphics from an external source, Publisher will ask you to insert the disk. If you used system fonts that cannot be embedded, Publisher will display a dialog box in which you may click the OK button for the purposes of this project. When the confirming dialog box displays, point to Print a composite.**

*After Publisher finishes packing your publication, a confirming dialog box displays (Figure 3-69). Both print check boxes are selected.*

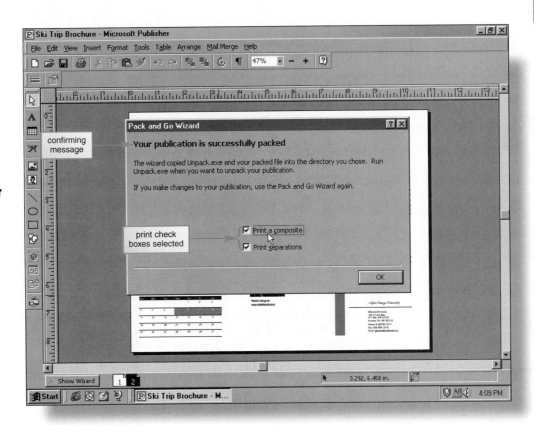

**FIGURE 3-69**

**5** **If necessary, click both print check boxes so neither one is selected. Point to the OK button.**

*The check boxes display without the check marks (Figure 3-70). You already have printed the brochure and unless you are actually submitting this publication to a printing service, a separation print is unnecessary. If you want to see what the separations look like, you may print them.*

**6** **Click the OK button.**

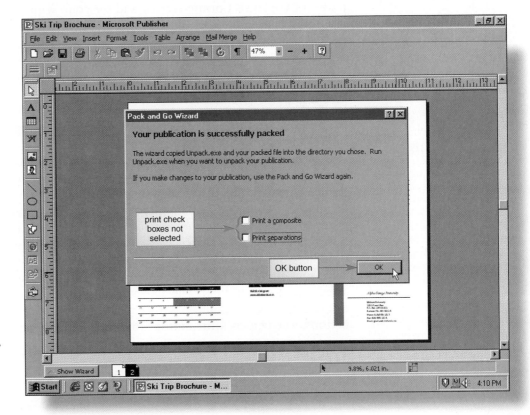

**FIGURE 3-70**

The files are saved on the disk in drive A. Publisher names and numbers the packed files and adds a **.puz extension**. For example, the first file will be named Packed01.puz, the second file will be Packed02.puz, and so on. If you make changes to the publication after packing the files, be sure to run the Pack and Go Wizard again so the changes are part of the packed publication.

## Using PostScript Files

If your printing service does not accept Publisher files, you can **hand off**, or submit, your files in PostScript format. **PostScript** is a page definition language that describes the document to be printed in language that the printer can understand. The PostScript printer driver includes a page definition language translator to interpret the instructions and print the document on a printer or a PostScript output device, such as an image setter. Because you cannot open or make changes directly to a PostScript file, everything in the publication must be complete before saving it.

Nearly all printing services can work with some type of PostScript files, either regular PostScript files, known as **PostScript dumps**, or **Encapsulated PostScript** (**EPS**) files, which are graphic pictures of each page. If you hand off a PostScript file, you are responsible for updating graphics, including the necessary fonts, and ensuring that you have all the files your printing service needs. Publisher includes several **PostScript printer drivers** and their description files (PPDs) to facilitate printing at the publisher. You must install a PPD before saving in PostScript form. Because the most common installation of Publisher is for a single user in a desktop environment, this project will not take you through the steps involved to install a PostScript printer driver. That process would necessitate using original operating system disks and a more thorough knowledge of PostScript printers. Ask your printing service representative for the correct printer driver, and see your Windows documentation for installing it. Then use the Save As command on the File menu to save the publication in PostScript format. Another question to ask your printing service is whether or not it performs the **prepress tasks** or a **preflight check**. You may be responsible for making color corrections, separations, setting the printing options, and other printing tasks.

# Working with Multiple Publications

One of the impressive features of modern operating systems is multitasking. **Multitasking** is the capability of the computer to perform more than one process or task at a time. Earlier operating systems had to close one program before opening another. The computer's **central processing unit** (**CPU**), could not store multiple jobs in memory. Advances in technology and consumer demand, however, have made multitasking an everyday occurrence.

The Windows taskbar is the best way to illustrate the concept of multitasking. The programs and applications currently running on your computer are displayed as buttons on the taskbar. The active window, or the one you currently are using, displays as a recessed button. Other running applications display as nonrecessed buttons. You can click the buttons to switch between applications.

**More** *About*

## Submitting PostScript Files

If you decide to hand off a PostScript dump to an outside printer or service bureau, include a copy of the original document as well — for backup purposes. Many shops are slowly changing over from Macintosh-based to cross-platform based operations. If something happens, the printer technician can correct the error from the original without another trip by you to the print shop.

**More** *About*

## Opening Multiple Publications

In many word processing programs, you can open more than one document within the same window of the application. For instance, in Microsoft Word, the New button on the Standard toolbar opens another document in the same window, and the Window menu displays the titles of all open documents. Publisher's workspace is too graphic-intensive to open two publications in the same window, so you must open a second session of Publisher to work with two different documents.

## Opening Multiple Sessions of Publisher

Multitasking also may include running multiple copies or **sessions** of the same program. Publisher's workspace can hold only one publication at a time; however, if you want to copy or move items between two publications, you do not have to place objects on the Clipboard, close the current publication, and then open the next one. You can run, or **thread**, two sessions of Publisher at the same time. **Threading** means the operating system uses the same set of instructions to run both copies of the software. Therefore, you can continue to enter commands in one session without waiting until the previous session has finished processing. Even if you merely want to view two publications — for purposes of checking the consistency between your letterhead and business cards, for example — running multiple sessions makes the task much easier.

The next sequence of steps illustrates how to open a second session of Publisher with the first session still running, and how to create a simple response postcard.

 **To Thread Multiple Sessions of Publisher**

**1** **With the brochure still displaying, click the Start button on the taskbar. Point to Programs on the Start menu and then click Microsoft Publisher on the Programs submenu. In the Catalog dialog box, point to the Blank Publications tab.**

*Publisher opens a second session (Figure 3-71). Notice the Publisher button for the brochure is still on the taskbar, but not recessed.*

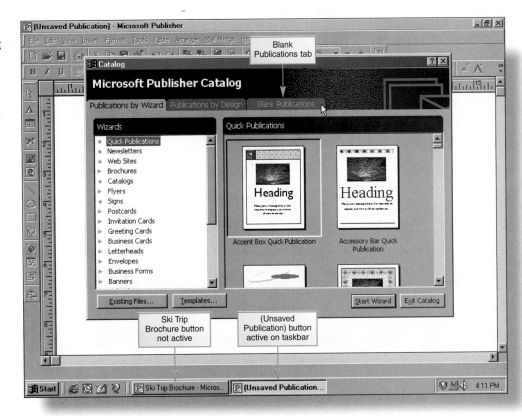

**FIGURE 3-71**

**② Click the Blank Publications tab and then click Postcard in the Blank Publications pane. Point to the Create button.**

*Postcard is selected (Figure 3-72). The Blank Publications tab displays previews of typical Publisher publications without any placed objects.*

**③ Click the Create button. When the postcard displays in the workspace, click the Hide Wizard button.**

*A blank postcard displays in the workspace. The new publication's file name displays as a button on the taskbar, along with the button containing the brochure's file name. Because the blank publication is in the active window, its button is recessed.*

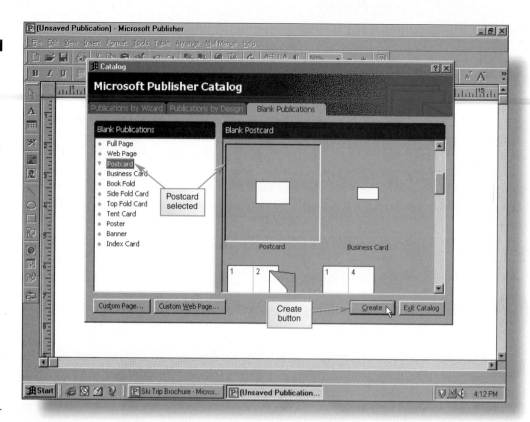

**FIGURE 3-72**

Occasionally, when you try to open an existing publication, you may get a message that the file is being used in another Publisher session. If this happens, one of two things may have taken place: either another user has opened the publication in a network or shared environment, or you may already have opened the file yourself. You cannot open the same file twice. If you really want two copies of the same publication, copy the file to another location, or save it with a different name.

## Copying Objects between Publications

The postcard should contain the same logo and return address as the brochure. With two sessions of Publisher open, it is easy to copy or move objects from one publication to another. Perform the following steps to copy the logo and address from the brochure to the postcard.

## TO COPY OBJECTS BETWEEN PUBLICATIONS

**1** Click the Ski Trip Brochure button on the taskbar. If necessary, click the page 1 icon on the status bar and then zoom to display the whole page.

**2** Click the return address in the center panel and then SHIFT-click the Organization Name Text Frame. SHIFT-click the small logo.

**3** Click the Group Objects button and then click the Copy button on the Standard toolbar. Click the Unsaved Publication button on the taskbar and then click the Paste button on the Standard toolbar.

**4** Click the Rotate Left button and drag the object onto the postcard so it is completely visible. SHIFT-drag the lower-right sizing handle until the grouped object fills approximately one-fourth of the postcard.

*The return address and logo display on the postcard (Figure 3-73). You may save the postcard with the name, Ski Trip Postcard on your floppy disk and then print if desired.*

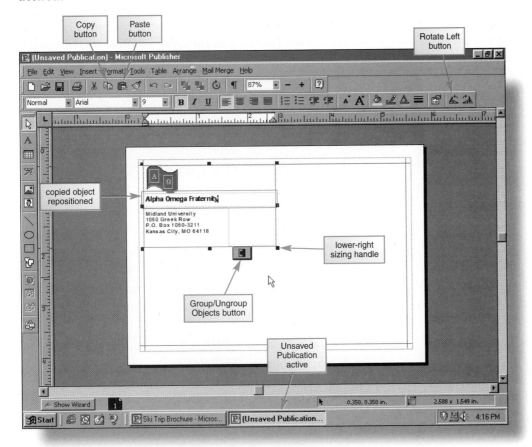

**FIGURE 3-73**

If you want to view both publications at the same time, the taskbar shortcut menu gives you options to **tile** windows vertically or horizontally. When publications display in one half of the screen, they are more difficult to read and edit, but checking design elements or moving and copying objects between publications may be easier. For more information about sizing and moving windows, see the Windows documentation.

C A S E   P E R S P E C T I V E   S U M M A R Y

Alpha Omega is thrilled with the result of the brochure and is ready to take your files to the printing service. The logo, on both the front and back panels, with its grouped shape and symbols enhances the brochure. The photographs from the lodge add to the brochure's appeal. On the inside, the sign-up form can be filled in and detached easily. You and the fraternity made good choices about the printing service, the paper, and color. The printer agrees with your choice of white text on the blue background. It should be a great ski trip!

# Project Summary

Project 3 introduced you to the brochure medium. You learned about the use of photographs versus images, and how to insert a photograph from a file. After entering new text and deleting unwanted objects, you created a logo from scratch using a custom shape and symbols grouped in the workspace. With the Size and Position command, you learned how to place a calendar on the brochure, along with a sign-up form. You also learned about design and printing considerations such as overlapping, separations, color libraries, paper types, and costs. In anticipation of taking the brochure to a professional publisher, you previewed and printed your publication and then used the Pack and Go Wizard to create the necessary files. Finally, you threaded multiple sessions of Publisher to copy objects from the brochure to the postcard.

# What You Should Know

Having completed this project, you now should be able to perform the following tasks:

▶ Choose a Commercial Printing Tool *(PUB 3.50)*
▶ Copy Objects between Publications *(PUB 3.57)*
▶ Create a Brochure Using a Wizard *(PUB 3.8)*
▶ Create a Mirrored Copy of the Heading *(PUB 3.33)*
▶ Create a Shape for the Logo *(PUB 3.20)*
▶ Create a Symbol Text Frame for the Logo *(PUB 3.23)*
▶ Create a Symbol Text Frame Using Copy and Paste *(PUB 3.27)*
▶ Delete Text Frames *(PUB 3.14)*
▶ Edit Text in the Brochure *(PUB 3.10)*
▶ Edit the Calendar *(PUB 3.44)*
▶ Edit the Font Color *(PUB 3.36)*

▶ Edit the Sign-Up Form *(PUB 3.37)*
▶ Finish Replacing the Photographs *(PUB 3.18)*
▶ Group and Position the Logo Objects *(PUB 3.30)*
▶ Insert a Photograph from a File *(PUB 3.15)*
▶ Insert and Position a Calendar *(PUB 3.39)*
▶ Insert Clip Art Using a Keyword Search *(PUB 3.17)*
▶ Prevent Objects from Overlapping *(PUB 3.42)*
▶ Preview the Brochure Before Printing *(PUB 3.47)*
▶ Print the Brochure *(PUB 3.47)*
▶ Save a Brochure *(PUB 3.19)*
▶ Start Publisher *(PUB 3.7)*
▶ Thread Multiple Sessions of Publisher *(PUB 3.55)*
▶ Use the Pack and Go Wizard *(PUB 3.51)*

# *Apply Your Knowledge*

➕ **Project Reinforcement at www.scsite.com/off2000/reinforce.htm**

## *1* Editing a Publication

**Instructions:** Start Publisher. Open the publication named, apply-3, from the Data Disk. See the inside back cover of this book for instructions for downloading the Data Disk or see your instructor for information on accessing the files required for this book. The edited publication is shown in Figure 3-74.

**2001 Summer Concert Series**

*This year's Summer Concert Series promises to be the best yet. The Performing Arts Center has brought in some of the more gifted and talented conductors from across the United States. Whether you want to hear the latest Broadway medley or Strauss's "Also Sprach Zarathustra" used in 2001-A Space Odyssey, the 2001 Summer Concert Series will entertain and delight you.*

2001 Summer Concert Series
1728 Nottingham Drive
Bennington, VT 05421

**The Performing Arts Center**

Music Among the Maples

**Fredrick Montgomery**
Director of the Vermont Symph
Orchestra for the last five year

**Natalie Pleasanton**
The first woman conductor of t
Vermont Pops Orchestra

**The Bennington Five**
The newest member of the ser

**(a) Page 1 of Tri-Fold Brochure**

**(b) Page 2 of Tri-Fold Brochure**

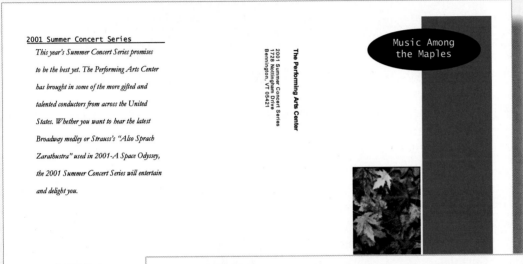

The Concerts

**The Classical Series:** Performed by the Vermont Symphonic Orchestra, the Classical Series has been the mainstay of the summer repertoire since the series' inception in 1984. This 80-piece orchestra, made up of professional and semiprofessional musicians, has performed all over the northeast. This year's theme is music of late nineteenth and twentieth century composers.

**The Broadway Series:** The Pops Orchestra is back by popular demand playing show tunes by famous duos. Performances of music by Rogers & Hammerstein and Lerner & Lowe highlight this family-oriented series.

**The Jazz Series:** The Bennington Five brings its unique interpretation of jazz greats Duke Ellington and Count Basie to the Summer Concert Series. Don't miss this newest addition.

*For more information, visit our Web site at www.arts.bennington.vt.org*

Friday and Saturday evening concerts begin at 8:00 p.m. Sunday matinees at 3:00 p.m.

**June 2001**

| Sun | Mon | Tue | Wed | Thu | Fri | Sat |
|-----|-----|-----|-----|-----|-----|-----|
|  |  |  |  |  | 1 | 2 |
| 3 | 4 | 5 | 6 | 7 | 8 | 9 |
| 10 | 11 | 12 | 13 | 14 | 15 | 16 |
| 17 | 18 | 19 | 20 | 21 | 22 | 23 |
| 24 | 25 | 26 | 27 | 28 | 29 | 30 |

**July 2001**

| Sun | Mon | Tue | Wed | Thu | Fri | Sat |
|-----|-----|-----|-----|-----|-----|-----|
| 1 | 2 | 3 | 4 | 5 | 6 | 7 |
| 8 | 9 | 10 | 11 | 12 | 13 | 14 |
| 15 | 16 | 17 | 18 | 19 | 20 | 21 |
| 22 | 23 | 24 | 25 | 26 | 27 | 28 |
| 29 | 30 | 31 |  |  |  |  |

**August 2001**

| Sun | Mon | Tue | Wed | Thu | Fri | Sat |
|-----|-----|-----|-----|-----|-----|-----|
|  |  |  | 1 | 2 | 3 | 4 |
| 5 | 6 | 7 | 8 | 9 | 10 | 11 |
| 12 | 13 | 14 | 15 | 16 | 17 | 18 |
| 19 | 20 | 21 | 22 | 23 | 24 | 25 |
| 26 | 27 | 28 | 29 | 30 | 31 |  |

**Order Summer Concert Series Tickets**

Enter the number of tickets you wish to purchase in the boxes.
All orders are filled using best seating available.

**Classical Series**
☐ June 8
☐ July 22
☐ August 18

**Broadway Series**
☐ June 17
☐ July 21
☐ August 10

**Jazz Series**
☐ June 16
☐ July 13
☐ August 19

**Season Tickets**
☐ Friday Series
☐ Saturday Series
☐ Sunday Matinee Series

Name
Address

Telephone

**Method of Payment**
☐ Check
☐ Bill Me
☐ Visa
☐ MasterCard
☐ American Express

Credit Card #                    Exp. date
Signature

**The Performing Arts Center**
Ticket Hotline: 802-555-8484

2001 Summer Concert Series
1728 Nottingham Drive
Bennington, VT 0542

**FIGURE 3-74**

*(continued)*

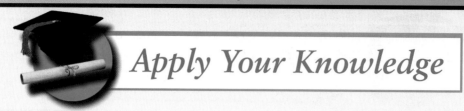

## *Apply Your Knowledge*

### Editing a Publication *(continued)*

**Instructions:** Perform the following tasks.

1. With page 1 displayed, Click the Show Wizard button and then click Customer Address in the Brochure Wizard pane. Choose to display placeholder text for the customer address. Hide the Wizard.

2. On page 1, make the following text changes, using the zoom features as necessary:
   a. Click the text, Seminar or Event Title. Type Music Among the Maples to replace the text.
   b. Drag through the text, Business Name. Type The Performing Arts Center to replace the text.
   c. Click the return address. Press F9 to magnify it. Press CTRL+A to select all the text. Type 2001 Summer Concert Series and then press the ENTER key. Type 1728 Nottingham Drive and then press the ENTER key. Type Bennington, VT 05421 to finish the address.
   d. Scroll down to display the mailing address. Delete the mailing address text frame by right-clicking the frame and then clicking Delete Object on the shortcut menu.

3. In the left panel, double-click each of the three graphics, one at a time. Use the keywords, violin, conductor, and entertainment, respectively, to search for pictures similar to Figure 3-74.

4. Click the page 2 icon on the status bar. Delete the text frame in the center panel by clicking Delete Object on the shortcut menu. Delete the picture and its caption.

5. SHIFT-drag the blue rectangle from the center panel to the left panel, left of the text.

6. Click the Design Gallery Object button on the Objects toolbar. Click Calendars on the Objects by Category tab. Insert a Borders style calendar.

7. On the Format menu, click Size and Position. Enter the following measurements: Width: 3.4 inches; Height: 2 inches; Horizontal: 3.8 inches; and Vertical: .5 inches.

8. Click the calendar's smart object Wizard button and then click Dates in the Wizard pane. Click the Change Dates button. Use June 2001 as the month and year. Close the Calendar Creation Wizard.

9. Click the Copy button on the Standard toolbar. Click the Paste button on the Standard toolbar twice, then drag the copies down, one at a time, to fill the center panel. Repeat Step 8 for each of the two new calendars to adjust the dates as shown in Figure 3-74.

10. Make the following changes to the dates listed in Figure 3-74 for each concert series:
    a. Click the calendar cell for the first date listed in the Classical series. Click the Fill Color button and then click Accent 1 (Blue) in the Scheme colors. Repeat for the other two Classical series dates.
    b. Click the calendar cells for the dates listed in the Broadway series, one at a time. Use the Fill Color button to change each of the three dates to Accent 3 (Orange).
    c. Click the calendar cells for the dates listed in the Jazz series, one at a time. Use the Fill Color button to change each of the three dates to Accent 4 (RGB (204, 204, 204)).
    d. For each blue text frame in the calendar, click the cell and change the font color to white.

11. Run Check Spelling and Design Checker. Correct errors if necessary.

12. Click File on the menu bar and then click Save As. Use the file name, Concert Series Brochure.

13. Click Tools on the menu bar, click Commercial Printing Tools, and then click Color Printing. When the Color Printing dialog box displays, click Process colors (CMYK) and then click the OK button.

14. With a floppy disk in drive A, click File on the menu bar. Click Pack and Go and then click Take to a Commercial Printing Service on the Pack and Go submenu. Click the Next button at each step.

15. When the wizard completes the packing process, if necessary click the Print a composite check box to select it. The brochure will print on two pages.

# In the Lab

## *1* Creating a Brochure Layout with One Spot Color

**Instructions:** Start Publisher and perform the following tasks to create the one spot color brochure shown in Figures 3-75a and 3-75b.

1. In the Catalog, click the Accent Box Informational Brochure. Click the Start Wizard button. As the wizard panes display, click the Next button. When the Customer Address Wizard pane displays, click Yes. When the Form Wizard Pane displays, click Response form.

2. Edit the text frames as shown in Figure 3-75a.

3. Double-click the graphic on the front panel. Insert a clip using the keyword, oil.

4. Click the Custom Shapes button on the Objects toolbar. Click the arrow shape that points upward. In the workspace, SHIFT-drag an arrow approximately two inches square. Use the Fill Color button to choose Accent 1 (Medium Blue). Click the Rotate Right button on the Formatting toolbar.

5. Drag a text frame in the workspace approximately .35 inch square. Use the Fill Color button to choose Accent 1 (Medium Blue). Use the Font Color button to choose Accent 5 (White). Type G in the text frame. On the Format menu, point to AutoFit Text and then click Best Fit.

6. Copy the text frame three times. Drag each copy away from the original. Replace the text in each copy with the letters O, A, and L, respectively.

7. Drag the text frames on top of the large arrow so they display diagonally across the arrow as shown in Figure 3-75a. Click the G text frame and then SHIFT-click each of the other letters. SHIFT-click the large arrow itself, away from the letters. Group the objects to create a composite logo. Drag the logo to the empty space above the picture.

8. Click the Response form (page 2). Make the text changes as indicated in Figure 3-75b.

9. Click Tools on the menu bar and then point to Commercial Printing Tools. Click Color Printing. When the Color Printing dialog box displays, click Spot Color(s).

10. Save the publication using the file name, GOAL Brochure. Print a copy.

**FIGURE 3-75a**

### Would you like to work for GOAL?

Check the appropriate boxes and then mail this form to the address below.

Describe your area of interest.

- ☐ Production
- ☐ Research
- ☐ Information Technology

Describe yourself.

- ☐ Self-starter
- ☐ Team-player
- ☐ Problem-solver

Describe your education.

- ☐ Technical school
- ☐ 4-year college/university
- ☐ Graduate school

Would you be willing to relocate?

- ☐ United States
- ☐ Locations abroad
- ☐ Undecided

Comments:

**FIGURE 3-75b**

# *In the Lab*

## 2 Creating a CD Liner

**Instructions:** Perform the following tasks to create the two-panel, two-sided CD liner as shown in Figures 3-76a and 3-76b.

1. Start Publisher. If the Catalog does not display, click File on the menu bar and then click New.
2. Under the Labels wizards, select Compact Disc. Select Compact Disc Case Liner and then start the wizard.
3. When asked for a color scheme, click Glacier and then click the Finish button.
4. In the left panel, click the outermost rectangle and resize it to fill the entire panel.
5. Edit the text in both panels as shown in Figure 3-76a.
6. Select the large rectangle border in the right panel. Press CTRL+T to make the rectangle transparent, in preparation for the watermark.
7. Edit the picture in the right panel using the Clip Gallery. Search using the keyword, guitar.
8. Copy the graphic using the Copy button on the Standard toolbar.
9. Insert a new blank page to follow page 1. Using the View menu, go to the background.
10. Paste the picture from page 1 on the background. Drag it to the left panel and SHIFT-drag a corner sizing handle, resizing so it fills the entire panel.
11. Click the Clip Gallery Tool button on the Objects toolbar. Drag a large square to fill the right panel of the background. After you release the mouse button, the Clip Gallery will display. Search for an appropriate line drawing graphic for the watermark effect using the keyword, music.
12. On the Format menu, choose to recolor the picture. In the Color list, choose Accent 3.
13. Go to the foreground of page 2.
14. Create a large text frame in the left panel. Make it transparent so the picture shows through. Choose a font color of white. Type the text as shown in Figure 3-76b.
15. Using the Design Gallery Object button, insert a Voyage style table of contents. Use the Size and Position dialog box to place it exactly as follows: Width: 3.4; Height: 4.5, Horizontal: 5.4; and Vertical .1 in the right panel. Make it transparent. Edit the table of contents as shown in Figure 3-76b.

**FIGURE 3-76a**

*In the Lab*

16. Save the publication on a floppy disk using the file name, Guitar CD Liner.

17. Print a copy of the CD liner, one page at a time. Use duplex printing. The default settings print the liner in the middle of an 8½-by-11-inch piece of paper, with crop marks. Trim the printout.

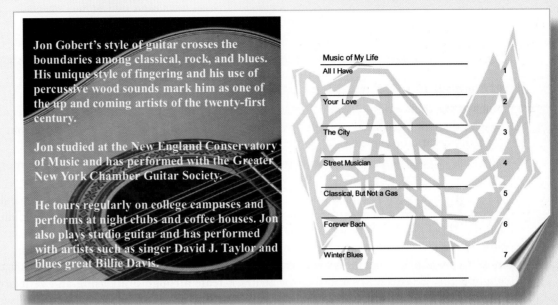

Jon Gobert's style of guitar crosses the boundaries among classical, rock, and blues. His unique style of fingering and his use of percussive wood sounds mark him as one of the up and coming artists of the twenty-first century.

Jon studied at the New England Conservatory of Music and has performed with the Greater New York Chamber Guitar Society.

He tours regularly on college campuses and performs at night clubs and coffee houses. Jon also plays studio guitar and has performed with artists such as singer David J. Taylor and blues great Billie Davis.

Music of My Life

All I Have ........... 1

Your Love ........... 2

The City ........... 3

Street Musician ........... 4

Classical, But Not a Gas ........... 5

Forever Bach ........... 6

Winter Blues ........... 7

**FIGURE 3-76b**

# 3 Creating a Postcard

**Instructions:** Start Publisher and perform the following tasks. *Note:* If you did not complete In the Lab 1, replace Steps 2 through 4 below with Steps 4 through 7 from the In the Lab 1 exercise.

1. In the Catalog, choose a postcard from Blank Publications.

2. Insert the floppy disk you used for the In the Lab 1 exercise. Start another session of Publisher, and open the GOAL Brochure.

3. When the GOAL Brochure displays, copy the composite logo on the front panel. Close the Publisher window without saving.

4. If necessary, click the Unsaved Publications button on the taskbar to display the postcard once again. Paste the logo from the Clipboard.

5. Size the selected logo as follows: Width: .63; Height: .53; Horizontal: .35; Vertical .35 and then create text frames — one for the return address and one for the message. Type the text from Figure 3-77 in the text frames.

6. Save the publication on a floppy disk with the file name, GOAL Postcard. Print a copy.

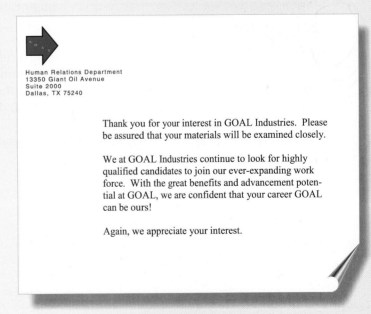

Human Relations Department
13350 Giant Oil Avenue
Suite 2000
Dallas, TX 75240

Thank you for your interest in GOAL Industries. Please be assured that your materials will be examined closely.

We at GOAL Industries continue to look for highly qualified candidates to join our ever-expanding work force. With the great benefits and advancement potential at GOAL, we are confident that your career GOAL can be ours!

Again, we appreciate your interest.

**FIGURE 3-77**

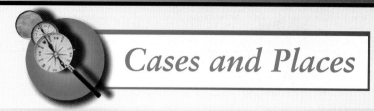

# Cases and Places

The difficulty of these case studies varies:
▶ are the least difficult; ▶▶ are more difficult; and ▶▶▶ are the most difficult.

**1** ▶ Use the Calendar Wizard to make a lunch calendar for your school's cafeteria or student union lunchroom. Pick a design and color scheme using a full-page calendar for the current month. Use a small font to display the special of the day below the date. Include your school's name and address. Print using landscape orientation.

**2** ▶ You have recently joined Success America, Incorporated as the new in-house desktop publisher. You are to design a tri-fold event brochure for their October 2001 training event in Indianapolis. The theme will be "Every American Can Win." Featured speakers will include former U.S. Senator Charles Goolsby, television news anchor Holly Schulke, and prominent businessman Dennis Louks. Your employer wants to mail the brochures to potential attendees. The company logo is a blue triangle with a white Sigma $\Sigma$ (Greek S) symbol in the center. Create a rough draft using an Event brochure that includes a sign-up form with a placeholder for the customer address. The technical writer will send you content for the stories at a later date.

**3** ▶▶ Using the Blank Publications tab of the Publisher Catalog, recreate your school or company logo, as closely as possible, on a full-page publication. Use the Custom Shapes button, fill and font colors, text frames and symbols to match the elements in your logo. You may also use WordArt. Ask your instructor or employer for clip art files, if necessary. Use the scratch area to design portions of the logo and then layer and group them before dragging them onto the publication.

**4** ▶▶ Bob Bert of Bert's Beanery has hired you to "spice up" and modernize the look of the restaurant's menu. You decide to use a menu wizard to create a full color menu for publication at a local copy shop. Bob wants special attention paid to his famous "Atomic Chili®," which is free if a diner can eat three spoonfuls without reaching for water. You will find the registered trademark symbol in the Insert Symbol dialog box. Bob serves salads, soups, and sandwiches a la carte. He has several family specials, as well as combo meals.

**5** ▶▶▶ Visit or call several local copy shops or commercial printers in your area. Ask them the following questions: What kind of paper stock do your customers choose for brochures? What is the most commonly used finish? Do you support all three color processes? Will you accept files saved with Microsoft Publisher Pack and Go, or EPS files? What prepress tasks do you perform? Use a blank publication in Publisher to create a table with the Table Frame tool on the Objects Toolbar. Insert the questions down the left side. Insert the names of the print shops across the top. Fill in the grid with the answers they provide.

Microsoft **Publisher 2000**

Microsoft Publisher 2000

# Creating Web Sites with Publisher 2000

Recall that in Project 3, you created a tri-fold brochure for the Alpha Omega Fraternity Ski Trip. Recently, you have been surfing the Internet and have discovered that many Web sites include brochures with sign-up forms that permit electronic registration. The fraternity now has asked you to publish its brochure on the Web, with some multimedia enhancements, as well as an interactive sign-up form. To accomplish this, you must create a Web site from the publication and insert sound, video, and appropriate submission hyperlinks on the site.

To complete this Web Feature, you will need the brochure created in Project 3 so that you can create the necessary HTML files and then edit the resulting Web pages. (If you did not create the project example, see your instructor for a copy.)

# Introduction

Publisher provides several techniques for creating Web pages and Web sites. You may save any Publisher publication as an HTML file so that it can be **posted**, or uploaded, to the Web and viewed by a Web browser, such as Internet Explorer. You also can start a new Web page by using a Publisher wizard. A **Web site** is group of pages linked together with an interface called a **front page** or **home page.** The front page contains hyperlinks to other pages in the site.

If you have an existing Publisher publication, you can convert it quickly to a Web page using Publisher's conversion option. If you do not have an existing Publisher publication to convert, you may create a new Web page by using the **Web Page Wizard**, which provides customized templates you can modify easily. In addition to these Web tools, Publisher has many other Web page authoring features. For example, you can insert hyperlinks, sound, video, pictures, and HTML code fragments into your publications.

Once complete, you may **publish** or make your Web page or Web site available to others on your network, intranet, or the World Wide Web. Publisher will post your page(s) for you if you are connected to a **host**, which is a computer that stores Web pages. Your host may be an **intranet**, which is a local network that uses Internet technologies, or it may be an **Internet service provider (ISP)**, that provides space for Web pages. Either way, you will need to know the exact address of the location, your user name, and your password to actually post the pages. You can complete this project and view it with a browser, however, even without an online connection.

If you decide to publish your Web site and have an online connection to your ISP or intranet, you may choose from three posting methods. First, if your ISP supports the concept of Web folders, you may save the publication directly to a Web folder.

Second, Publisher can save the Web files in an FTP location on your host computer. **FTP (file transfer protocol)** is a program that sends copies of files, sounds, and graphics to the ISP. If supported by your ISP, FTP locations may be listed with other storage locations on your computer. Both Web folders and FTP are explained in detail in Appendix B. The third way to publish to the Web is to post the saved files yourself, using Microsoft's Web Publishing Wizard or the FTP program of your choice.

Using Publisher's Convert to Web Site feature, the Ski Trip Brochure created in Project 3 will be converted to an interactive Web site for online viewing and registration. The following pages illustrate the steps to save your Web site in a folder on a floppy disk ready for posting. Then, check with your instructor for the best way to post your files to the Web. No matter which of the three posting methods you use to publish — or even if you do not plan to publish at all — you may preview your site using any standard Web browser.

**FIGURE 1a**

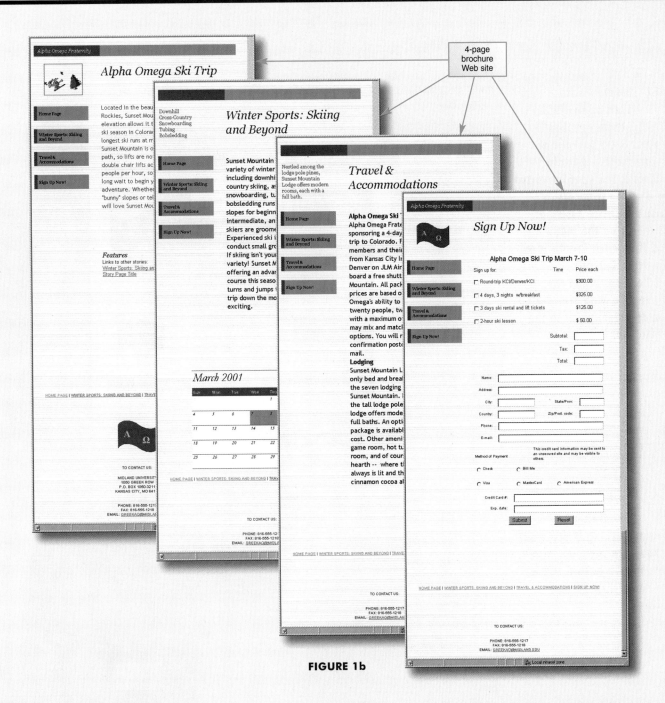

FIGURE 1b

# Brochure to Web Site Conversion

A tri-fold brochure, such as the one created in Project 3, has two pages and a total of six panels (Figure 1a). When converted to a Web site, the left fold-in panel from page 1 becomes the first page of the Web site (Figure 1b). The three panels from page 2 of the brochure become pages 2, 3, and 4 of the Web site. The color schemes and design style carry over, and the extra graphic and text frames are stored for optional insertion. The Web site pages are preset to 6-inches wide and 14-inches tall to display easily on most monitors.

Publisher provides the options of designing the layout yourself or using the Web Site Wizard. This Web Feature illustrates using the Web Site Wizard and then editing and customizing the layout. Perform the steps on the next page to convert the tri-fold brochure to a Web site.

### More About 2000

## Web Site Design

Publisher's Web site conversion process uses proven design strategies to create a well-designed Web site that is easy to navigate and view. For more information on designing Web sites, visit the Web Design Web page (www.scsite.com/web/SCWebDes.htm) and click Web Page Design.

**Steps** ## To Convert a Brochure to a Web Site

**1** **Start Publisher and then open the Ski Trip Brochure created in Project 3. (If you did not create the brochure in Project 3, see your instructor for a copy.) If necessary, close the Office Assistant. Click File on the menu bar and then click Create Web Site from Current Publication. When the Convert To Web Site dialog box displays, point to the OK button.**

*The Convert To Web Site dialog box displays (Figure 2). Publisher offers two ways to create the Web site. The option for using the Web Site Wizard is selected.*

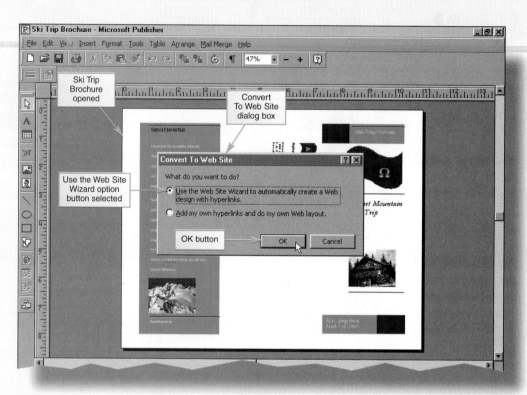

**FIGURE 2**

**2** **Click the OK button. If a dialog box displays asking if you want to save the brochure again, click the No button. Click the Show/Hide Wizard button.**

*Page 1 of the 4-page Web site displays (Figure 3).*

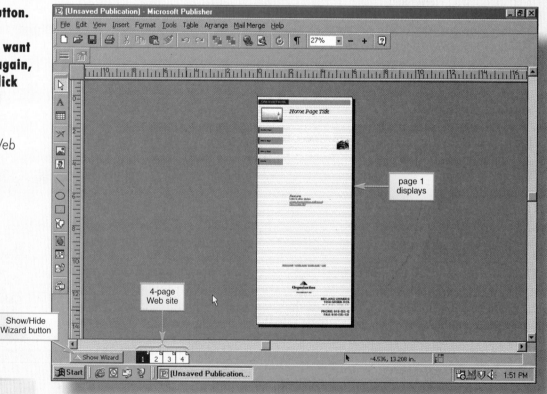

**FIGURE 3**

**Other Ways**

1. In Brochure Wizard pane, click Convert to Web

For a full Web page to display, the magnification is very small. Recall that you can use the F9 key to toggle to 100% magnification to facilitate reading and editing.

# Web Properties

Web sites and pages have several unique characteristics when published to the Web. Some of these special characteristics involve naming conventions; others are related to Internet search engines. Additionally, many Web pages include audio background. Publisher's Web Properties dialog box allows you to set all these special features.

## Editing Web Properties

One of the most marketable features of Web sites relates to Internet search engines. **Search engines** are programs that locate sites based on keywords entered by users. Registering your site with national search engines helps users locate your site quickly. Once located, search engines sometimes display a short description of the Web site for users to read before they click the hyperlink to jump to the site itself.

The first page of your Web site is commonly named **index.html**. This enables your ISP to display this page first when users click the link to your site. The index page usually displays a more descriptive, internally coded title on the Web title bar, however.

Publisher stores the keywords, description, and title in internal, HTML code called **tags**. Search engines use tags in the search process.

Finally, Publisher can provide sounds or music for your Web page. Publisher saves the linked sound file with the pages and graphics of your Web site and automatically generates the internal HTML code and tags necessary to play the sound. You may choose to have the sound or music play once or **loop** continually.

Perform the following steps to edit the Web properties of the first Web page.

**More About**

### Search Engine Keywords

For more information about using keywords to attract search engines, and therefore visitors to your Web site, visit the HTML More About Web page (www.scsite.com/html/more.htm) and click HTML tags.

---

 **Steps** **To Edit Web Properties on Page 1**

---

**1** **Click File on the menu bar and then click Web Properties. When the Web Properties dialog box displays. If necessary, click the Site tab. Type** ski, Alpha Omega, Sunset Mountain **in the Keywords text box. Press the TAB key. In the Description text box, type** Alpha Omega Fraternity is sponsoring a ski trip to Sunset Mountain, March 7-10, 2001. **Point to the Page tab.**

*The text displays in the Keywords and Description text boxes (Figure 4).*

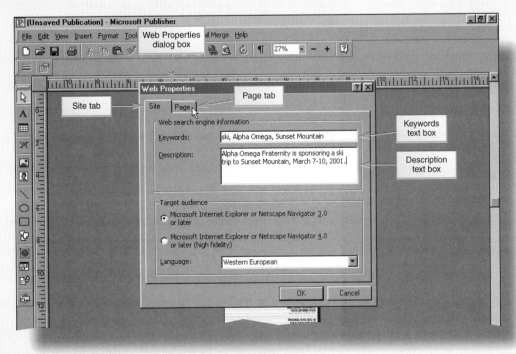

**FIGURE 4**

**2** **Click the Page tab. Press the TAB key twice to move to the Title text box. Type** Alpha Omega Ski Trip **to replace the text. Point to the Browse button.**

*The new text for the Web page title displays (Figure 5).*

**3** **Click the Browse button. When the Background Sound dialog box displays, double-click the file name, wnter_01 in the list of files. When the Web Properties dialog box again displays, click the OK button.**

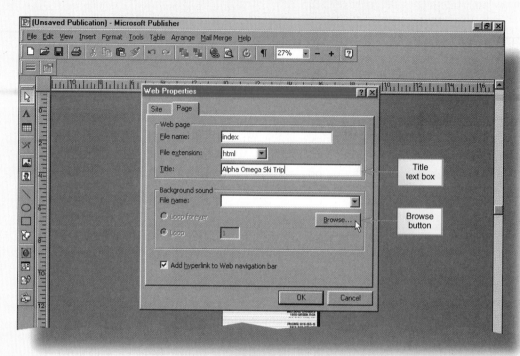

**FIGURE 5**

*If the file wnter_01 is not available, select an appropriate clip from your list. Depending on your installation of Publisher, the music clips may be located on the Publisher CD-ROM. See your instructor for the location of additional music clips.*

*Other* Ways

1. Web Site Wizard pane, click Background Sound, click Select Sound
2. Insert HTML code fragment

*More* About

**Navigating**

The major reason visitors leave Web sites is because they cannot find what they are looking for. Publisher's navigation bar provides a highly visible and easy way to navigate through the Web site, but other navigation tools can be imported or created from scratch. For more information on navigation, visit the HTML More About Web page (www.scsite.com/html/more.htm) and click Menu Bars.

The address of your Web site itself is dependent on your ISP, but in general, the address is made up of the Web protocol prefix, the service provider domain name, and then your site name or path. It is common practice to use the site name as the Web folder name or FTP location name that holds all the files related to your Web site. For instance, if your Web site is called MySite, the address would include the usual prefixes (http://www.), then the name of your ISP, and then a slash followed by the word, MySite. Page 1 of your Web site would display automatically as a kind of index page to browse the rest of your site. Because of this, Publisher assigns page 1 of your Web site the file name of index.html.

# Editing Web Objects

The next step is to edit the specific objects in the Web site. Not only must you customize the graphics and placeholder text supplied by the wizard, but some format changes also are necessary. You may decide to reinsert some of the objects from the original brochure. The hyperlinks and command buttons also need to be edited.

## Editing Web Site Text Frames

Several text frames in the Web site need to be edited to customize the Web site and make it easier to read and navigate. Publisher's Web Site Wizard added a design element during conversion called a Web navigation bar. The **navigation bar** (Figure 6) provides automatic links to the other pages in the Web site. Editing the text of the navigation bar on page 1 also edits the titles on the other pages of the Web site. Other text frames to edit include the text frame on page 1 that contains the white text of the original brochure. You will change the font color to black. The large text frames on each page need to fill the space of the longer Web page. You will use the AutoFit Text feature to make those adjustments. Finally you will edit some place-holder text frames in the Web site.

Perform the following steps to edit the text frames.

### TO EDIT THE TEXT FRAMES IN THE WEB SITE

**1** Click the first navigation bar on the left side of page 1. Press the F9 key.

**2** Click the text on the second navigation bar. Type `Winter Sports:` `Skiing and Beyond` to replace the text. Repeat the process to edit the third and fourth navigation bars as shown in Figure 6.

**3** Click the area to the right of the navigation bar. Press CTRL+A to select all the text. Click the Font Color button on the Formatting toolbar, and then click Main (Black) in the Scheme colors. To turn on the AutoFit Text feature, click Format on the menu bar, point to AutoFit Text, and then click Best Fit.

**4** Click page 2 on the status bar and then scroll to display the text above the navigation bar. Click the placeholder text above the navigation bar. Type the following list pressing the ENTER key after each item: `Downhill`, `Cross-Country`, `Snowboarding`, `Tubing`, `Bobsledding`. See Figure 1b.

**5** Click the story on page 2 and then press CTRL+A to select all the text. AutoFit the text as described in Step 3.

**6** Click page 3 on the status bar and then click the text in the upper-left corner. To replace the existing text, type `Nestled among the lodge pole pines,` `Sunset Mountain Lodge offers modern rooms, each with a full bath.`

**7** Click the story on page 3 and then press CTRL+A to select all the text. AutoFit the text as described in Step 3.

**8** Click page 1 on the status bar.

*Page 1 displays (Figure 6). Titles for pages 2, 3, and 4 display in the navigation bars. Each story text frame is enlarged to fit the available space.*

### More About 2000

### Web Page Formatting

Formatting not supported by HTML will display as plain text or graphics in your Web site. For example, you cannot emboss, shadow, or engrave characters; and you cannot change line spacing, margins, or set tabs. WordArt objects become graphics. You can, however, display bold, italic, and underline, and adjust font sizes of characters.

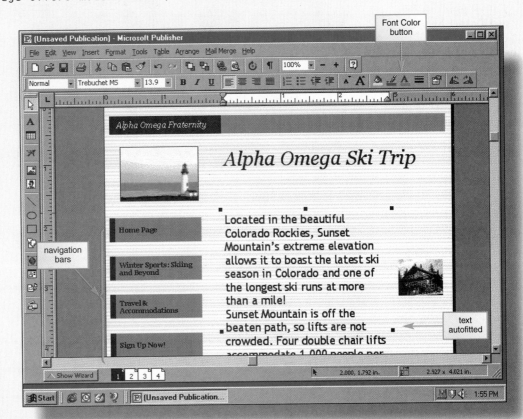

**FIGURE 6**

### Inserting Extra Content

When Publisher converted the tri-fold brochure to a Web site, not all of the graphics and text frames were used. Some were unnecessary, like the mailing address. Others did not fit the Web design template. You always have the option of reinserting these objects. During the conversion process, Publisher creates an additional tab in the Design Gallery called the **Extra Content tab** to store unused objects from the original publication.

The following steps replace the generic organization logo with the Alpha Omega logo from the brochure.

*Steps* **To Insert Extra Content**

**1** **Scroll to the lower portion of page 1. Right-click the organization logo and then click Delete Object on the shortcut menu. Click the Design Gallery Object button on the Objects toolbar. When the Design Gallery dialog box displays, click the Extra Content tab. If necessary, scroll to display the Alpha Omega logo. Click the logo and then point to the Insert Object button.**

*The Alpha Omega logo is selected on the Extra Content tab (Figure 7). The Content from Your Publication pane contains previews of each object.*

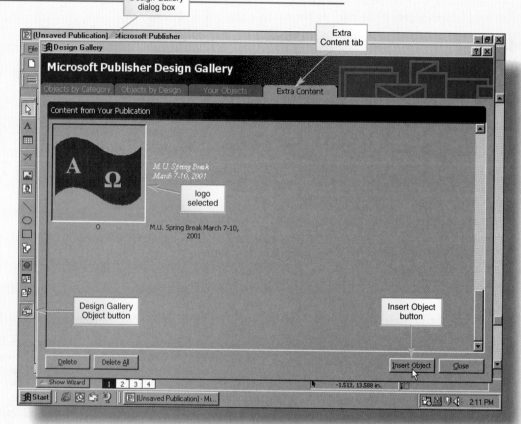

**FIGURE 7**

**2** **Click the Insert Object button.** Resize the logo and drag it to fit the space left by the deleted organization logo. If Publisher warns you the logo overlaps or is too close to other objects, make it smaller or move it as necessary. With the logo still selected, click the Copy button on the Standard toolbar.

*The Alpha Omega logo displays on page 1 (Figure 8).*

**3** **Click page 4 on the status bar and then** scroll to the top of the page. Delete the organization logo in the upper-left corner of the page as described in Step 1. Click the Paste button on the Standard toolbar then resize and drag the Alpha Omega logo to replace the organization logo.

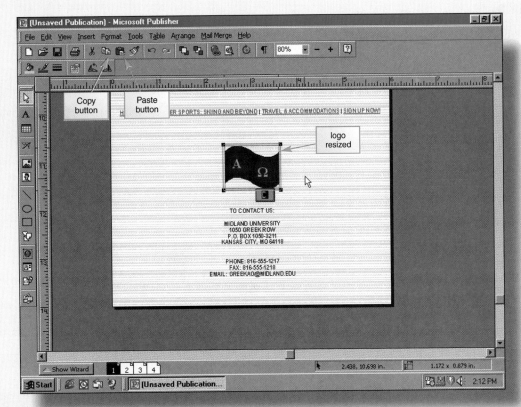

**FIGURE 8**

## Animation

Editing animation objects is similar to editing other graphics and clip art. When Publisher converted the brochure to a Web site, it added an animated graphic to page 1. In the Clip Gallery, these animated graphics are called **Motion Clips.** Available to both Web and print publications, animation not only draws attention to a page, but also serves as a source of entertainment. Most animated clip files are .gif files as opposed to movies or streaming video. You may recall from Project 3 that **.gif files** are graphic interchange format files that are published easily to the Web. The Clip Gallery contains many animated .gif files from which you may choose. You cannot preview an animated .gif file directly in your publication, but you can preview it using a browser. Or, if the .gif file came from the Clip Gallery, you can play it there.

Follow the steps on the next page to edit the animated graphic on page 1 of the Web site.

### Other Ways

1. On Insert menu click Design Gallery Object

### Animation

Animated graphics can be created using many different application programs, as well as programming tools such as JavaScript. For more information on animated graphics for the Web, visit the Publisher 2000 More About Web page (www.scsite.com/pub2000/more.htm) and click Animation.

## To Edit the Animation

**1** **Click page 1 on the status bar to display the first page of the publication. Double-click the graphic of the lighthouse in the upper-left corner. When the Insert Clip Art window displays, if necessary, click the Motion Clips tab. Click the Search for clips text box. Type** ski **and then press the ENTER key. When the previews display, right-click the picture of the downhill skier and then point to Insert on the shortcut menu.**

*The selected graphic displays in a blue frame (Figure 9). If the graphic shown in Figure 9 is not available, pick a suitable one from your clips or ask your instructor for the location of the Microsoft Shared Clip Art folder and then use the Import Clips button. The name of this specific file is ag00420_.gif.*

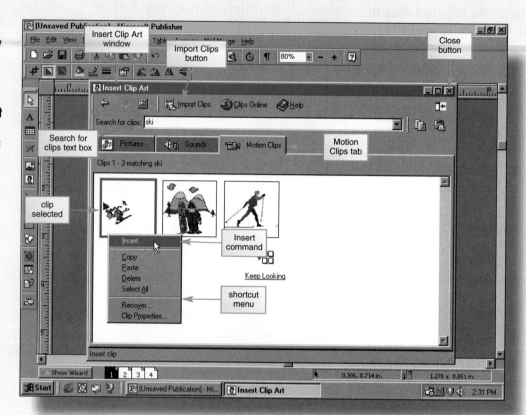

**FIGURE 9**

**2** **Click Insert on the shortcut menu, then close the Insert Clip Art window by clicking the Close button.**

1. On Insert menu point to Picture, click Clip Art
2. Right-click graphic, point to Change Picture, point to Picture, click Clip Art

With Publisher, you may insert sound and video objects created by other programs. These files, which use file extensions such as .mid, .wav, or .avi, become embedded in your publication. Viewing or playing them requires that the user double-click them.

### Using Hyperlinks and Command Buttons

The final group of Web objects to edit includes hyperlinks and command buttons. A **hyperlink** is a portion of text or a graphic that, when clicked, allows a user to jump easily and quickly to other objects or Web pages. Text hyperlinks usually are identified by a distinctive color or underline. Graphic hyperlinks, or **hot spots,** are identified by a change in the mouse pointer when it moves over the spot. After a text hyperlink has been clicked, or **followed,** by the reader, its color changes.

The Alpha Omega Ski Trip Web site contains hyperlinks to each page in the site and a link to the fraternity's e-mail. The navigation bar assigns the links to each page in the site automatically; however, the e-mail links must be created. Publisher's Standard toolbar contains an **Insert Hyperlink button** to help you create hyperlinks. The Objects toolbar contains a **Hot Spot button**. The **Hyperlink dialog box** (Figure 10) assigns the destination of the hyperlink. Many Web sites display links to more information, sponsors, or favorite sites. The four choices include: A Web site or file on the Internet, Another page in your Web site, An Internet e-mail address, and A file on your hard disk.

The Alpha Omega Ski Trip Web site contains two command buttons in the electronic sign-up form. A **command button** is a button that, when clicked, performs a task such as submitting information from an electronic form, or clearing information previously entered by the user. As with inserting hyperlinks, the **Command Button Properties dialog box** contains options for submitting and retrieving data using Web pages and e-mail addresses (Figure 12 on the next page).

Perform the following steps to edit the hyperlinks and command buttons on the Web pages.

## More About

### Dead Links

A dead link is a hyperlink or hot spot that does not lead to an active Web page when clicked. Visitors become annoyed and leave Web sites when dead links are encountered. Many tools exist to check your Web site for viable links and hot spots. For a partial listing of available tools on the Web, visit the HTML More About Web page (www.scsite.com/html/more.htm) and click Web Page Testing.

---

 **To Edit the Hyperlinks and Command Buttons**

**1** Scroll to the bottom of page 1. Drag through the text, **GREEKAO@MIDLAND.EDU** and then click the Insert Hyperlink button on the Standard toolbar. When the Hyperlink dialog box displays, point to the An Internet e-mail address option button.

*The Hyperlink dialog box displays (Figure 10). The An Internet e-mail address option makes a hyperlink connection to e-mail.*

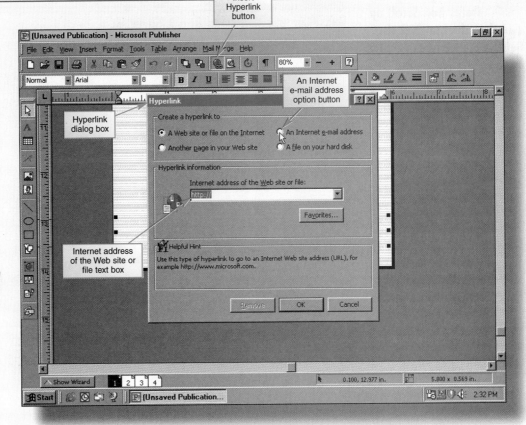

**FIGURE 10**

**2** Click An Internet e-mail address and then click the Internet address of the Web site or file text box. Type GREEKAO@MIDLAND.EDU to replace the text. Click the OK button.

*The text on the Web page changes to a hyperlink (Figure 11). The e-mail addresses on pages 2, 3, and 4 also change.*

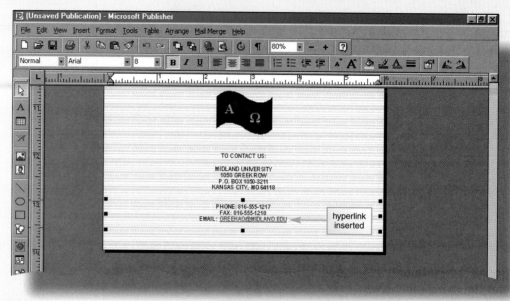

**FIGURE 11**

**3** Click page 4 on the status bar. Scroll up and then double-click the Submit button in the center of the page. When the Command Button Properties dialog box displays, point to Send data to me in e-mail.

*The Command Button Properties dialog box displays (Figure 12).*

**4** Click Send data to me in e-mail. Click the Send data to this e-mail address box arrow and then click GREEKAO@MIDLAND.EDU in the list. Click the OK button.

*The Send data to me in e-mail option maintains a list of recently used addresses.*

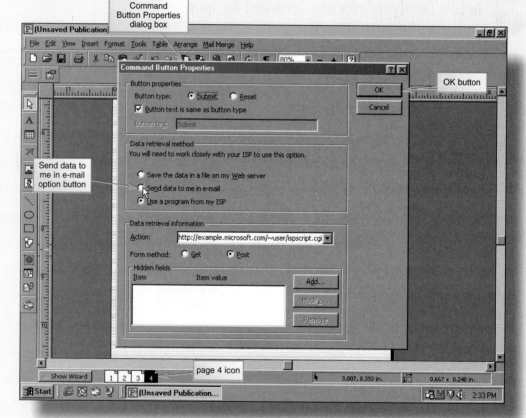

**FIGURE 12**

1. Right-click text, click Hyperlink on shortcut menu
2. On Insert menu click Hyperlink
3. Press CTRL+K

Some ISP servers cannot send user data using a Publisher-supplied script, but most can accept user input and send it in an e-mail message. When the Web site user clicks the **Submit button**, form responses are sent to the e-mail address you supply. The **Reset button** automatically clears all input boxes on the form.

# Viewing a Web Site

You may want to view the Web site in your default Web browser to see how it looks. When the brochure was converted to a Web site, Publisher added a Web Page Preview button (Figure 13). When working with Web files, the buttons on the tool-bars change to provide additional Web authoring features.

Perform the following steps to view the Web site in your default browser.

## Steps  To View a Web Site in a Browser

### 1  Click the Web Page Preview button on the Standard toolbar.

*Publisher opens your Web browser in a separate window and displays the first page of your Web site (Figure 13). The animation and sound play. You may click the links to check navigation.*

### 2  Close the Web browser window by clicking the Close button.

*The browser window closes and the Publisher window redisplays.*

**FIGURE 13**

If you are satisfied with the way your Web site looks and navigates, proceed to the next sequence of steps, which save on a floppy disk all the files related to your site.

**Other Ways**

1. On File menu click Web Page Preview
2. Press CTRL+SHIFT+B

# Saving a Web Site

You may recall from Project 1 that Publisher suggests saving Web pages and Web sites in separate folders. The folder for the brochure Web site will contain the linked pages, graphics, sounds, and motion clips. You also need to save the publication as a Publisher file for future editing. Perform the steps on the next page to save the Web site files.

**To Save the Web Site Files**

**1** If necessary, insert a floppy disk in drive A. Click File on the menu bar and then click Save as Web Page. Select 3½ Floppy (A:) in the Look in list. Point to the Create New Folder button.

*The Save as Web Page dialog box displays (Figure 14). The pages, graphics, animation, and sounds will save on the floppy disk in drive A.*

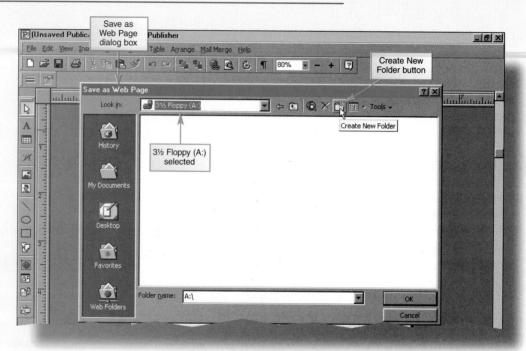

**FIGURE 14**

**2** Click the Create New Folder button. When the New Folder dialog box displays, type Web Brochure Files in the Name text box. Point to the OK button.

*The new folder name displays in the Name text box (Figure 15).*

**3** Click the OK button in the New Folder dialog box, and then click the OK button in the Save as Web Page dialog box.

*The saved files are ready to post to the Web.*

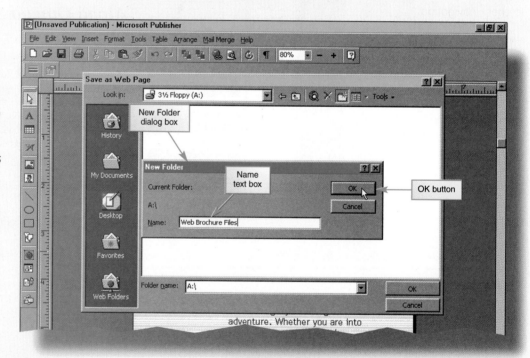

**FIGURE 15**

Talk to your instructor about making this Web site available to others on your network, intranet, or the World Wide Web (see Appendix B). When you publish the site, do not forget to send all the files in your folder so the links, animation, and sound work correctly.

## Saving the Publication

You should save the publication for future editing. The Web folder contains HTML files, which are not directly accessible in Publisher. It is also a good idea to give the Web version of the brochure a different file name than the print version. Follow these steps to save the publication and then quit Publisher.

### TO SAVE THE PUBLICATION AND QUIT PUBLISHER

**(1)** With a floppy disk still in drive A, click File on the menu bar and then click Save As.

**(2)** When the Save As dialog box displays, select 3½ Floppy (A:) in the Look in list.

**(3)** In the File name text box, type Ski Trip Web Brochure to save the Web publication with a new name and then click the OK button.

**(4)** Click the Close button on the Publisher title bar.

---

## CASE PERSPECTIVE SUMMARY

Alpha Omega Fraternity is pleased with your work on its ski trip Web site. The site is easy to navigate, and the animation and sound create a multimedia enticement to hit the slopes. The fraternity verifies the electronic submission policy of its ISP and then posts your pages to the host computer. The brochure looks great on the Web, and the fraternity is eagerly awaiting electronic registrations.

---

## Web Feature Summary

This Web Feature introduced you to creating a Web site by saving an existing Publisher publication as a Web site or HTML files. You also edited the Web site properties, text frames, sounds, animation, hyperlinks, and command buttons in anticipation of publishing the brochure to the Web. Finally, you saved all the related files in a folder for later posting.

## What You Should Know

Having completed this project, you now should be able to perform the following tasks:

▶ Convert a Brochure to a Web Site *(PUBW 1.4)*
▶ Edit the Animation *(PUBW 1.10)*
▶ Edit the Hyperlinks and Command Buttons *(PUBW 1.11)*
▶ Edit the Text Frames in the Web Site *(PUBW 1.7)*
▶ Edit Web Properties on Page 1 *(PUBW 1.5)*
▶ Insert Extra Content *(PUBW 1.8)*

▶ Save the Publication and Quit Publisher *(PUBW 1.15)*
▶ Save the Web Site Files *(PUBW 1.14)*
▶ View a Web Site in a Browser *(PUBW 1.13)*

*In the Lab*

## 1 Publisher Tutorials

**Instructions:** Start Publisher. Open any existing publication or begin a new blank publication. Click Help on the menu bar and then click Publisher Tutorials. When the Microsoft Publisher - Tutorial window displays, click the graphic as directed on the screen, to display the topics. Click the topic entitled, Creating a Web site. Use the page buttons at the bottom of the tutorial window to read each screen. Right-click any page and then click Print on the shortcut menu. When the Print dialog box displays, click All in the Print range area. Click As laid out on screen and then click the OK button. Close the tutorial and Help windows. Quit Publisher without saving.

## 2 Creating a Web Site from a Price List Brochure

**Problem:** Small businesses are starting to maintain advertising Web sites complete with product descriptions, links to manufacturers, prices lists, and even maps to their location. Using the Blocks Price List Brochure Wizard, create a Web site template to show a local company what might be involved in maintaining a Web site.

**Instructions:** Perform the following tasks.

1. Start the Blocks Price List Brochure Wizard. Accept all preset values.
2. Print a copy of both pages of the brochure.
3. Click File on the menu bar and then click Create Web Site from Publication. Click the option to use a Web Site Wizard to automatically create a Web design with hyperlinks. You do not need to save the publication at this point.
4. In the Web Site Wizard pane, click Background Sound, and then click Select Sound. Browse to select an appropriate music clip to add to the Web site.
5. On page 1 double-click the upper-left graphic and then pick an animated graphic on the Motion Clips tab.
6. In the center of page 1, a text frame provides links to other stories. Type the address of your school's Web site and then insert a hyperlink.
7. Preview the Web site. Check all links.
8. Click File on the menu bar and then click Print. Print each page of the site. Compare the printouts of the brochure versus the Web site. Note Extra Content items and story placement. Look for blank areas that could display a map.

## 3 Creating a Web Page with Hyperlinks

**Problem:** You have decided to create your own personal Web site using a Web Site Wizard.

**Instructions:** Perform the following tasks.

1. Start Publisher. In the Catalog, click the Web Sites on the Publication by Wizard tab. Use the design style you like best.
2. Personalize the Web site by editing the text frames and graphics. Read the wizard's suggestions for content. Consider creating a link to your resume on the school's Web site. The Send data to me in e-mail option maintains a list of recently used addresses.
3. Insert a new page to the Web site using the Insert menu. Rename the link on the navigation bar created by Publisher.
4. Edit the Web properties to add your name and interests as keywords for search engines.
5. Add a background sound to page 1.
6. Save your publication for posting to the Web. Preview your site using a browser.
7. Ask your instructor for directions on posting your Web page so others may have access to it.

Microsoft Publisher 2000

## PROJECT 4

# Personalizing and Customizing a Publication with Information Sets

You will have mastered the material in this project when you can:

- Start Publisher with a blank publication
- Edit publication margins
- Use layout and ruler guides effectively
- Define personal information sets and components
- Edit a personal information set
- Understand letterhead production techniques
- Create a letterhead using background effects
- Explain the difference among tints, shades, patterns, and gradients
- Insert personal information components
- Insert and edit a logo
- Explain character spacing techniques
- Format text using the Measurements toolbar
- Describe the various graphic formatting options
- Understand and apply styles to a publication
- Create a business card
- Create a coupon
- Create an envelope
- Explain the merge process
- Create an address list
- Create a label
- Understand the use of field codes
- Merge an address list with a main document

# Branding for Success
## A Perfect Blend of Text, Graphics, Tints, and Styles

Many of life's most rewarding pleasures come from blending constituent parts, resulting in a mixture that is better than the individual components. Look at the results of combining fresh ingredients to yield a scrumptious recipe. Consider how people of numerous ethnic groups have blended to constitute the population of the United States. Cement, sand, gravel, and water form concrete. Integrating elements can increase strength. Steel results from a combination of iron, carbon, and molybdenum. In a suite of applications such as Office 2000, users can achieve great results with less effort because the programs look and work alike. The complete capabilities of Publisher allow business or home users to create text frames as in word processing software; draw tables, perform mathematical and statistical operations, and embed charts as in spreadsheet software; and build databases for use with mass mailings, billings, and customer accounts as in database software. Merging these features and transferring objects between publications provides an efficient business tool.

Large corporations and small businesses alike realize that their most important assets are their customers, brands, logos, and slogans. The brand is a distinguishing name and/or symbol. The symbol a business chooses differentiates it from all other businesses and structures its presence in the marketplace. By developing strong and consistent images, these brands can

efficient
business tool

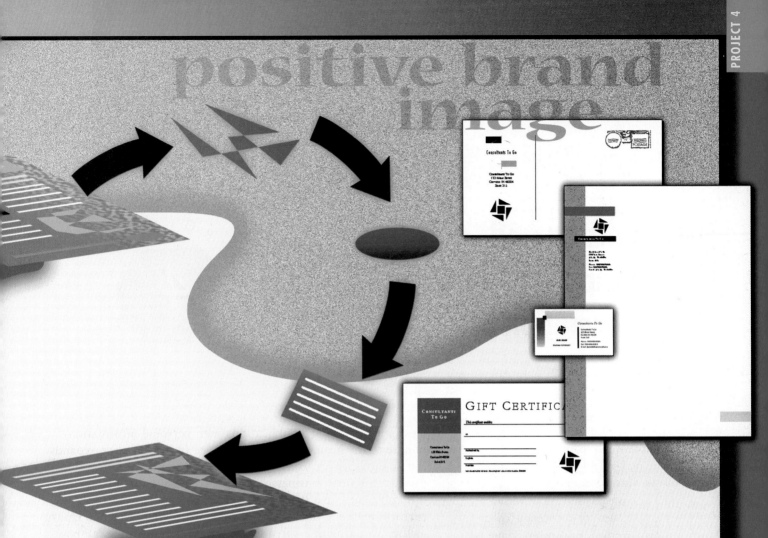

help generate continued revenue and success. Creating a positive brand image is an important component of every business; it lays a foundation for future company growth and represents all its internal and external characteristics. A slogan can cause those who hear it and read it to keep a company or product in mind when making buying choices.

As entrepreneurs are well aware, they must assume the responsibility and the risk for a business operation with the expectation of making a profit. The entrepreneur generally decides on the product, acquires the facilities, and brings together the labor force, capital, and production materials. If the business succeeds, the entrepreneur reaps the reward of profits; if it fails, he or she takes the loss. When beginning your own business, services are available locally and online that can help you get started, but having the required tools helps you expand the possibilities without great expense.

Publisher is that tool. To illustrate some of the business features of Publisher, you will produce a brand design for a small copy service company in this project by creating letterhead, business cards, envelopes, labels, and a coupon using the personal information set. Choosing from the Design Gallery, you will insert a logo for this company. When starting a business, your logo identifies and represents your company; it gets you noticed, and helps clients remember you.

Handing out a business card is like shaking hands. The business card is your first opportunity to present yourself and represent your company. It should reflect the style of your company as well as providing the necessary information required to reach you. Your letterhead typically is used for official business communications; it conveys company information, and quickly establishes a formal and legitimate mode of correspondence. Letterhead, envelopes, and business cards should coordinate, thus providing a unifying identity. Be original, dare to be different, and find the style that sets you apart as a unique and innovative business. Brand for success.

Microsoft Publisher 2000

# Personalizing and Customizing a Publication with Information Sets

PROJECT 4

CASE PERSPECTIVE

CopyCat Creations just opened its doors! A small business specializing in printing and duplicating, CopyCat Creations is located near campus in a strip mall with several professional offices. The company expects to acquire a lot of business from the university where the need for duplicating, collating, and binding is extensive. Some business will come from local merchants that will want CopyCat Creations to print their letterhead, business cards, and mailing labels, and to provide copying services for them.

Because you have desktop publishing experience, you are hired to design the letterhead, business cards, and envelopes for CopyCat Creations and then create a database of the initial customers. The office manager, Tony Manderino, also wants a two-for-one coupon for the grand opening.

You decide to create a personal information set, complete with color scheme and logo for CopyCat Creations. You enter the data and create the publications using items from the Design and Clip Art Galleries, as well as the Microsoft Publisher Catalog.

## Introduction

Customizing desktop publications with personal information unique to the business, organization, or individual user expands the possibilities for using Publisher as a complete application product for small businesses. People create large text frames and use Publisher like a word processor. Others create a table and perform mathematical and statistical operations or embed charts as they would with a spreadsheet. Still others create a database, using Publisher for mass mailings, billings, and customer accounts. Publisher's capability of merging these features and transfering objects between publications makes it an efficient tool in small business offices — without the cost and learning curve of some of the high-end dedicated application software.

## Project Four — Creating Letterhead, Business Cards, and Envelopes

To illustrate some of the business features of Microsoft Publisher, this project presents a series of steps to create a letterhead, business card, envelope, and coupon using a personal information set for a company as shown in Figure 4-1. Additionally, it demonstrates the creation and use of a simple database, the sort a small business would use to keep track of its customers.

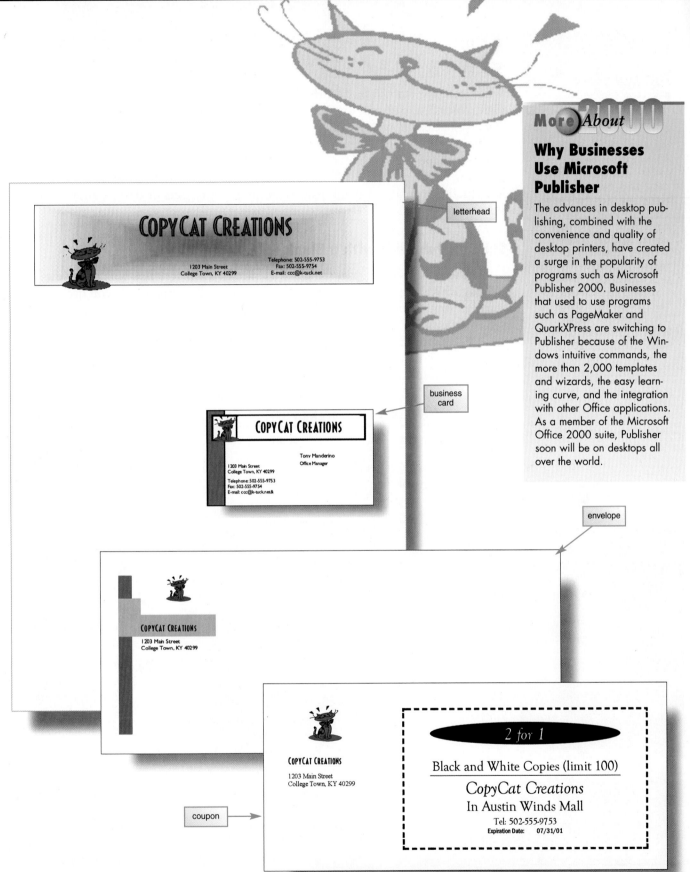

letterhead

business card

envelope

coupon

**FIGURE 4-1**

## More About

### Full and Short Menus

The figures in this book normally display the full menu. If a menu on your screen looks different, it may be because you are looking at the short menu. Click the arrows at the bottom of a short menu to display its full version. Your menu may differ in order of commands, because Office has promoted commands you use frequently. To restore the menu to its original state, on the Tools menu click Options, and then click the Reset Usage Data button. See Appendix C for more information on the menus in Publisher 2000.

# Setting Up a Blank Publication Page

When you first start Publisher, the Catalog displays. With its many wizards and templates, most users choose an item from the Catalog and then begin editing. It is not always the case, however, that a wizard will fit every situation. Sometimes you want to think through a publication while manipulating objects on a blank page, trying different shapes, colors, pictures, and effects. Other times you may have specific goals for a publication that do not match any of the wizards. In these cases, Publisher makes available a blank page with no preset objects or design, allowing you to start from scratch.

## Starting Publisher with a Blank Publication

In the Publisher Catalog, the **Blank Publications tab** contains blank previews for full pages, Web pages, cards, posters, and banners. Additionally, if you decide to start Publisher each time with a blank page, you can use the Options command on the Tools menu (Figure C-2 on page PUB C.1).

The preset page options for a full page include an 8½-by-11-inch publication with one-inch margins. Perform the following steps to start Publisher and choose a blank publication from the Catalog.

### TO START PUBLISHER WITH A BLANK PUBLICATION

**1** Click the Start button on the taskbar.

**2** Point to Programs on the Start menu and then click Microsoft Publisher on the Programs submenu.

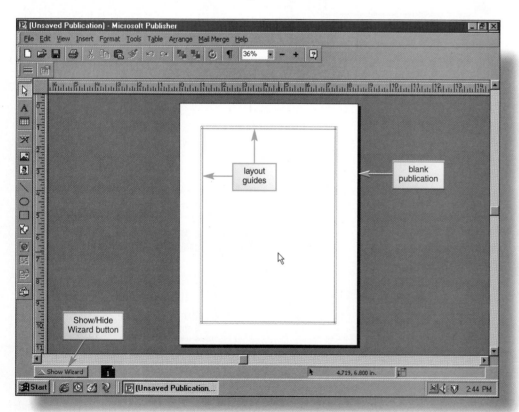

FIGURE 4-2

**3** If the Catalog does not display, click File on the menu bar and then click New.

**4** Click the Blank Publications tab in the Catalog dialog box.

**5** Double-click the Full Page preview. When the blank full page displays in the workspace, click the Hide Wizard button on the status bar. If the Office Assistant displays, click Hide the Office Assistant on the Help menu.

*The blank full page displays in the workspace (Figure 4-2).*

## Setting Publication Margins Using Layout and Ruler Guides

Publisher displays each publication with layout guides around the edge of the page as a sort of margin (Figure 4-2). This is not to say that you cannot position objects closer to the edge of the paper — if your printer is capable of printing close to the edge. The guides are there to help you edit object placement and alignment. The size of the printing area, or **printable region**, varies among printers and depends on paper sizes. Most printers have a small area around the edge of the paper that they cannot use. On a desktop printer, the printable region may include the space up to three-tenths of an inch from the edge; others may require five-tenths to seven-tenths of an inch. If you know your printer's nonprintable region, you can ensure that the printing area is large enough to include everything on each page. If your publication is destined for a commercial printer, you should consult the print professional about printable regions.

The size of the paper also makes a difference. Labels, envelopes, and business cards display a variety of different margins in Publisher depending on the number of copies per sheet and the size of the publication. Web pages, designed for electronic publication rather than print, display layout guides at the edge of the publication page.

You learned in Project 1 that Publisher's boundaries and guides help you align and position objects on the page. To help preview what your publication will look like when printed, the View menu allows you to hide these lines. During the creation/editing process, however, the lines are very helpful. Recall that **layout guides** are the nonprinting blue and pink dotted lines that display on the pages of a publication. These guides reside on the background and repeat on each page of a publication, serving as a template for uniformity in multipage publications. Additionally, when more than one person works on a publication, the final product has a consistent look. The layout guides organize text, pictures, and other objects into straight columns and rows. Green dotted lines are **ruler guides** used for alignment. Added to individual pages on an as-needed basis, ruler guides also help align objects.

Perform the following steps to change the top margin to one-half inch and set a ruler guide at two inches by editing the layout and ruler guides.

### More About

### The Workspace

If the buttons and toolbars on your screen are distracting to you, or if you merely want to increase the size of the workspace, you can hide the buttons and toolbars. On the View menu, point to Toolbars, and then click each toolbar name on the Toolbars submenu to turn it on or off. You also can hide the rulers using the View menu, thus increasing the size of the workspace.

### More About

### Printer Problems

If your printer stops short of printing the entire page, resulting in only the top portion of the publication printing, it may be a memory problem. Some printers do not have enough memory to print a wide variety of images and color. Consider printing a single page at a time, changing the color scheme to black and white, printing the text and graphics separately on the same printed page, or optimizing the printer memory.

---

 ## To Edit the Layout and Ruler Guides

**1** **If the rulers do not display, click View on the menu bar and then click Rulers. If the layout guides do not display, click View on the menu bar and then click Show Boundaries and Guides. Click Arrange on the menu bar. Point to Layout Guides.**

*The Arrange menu displays (Figure 4-3).*

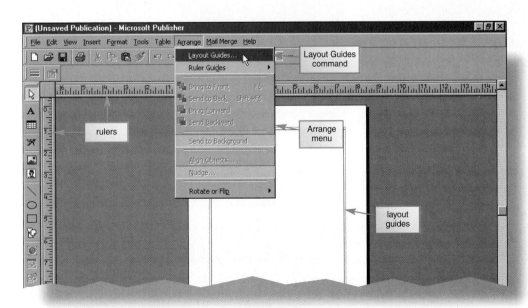

**FIGURE 4-3**

**(2)** **Click Layout Guides. When the Layout Guides dialog box displays, press the TAB key twice to select the text in the Top text box. Type .5 and then point to the OK button.**

*The Top text box displays .5 for a one-half inch margin (Figure 4-4).*

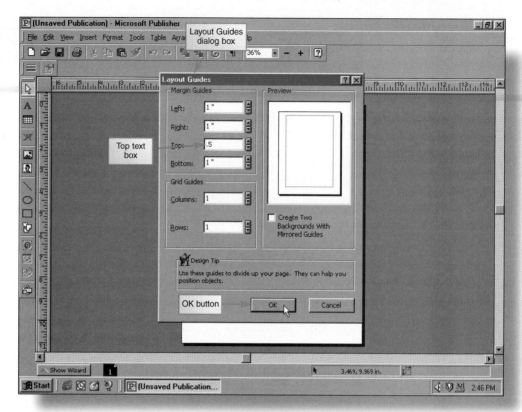

**FIGURE 4-4**

**(3)** **Click the OK button. Point to the Horizontal Ruler at the top of the workspace.**

*The top margin of the publication displays with a .5-inch margin (Figure 4-5). The mouse pointer changes to a double-headed arrow when positioned on the Horizontal Ruler.*

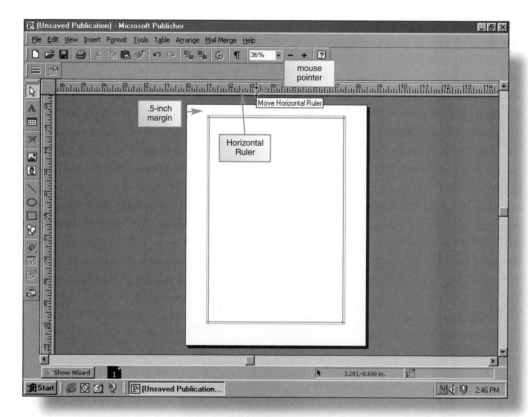

**FIGURE 4-5**

**4** **SHIFT-drag the ruler guide to the 2-inch mark on the Vertical Ruler.**

*The green dotted ruler guide displays horizontally two inches from the top of the page (Figure 4-6).*

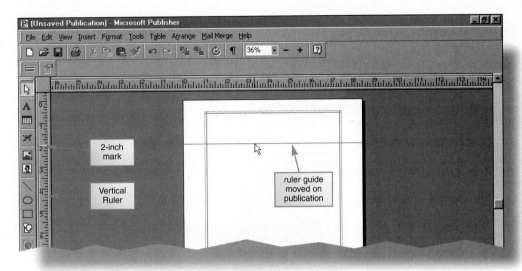

FIGURE 4-6

In addition to the page margins, each object on the page has its own individual boundary margins. For instance, text frames are preset with a 0.04-inch margin, which means that text on all four sides begins 0.04 inch from the edge of the frame, and thus away from any other object snapped to the text frame.

# Personal Information Sets

Recall that in Project 2 you learned that a personal information set is a set of fields, or **components**, containing information about a person, a business, or an organization — components that Publisher maintains for use across publications. Many of the wizards create personal information text frames or components that incorporate the data from the personal information set. Publications created from scratch also can integrate a personal information set by including one or more of the components in the publication. For example, you can save your name, address, and telephone number in the personal information set. It then automatically displays when inserted by you or by a wizard. A company could save its organizational data for use in a variety of publications.

Publisher provides four different, independent personal information sets for use in business and home: Primary Business, Secondary Business, Other Organization, and Home/Family. Although every new publication has the Primary Business personal information set selected by default, it is easy to apply a different personal information set to the publication.

Each personal information set contains eight components: Personal Name, Job Title, Organization Name, Address, Tag line, Phone/Fax/E-mail, Logo, and Color Scheme. When you install Publisher, the personal information components contain default information. You can change the information in any component, however.

## Editing the Personal Information Set

When you first install Publisher, the personal information components contain preset, generic information for each of the four sets. If you edit a text frame containing personal information, you change that publication only. To affect changes for all future publications, you edit the components through the Edit menu. You can edit the information set at any time — before, during, or after performing other publication tasks.

*Other Ways*

1. To insert ruler guides, on Arrange menu click Ruler Guides
2. To edit layout guides, on View menu click Go to Background, SHIFT-drag guide
3. To edit layout guides, press CTRL+M, SHIFT-drag guide

*More About 2000*

## Choosing a Personal Information Set

Each wizard in Publisher allows you to choose which personal information set you want to use. Simply click the Show Wizard button on the status bar at any time during the editing process. The upper wizard pane displays a Personal Information option. You then may choose any of the four sets.

Perform the following steps to edit the Primary Business personal information set. You will add text and a color scheme. The logo will be inserted later in the project.

 **Steps** **To Edit a Personal Information Set**

**1** **Click Edit on the menu bar and then point to Personal Information.**

*The Edit menu displays (Figure 4-7).*

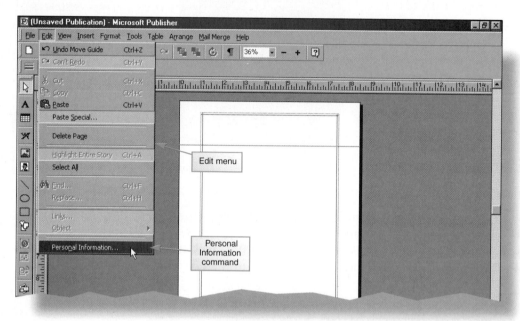

**FIGURE 4-7**

**2** **Click Personal Information. When the Personal Information dialog box displays, if necessary, click Primary Business and then press the TAB key.**

*The personal information set for the Primary Business displays (Figure 4-8). The Name text box is selected.*

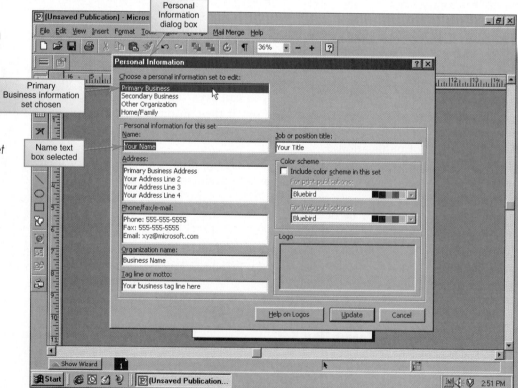

**FIGURE 4-8**

**3** **Type** Tony Manderino **in the Name text box and then press the TAB key.**

*The new name displays in the Name text box (Figure 4-9). The Address text box is selected.*

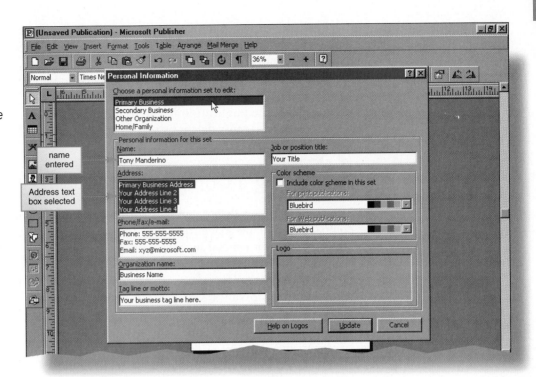

FIGURE 4-9

**4** **Repeat Step 3 to enter the data from Figure 4-10 in each of the text boxes. Press the TAB key to progress from one text box to the next. Click Include color scheme in this set to select it. Point to the Update button.**

*The completed text boxes display (Figure 4-10). The Bluebird color scheme will be included in the Primary Business personal information set.*

**5** **Click the Update button.**

*The blank publication displays.*

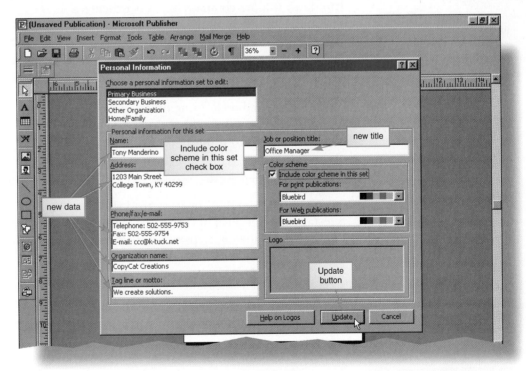

FIGURE 4-10

You can edit any of Publisher's four personal information sets in the Personal Information dialog box. It is not necessary to save the publication in order to save the changes to the set. When you click the Update button, Publisher uses the displayed set in the current publication.

1. In publication, edit personal information text frame
2. In wizard, click Show Wizard, click Personal Information, click Update button

Publisher provides four different sets for your convenience in maintaining alternate information about your business; a second or related business, such as a major supplier or home business; an outside organization for which you maintain information, such as scouting or sports; and your personal home/family information.

To remove a personal information component in a single publication, you can delete it from the publication itself. To remove a personal information component permanently, you must delete its text from the Personal Information dialog box.

# Creating a Company Letterhead

In many businesses, **letterhead** is preprinted stationery with important facts about the company and blank space to display the purpose of the correspondence. Letterhead, typically used for official business communication, is an easy way to convey company information to the reader and quickly establish a formal and legitimate mode of correspondence. The company information displays in a variety of places — across the top, down the side, or split between the top and bottom. Although most business letterhead is 8½-by-11-inches, other sizes are becoming more popular, especially with small agencies and not-for-profit organizations.

Generally, it is cost effective for companies to outsource their letterhead. Designing the letterhead in-house and then sending the file to a commercial printer saves design consultation time, customization, and money. Large firms order thousands of copies at a time, as the data seldom changes. Black-and-white or spot-color letterhead is more common and less expensive than composite or process color.

Sometimes preprinted letterhead may not be purchased because of its expense, color, or limited quantity. In these cases, companies can design their own letterhead and save it in a file. Employees open the letterhead file, create the rest of their document, and then save the finished product with a new name — thus preserving the original letterhead file. Alternately, businesses may print multiple copies of their letterhead only; and then, using other application software, prepare documents to print on the letterhead paper. All of these types of letterhead production can be used in any combination to produce professional publications.

## The Letterhead Background

The background of the letterhead shown in Figure 4-1 on page PUB 4.5 contains a rectangle, positioned at the top of the page, with a distinctive gradient fill color. Perform the following steps to create the rectangle and fill it with a gradient effect.

## Publisher 98 Updates

In Publisher 98, personal information sets could be updated only from a publication. In Publisher 2000, the Edit menu has a command for updating personal information. If you want to reinstate Publisher 98's capability to update automatically, on the Tools menu click Options, and then click the User Assistance tab. Click the Update personal information when saving check box. See Appendix C for more information on the Options dialog box.

## Online Paper Suppliers

For more information on where to obtain supplies for printing publications such as a company letterhead, visit the Word 2000 More About Web page (www.scsite.com/wd2000/more.htm) and then click Online Office Supplies.

## Zooming

If you have a Microsoft IntelliMouse®, you can zoom in and out of a publication by holding the CTRL key while rotating the wheel forward or backward. To learn other features of the IntelliMouse, click the Start button on the taskbar, point to Programs, point to Microsoft Hardware, point to Mouse, and then click Intellipoint Online User's Guide.

**To Create the Letterhead Background**

**1** **Click the Rectangle Tool button on the Objects toolbar and then point to the upper-left corner of the page margin represented by the layout guide.**

*The mouse pointer changes to a crosshair in preparation for drawing a rectangle (Figure 4-11).*

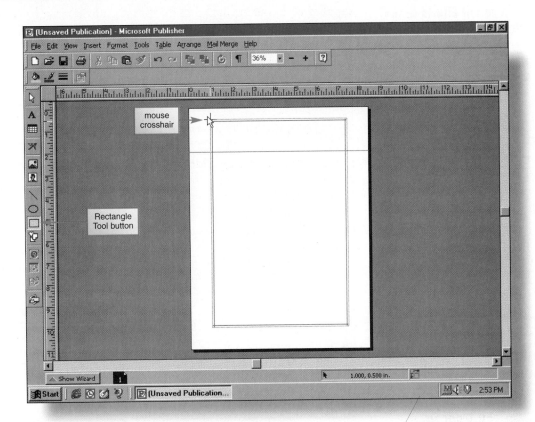

**FIGURE 4-11**

**2** **Drag down and right from the layout guide to the right margin at the ruler guide. After releasing the mouse button, point to the Fill Color button on the Standard toolbar.**

*The rectangle snaps to the guides and displays selected with its sizing handles (Figure 4-12).*

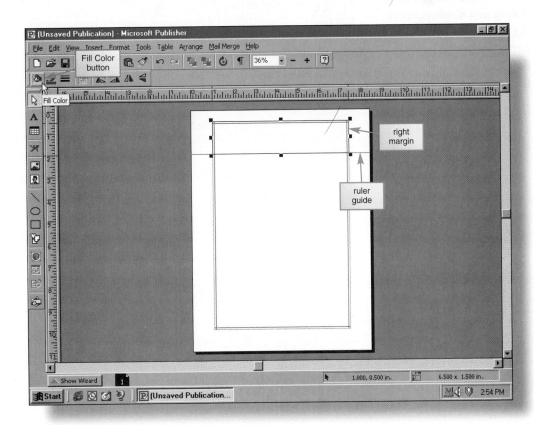

**FIGURE 4-12**

**3** **Click the Fill Color button and then point to Fill Effects in the Fill Color button menu.**

*The Fill Color button menu displays (Figure 4-13).*

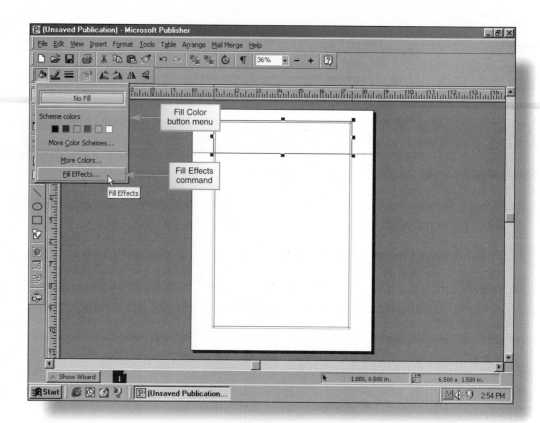

**FIGURE 4-13**

**4** **Click Fill Effects. When the Fill Effects dialog box displays, click the Gradients option button and then point to the Base color box arrow in the Color frame.**

*The Gradients option button is selected (Figure 4-14). The available gradient patterns display in the Style bar.*

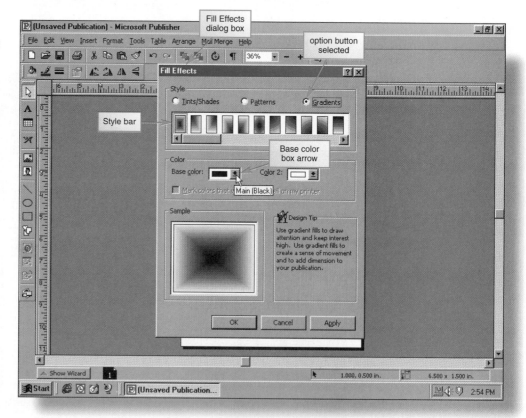

**FIGURE 4-14**

**5** **Click the Base color box arrow and then point to Accent 3 (Orange) in Scheme colors.**

*The Base colors display (Figure 4-15).*

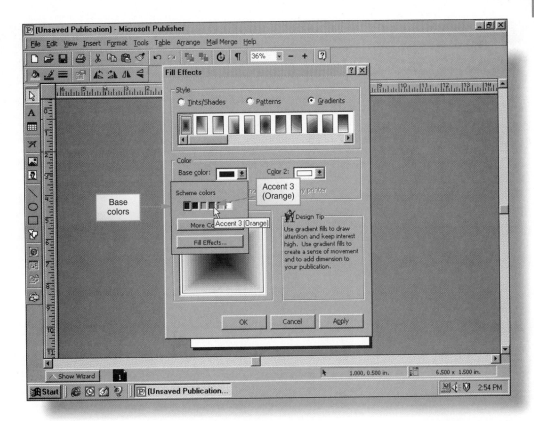

**FIGURE 4-15**

**6** **Click Accent 3 (Orange) and then point to the OK button.**

*The sample of the gradient orange background for the rectangle displays (Figure 4-16).*

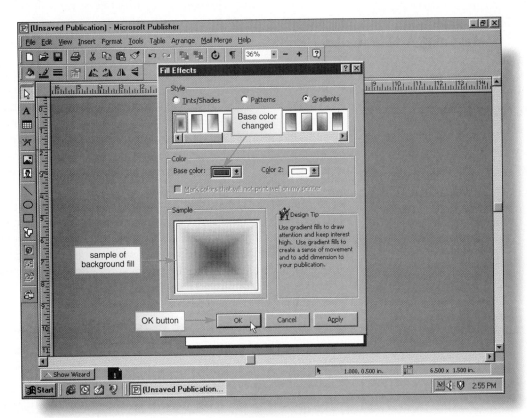

**FIGURE 4-16**

**7** **Click the OK button and then press the F9 key to enlarge the display.**

*The rectangle displays with the orange gradient fill effect (Figure 4-17).*

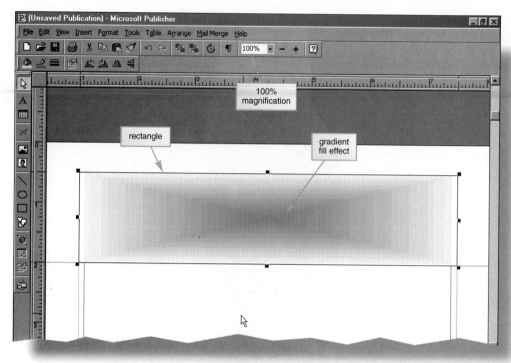

FIGURE 4-17

Publisher offers three styles of fill effects: tints/shades, patterns, and gradients. A **tint** is a gradation of a color with reference to its mixture with white. A **shade**, on the other hand, is a mixture of a base color and black. You use tints and shades to create a more sophisticated color scheme. Tints and shades are incremented in ten-percent intervals. For example, the first tint of red is nine parts red and 1 part white. Therefore, Publisher displays 10 tints and 10 shades of each basic color in its Styles bar.

**Patterns** behind shapes or large areas add subtle contrast and create an illusion of texture and depth. Patterns include variations of repeating designs such as lines, stripes, checks and bricks. Publisher uses the base color and a second color to create the pattern. Patterns destined for commercial printing are usually more expensive than tints and shades, because they increase the time its takes to image the file to film.

Publisher suggests using **gradient** fills to draw attention and heighten interest. Gradient fills create a sense of movement and add dimension to a publication. A gradient uses tints or shades of one color to create a special pattern of increased shading with another color, usually white. Publisher displays more than 40 available gradients with patterns ranging from stars and swirls to arrows to three-dimensional abstractions.

## Inserting and Formatting Personal Information Components

The letterhead contains three text frame components from the personal information set: the Organization Name, the Address, and the Phone/Fax/E-mail text frames. When you insert a component, Publisher places it in the center of the screen with a preset font and font size. You may then move it and format the text as necessary. Applied formatting affects the current publication only.

Perform the following steps to insert and format personal information components in the letterhead.

**Steps** ## To Insert and Format Personal Information Components

**1** **Click Insert on the menu bar. Point to Personal Information and then point to Organization Name on the Personal Information submenu.**

*The Insert menu and the Personal Information submenu display (Figure 4-18).*

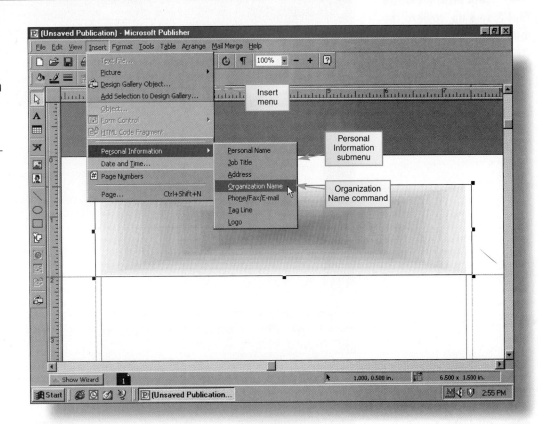

**FIGURE 4-18**

**2** **Click Organization Name. When the text frame displays, press CTRL+A to select all the text. Click the Center button on the Formatting toolbar and then point to the border of the text frame.**

*The Organization Name Text Frame displays and the mouse pointer changes to the Mover (Figure 4-19).*

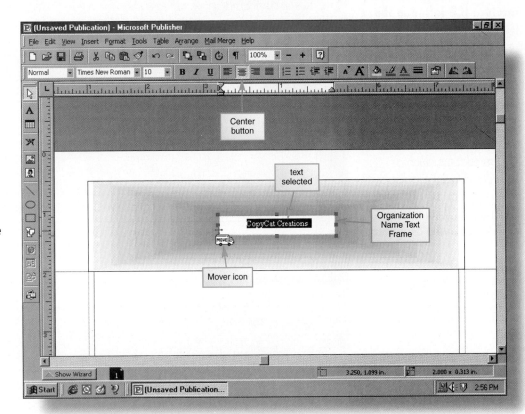

**FIGURE 4-19**

**3** Drag the Organization Name Text Frame up, toward the top of the rectangle. Press CTRL+T to make the text frame transparent. Point to the Font box arrow.

*The text is selected (Figure 4-20).*

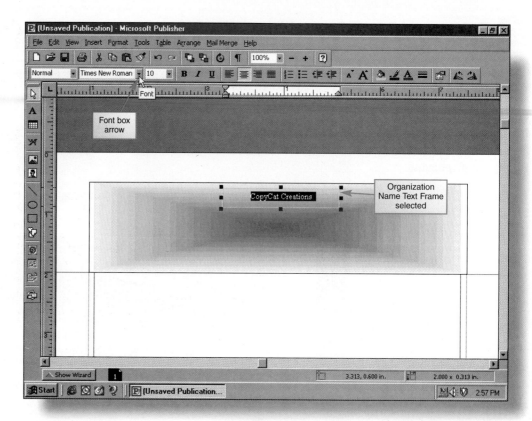

**FIGURE 4-20**

**4** Click the Font box arrow and then click Decotura ICG Inline in the list. If you do not have the Decotura font, choose a similar font. Point to the Organization Name Text Frame again.

*The text changes to Decotura ICG Inline (Figure 4-21). Variegated fonts, such as Decotura ICG Inline, display characters that are not solid, allowing the fill color to partially display in the character.*

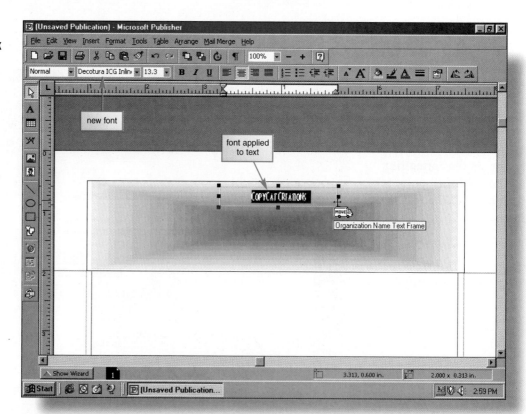

**FIGURE 4-21**

**5** Right-click the Organization Name Text Frame and then point to Change Text on the shortcut menu. Point to AutoFit Text on the Change Text submenu and then point to Best Fit on the AutoFit Text submenu.

*The AutoFit Text submenu displays (Figure 4-22).*

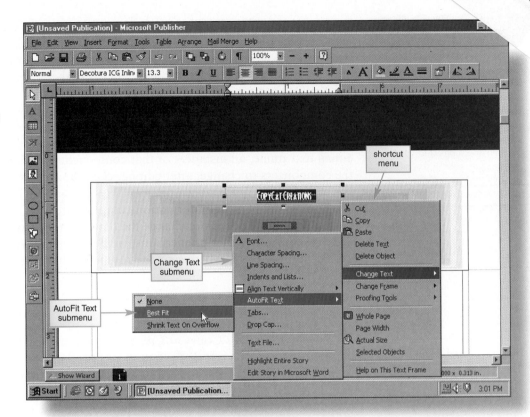

**FIGURE 4-22**

**6** Click Best Fit. Repeat Steps 1 through 3 to insert the Personal Information components for the Address Text Frame and Phone/Fax/E-mail Text Frame. Position the frames approximately as shown in Figure 4-23. Do not change the font or AutoFit settings on the Address and Phone/Fax/E-mail Text Frames.

*The inserted components display (Figure 4-23).*

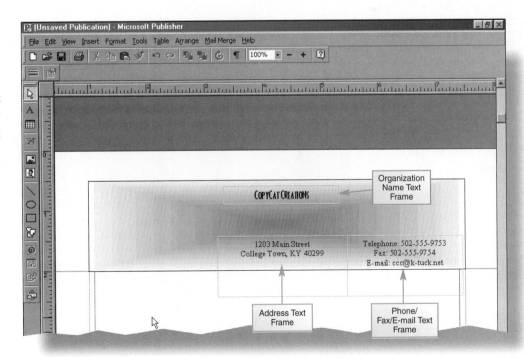

**FIGURE 4-23**

*Other* Ways

1. Click Show Wizard button, click Personal Information, click Insert Component

### More About

### AutoCorrect

The AutoCorrect feature is part of Microsoft's IntelliSense™ technology and is built into all of the Office 2000 applications. On the Tools menu, you can set AutoCorrect to capitalize the first letter in a sentence and the first letter of the days of the week automatically. You also can correct automatically two initial capital letters, as well as accidental use of the CAPS LOCK key. AutoCorrect's most powerful feature, however, allows you to insert your own typical errors for automatic correction.

Many times, e-mail addresses display with red wavy underlines. This flagged text, as discussed in Project 2, means Publisher did not find the word in its dictionary. Flagged words are not necessarily misspelled. Right-clicking the text and then clicking Ignore on the shortcut menu will cause the wavy line not to display.

You can place a component many times in a publication, as long as you use separate text frames each time. If you change the information in a personal information component, all components of that type will change or synchronize in the current publication. For example, if you edit the address in a personal information e-mail text frame, all instances of that component will change. If you do not want all the components to change, after editing, click the Undo button on the Standard toolbar to cancel the synchronization.

Editing any personal information component except the logo changes the current publication only. It does not change the data in the Personal Information dialog box, nor does it change other publications using the component. When you save a publication, Publisher asks whether or not to update the logo, as you will see in the next series of steps.

### The CopyCat Creations Logo

The letterhead for CopyCat Creations contains a picture of a cat. The graphic, placed in front of the rest of the letterhead, overlaps the bottom edge of the rectangle to intentionally break the border for a visual effect. In order to make the graphic become a part of the personal information set, you must use a logo object from the Design Gallery and then save the publication with the edited logo.

Perform the following steps to insert a logo in the publication.

### Steps To Insert a Logo

**1** **Click Insert on the menu bar. Point to Personal Information and then point to Logo on the Personal Information submenu.**

*The Personal Information submenu displays (Figure 4-24).*

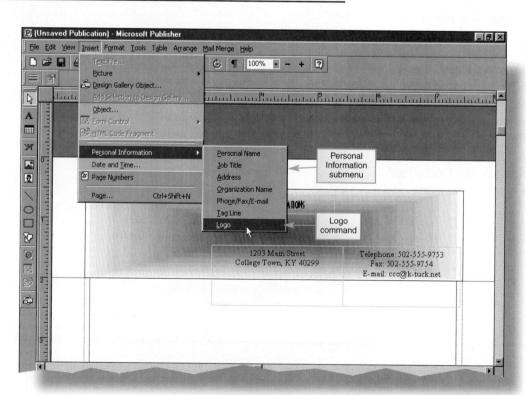

**FIGURE 4-24**

**2** Click Logo. When the logo displays in the publication, point to the smart object Wizard button.

*The logo placeholder displays in the publication (Figure 4-25).*

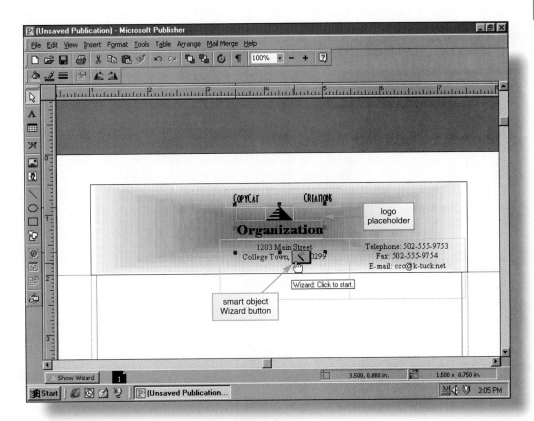

FIGURE 4-25

**3** Click the smart object Wizard button. When the Logo Creation Wizard dialog box displays, point to Picture file that I already have.

*The Logo Creation Wizard dialog box displays options in the top pane and explanations with choices in the bottom pane (Figure 4-26).*

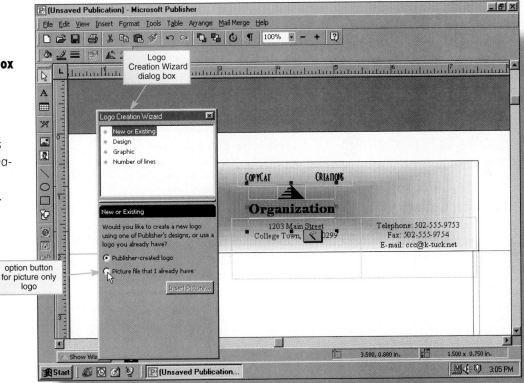

FIGURE 4-26

**4** Click Picture file that I already have and then point to the Close button on the Logo Creation Wizard title bar.

*The logo changes to a picture only format (Figure 4-27).*

**5** Click the Close button.

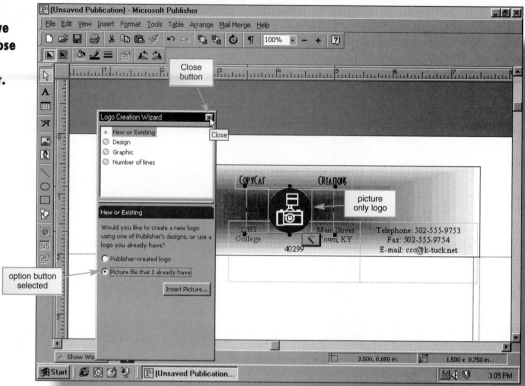

FIGURE 4-27

Other Ways

1. On Insert menu click Design Gallery Object, click Logos
2. On Insert menu click Personal Information, click Logo

## To Finish Editing the Logo

Perform the following steps to finish editing the logo by choosing a graphic for CopyCat Creations.

### TO EDIT THE LOGO

**1** Double-click the graphic.

**2** If necessary click the Pictures tab in the Insert Clip Art window and then click the Search for clips text box.

**3** Type cat in the Search for clips text box and then press the ENTER key.

**4** Scroll to locate the picture of the cat shown in Figure 4-28 or another appropriate graphic.

**5** Right-click the graphic and then click Insert on the shortcut menu.

**6** Close the Insert Clip Art window by clicking its Close button.

*The graphic is inserted into the logo (Figure 4-28).*

**More About**

**Adding Graphics to the Design Gallery**

The Design Gallery maintains a Your Objects tab to which you may add objects for use in other publications, such as edited graphics or multiple logos. The Your Objects tab is similar to the Extra Content tab created with the leftover objects from a print to Web conversion. Each publication has its own design set and categories, but you may browse to borrow design sets from other publications using the Options button on the Your Objects tab.

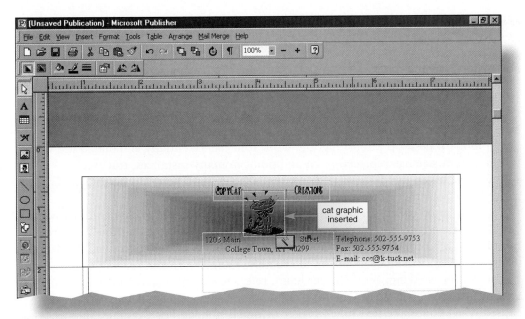

**FIGURE 4-28**

More About 2000

**Toolbars**

If you are vision impaired, you may want to display larger toolbar buttons. On the View menu, point to Toolbars, and then click Options on the Toolbars submenu. Large icons, ScreenTips, and options for animations are in the Toolbar Options dialog box.

# Using the Measurements Toolbar

In earlier projects, graphics were formatted by using the sizing handles to resize or by using the Mover to reposition the graphic. You learned that the Size and Position command on the Format menu is another way to precisely place objects in publications. A third way, using the **Measurements toolbar**, not only sets the location and size of an object, but sets the angle of rotation, as well. If the object is text, the Measurements toolbar offers additional character spacing or typesetting options. Accessed either through the View menu or by double-clicking one of the Object boxes on the status bar, the Measurements toolbar is a floating toolbar with nine text boxes. Entries can be typed in each box or chosen by clicking the appropriate arrows. Table 4-1 lists the boxes available on the Measurements toolbar, their purpose, and their preset unit of measurement.

**Table 4-1 Measurements Toolbar Boxes**

| TOOLBAR SYMBOL | BOX NAME | PURPOSE | PRESET UNIT OF MEASUREMENT |
|---|---|---|---|
| x | Horizontal Position | Horizontal distance from the upper-left corner of the page to the upper-left corner of the object | Inches |
| y | Vertical Position | Vertical distance from the upper-left corner of the page to the upper-left corner of the object | Inches |
| (width icon) | Width | Width of object | Inches |
| (height icon) | Height | Height of object | Inches |
| (rotation icon) | Rotation | Rotate the object counterclockwise from the original orientation | Degrees |
| aaa | Text Scaling | Width of the text | Percent |
| ‹A› | Tracking | General space between characters | Percent |
| A/V | Kerning | Subtle space between paired characters | Point size |
| A↕ | Line Spacing | Vertical spacing between lines of selected text | Space (1 for single) |

## Character Spacing Techniques

Early typesetters were limited to just a few typefaces and sizes of type. The only way to change the spacing between characters was to insert or remove metal on each side of a piece of type. To stretch a title across the top of a page, they inserted several equally sized pieces of metal between each character. To position characters closer together, some typesetters actually used a knife to shave bits of lead from the sides of wide characters. The resulting overhang was called a **kern**.

In modern desktop publishing, the word font has essentially eliminated the word typeface, font size has replaced pitch and point in many instances, tracking and scaling have taken the place of proportional spacing, and kern has become a verb referring to both the subtraction and addition of subtle spacing.

**Scaling**, often called shrinking or stretching, is the process of changing the width of characters in text frames. You may remember from Project 2 that the WordArt toolbar has a button for scaling; however scaling also is available for any text frame using the Measurements toolbar or, alternately, using Character Spacing on the Format menu. **Tracking**, on the other hand, refers to the adjustment of the general spacing between characters. Tracking text compensates for the spacing irregularities caused when you make text much bigger or much smaller. For example, smaller type is easier to read when it has been tracked loosely. Tracking both maintains the original height of the font and overrides adjustments made by justification of the margins.

**Kerning**, or track kerning, is a special form of tracking related to pairs of characters that may appear too close together, even with standard tracking. For instance, certain letters such as T, V, W, and Y, often are kerned when they are preceded or followed by A, a, e, or o. **Automatic kerning** is applied to 14-point text and above. Text in smaller point size usually does not need to be kerned. With **manual kerning** Publisher lets you choose from normal, expanded, and condensed kerning for special effects. Kerning fine-tunes the amount of space between specific character pairs that would otherwise appear to be too close together or too far apart.

Perform the following steps to set the location of the graphic and to adjust the tracking of the text, CopyCat Creations, using the Measurements toolbar.

### More About
### Rotating

The Rotation text box on the Measurements toolbar allows you to enter any degree of rotation from -360 to +360. Positive numbers rotate counterclockwise. Negative numbers rotate clockwise and are converted on the toolbar to their corresponding positive number. For instance an entry of -90 is converted to 270 (360 minus 90) and the object is rotated 90 degrees clockwise. You can rotate any object or grouped objects, including text, for special effects.

## Steps To Format Using the Measurements Toolbar

**1** **If necessary, click the logo to select it and then double-click the Object Position box on the status bar. When the Measurements toolbar displays, point to the Horizontal Position text box.**

*The Measurements toolbar displays (Figure 4-29). Your displayed measurements may differ.*

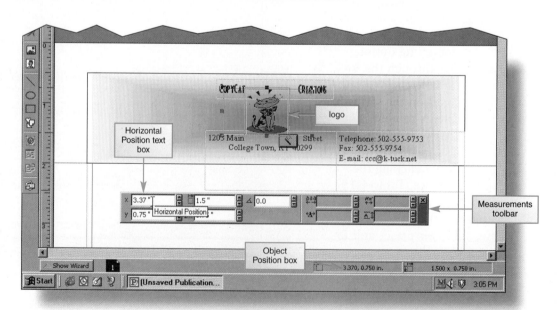

**FIGURE 4-29**

**2** Drag through the measurement in the Horizontal Position text box and then type 1 to replace the measurement.

*The measurement displays in the Horizontal Position text box (Figure 4-30).*

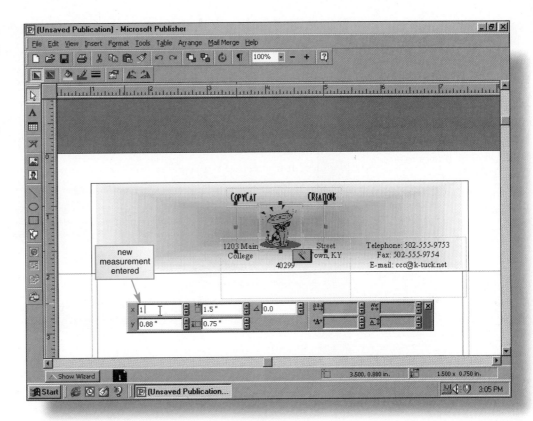

new measurement entered

**FIGURE 4-30**

**3** If necessary, move the measurements toolbar. Enter the values shown in Figure 4-31. Press the TAB key to progress from one text box to the next. When finished, point to the Organization Name Text Frame.

*The Measurements toolbar displays the values for the graphic (Figure 4-31).*

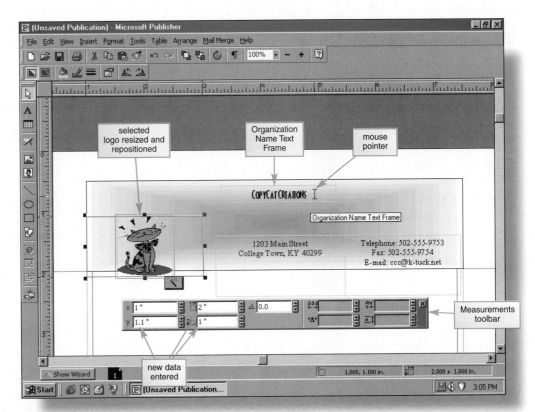

selected logo resized and repositioned

Organization Name Text Frame

mouse pointer

Organization Name Text Frame

Measurements toolbar

new data entered

**FIGURE 4-31**

**4** Drag through the text CopyCat Creations. Point to the Horizontal Position text box.

*The Measurements toolbar changes to reflect the values for the heading (Figure 4-32). Notice that the character spacing text boxes now are available.*

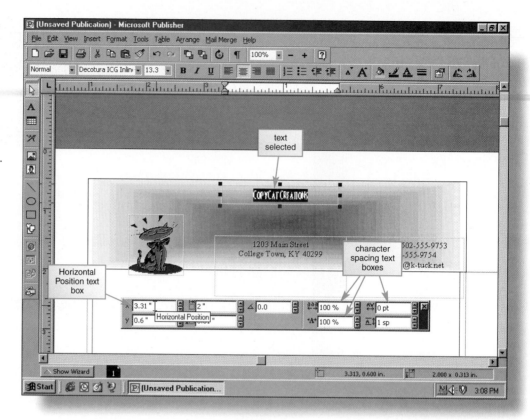

**FIGURE 4-32**

**5** Drag through the measurement in the Horizontal Position text box and then type 2.5 to replace the text. Press the TAB key to proceed to each measurement box, entering the values shown in Figure 4-33. When finished, point to the Close button on the Measurements toolbar.

*The values for the heading display (Figure 4-33).*

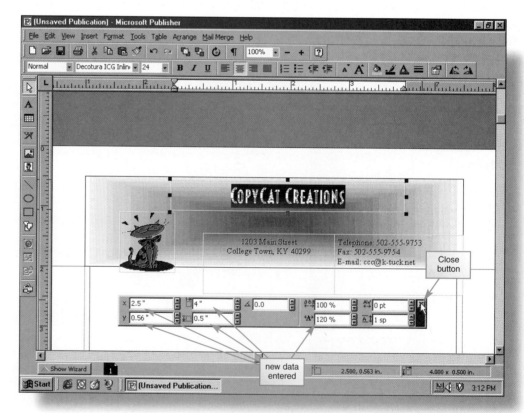

**FIGURE 4-33**

**6** **Click the Close button on the Measurements toolbar.**

*Spacing is increased between the letters of the title (Figure 4-34).*

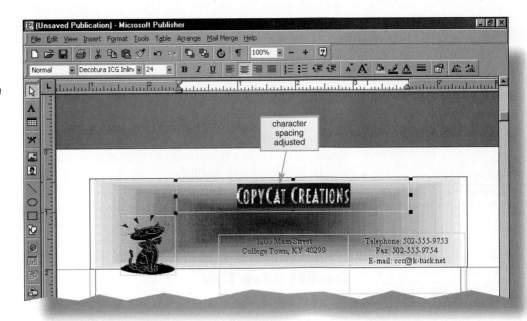

**FIGURE 4-34**

**Other Ways**

1. On View menu click Toolbars, click Measurements
2. On Format menu click Character Spacing
3. To increase the kerning, press CTRL+SHIFT+]
4. To decrease the kerning, press CTRL+SHIFT+[

Yet another set of formatting options is available for graphics. You can recolor, scale, or crop the graphic when you click Change Picture on the shortcut menu of any picture frame.

**Recoloring** means making a large-scale color change to the entire graphic. When chosen, the color applies to all parts of the graphic, with the option of leaving the black parts black. It is an easy way to convert a color graphic to a black and white line drawing in order to print more clearly. The reverse is also true; if you have a black and white graphic, you can convert it to a tint or shade of any one color.

**Scaling**, when it applies to graphics, means changing the vertical or horizontal size of the graphic by a percentage. Scaling can create interesting graphic effects. For example, a square graphic could become a long thin graphic suitable for use as a single border, if the scale height were increased to 200% and the scale width were reduced to 50%. Caricature drawings and intentionally distorted photographs routinely use scaling. Used for resizing, scaling is appropriate for subtle changes to make a graphic fit in tight places.

**Cropping** is cutting out part of a graphic. When cropping is chosen, Publisher changes the mouse pointer to the Scissor icon allowing you to cut from any of the eight sizing handles. Additionally, cropping can cut down a large graphic in order to focus on a specific part, or eliminate a border or caption that came with the picture.

# Using Styles

Formatting changes applied to one instance of a personal information component are not saved to the personal information set in Publisher. In other words, personal information components insert text only. You have to apply formatting every time you use them. If you want to save formatting for use in future publications, Publisher uses a concept called styles, as do many word processing applications. A **style** is a set of formatting characteristics that you apply to text to change its appearance quickly. A style contains all text formatting information: font and font size, font color, indents, character and line spacing, tabs, and special formatting, such as

**More About**

**Graphic Drawing Programs**

Publisher supports the direct editing of objects drawn in Microsoft Paint, Microsoft PhotoDraw, Microsoft Photo Editor, MS Draw, Microsoft Picture It!, and others. Instead of inserting the object as a picture, you use the Paste Special command on the Edit menu. The object then can be linked or embedded to launch the drawing application when you edit the graphic. See the Integration Project for examples of object linking and embedding (OLE).

## Fonts

If you use TrueType fonts, Publisher uses the same font to display text on the screen and on the printout. TrueType font names are preceded by TT in the Font box on the Formatting toolbar. TrueType fonts are installed automatically when you set up Windows. If you use non-TrueType fonts, try to use a screen font that matches your printer font. If a matching font is not available or if your printer driver does not provide screen font information, Windows chooses the screen font that most closely resembles the printer font.

numbered lists. When you apply a style, you apply a whole group of formats in one step. For example, you may want to format the Web page address of a company to make it stand out. Instead of taking four separate steps to format the address as underlined, blue, 16-point, and center-aligned, you can achieve the same result in one step by applying a saved style. The formatting changes affect the entire paragraph.

Publisher installs a predefined Normal style as 10-point Times New Roman, flush-left. Other text styles can come from a variety of sources. You can define your own styles in Publisher, import text styles from other publications, or use text styles you have saved in a template. For example, styles from Microsoft Word documents can be imported into Publisher.

Using a style is easier than using the Format Painter when you have multiple pages or multiple documents. You do not have to search for the text with the formatting you like, click the Format Painter, and then return to new text. Rather, you can choose the preferred style from the Formatting toolbar.

### Creating a New Style

The organization name located in the letterhead has specific formatting that the company would like to become part of its unique identity. Once created, you can import the style from the letterhead to the business card, coupon, and envelope.

Perform the following steps to create a new text style from the letterhead organization name text frame example and name it CopyCat.

 **To Create a New Text Style by Example**

**1** Click the text, **CopyCat Creations**, in the Organization Name Text Frame. Point to the Style box on the Formatting toolbar.

The text frame is selected (Figure 4-35).

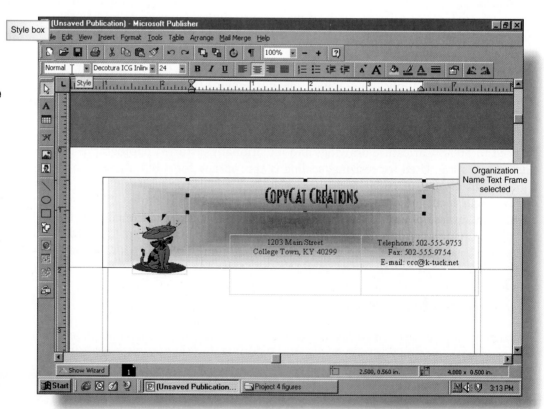

**FIGURE 4-35**

**2** **Click the Style box. Type** `CopyCat` **to replace the word Normal and then press the ENTER key. When the Create Style By Example dialog box displays, point to the OK button.**

*The Create Style By Example dialog box displays with the new style name (Figure 4-36). The sample displays the font, size, and character spacing settings of the example text.*

**3** **Click the OK button.**

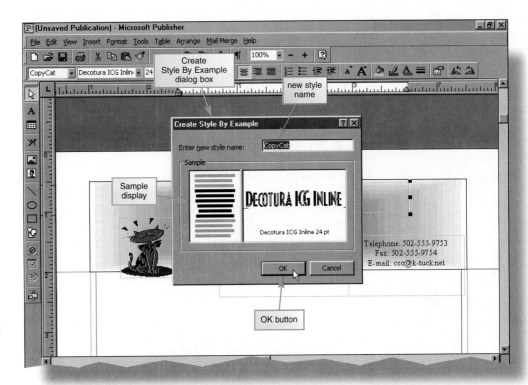

FIGURE 4-36

Styles are saved when the publication is saved. You will import the CopyCat style later in this project.

## Saving and Printing the Letterhead

The CopyCat Creations letterhead is complete. It is time to save the publication and begin work on the business card. For a detailed example of the procedure summarized below, refer to pages PUB 1.26 through PUB 1.28 in Project 1.

### TO SAVE AND PRINT THE LETTERHEAD

**1** Insert your floppy disk into drive A.

**2** Click the Save button on the Standard toolbar.

**3** When a message displays asking if you want to save the logo, click the Yes button.

**4** When the Save As dialog box displays, type `CopyCat Letterhead` in the File name text box. Do not press the ENTER key.

**5** Click the Save in box arrow and then click 3½ Floppy (A:).

**6** Click the Save button in the Save As dialog box.

**7** Click the Print button on the Standard toolbar.

*Publisher saves the publication on a floppy disk in drive A with the file name, CopyCat Letterhead, and then prints a copy on the printer. The letterhead is shown in Figure 4-1 on page PUB 4.5.*

Other Ways

1. On Format menu click Text Style, edit formatting

## More About 2000

### Embedding Fonts

When you take your Publisher file to a commercial printing service, the printing service needs to have the fonts you used in your publication correctly. To embed the fonts, on the Tools menu, point to Commercial Printing Tools, and then click Fonts on the Commercial Printing Tools submenu. In the Fonts dialog box, you will see options for embedding the entire font set, or a subset. You also will see a list of the necessary fonts and their legal restrictions, if any. Publisher supplied fonts have no license restrictions; however, if you use outside fonts, your printing service may need to purchase a copy.

The logo is saved with the publication and becomes part of the personal information set for the Primary Business. Publisher creates a file named BIZ1LGO.JSP, stores it in the default folder for Microsoft Office Applications, and **associates** it with the personal information set, which means that the set will always look to that file for the logo. Each of the four personal information sets may contain a different logo.

# Business Cards

Another way companies are saving money on publishing costs is by designing their own business cards. A **business card** is a small publication, 3½-by-2-inches, printed on heavy stock paper. It usually contains the name, title, business, and address information for an employee, as well as a logo, distinguishing graphic, or color to draw attention to the card. Many employees want their telephone, pager, and fax numbers on their business cards in addition to their e-mail and Web page addresses, so that colleagues and customers can reach them quickly.

Business cards can be saved as files to send to commercial printers or printed by desktop color printers on special perforated paper.

## The Business Card Wizard

Because the personal information set contains information about CopyCat Creations, using a **Business Card Wizard** is the quickest way to create a business card. Not only does the wizard set the size and shape of a typical business card, it also presets page and printing options for the easiest production.

The next sequence of steps uses the Business Card Wizard to produce a business card for the office manager at CopyCat Creations. The Wizard automatically uses information from the personal information set created earlier in this project. For a detailed explanation of the steps required to begin a publication using the Catalog and a wizard, see pages PUB 1.11 through PUB 1.13 in Project 1. Perform the following steps to create a business card using a wizard.

### TO USE THE BUSINESS CARD WIZARD

1. Click File on the menu bar and then click New.

2. When the Microsoft Publisher Catalog dialog box displays, click Business Cards.

3. Double-click the Accent Box Business Card preview.

4. If a dialog box displays asking you to save the letterhead again, click the No button.

5. When the business card displays, click the Finish button in the Business Card Wizard pane.

6. Click the Hide Wizard button on the status bar.

*The Personal Information components display in the business card, as does the CopyCat logo (Figure 4-37).*

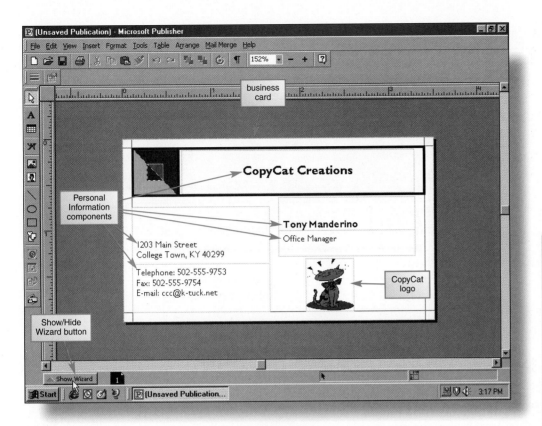

**FIGURE 4-37**

## Editing the Business Card

The Business Card Wizard uses information from the Primary Business personal information set. The wizard places typical business card fields in appropriate places in the publication. Editing the layout customizes the business card even further. The term **layout** refers to both the process and the result of planning and arranging objects in a publication. Sending objects behind other objects, layering, and aligning objects are part of editing the layout.

The steps on the next page edit the business card to repeat the orange rectangle element from the letterhead, as well as the broken border style. A guide from the Vertical Ruler helps place the rectangle and align text frames. The CopyCat logo displays in front of the rectangle.

**To Edit the Business Card**

**1** **Click the upper-left corner of the rectangle at the top of the business card to select it. Press CTRL+T to change the rectangle's transparency.**

*The rectangle, no longer transparent, displays its white fill color (Figure 4-38).*

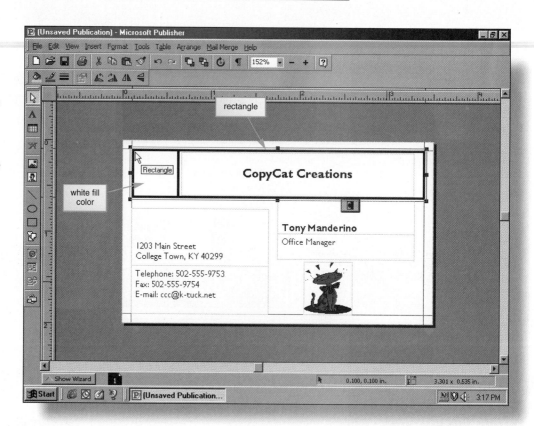

**FIGURE 4-38**

**2** **From the left side of the workspace, SHIFT-drag the Vertical Ruler approximately to the .375 (or three-eights inch) position on the Horizontal Ruler.**

*The ruler guide displays at .375 from the left margin (Figure 4-39).*

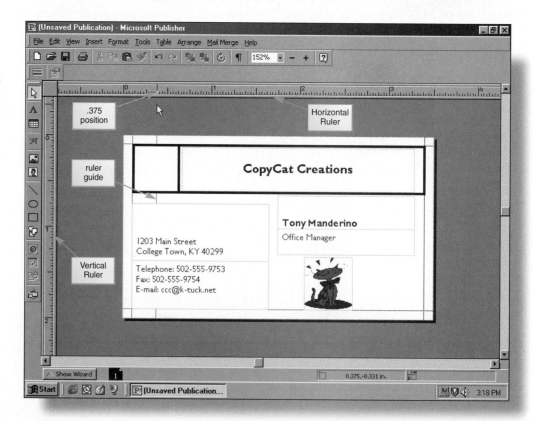

**FIGURE 4-39**

**3** Click the Address Text Frame and then SHIFT-click the Phone/Fax/E-mail Text Frame. Drag the selected text frames to the right of the green ruler guide. Point to the Rectangle Tool button on the Objects toolbar.

*The two text frames display to the right of the ruler guide (Figure 4-40).*

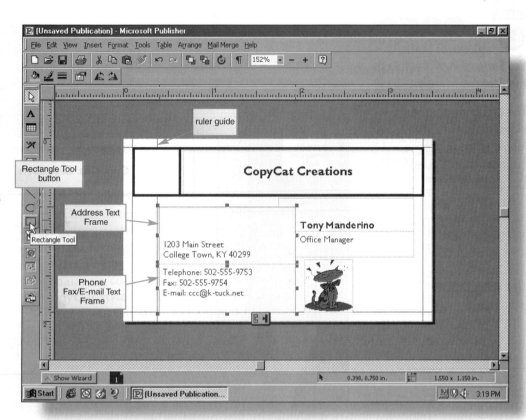

**FIGURE 4-40**

**4** Click the Rectangle Tool button and then drag a rectangle from the upper-left edge of the business card to the lower edge at the green ruler guide. Click the Fill Color button on the Formatting toolbar and then point to Accent 3 (Orange) in Scheme colors.

*The new rectangle is selected (Figure 4-41).*

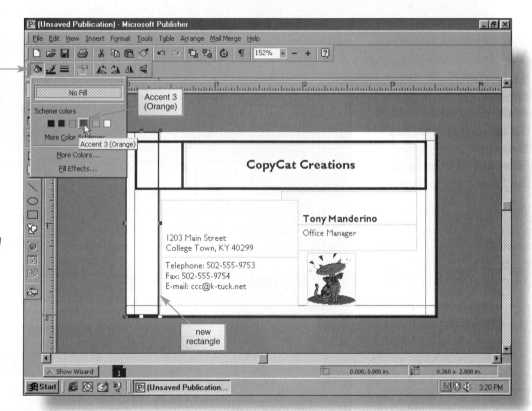

**FIGURE 4-41**

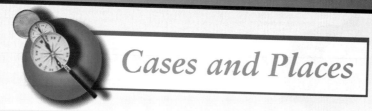

# Cases and Places

**5** ▶▶ You are the teaching assistant for a distance learning computer application course. The lead instructor has asked you to design a fancy heading for the virtual office hours chat room. Use what you have learned about customizing with backgrounds, fill effects, tracking, scaling, kerning, and layering to design a banner heading. Be sure to include the name of the course, the instructor, virtual office hours, and perhaps a graphic. When you are finished, save the file as a publication, and then, on the File menu, choose Create Web Site from Current Publication. Choose Yes to run the design checker when prompted. Publisher will convert overlapping text frames to graphics and warn of long downloading times. Choose to continue at each prompt. View the Web site with your browser.

**6** ▶▶▶ You currently are seeking employment in your field of study. You already have prepared a resume and would like to send it to a group of potential employers. You decide to design a cover letter to send with the resume. Obtain a recent newspaper and cut out five classified advertisements pertaining to your field of study. Create the cover letter for your resume as a main publication to merge with a data source. Be sure the cover letter has an attractive letterhead containing your name, address, and telephone number, as well as a logo from the Design Gallery. Use the information in the classified ads for the address list. Insert the personal information components as the inside mailing address underneath the letterhead. Create a large text frame for the body of your letter. Merge the letter with the address list and print all five copies. Turn in the want ads with your printouts.

**7** ▶▶▶ If Microsoft Access is installed on your system, you can use it to create a data source and then merge that file with a publication. Start Access and then create the table in Project 4 on page PUB 4.46 as an Access database table. You may need to use Help in Access to assist you in the procedure for creating and saving a database that contains a table. Quit Access. Start Publisher. Open an envelope wizard of your choice. Begin the mail merge process as discussed in Project 4. When specifying the data source, change the file type to MS Access Database and then click the database name of the file you created in Access. Insert the fields from the data source in the mailing address text frame. Print the merged envelopes.

Microsoft Publisher 2000

PROJECT

5

# Creating Business Forms and Tables

You will have mastered the material in this project when you can:

- List common business forms
- Create an invoice template
- Compare the Select All command to the Pointer Tool
- Move objects incrementally with the Nudge command
- Format drop caps
- Identify tools on the ruler
- Set a tab stop
- Define the difference between tab and indent
- Insert the system date
- Create and format tables
- Navigate through table cells to enter data
- Merge cells and insert a cell diagonal
- Use the Fill command
- Insert columns and rows in a table
- Attach a publication to an e-mail message
- Understand electronic forms
- Insert a Web masthead
- Insert a hot spot
- Insert Web form controls
- Align objects

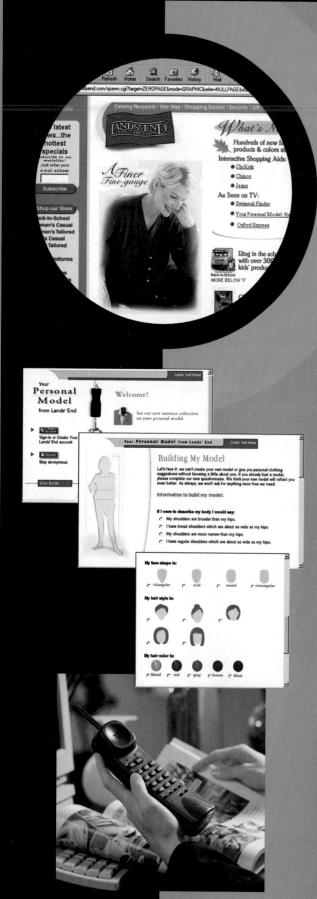

# Put the Shirt on Your Back

## Shop Online with a Personal Model

S hop 'til you drop has a new connotation in today's virtual world of e-commerce. Shopping on the Internet for everything from vitamins to cream puffs can be a piece of cake.

Things can be a bit more complicated, however, when it comes to buying clothes on the Net. After all, you cannot try on a pair of jeans or see if a green sweater clashes with your red hair when you are shopping online. This logistical problem can be frustrating to shoppers who are expected to spend $13 billion online for apparel by 2003.

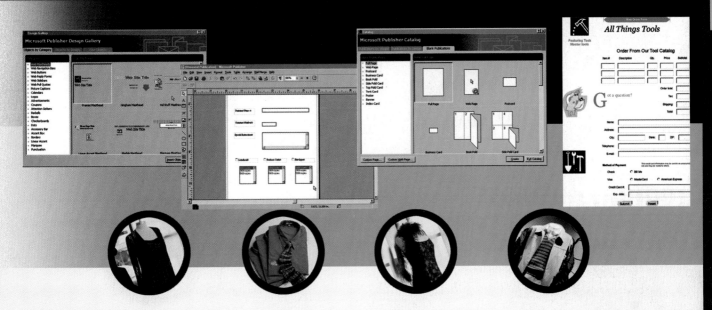

Lands' End has come up with a solution to these virtual shopping woes. This Wisconsin-based direct merchant of traditional, casual clothes has developed Your Personal Model, a personalized 3-D representation of female customers that selects the most flattering clothes for their figures, suggests specific outfits for various occasions, and provides an online dressing room to try on the garments.

Shoppers begin their Your Personal Model shopping adventure by answering several questions regarding their physical features. For example, they select specific skin tones, face shapes, hairstyles, and hair colors. They then give their models a name, save their profiles for future shopping sprees, and proceed to the Welcome Page.

At this point, their models appear along with custom outfits designed for their bodies and for their lifestyles. The site might suggest women with broad shoulders and hips wear gray Chinos and a beige sweater set for a casual workplace and a simple black knit dress for an informal weekend party.

The next step is to take these garments to The Dressing Room. There, the shoppers can view the particular clothes on their models. They even can mix and match outfits and change colors. The site gives advice on choosing the proper size and then places the items in the customers' virtual shopping carts.

Ordering is easy. If they use Your Personal Model, the contents of their shopping carts

display automatically in an order form. Otherwise, they can use the table found in the Lands' End Intelligent Order Blank and input an item number in each table row and then indicate size, color, quantity, and the desire for a monogram or a gift box.

Likewise, you will create a form in this Publisher project that allows customers of a small business to reorder supplies online. The reorder form contains text boxes, check boxes, and list boxes to facilitate ordering. In addition, you will create the Web page where clients can use the automated ordering process. Using the Design Gallery, you will select the appropriate masthead and then insert the company logo. Then, you will publish the page to the World Wide Web.

Gary C. Comer, an avid sailor and advertising copywriter, founded Lands' End in 1961 in Chicago to sell sailing equipment and hardware via a catalog. In the 1970s, the company's focus switched to clothing. Today, Lands' End features apparel for men, women, and children, along with luggage and home furnishings. It is the second largest apparel mail-order company with sales of more than $1.37 billion to its 6.1 million customers. The Lands' End Web site (www.landsend.com) was unveiled in 1995 and receives 15 million visitors yearly.

*Fortune* magazine has included Lands' End in its Top 100 Best Companies to Work For list. Indeed, these employees' efforts can help you shop online to your heart's content.

Microsoft **Publisher 2000**

# Microsoft Publisher 2000

# Creating Business Forms and Tables

P R O J E C T

5

CASE PERSPECTIVE

CopyCat Creations has hired you to work 20 hours a week to design in-house business forms, as well as to provide customer publishing support. You already have designed the letterhead, business cards, envelopes, and labels for this small business that specializes in printing and duplicating. The company has begun to acquire business from the local university and area merchants. CopyCat Creations now needs an invoice template and a fax cover.

Tony Manderino, office manager, has been working with several repeat customers who would like to automate their reordering process for quicker turnaround and delivery. You decide to present him with a sample Web reorder form. Mr. Manderino also wants you to send him a copy of the work schedule for the month of April, via e-mail, as soon as you finish it.

You decide to use CopyCat Creations' personal information set and Publisher wizards to design the business forms, and the table feature to create a work schedule. Publisher's Web Form Control contains the types of Web objects you will need to make a presentation to Mr. Manderino. Customers are waiting!

## Introduction

Computers commonly are used to produce modern business forms, such as invoices, statements, purchase orders, expense reports, fax covers, time records, and inventory lists. Not only do computers make it easy to maintain a consistent look and style for business forms, but they update and manipulate the forms more quickly and inexpensively than manual processing. Some of Publisher's forms typical to business applications are defined below.

An **invoice** is an itemized list of goods or services, stating quantities, prices, fees, and other charges with a request for payment. Invoices usually accompany delivered orders; occasionally they are mailed to customers. A **statement** is a form sent to customers at regular intervals, displaying a compilation of invoices, charges, and payments. A formal request to buy a product from a vendor and bill it to a business account is called a **purchase order**. When employees travel or entertain for business purposes they prepare an **expense report** as a means of itemizing incurred business expenses for reimbursement. A **fax cover** is a cover sheet for a facsimile transmission to send images over telephone lines. Companies use **timecards** or time records to keep track of the exact time employees begin and end their workdays for payroll purposes. An **inventory list** may take any of several different forms, but usually includes fields for quantities, serial numbers, descriptions, warranties, and values.

## Project Five — Creating Business Forms and Tables

Project 5 illustrates the generation of several business forms including an invoice, a fax cover, a work schedule, and a Web electronic order form as shown in Figure 5-1.

**(a) Work Schedule Table**

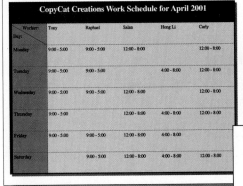

**(b) Electronic Order Form**

**(d) Fax Cover**

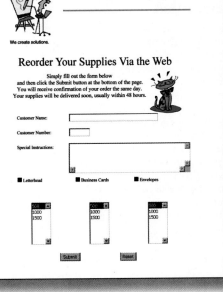

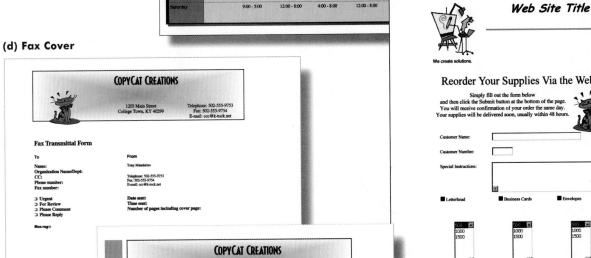

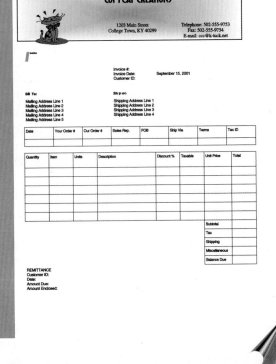

**More About 2000**

## Firsts in Desktop Publishing

The first author to submit a typewritten manuscript to a publisher was Mark Twain. He typed his book, *The Adventures of Huckleberry Finn*, on a Linotype machine in 1885. Unfortunately, even after investing several thousands of dollars in the Linotype technology, the invention of the typewriter quickly made it obsolete. Mark Twain lost money on the Linotype, but Huck Finn is here to stay.

**(c) Invoice**

**FIGURE 5-1   Business Forms**

The invoice and fax cover will print on the letterhead created in Project 4, as templates with fields for individualizing the customer data and charges. The work schedule is a formatted table to display the days of the week and employee hours. The order form is a Web page for repeat customers to order typical supplies, quickly and easily.

## Starting Publisher

Follow these steps to start Publisher or ask your instructor how to start Publisher for your system.

### TO START PUBLISHER

**1** Click the Start button on the taskbar.

**2** Point to Programs on the Start menu.

**3** Click Microsoft Publisher on the Programs submenu.

**4** If the Catalog dialog box does not display, click New on the File menu.

*Publisher displays the Catalog dialog box.*

# Creating an Invoice Template

Invoices come in a variety of styles and sizes. Some invoices are handwritten on generic invoice pads, while others may be multipart carbonless forms sold commercially. Most invoices have several things in common. First, they display the name of the company, its location, and contact information. Invoices generally include the creation date, an invoice number, and the name of the customer to whom the invoice is presented. Invoices may contain different addresses for billing and shipping. Finally, invoices display quantities, descriptions, prices, taxes, and totals.

While larger businesses may use accounting programs, point-of-sale terminals, or transaction processing systems to create invoices automatically from inventory databases or work records, smaller businesses that use a computer system to keep track of billing and customers usually generate invoices on an as-issued basis. That means that when a customer orders an item, an employee accesses an **invoice template** on the computer, filling in the parts of the invoice that change. Once saved, this data-enriched template becomes an **instance** of the invoice.

## Creating an Invoice Template

Using a Publisher Invoice wizard along with the letterhead and personal information set created in Project 4, you will create an invoice template for CopyCat Creations' employees to complete on the screen.

The Business Forms wizard creates a publication with company information and invoice objects. Because you want to copy only the invoice objects, you will use the SHIFT-click method to select the multiple company information objects and delete them. Then you can use the Select All command to copy the remaining invoice objects. The **Select All command** is an easy way to copy or move all the objects on a page from one location to another. You will copy the invoice object frames, as a group, and paste them onto the letterhead. If you did not complete Project 4, see your instructor for a copy of the letterhead file. Perform the following steps to create an invoice template.

**To Create an Invoice Template**

**①** **With the Catalog displayed, click Business Forms on the Publication by Wizard tab, and then click Invoice in the Business Forms list. Scroll to display the Straight Edge Invoice in the Invoice Business Forms pane. Point to Straight Edge Invoice.**

*The Catalog dialog box Invoice Business Forms display (Figure 5-2). Your previews of business forms may vary.*

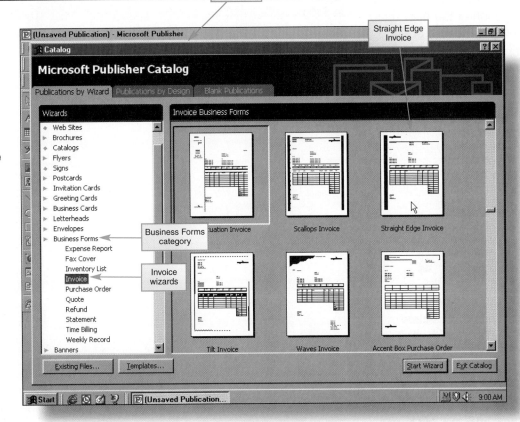

**FIGURE 5-2**

**②** **Double-click Straight Edge Invoice. When the Business Form Wizard displays, click its Finish button and then click the Hide Wizard button. If the Office Assistant displays, click Hide the Office Assistant on the Help menu. Point to the horizontal line near the top of the page.**

*The Straight Edge Invoice displays in the workspace (Figure 5-3).*

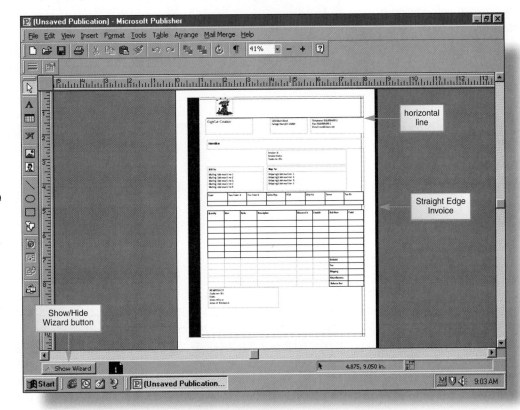

**FIGURE 5-3**

**3** **Click the horizontal line. SHIFT-click the logo above the line. Then, SHIFT-click each of the three personal information components at the top of the page.**

*The five objects display selected (Figure 5-4). Your publication may display a different logo.*

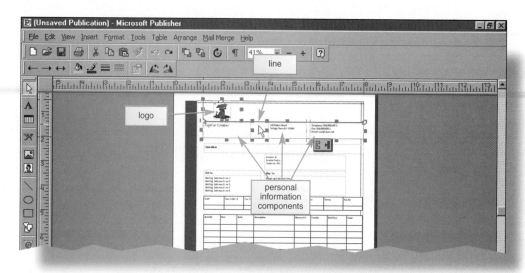

FIGURE 5-4

**4** **Right-click the selected objects, and then click Delete Object on the shortcut menu. If a Publisher dialog box displays asking if you want to change to a design that does not include a logo, click the Yes button.**

*The invoice displays without the personal information at the top (Figure 5-5).*

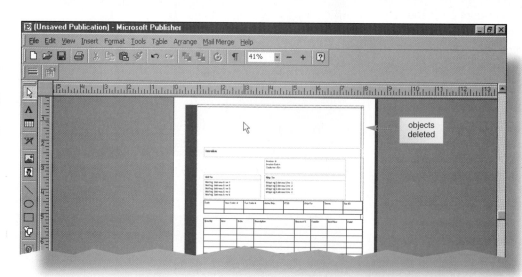

FIGURE 5-5

**5** **Click Edit on the menu bar and then point to Select All.**

*The Select All command is equivalent to SHIFT-clicking each individual object (Figure 5-6).*

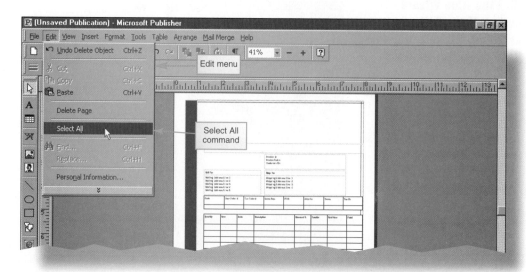

FIGURE 5-6

**6** **Click Select All, click the Group Objects button, and then point to the Copy button on the Standard toolbar.**

*The grouped object displays (Figure 5-7).*

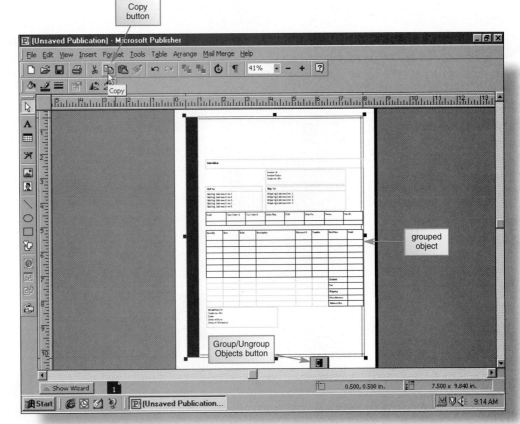

FIGURE 5-7

**7** **Click the Copy button. Insert your floppy disk from Project 4 into drive A and then point to the Open button on the Standard toolbar.**

*The grouped object is copied to the Clipboard in preparation for pasting onto the letterhead (Figure 5-8). If you did not complete Project 4, see your instructor for a copy of the letterhead file.*

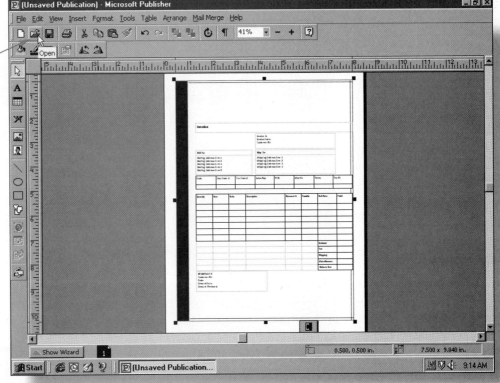

FIGURE 5-8

**8** Click the Open button. When the Open Publication dialog box displays, click the Look in box arrow, click 3½ Floppy (A:) in the Look in list and then point to the file name, CopyCat Letterhead.

*The list of files on drive A displays (Figure 5-9).*

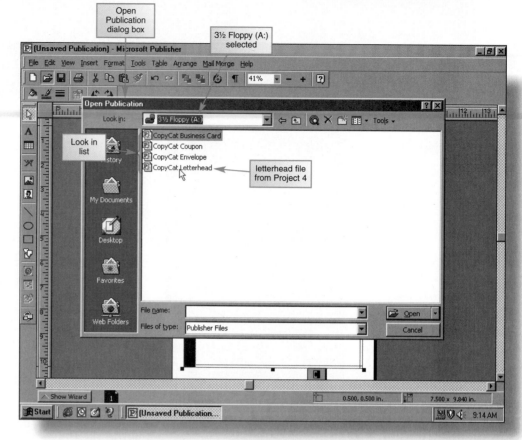

**FIGURE 5-9**

**9** Double-click CopyCat Letterhead. When a Publisher dialog box displays asking if you want to save the current publication, click the No button. When the letterhead displays, point to the Paste button on the Standard toolbar.

*Publisher displays the CopyCat Letterhead file in the workspace (Figure 5-10).*

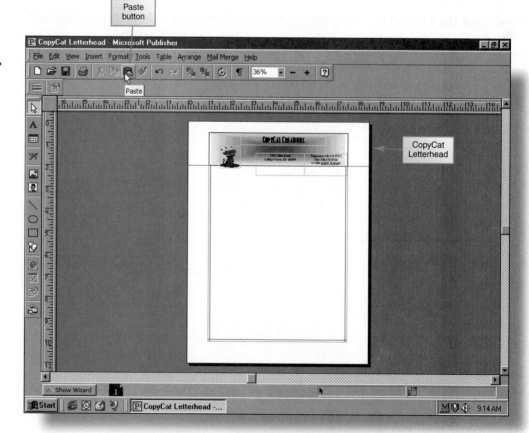

**FIGURE 5-10**

**Click the Paste button.**

*The grouped object displays in the publication (Figure 5-11). Your grouped object may paste to a slightly different position depending on your monitor.*

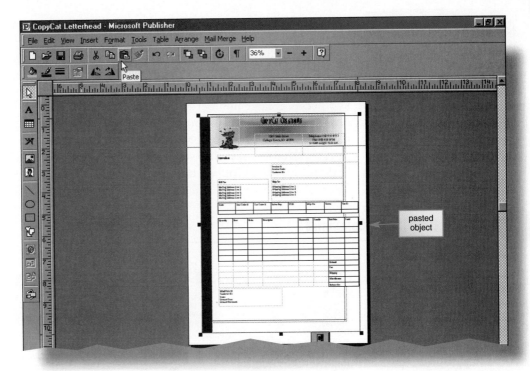

pasted object

**FIGURE 5-11**

Automating business forms such as invoices and monthly statements can be expedited even further by merging. As you learned in Project 4, Publisher's capability of using an external data source can facilitate the processing of standard forms and letters. If a company uses a database such as Microsoft Access to store charges, they can merge the business form with the data source. Field codes corresponding to those in the database can be inserted into the appropriate text frames, then all the forms will be updated, computerizing the process even more.

# Formatting the Invoice Template

Formatting the invoice template involves positioning the grouped object higher on the page, making the word, Invoice, more prominent, and inserting a date. In the next sequence of steps, you will learn how to move objects using the Nudge command. Then, you will create a large dropped initial capital letter called a drop cap. Finally, you will create a tab stop to position a formatted date field that automatically updates each time you open the publication.

## Using the Nudge Command

Recall that many ways exist to move objects to exact places within a publication depending on the object and the specifics of the resizing or moving needs. You learned how to use the sizing handles and the Mover when you want to drag an object to a general location or snap an object to a guide. You learned how to use the Size and Position command when you can identify the width, height, and location in inches. Then, in Project 4, you used the Measurements toolbar to set the angle of rotation and character spacing in combination with the measurements of an object.

---

**Other Ways**

1. To delete, press DELETE
2. To open, press CTRL+O
3. To group, press CTRL+SHIFT+G
4. To copy and paste, press CTRL+C, press CTRL+V

**More About**

## Customizing Color Schemes

Not only can you select a color scheme for each personal information set, you also can create an unlimited number of new color schemes and name them for future use. On the Format menu, click Color Scheme. In the Available schemes list, click the standard color scheme you want to start with, and then click the Custom tab. Create a custom scheme by changing one or several of the colors in the New boxes and then click the Save Scheme button. If you open a publication from an earlier version of Publisher, Publisher can save the colors on the publication as a custom color scheme.

**Zooming**

You can type any number between 10 and 400 in the Zoom box on the Standard toolbar.

One final way to position objects, by moving them in small increments, is to use the **Nudge command**. All objects display on a monitor using patterns of lighted dots. Each lighted dot is called a picture element, or **pixel**. The **resolution**, or clarity, of an object is related directly to the number of pixels the monitor can display and the distance between each pixel. Pixels can vary in size from one type of monitor to another. A greater number of pixels per inch results in a higher resolution. The Nudge command moves an object one pixel at a time — a smaller unit than is allowed by any of the other positioning methods.

Perform the following step using the Nudge command with directional arrow keys to move the grouped object closer to the letterhead banner.

 **To Use the Nudge Command**

**1** **With the grouped object still selected, press and hold the ALT key and then press the UP ARROW key several times. Press ALT + the appropriate arrow key to move the black rectangle approximately one pixel left of the letterhead banner.**

The grouped object displays aligned on the top of the letterhead banner and slightly to the left (Figure 5-12). Notice that the selected object moves a small increment each time you press the ALT+ARROW key.

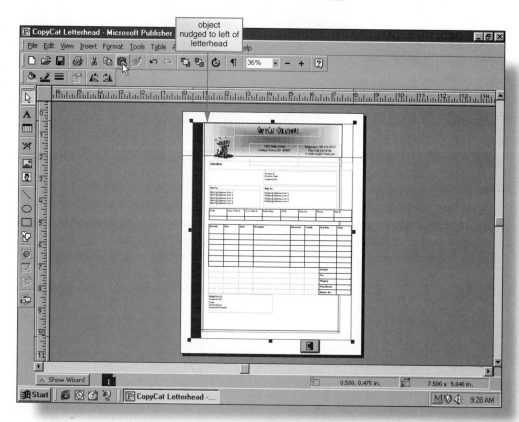

**FIGURE 5-12**

1. On Arrange menu click Nudge

Most monitors can display the screen image at various pixel resolutions. The most common resolutions are 640 by 480, 800 by 600, and 1024 by 768 pixels. Many people prefer a screen resolution of at least 800 by 600 when working with desktop publishing and graphics programs. At 100% magnification, on an **SVGA** (super video graphics array) device, with a monitor resolution of 800 by 600, a pixel is approximately 0.01 inch. Note that the distance a pixel represents increases as you zoom in closer, which means that the Nudge command will represent a smaller movement at higher magnifications.

## Using a Drop Cap

A dropped capital letter, or **drop cap,** is a decorative large initial capital letter extending down below the other letters in the line. A drop cap displays larger than the rest of the characters in the line or paragraph and commonly is used to mark the beginning of an article or text frame. If the text wraps to more than one line, the paragraph typically wraps around the dropped capital letter. You can format up to 15 contiguous letters and spaces as drop caps at the beginning of each paragraph.

Perform the following steps to create a dropped capital letter I in the word, Invoice, and to change the rectangle color to match.

 *Steps*

## To Format with a Drop Cap

**1** **Click the text, Invoice, below the logo and then press the F9 key to increase the magnification. Click Format on the menu bar and then point to Drop Cap.**

*The Format menu displays (Figure 5-13).*

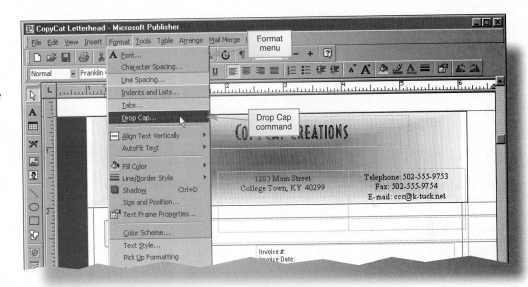

**FIGURE 5-13**

**2** **Click Drop Cap. When the Drop Cap dialog box displays, if necessary, click the Drop Cap tab. In the Available drop caps list, scroll and then point to a drop cap style with an italicized orange I.**

*The Available drop caps list displays using colors from the color scheme of the publication (Figure 5-14). Your list may vary.*

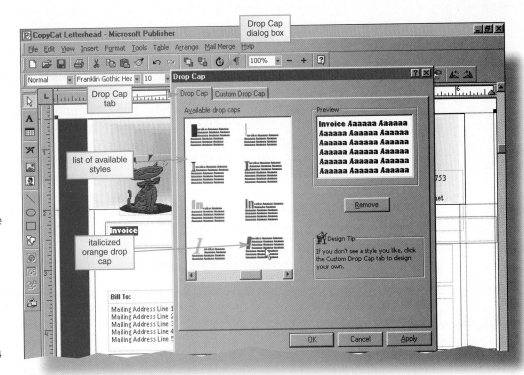

**FIGURE 5-14**

**3** **Double-click the italicized orange drop cap style. Click the black rectangle, click the Fill Color button, and then click Accent 3 (Orange).**

*The word Invoice displays with an orange drop cap that matches the color of the rectangle (Figure 5-15).*

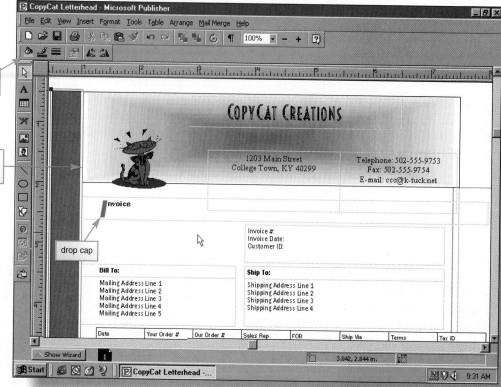

FIGURE 5-15

**Commercial Printing Tools**

On the Tools menu, the Commercial Printing Tools submenu gives you four commands to assist you in preparing your publication for outside printing. **Color Printing** allows you to select a color-printing scheme such as RGB or spot color. **Graphics Manager** gives commercial printers comprehensive information about every graphical component in a publication. You can change the status of an image from embedded to linked, allowing the printer to enhance images while retaining the integrity of the original graphic. **Trapping** allows you to set the percentages and color thresholds for trapping objects. You can choose general settings for the publication or Per Object Trapping. **Fonts** can be completely embedded or subsetted for the commercial printer.

Publisher allows you to tailor the capital letter's appearance, formatting its font, style, color, and size using the **Custom Drop Cap tab** in the Drop Cap dialog box. You also may specify the number of lines to wrap in front of the drop cap. When you create a custom drop cap, the custom style is added to the Available drop caps list in the Drop Cap sheet. You can use this style to create other drop caps in the current publication. Another option is to use an **Up cap**, which extends above the paragraph, rather than sinking into the first few lines of the text.

Drop caps deserve special consideration if you are sending the file to a commercial printer. A file prepared for commercial submission includes all fonts from the publication. If you use only a small number of characters from a font, as in drop caps or for headlines, you can have Publisher embed only the characters you used from the font. Embedding only part of a font is called **subsetting**. The advantage of font subsetting is that it decreases the overall size of your file. The disadvantage is that it limits the ability to make corrections at the printing service. If your printing service does not have the full font installed on its computer, corrections can be made using only the characters included in the subset. Using the Fonts command on the Format menu, you are able to turn on font subsetting so that all the fonts you use in your publication will be subsetted when you embed them.

## Working with Tabs and Markers

To make the invoice template as user-friendly as possible, it is important to help the user enter data in the correct places as much as you can. Text frames with exact margin settings help the user identify where to place the text as well as the typical length of the entry. One way to position the insertion point inside the text frame, at the correct spot, is with **tabs**. The ruler contains several tools to help you set text frame margins, indents, and tabs. Table 5-1 explains the functions of the tools displayed in Figure 5-16 and how to change them.

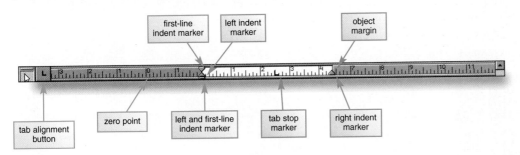

**FIGURE 5-16**

| Table 5-1 | Ruler Tools | | |
|---|---|---|---|
| **TOOL NAME** | **DESCRIPTION** | **HOW TO CHANGE** | **OTHER WAYS** |
| First-line indent marker | The position at which paragraphs begin | Drag to desired location | On Format menu click Indents and Lists |
| Left and first-line indent marker | A small rectangle used to move both markers at once | Drag to desired location | On Format menu click Indents and Lists |
| Left indent marker | The left position at which text will align in a paragraph | Drag to desired location | On Format menu click Indents and Lists |
| Object margins | Gray indicates the area outside the object margin; white indicates the area inside the object margin | Resize object | On Format menu click Text Frame properties |
| Right indent marker | The right position at which text wraps to the next line | Drag to desired location | On Format menu click Indents and Lists |
| Move Both Rulers button (tab alignment button) | Displays the current alignment setting: left, right, center, or leader | Click to toggle choice | Double-click tab stop marker |
| Tab stop marker | Displays the location of a tab stop | Click to create; drag to move | On Format menu click Tabs |
| Zero point | A ruler setting commonly used to measure distances from the upper-left corner of a page or object | SHIFT+right-click ruler at desired location | SHIFT+right-drag to move both horizontal and vertical zero points |

The triangles and rectangles on the ruler are called **markers**. You drag markers to any place on the ruler within the object margin. You can click a marker to display a dotted line through the publication to see in advance where the marker is set. Markers are paragraph-specific, which means that the tabs and indents apply to the whole paragraph. If you are typing a long passage of text, pressing the ENTER key carries forward the paragraph formatting.

Recall that the Show Special Characters button (Figure 5-17 on the next page) on the Standard toolbar makes visible special nonprinting characters to help you format text passages, including tab characters, paragraph marks, and end-of-frame marks.

Perform the steps on the next page to add a tab stop to the text frame that contains the Invoice #, Invoice Date, and Customer ID. A **tab stop** will ensure that the data is properly aligned when entered by the user.

**To Insert a Tab Stop for the Date**

**1** **Click the text frame that contains Invoice #, Invoice Date, and Customer ID. Press CTRL+A to select all the text. Click the Show/Hide Special Characters button on the Standard toolbar. Point to the 1.25″ position on the Horizontal Ruler.**

*The paragraph marks display in the text frame (Figure 5-17). Each line of this text frame is a paragraph. The end-of-frame markers display as embellished circles.*

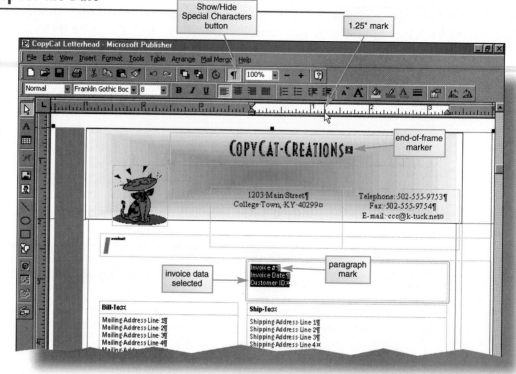

**FIGURE 5-17**

**2** **Click the Horizontal Ruler at the 1.25″ position. Click outside the selected area to remove the highlight and then click just to the left of the paragraph mark in the first line. Press the TAB key. Repeat the process to insert a tab stop in the other two lines of the text frame.**

*The tab stop marker displays on the Horizontal Ruler, and the nonprinting tab characters display in each line to indicate the position of the tab stop (Figure 5-18). Removing the highlight returns the mouse pointer to an I-beam, making it easier to edit text.*

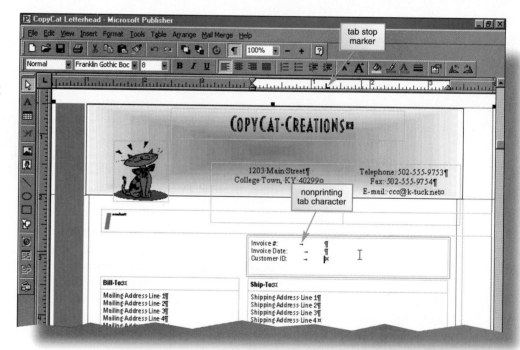

**FIGURE 5-18**

**Other Ways**

1. Double-click Horizontal Ruler
2. Right-click text frame, point to Change Text on shortcut menu, click Tabs on Change Text submenu
3. On Format menu click Tabs

Sometimes it is difficult to determine whether to use tab stops or indents. Use **tab stops** when you want to indent paragraphs as you go or when you want a simple column. You may want to tab the first line in a single paragraph, or add leaders (dots or dashes), as in a table of contents. Using the TAB key to indent the first line of each paragraph in a long passage of text is inefficient, however, because you must press it each time you begin a new paragraph. In those cases, it is better to use an **indent** because it automatically carries forward when you press the ENTER key. Use indents when you want the lines in a paragraph to be automatically adjusted for you, or when you want to indent all the lines in a paragraph without inserting tab stops at the beginning of each line.

The final step to format the Invoice template is to add a date that updates automatically each time you open the template.

## Inserting the System Date

When creating an invoice, the date is an important piece of information. To always print the correct date, and to save time and keystrokes each time you create an instance of the invoice, you will create a field that Publisher will update from the operating system. As part of its system administration functions, Windows keeps track of the date and time using a battery inside the processing unit. Besides the internal needs of the operating system to monitor performance, this date and time can be used by application software, not only to track the date and time of file creation and modification, but as an accessible field of information. Most Windows application software packages, including Publisher, can access the **system date and time** in order to display the current data as fixed text or to create an automatically updating field. That way, each time you access the file, the date will be correct.

### The Tabs Dialog Box

When you are editing a text frame or table, the Format menu contains a Tabs command to display a Tabs dialog box. You can use the Tabs dialog box to change an existing tab stop's alignment or position. You also can place leader characters in the empty space occupied by the tab. Leader characters such as a series of dots, often are used in a table of contents to precede the page number. Simply click the desired leader in the Leader area of the Tabs dialog box.

 **To Insert a System Date**

**1** Click just to the left of the paragraph mark on the Invoice Date line. Click Insert on the menu bar and then point to Date and Time (Figure 5-19).

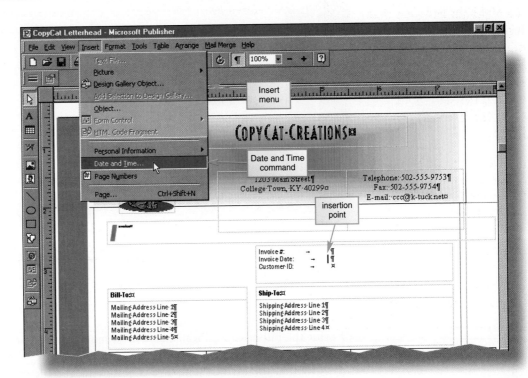

**FIGURE 5-19**

**2** **Click Date and Time. When the Date and Time dialog box displays, click the format, January 24, 2001 (or the current date on your screen). If necessary, click Update automatically to select the check box. Point to the OK button.**

*The Date and Time dialog box displays (Figure 5-20). Your screen most likely will not show January 24, 2001; instead, it will display the current system date stored in your computer according to the highlighted format.*

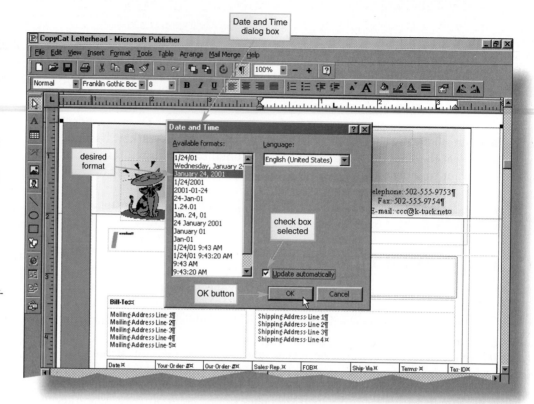

FIGURE 5-20

**3** **Click the OK button.**

*Publisher displays the current system date (Figure 5-21).*

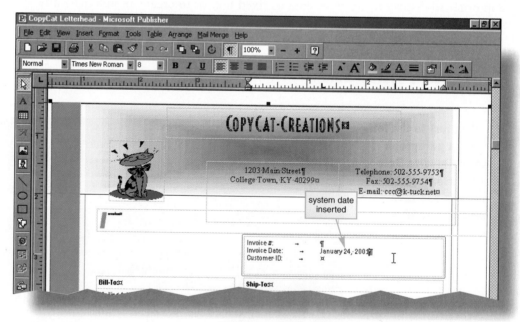

FIGURE 5-21

You may insert a system date, a system time, or both in a text frame or table cell. In addition, you can determine the language and format you want. When you open or print the publication, Publisher will update the date or time you inserted to reflect the current date or time.

Now that the invoice template is complete, the file can be used to generate instances on an as-needed basis. Complete the following steps to save and print the invoice template.

## Saving and Printing the Invoice Template

To maintain a clean letterhead file and to create a template for daily use, you should save this file with a different name. For a detailed explanation of the procedure summarized below, refer to pages PUB 1.26 through PUB 1.28 in Project 1.

### TO SAVE AND PRINT THE INVOICE TEMPLATE

**1** Insert a floppy disk into drive A.

**2** Click File on the menu bar and then click Save As.

**3** When the Save As dialog box displays, type CopyCat Invoice Template to replace the previous name in the File name text box. Do not press the ENTER key.

**4** If necessary, click the Save in box arrow and then click 3½ Floppy (A:).

**5** Click the Save button in the Save As dialog box.

**6** Click the Print button on the Standard toolbar.

*Publisher saves the publication on a floppy disk in drive A with the file name, CopyCat Invoice Template, and then prints a copy on the printer. The completed invoice template is shown in Figure 5-1 on page PUB 5.5.*

# Creating a Fax Cover

A **facsimile**, or **fax**, is an image or document transmitted and received over telephone lines. A fax either is created on a computer and sent with a modem and fax software, or on stand-alone machines the image is scanned optically and converted into digitized data. Most people include a **fax cover**, or **cover page**, to identify the sender, receiver, date, telephone/fax numbers, and the number of pages. Some fax covers include a short message about the contents of the fax. When companies receive a fax, the fax cover quickly identifies for whom the fax is intended and how many incoming pages accompany the cover.

Publisher is a good tool for creating a business form such as a fax cover for several reasons. Fax covers can be filled out on the screen and either printed or sent directly to the fax modem. Like the previous invoice, Publisher provides the flexibility of tailoring the fax cover with information specific to a company — such as business hours, days of the week, and information sets — then using it as a template over and over again. Multiple generic copies can be produced inexpensively both for customers and for employees to fill out when sending a fax. Finally, Publisher's merging capabilities can pull the information from most databases automatically and produce fax covers to each address in a data source, if so desired.

## Creating a Fax Cover Using the Business Form Wizard and Pointer Tool

The fax cover, like the invoice in this project, is a compilation of the company letterhead and a Publisher wizard. This time, however, you will use the Pointer Tool button on the Objects toolbar to select objects from the fax cover created by the wizard. Recall that you have used the SHIFT-click method to select multiple objects and the Select All command to select every object in the publication. The **Pointer Tool button** on the Objects toolbar allows you to draw a box around specific objects you want to select together or group. The Pointer Tool is the same as the mouse pointer when no other Objects toolbar button has been selected, making it simple to use. Dragging the mouse creates a selection box on the screen. Releasing the mouse button selects all the objects inside the box, as you will see in the steps on the next page.

### More About

### Entering Two-Digit Years

If you choose a date format that displays only a two-digit year, be careful. Dates entered as 00 through 29 are interpreted as the years 2000 through 2029. Two-digit years entered as 30 through 99 are interpreted as 1930 through 1999. Should you later change the date format, you could be displaying a date that is 100 years off.

### More About

### Special Characters

Tab characters, paragraph marks, end-of-frame and end-of-story marks, some special hyphens, and space marks are special characters that can be displayed on your screen, but not printed in your publication.

### More About

### Firsts in Desktop Publishing

The first author to submit a manuscript electronically was Arthur C. Clarke. In 1968, he wrote *2001– A Space Odyssey* using a word processing package named WordStar on a Kaypro microcomputer. He submitted a disk to the publisher, and Hal 9000 became history.

**Microsoft Publisher 2000**

## Steps: To Select Objects Using the Pointer Tool

**1** Click File on the menu bar and then click New. When the Catalog displays, click Business Forms in the Wizards pane and then click Fax Cover. If necessary, scroll down and then point to the Accessory Bar Fax Cover preview in the Fax Cover Business Forms pane.

*The Catalog dialog box and Fax Cover Business Forms display (Figure 5-22). Your list may differ.*

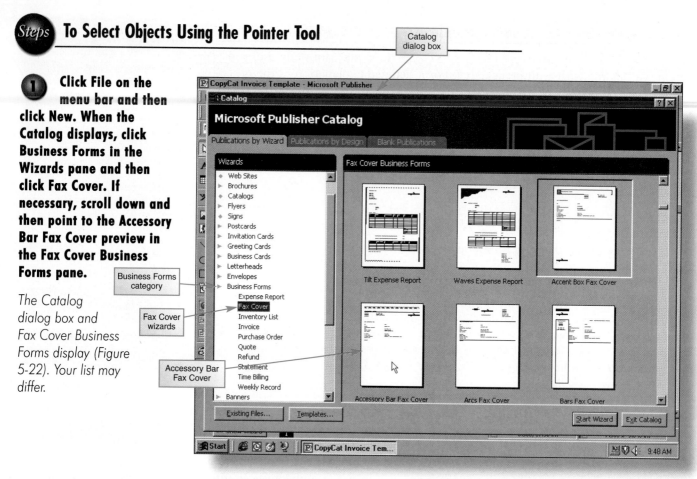

**FIGURE 5-22**

**2** Double-click Accessory Bar Fax Cover. When the publication displays, if necessary, click the Finish button in the Business Form Wizard, and then hide the wizard. Point to the margin above and to the left of the words, Fax Transmittal Form.

*Because you have not chosen any other object on the Objects toolbar, the Pointer Tool button is recessed (Figure 5-23). The mouse pointer displays as a left-pointing block arrow.*

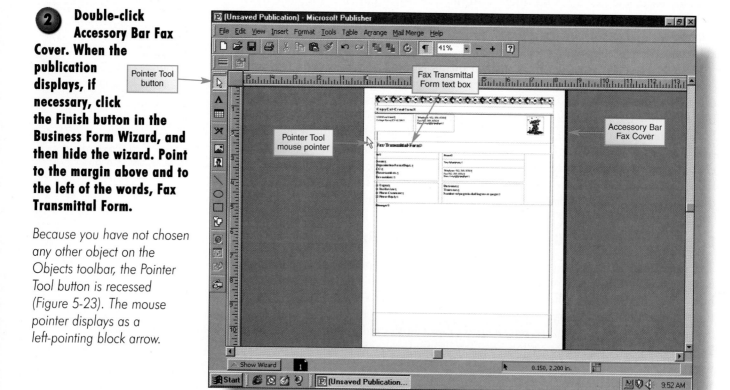

**FIGURE 5-23**

**3**  Diagonally drag down and to the right through the publication to include the entire large message text frame in the lower portion of the page. Release the mouse button. Point to the Copy button on the Standard toolbar.

*All the objects, from the Fax Transmittal Form text frame downward, display selected (Figure 5-24).*

**4** Click the Copy button.

*The objects are copied to the Clipboard.*

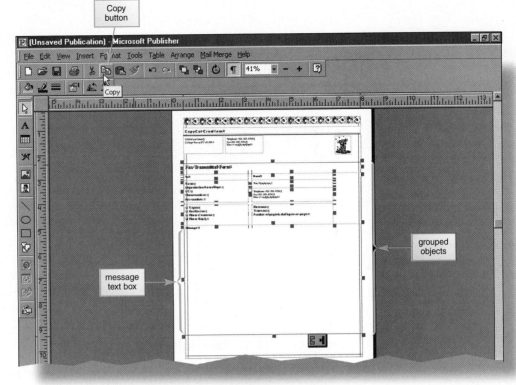

**FIGURE 5-24**

## Final Modifications of the Fax Cover

The final steps to complete the fax cover involve opening the letterhead, pasting the Wizard objects from the Clipboard, and then saving the fax cover as a template with a new name, just as you did with the invoice template.

### TO FINISH THE FAX COVER

**1** Click the Open button on the Standard toolbar. When the Open Publication dialog box displays, if necessary, click the Look in box arrow and click 3½ Floppy (A:).

**2** Double-click CopyCat Letterhead in the file list. When a Publisher dialog box displays asking if you want to save the current publication, click the No button.

**3** When the letterhead displays, click the Paste button on the Standard toolbar.

**4** Use the Nudge command to align the pasted objects at the left margin.

**5** Click File on the menu bar and then click Save As.

**6** When the Save as dialog box displays, type CopyCat Fax Cover in the File name text box. Do not press the ENTER key.

**7** If necessary, click the Save in box arrow and then click 3½ Floppy (A:).

**8** Click the Save button in the Save As dialog box.

**9** Click the Print button on the Standard toolbar.

*Publisher saves the publication on a floppy disk in drive A with the file name, CopyCat Fax Cover, and then prints a copy on the printer. The completed fax cover is shown in Figure 5-1 on page PUB 5.5.*

### File Attributes

The four accessibility attributes of a file in the Windows Operating System are Read-Only, Hidden, Archive, and System. **Read-Only** means the file cannot be changed or accidentally deleted. **Hidden** means that you cannot see or use the file unless you know its name. **System** indicates a system file, required by Windows to run properly. By default, system files are not shown in folder listings. Do not delete system files. The **Archive** option controls which files are backed up automatically in a complying application.

The fax cover is complete. You can protect this file and the invoice template file from accidental deletion, forcing users to save instances with a different name, by changing the **read-only attribute**. The Windows operating system provides a Properties command on every file's shortcut menu. If you want to protect the file, click the Read-only check box in the General sheet.

# Using Tables

You may recall that a Publisher table is a collection of rows and columns and that the intersection of a row and column is called a **cell**. Cells are filled with data.

Within a table, you easily can rearrange rows and columns, change column widths and row heights, and insert diagonal lines, pictures, and text. You can use the **Create Table command** to give the table a professional appearance. You can add a border to the entire table as well. For these reasons, many Publisher users create tables rather than using large text frames with tabs. Tables allow you to input data in columns as you would for a schedule, price list, a resume, or a table of contents.

### Creating a Work Schedule Table

Perform the following steps to draw the table for CopyCat Creations' work schedule and format it using the Create Table dialog box. The first step is to draw an empty table in a blank publication with the **Table Frame Tool button** on the Objects toolbar. You then will add a **shadow** to the table to give it a three-dimensional look.

 **To Create a Table**

**1** **Click the New button on the Standard toolbar. If Publisher asks you to save the previous publication, click the No button. Click the Hide Wizard button on the status bar and then point to the Table Frame Tool button on the Objects toolbar.**

*A new publication displays in the workspace (Figure 5-25).*

**FIGURE 5-25**

**2** Click the Table Frame Tool button. Drag the cross hair mouse pointer from the upper-left portion of the publication downward and to the right until the created frame is approximately six inches square.

*The frame of the table displays before you release the mouse button (Figure 5-26).*

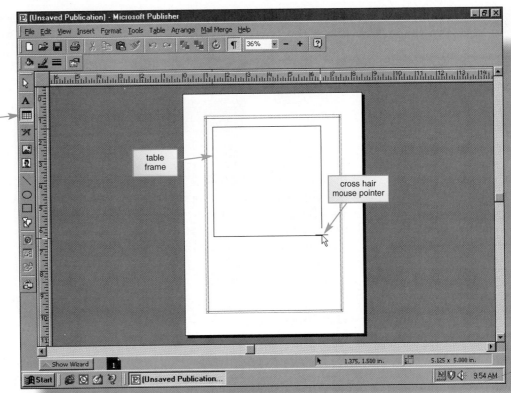

FIGURE 5-26

**3** Release the mouse button. When the Create Table dialog box displays, type 8 in the Number of rows box. Press the TAB key. Type 5 in the Number of columns box. Click the down scroll arrow in the Table format list box until List with Title 2 displays in the Table format list. Click List with Title 2 and then point to the OK button.

*The Create Table dialog box displays (Figure 5-27). The Table format list includes formats with and without titles.*

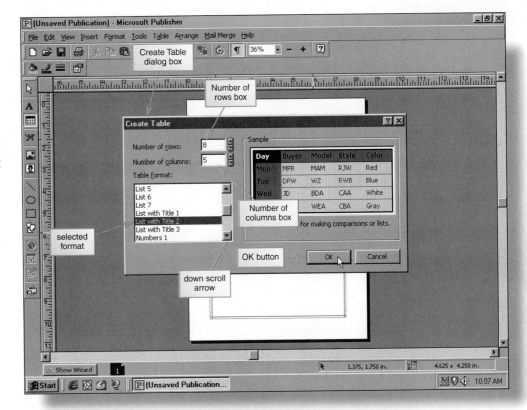

FIGURE 5-27

**4** **Click the OK button. Click the Zoom In button on the Standard toolbar twice. Press CTRL+D to add a shadow to the table.**

*The formatted table displays in the workspace (Figure 5-28).*

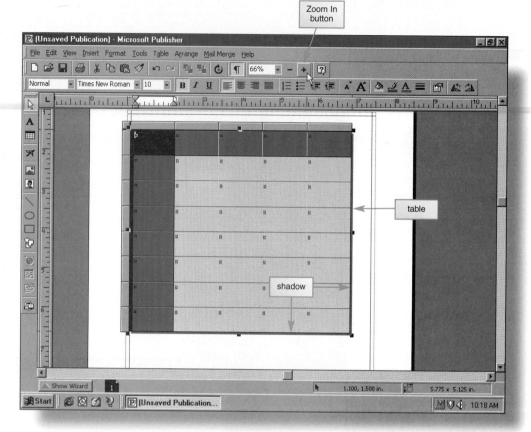

**FIGURE 5-28**

A table looks different from a text frame. When selected, Publisher tables display vertical and horizontal gray bars called **selector buttons** and light gray gridlines. The nonprinting gridlines display in the frame so you can see the rows and columns.

Tables are much like any other object in Publisher, except that each cell in a table is like a miniature text frame. Each cell is the same size, based on how large you draw the table, and how many rows and columns you choose. Cell heights automatically increase as inserted text wraps to the next line.

To format a table or data within a table, first you must select the cell(s) and then apply the appropriate formats. Table 5-2 describes techniques to select items in a table.

| Table 5-2 | Selecting Items in a Table |
|---|---|
| **ITEMS TO SELECT** | **ACTION** |
| Cell | Triple-click the cell or drag through the text |
| Column | Click the column's top selector button |
| Contiguous cells, rows, or columns | Drag through the cells, rows, or columns |
| Entire table | Click the table's corner selector button |
| Row | Click the row's left selector button |
| Text in next cell | Press the TAB key |
| Text in previous cell | Press the SHIFT+TAB keys |

## Merging Cells and Inserting a Cell Diagonal

The first row of the table will hold the title of the table. Publisher uses the **Merge Cells command** to create one large cell instead of several smaller ones.

The first cell in the second row will hold both the column heading and the row heading. Publisher uses the **Cell Diagonals command** to split the cell in half diagonally.

Perform the following steps to merge cells and create a cell diagonal.

**To Merge Cells and Create a Cell Diagonal**

**1** **Click the table to select it, and then click the left selector button for the first row. Click Table on the menu bar and then point to Merge Cells.**

*The Table menu displays, and the first row is selected (Figure 5-29).*

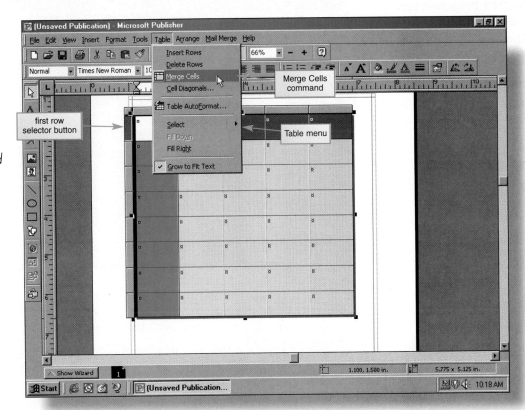

**FIGURE 5-29**

**2** **Click Merge Cells. Click the first cell in the second row. Click Table on the menu bar and then point to Cell Diagonals.**

*The first row displays as a single, large cell (Figure 5-30). The insertion point displays in the second row.*

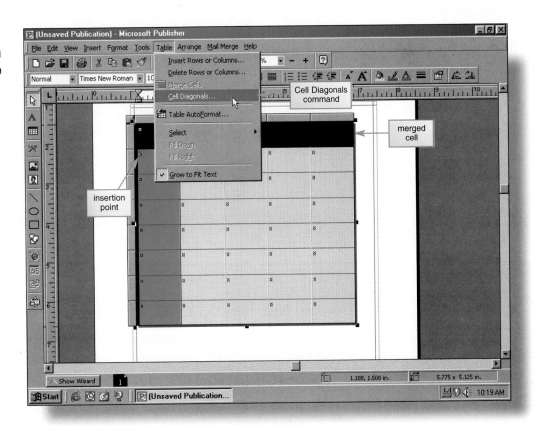

**FIGURE 5-30**

**3** **Click Cell Diagonals. When the Cell Diagonals dialog box displays, click Divide down, and then point to the OK button.**

*The Cell Diagonals dialog box displays (Figure 5-31). The Divide down option button is selected.*

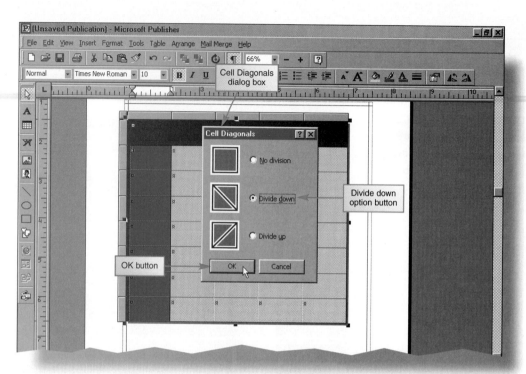

**FIGURE 5-31**

**4** **Click the OK button.**

*The cell is split into two cells with a diagonal line (Figure 5-32).*

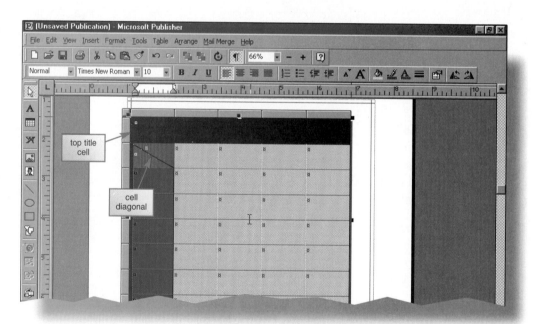

**FIGURE 5-32**

1. Right-click selected cells, point to Change Table on shortcut menu, click Merge Cells on Change Table submenu

## Entering Data into the Table

Efficiently navigating cells is an important skill when entering data into a table. To advance from one cell to the next, press the TAB key. To advance from one column to the next, also press the TAB key; do not press the ENTER key. The ENTER key is used to begin new paragraphs within a cell. To advance from one row to the next, press the DOWN ARROW key. Perform the following steps to enter the data into the table.

## TO ENTER DATA INTO A TABLE

**1** Click the top title cell of the table. Click the Center button on the Formatting toolbar. Click the Increase Font Size button on the Formatting toolbar five times. Type CopyCat Creations Work Schedule for April 2001 and then press the TAB key.

**2** Type Day: and then press the TAB key. Click the Bold button on the Formatting toolbar. Type Worker: and then press the TAB key.

**3** Continue to enter data as shown in Figure 5-33.

*The title, column headings, row headings, and Monday time periods display in the table (Figure 5-33).*

### The Ruler

When the insertion point is in a table, the ruler shows the boundaries of each column in the table. For example, in Figure 5-33, the first column displays a one-inch column width on the ruler.

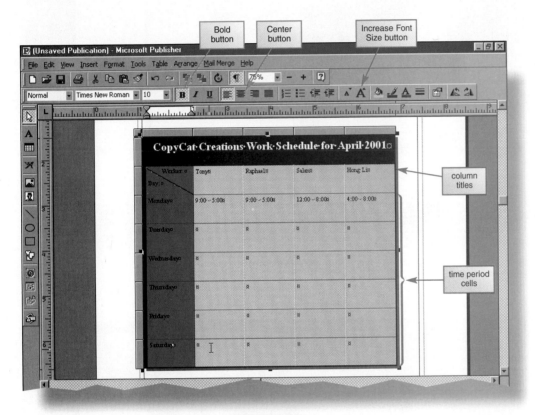

**FIGURE 5-33**

## Using the Fill Command

Publisher uses the Fill command to copy cell data quickly. Similar to the Fill command in spreadsheet applications, the **Fill command** in Publisher examines the contents of the first selected cell, and then copies the data to all other selected cells. You may Fill Down or Fill Right, depending upon the situation. Publisher's Fill command does not adjust the cells, create a series, or update relative references, as do most electronic spreadsheet programs; it simply is an extended copy command. As you will see in a following project about integration features, Publisher links or embeds worksheet tables that allow calculations and replications.

To edit a filled cell you may select the data or text in several different ways. Tabbing to an adjacent cell selects the whole cell automatically. You also can click the cell and press CTRL+A or the F8 key. Alternately, triple-clicking a cell selects all the text within it.

Perform the steps on the next page to use the Fill command and selection techniques to assist you in completing the table more efficiently.

**To Use the Fill Command**

**1** **Drag through the work schedule time cells for Tony.**

*The cells, including the first one with the data, are selected (Figure 5-34). You cannot use the selector button at the top of the column, because of the merged cell for the table title.*

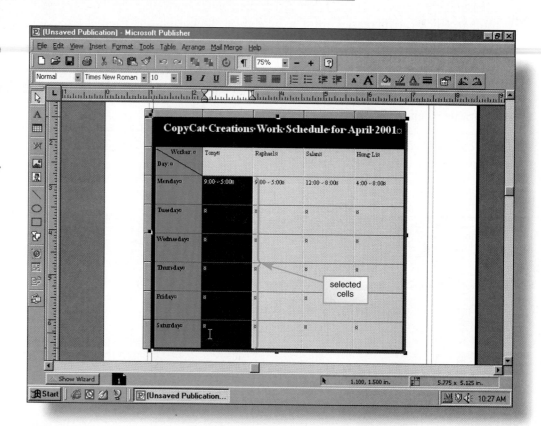

FIGURE 5-34

**2** **Click Table on the menu bar and then point to Fill Down.**

*The Table menu enables the Fill Down command when vertical cells are selected (Figure 5-35), or the Fill Right command when horizontal cells are selected.*

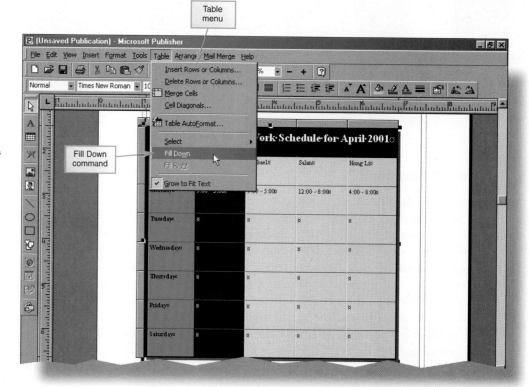

FIGURE 5-35

**3** **Click Fill Down.
Point to the
Saturday time cell for Tony.**

*The data is copied to the
adjacent cells (Figure 5-36).*

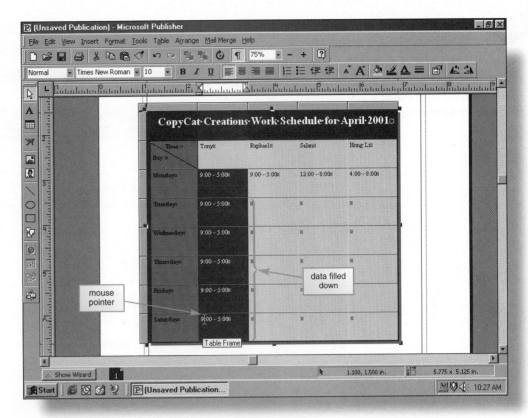

FIGURE 5-36

**4** **Triple-click the cell
for Tony on Saturday
and then press the DELETE
key.**

*The text no longer displays in
the cell (Figure 5-37).*

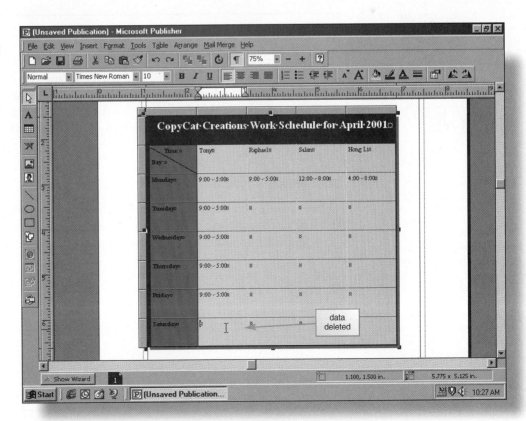

FIGURE 5-37

**5** Repeat Steps 1 through 4 to enter data for the other employees using the Fill Down command and the DELETE key as necessary.

*The completed table displays (Figure 5-38).*

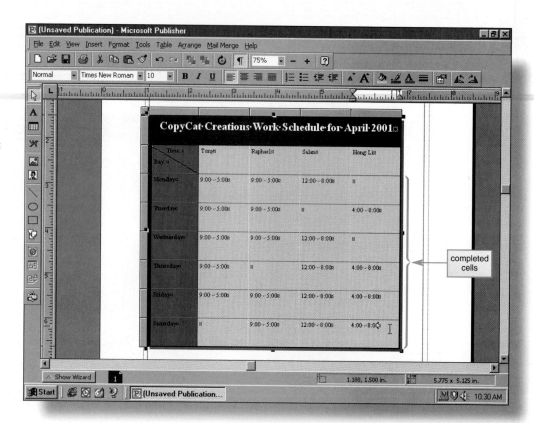

FIGURE 5-38

**Mouse Pointer Shapes**

The mouse pointer can change to one of more than fifteen different shapes. Besides the common I-beam, cross hair, and pointer, other mouse shapes such as the Resizer, the Mover, the Scissors, and the Rotator help you determine the possibilities for editing an object. You can turn these helpful mouse pointers on or off using the Options command on the Tools menu. See Appendix C, page PUB C.2 for more information.

The Fill command is faster than selecting a cell, clicking the Copy button, selecting the destination range of cells, and then clicking the Paste button. It is useful for contiguous copies and repetition across rows and columns in a table.

Editing data in a table involves deleting the text from a cell as you did in the previous steps, or manipulating an entire row or column, as you will see in the next series of steps.

### Inserting a Column

Sometimes you need to insert a row or column to display additional information. You can insert or delete entire rows or columns through the Table menu. Perform the following steps to insert a column in the work schedule table for a new employee.

## Steps To Insert a Column

**①** **Right-click any cell in the column with the heading Hong Li. Point to Change Table on the shortcut menu, and then point to Insert Rows or Columns on the Change Table submenu.**

*The Change Table submenu displays commands to insert and delete columns or rows (Figure 5-39).*

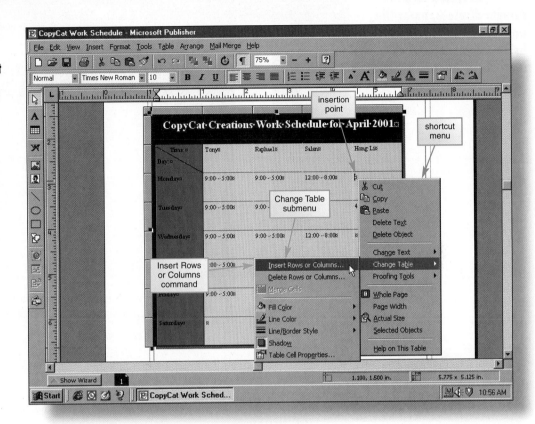

**FIGURE 5-39**

**②** **Click Insert Rows or Columns. When the Insert dialog box displays, click Columns and then click After selected cells. Point to the OK button.**

*Publisher will insert a column after the selected cell (Figure 5-40). The Number of columns text box displays a 1.*

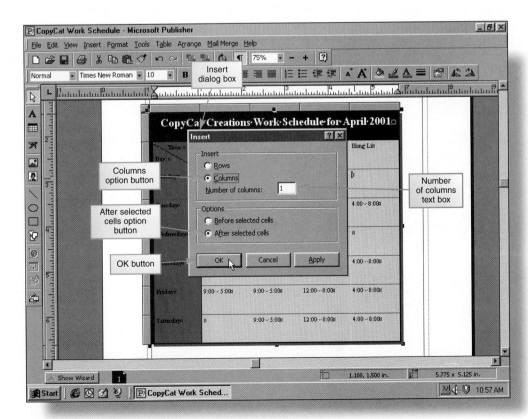

**FIGURE 5-40**

**3** **Click the OK button. When the new column displays, enter the data shown in Figure 5-41 using the techniques you learned in the previous steps.**

*The completed table displays (Figure 5-41).*

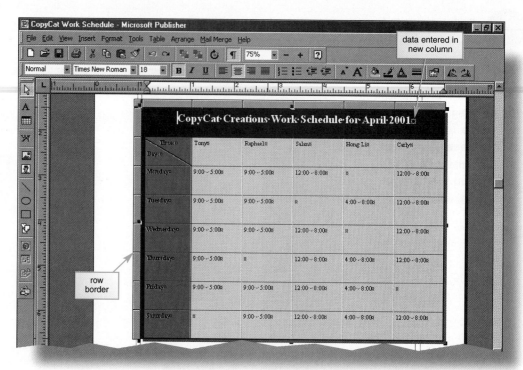

**FIGURE 5-41**

The Table menu contains a command called **Grow to Fit Text** (Figure 5-35 on page PUB 5.28) that displays a check mark when turned on. Table cells, except those diagonally split, automatically display all entered text if Grow to Fit Text is enabled. If you turn off the command, the table is locked and the extra text is stored in the cell's overflow area.

To resize manually the height of a row or the width of a column, you may point to a border in the gray selector buttons (Figure 5-41). When the Adjust mouse pointer displays, you may drag the column or row to the desired size.

### Saving the Table

Before sending a copy of the work schedule to the office manager, you should save the file by performing the following steps.

### TO SAVE AND PRINT THE WORK SCHEDULE TABLE

**1** Insert a floppy disk into drive A.

**2** Click File on the menu bar and then click Save As.

**3** When the Save As dialog box displays, type CopyCat Work Schedule in the File name text box. Do not press the ENTER key.

**4** Click the Save in box arrow and then click 3½ Floppy (A:).

**5** Click the Save button in the Save As dialog box.

**6** Click the Print button on the Standard toolbar.

*Publisher saves the publication on a floppy disk in drive A with the file name, CopyCat Work Schedule, and then prints a copy on the printer. The completed work schedule is shown in Figure 5-1 on page PUB 5.5.*

The final step is to send a copy of the work schedule in an e-mail message to the office manager.

# Attaching a Publication to an E-mail Message

E-mail messages by themselves have limited graphic capabilities, although that is beginning to change. As communication protocols and hardware improve, more and more formatting will be included in e-mail messages. Sending e-mail with attachments, however, is still the standard way to send documents and publications electronically with formatting and graphics. An **attachment** is a separate file electronically sent with a message to and from other computer users. A Publisher publication may be sent as an attachment for consultation purposes or when multiple employees work on the same publication. Many times publications are sent as attachments when forwarded to outside printing services.

Publisher's **Send command** automatically opens the system's preset e-mail software and creates an attachment of the current saved publication. Because Publisher is part of the Microsoft Office Suite of application software, the Send command usually activates an Outlook message. **Microsoft Outlook** is a **personal information management (PIM)** software package, integrated with Microsoft Office, which not only handles your e-mail, but also automates your desktop and communication, with tools for maintaining your appointment calendar, contacts, tasks, and notes. Some other examples of popular **e-mail handlers**, or electronic mail software packages, are **Microsoft Mail**, **Lotus cc:Mail**, and **Eudora**.

Most e-mail handlers — even on **intranets**, or internal networks — can send attachments. A few of the packages limit the file size of the attachments.

## Sending a Publisher File via E-mail

The following project steps direct you to send a message and attachment to the office manager. You may substitute your instructor's e-mail address if you actually want to send the message. Ask your instructor or network administrator for directions to complete these steps properly for your system. You can perform these steps, however, even if you have no Internet connection.

### Firsts in Desktop Publishing

UCLA Professor Leonard Kleinrock, sent the first electronic mail message in 1969 to a colleague at Stanford University. Today, Americans send more than 2.2 billion e-mail messages daily, as compared with fewer than 300 million pieces of first-class mail.

### E-mail

Several Web sites are available that allow you to sign up for free e-mail. For more information on signing up for free e-mail, visit the Publisher 2000 More About Web page (www.scsite.com/pub2000/ more.htm) and click Signing Up for E-mail.

## To Send a Publisher File via E-mail

**1 Click File on the menu bar and then point to Send.**

The File menu displays (Figure 5-42).

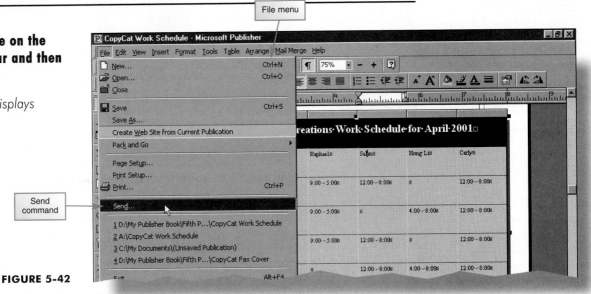

**FIGURE 5-42**

**2** **Click Send. If your system does not connect automatically to the Internet, a Choose Profile dialog box may display. If your system connects automatically to an intranet or the Internet, a password or login dialog box may display. Enter the required data and then click the OK button.**

*The Untitled - Message (Rich Text) window displays (Figure 5-43). Your system may display a different e-mail handler window.*

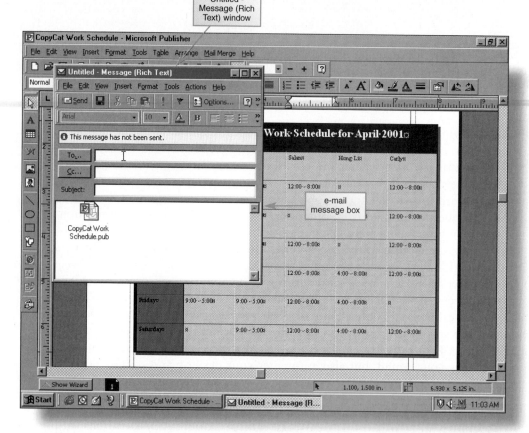

FIGURE 5-43

**3** **Type** Tony_ Manderino@ k-tuck.net **in the To text box. Press the TAB key twice or click in the Subject text box. Type** CopyCat Work Schedule **in the Subject text box. Press the TAB key or click in the message window.**

*The To and Subject text boxes display the entered data (Figure 5-44). You may use your instructor's e-mail address, if permitted. If a From text box displays, type your name or e-mail address in the text box.*

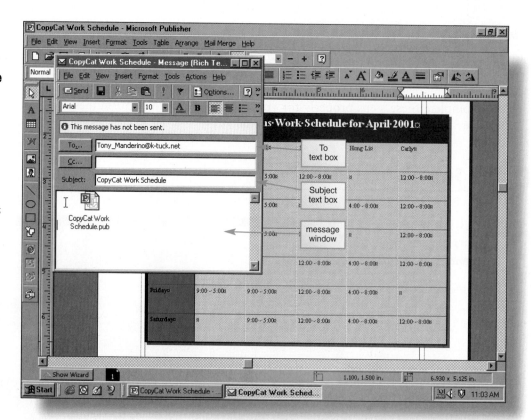

FIGURE 5-44

**4**  **Type** Dear Tony, **and then press the ENTER key. Type** Attached please find the work schedule you requested for April 2001. Let me know if you have any questions. **to complete the message. Point to the Send button.**

*The text will wrap to the next line and the **attachment icon** will move out of the way as you type (Figure 5-45).*

**5** **Click the Send button.**

*The message is sent with the attachment, and the publication again displays. If you were not connected to the Internet, the message is stored in Outlook's Outbox.*

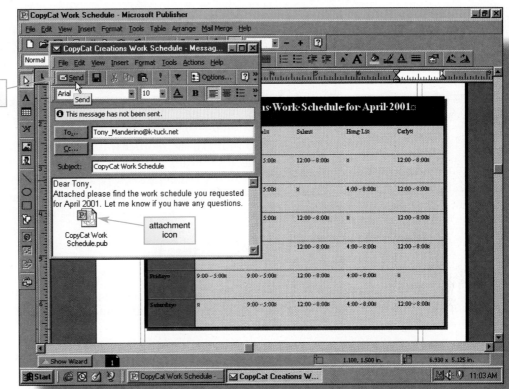

**FIGURE 5-45**

Multiple files can be attached to e-mail messages. Microsoft Office message windows contain an **Insert File button** on the Standard toolbar. When clicked, the Insert File button displays a dialog box that allows you to browse and select the file you want to attach. Additionally, Microsoft Office gives you the choice of either creating a file and then sending a message, or beginning with a message and then attaching a file.

# Web Pages with Electronic Forms

**Electronic commerce**, or **e-commerce**, has established itself in the business world as an inexpensive and efficient way to increase visibility and, therefore, sales. Customers visit, browse, make purchases, and ask for assistance at a Web Site, just as they would at a physical location.

An electronic form is used on a Web page to collect data from visitors. **Electronic forms** are used to request and collect information, comments, or survey data, and to conduct business transactions. An electronic form is made up of a collection of **form controls**, which are the individual buttons, boxes, and hyperlinks that let Web site visitors communicate with Web site owners. Electronic forms must include a submit button; otherwise Web site visitors cannot return their form data.

As e-commerce becomes more popular, desktop publishing theory must include electronic as well as print publishing concepts. Publisher's Design Gallery contains many electronic mastheads, navigation bars, Web buttons, and forms, designed to look good and load quickly on the Web. Additionally, the Form Object menu

*Other Ways*

1. To create new message, in Microsoft Outlook press CTRL+N
2. To attach new file, click Insert File button on Message window Standard toolbar

contains many features to assist in designing forms from scratch. Most desktop publishers use a combination of rapid form development techniques to tailor their Web site to suit their needs.

# Creating a Web Page from Scratch

You will create a sample Web reorder form in an effort to automate the company's reorder process. To make the reorder form display quickly, you will use a Design Gallery Web Masthead instead of the graphic-intensive letterhead, and then insert the appropriate electronic form controls. Clicking the graphic in the Web site will allow users to e-mail CopyCat Creations. After running the publication through the Design Checker, you will save both the publication and the Web files on a floppy disk.

## Inserting a Web Masthead

The Publisher Design Gallery has more than 20 Web mastheads. Most of the mastheads use personal information components as well as animated graphics. Perform the following steps to create a masthead on a blank Web page.

## Steps To Insert a Design Gallery Web Masthead

**1** **Click File on the menu bar and then click New. When the Catalog dialog box displays, click the Blank Publications tab and then point to Web Page in the Blank Full Page pane.**

*The Catalog dialog box displays previews of blank publications in the Blank Full Page pane (Figure 5-46).*

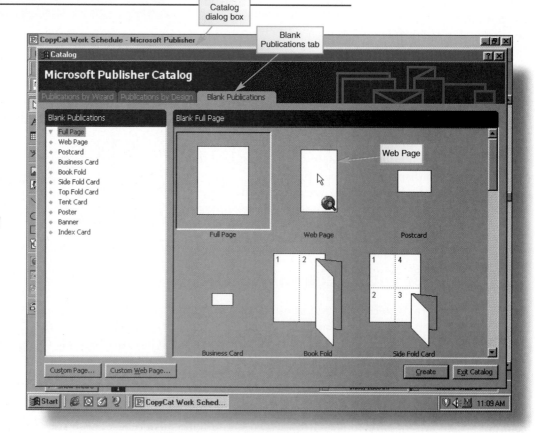

**FIGURE 5-46**

**3** **Type**
cc@k-tuck.net **in the Internet e-mail address text box and then point to the OK button.**

*The hot spot directs users to the e-mail address of the company (Figure 5-53).*

**4** **Click the OK button.**

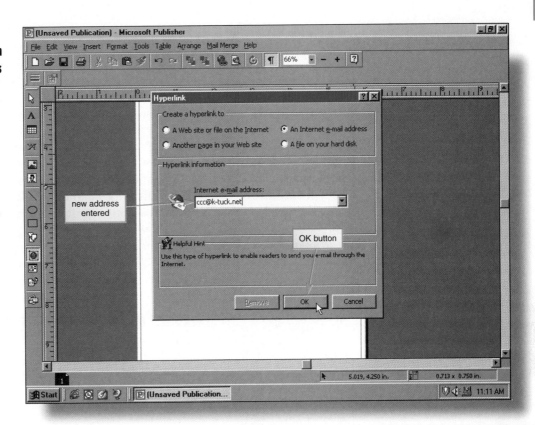

new address entered

OK button

**FIGURE 5-53**

The graphic now is a hot spot that, when clicked, opens the user's e-mail message window. Pointing to the hot spot, even during editing, now will display a hand mouse pointer and an e-mail ScreenTip with the e-mail address.

# Using Form Controls

**Form controls** are the individual boxes and buttons used by Web site visitors to enter data. The data from a form control is transmitted from the visitor to the site owner via a **submit button**. Publisher supports six types of form controls.

A **check box** is a square box that presents a yes/no choice. Selected, it displays a check mark or X. Several check boxes function as a group of related but independent choices. An **option button** is a round radio button that presents one choice. Selected, an option button circle displays filled in. When grouped, option buttons function like multiple-choice questions. The difference between an option button and a check box is that visitors can select only one option button within a group, but any number of check boxes. Check boxes and options buttons both display a label you can edit. Furthermore, you can choose to display either control selected or not selected at startup.

A **list box** presents a group of items in a list. Visitors can scroll to select from one or any number of choices in the list box. You determine the available choices and the number that may be selected when you set list box properties.

*Other* Ways

1. Select graphic, press CTRL+K

*More About*

**Internal Data Labels**

The name for a control can include any combination of alphabetic characters (A-Z, a-z), numbers (0-9), or underline symbols (_). It neither can begin with a number, nor can it contain spaces or special characters.

**More About**

### Web Objects with HTML

Publisher can accept code fragments that you have created in HTML. On the Objects toolbar, click the HTML Code Fragment button and then type or copy and paste your own HTML code to add an element such as a scrolling marquee, a counter, an ActiveX control, or a Java applet. For more information on Java applets, visit the JavaScript Web page (www.scsite.com/js/p1.htm).

If you want Web visitors to type information in a text box, you insert a form control called a **single-line text box**. Sensitive information, such as credit card information or passwords, can display with asterisks. A **multiline text box** provides a means of entering information by making available to the visitor a larger text box with multiple blank lines. Next to the text boxes, it is advisable to include text frames as instruction labels, to assist visitors in entering the correct information.

You must include a **submit command button** on every form. This button allows visitors to send you their form data. A **reset command button** is optional, but provides a way to clear form data and allow the Web visitor to start over. Command buttons can display any words in their visible labels, such as Send or Clear.

Form controls each have a logical, or **internal data label**, as well. This data label references and identifies the visitor-supplied information when submitted to the Web site owner. For instance, the label words, Customer ID, would accompany the visitor-supplied number in the e-mail submission. You may assign these internal data labels as well as other settings by clicking a **Properties button** that displays on the Formatting toolbar of each selected control or by double-clicking the control.

### Inserting Form Controls on the Web Reorder Form

The Web reorder form contains two single-line text boxes, one multiline text box, three check boxes, and three list boxes. Perform the following steps to add form controls to the Web reorder form.

*Steps* **To Insert Form Controls**

**1** **Scroll to display the middle portion of the Web page. Click the Form Control button on the Objects toolbar and then point to Single-Line Text Box on the Form Control button menu.**

*The six choices on the Form Control button menu display (Figure 5-54).*

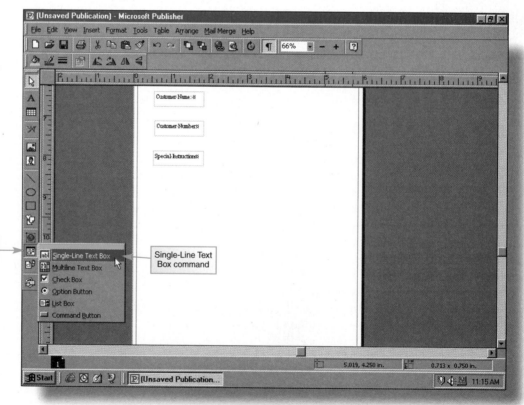

FIGURE 5-54

**2** Click Single-Line Text Box. Drag a frame approximately three-inches wide to the right of the Customer Name text frame. Release the mouse button.

*The text box displays in the publication (Figure 5-55). Your screen need not match the figure exactly; you will align the objects later in the project.*

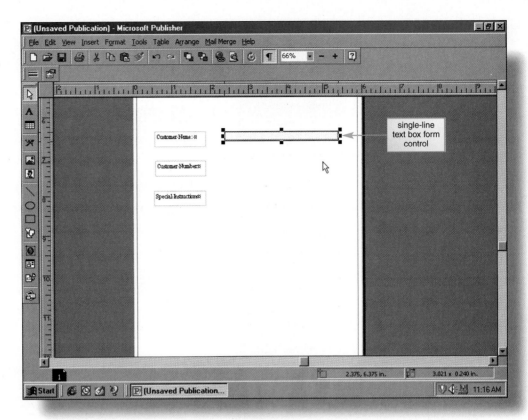

FIGURE 5-55

**3** Double-click the single-line text box. When the Single-Line Text Box Properties dialog box displays, enter the data as shown in Figure 5-56 and then point to the OK button.

*The Single-Line Text Box Properties dialog box displays with its data label and selected check box (Figure 5-56).*

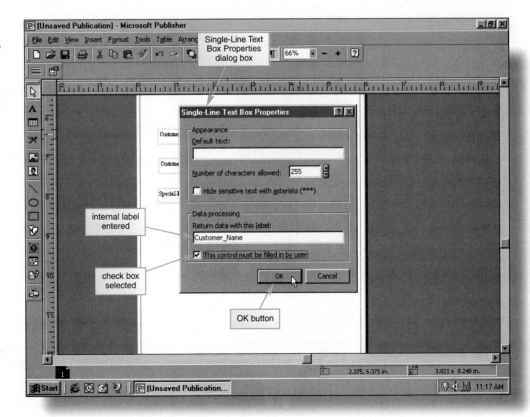

FIGURE 5-56

**4** Click the OK button. Repeat Steps 2 and 3 to create a slightly shorter text box for the **Customer Number text frame directly below the previous form control. Enter the data as shown in Figure 5-57 and then point to the OK button.**

*The Single-Line Text Box Properties dialog box for the Customer Number text frame displays (Figure 5-57). Customer numbers will be 10 characters in length. The Hide sensitive text with asterisks check box is selected.*

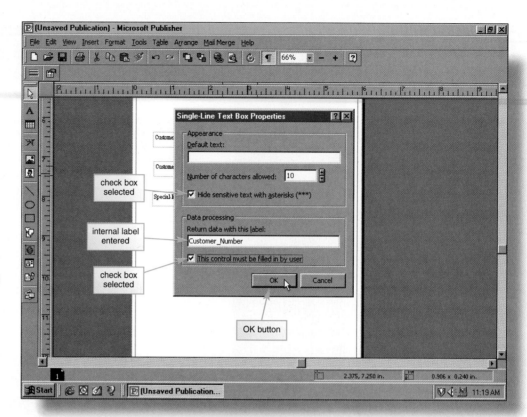

**FIGURE 5-57**

**5** Click the OK button. Click the Form Control button on the Objects toolbar and then point to Multiline Text Box.

*The Form Control button menu displays (Figure 5-58).*

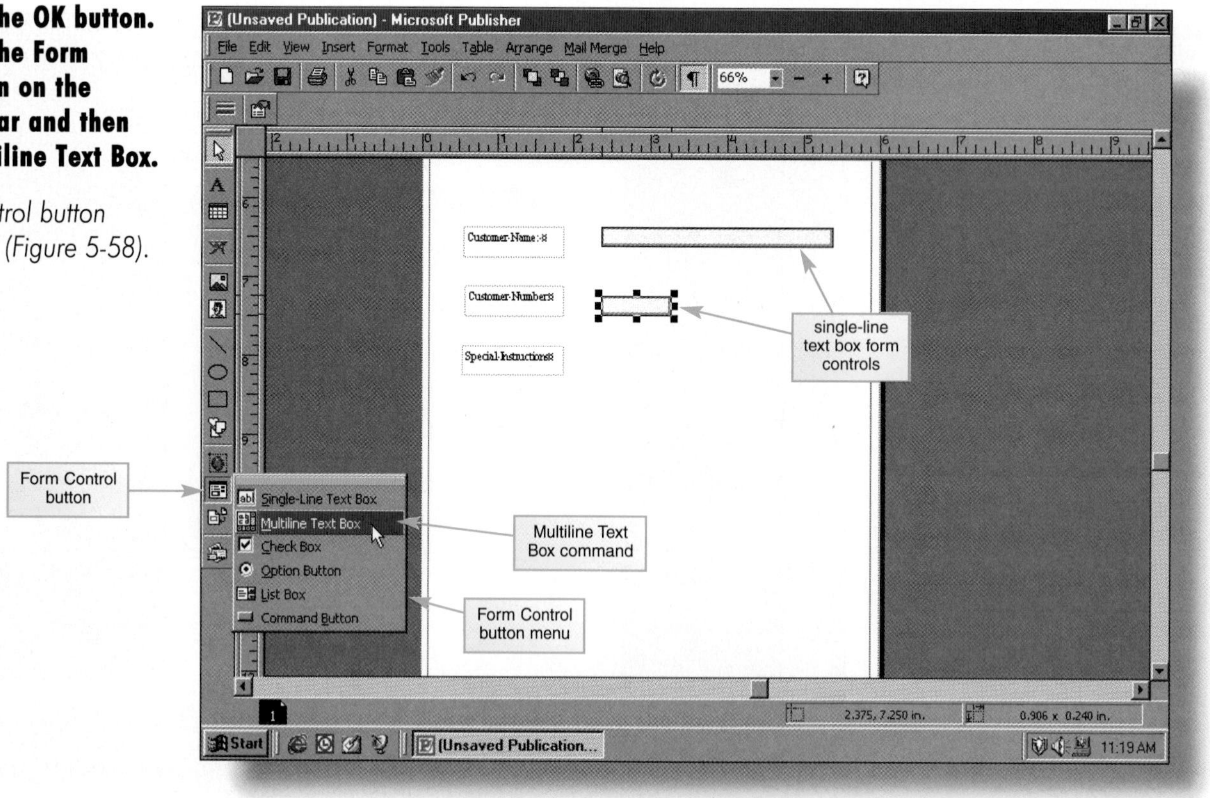

**FIGURE 5-58**

**6** **Click Multiline Text Box. Drag a frame approximately one-inch tall and three-inches wide. Double-click the multiline text box. When the Multiline Text Box Properties dialog box displays, type** Instructions **in the Return data with this label text box and then point to the OK button.**

*The Special Instructions text box will not contain any displayed or required information (Figure 5-59).*

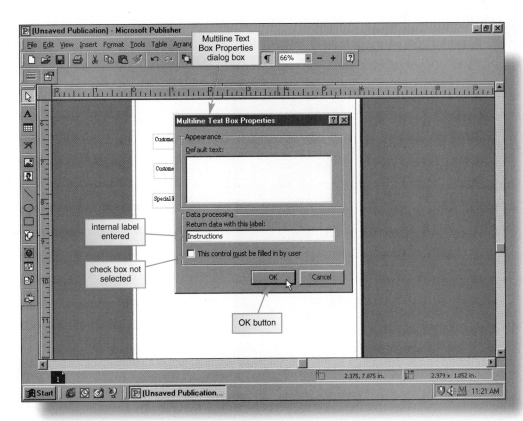

FIGURE 5-59

**7** **Click the OK button. Click the Form Control button on the Objects toolbar and then click Check Box on the Form Control button menu. Drag a frame below the other form controls, approximately one-quarter-inch tall and one and one-half-inches wide.**

*The check box form control displays in the publication (Figure 5-60). The dimensions need not match exactly.*

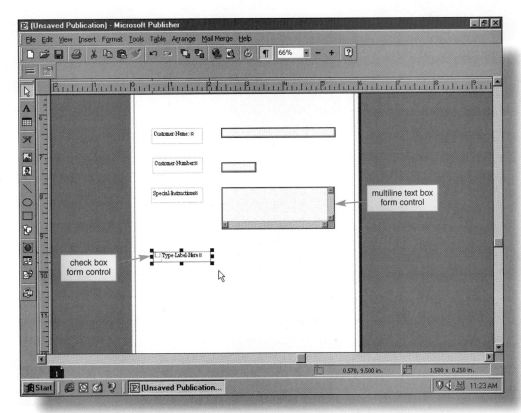

FIGURE 5-60

**8** Click the text, Type Label Here, and then type Letterhead to replace the text. Repeat the process to insert a check box for Business Cards and a check box for Envelopes in the publication, as shown in Figure 5-61.

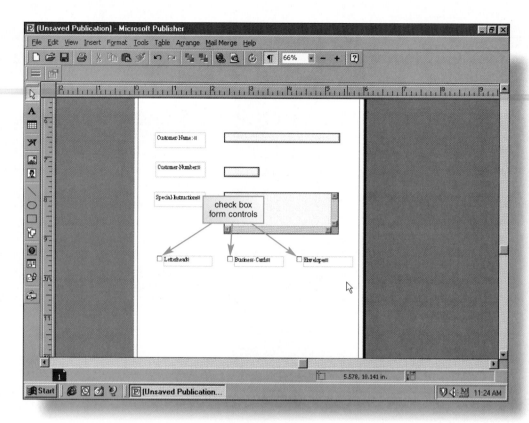

**FIGURE 5-61**

**9** Click the Form Control button on the Objects toolbar and then click List Box on the Form Control button menu. Below the Letterhead check box, drag downward to create approximately a one-inch frame. Release the mouse button.

*The list box form control displays (Figure 5-62).*

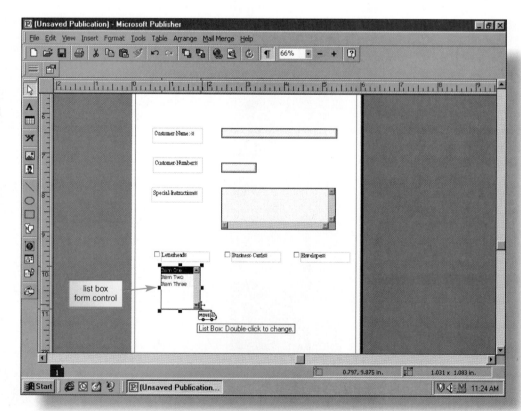

**FIGURE 5-62**

**10** Double-click the list box form control. When the List Box Properties dialog box displays, if necessary, click Item One in the Appearance list box and then point to the Modify button.

*The List Box Properties dialog box displays choices to Add, Modify, Remove, and move items up or down in the list (Figure 5-63).*

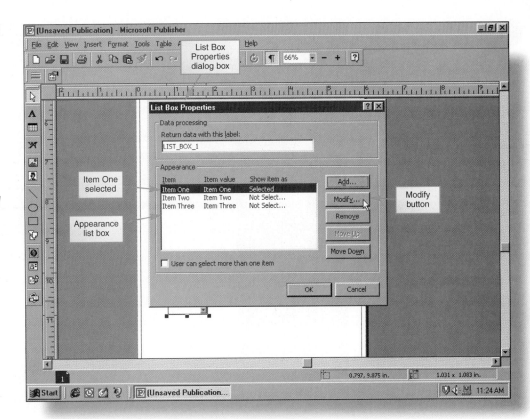

FIGURE 5-63

**11** Click the Modify button. When the Add/Modify List Box Item dialog box displays, type 1000 copies in the Item text box. Point to the OK button in the Add/Modify List Box Item dialog box.

*The Add/Modify List Box Item dialog box displays (Figure 5-64).*

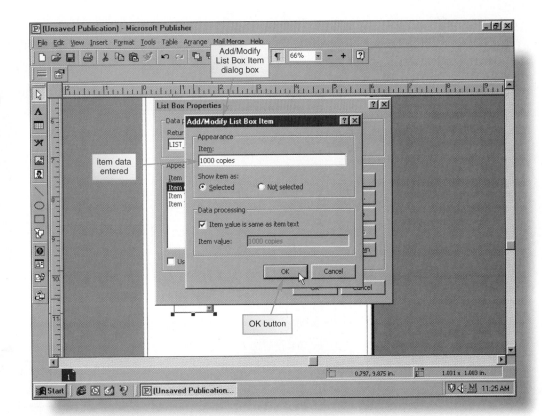

FIGURE 5-64

**12** **Click the OK button. When the List Box Properties box is visible again, repeat Step 11 on the previous page to enter** 2500 copies **for Item Two and** 5000 copies **for Item Three. Point to the OK button in the List Box Properties dialog box.**

*The three modified choices display in the Appearance list box (Figure 5-65).*

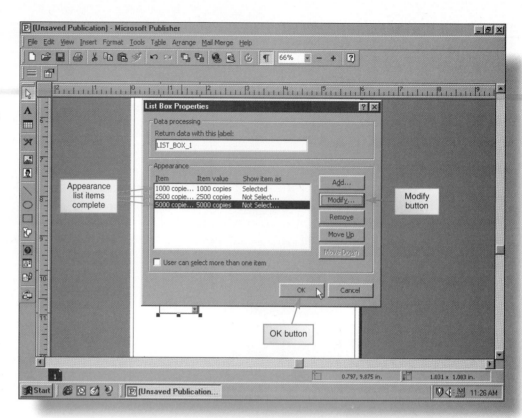

**FIGURE 5-65**

**13** **Click the OK button. With the newly created list box still selected, click the Copy button on the Standard toolbar. Click the Paste button on the Standard toolbar twice. Drag the copies to display below the other two check boxes as shown in Figure 5-66.**

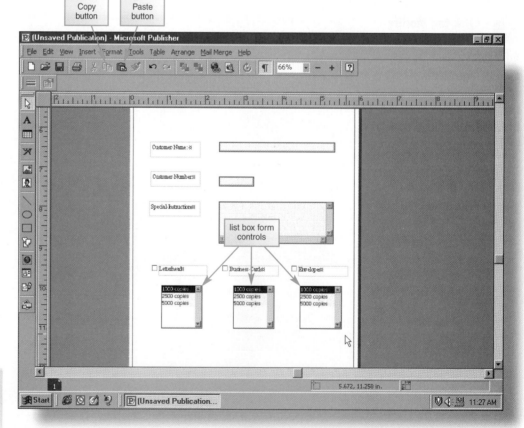

**FIGURE 5-66**

*Other* **Ways**

1. To insert, on Insert menu point to Form Control
2. To edit, click Properties button on Formatting toolbar

## Inserting Command Buttons on the Web Reorder Form

The next step is to insert a submit button and a reset button in the same manner you inserted the other controls. For a detailed example of the command button editing, refer to pages PUBW 1.11 and PUBW 1.12 in the Web Feature project.

### TO INSERT COMMAND BUTTONS

**1** Click the Form Control button on the Objects toolbar and then click Command Button on the Form Control button menu.

**2** Click the publication below the first list box.

**3** When the Command Button Properties dialog box displays, click Send data to me in e-mail to select it.

**4** Select the text in the Send data to this e-mail address text box. Type ccc@k-tuck.net to replace the text, and then click the OK button.

**5** When the publication again displays, click the Copy button on the Standard toolbar and then click the Paste button on the Standard toolbar to create another copy of the command button.

**6** Drag the copy to the right of the original button and then double-click it.

**7** When the Command Button Properties dialog box displays, click Reset to select it.

**8** Click the OK button. When the publication displays, click outside the Reset button to remove the selection.

*The command buttons display in the publication (Figure 5-67).*

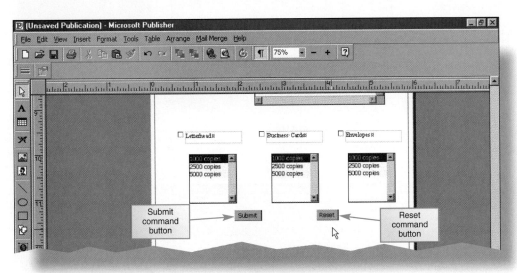

**FIGURE 5-67**

# Aligning Objects

To align the text frames and form controls on the Reorder form, you will use the Align command on the Arrange menu. The **Align command** offers left to right and top to bottom alignment choices. The Align command works only when more than one object is selected.

*Other Ways*

1. To insert, on Insert menu point to Form Control, click Command Button
2. To format, click Command Button Properties button on Formatting toolbar
3. To format, right-click control, click Command Button Properties on shortcut menu

### Aligning Objects in the Web Reorder Form

Perform the following steps to left-align the groups of text frames and text boxes on the Web reorder form. You also will center the check boxes vertically with their corresponding list boxes.

## To Align Objects

**1** Scroll to display the middle of the publication. If necessary, click the Pointer Tool button on the Objects toolbar. Drag a selection box around the text frames for Customer Name, Customer Number, and Special Instructions. Release the mouse button.

*All three text frames display selected (Figure 5-68). Recall that the Pointer Tool displays as the mouse pointer in the workspace.*

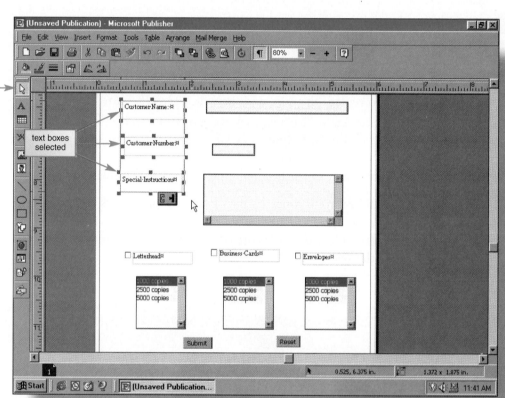

**FIGURE 5-68**

**2** Click Arrange on the menu bar and then point to Align Objects (Figure 5-69).

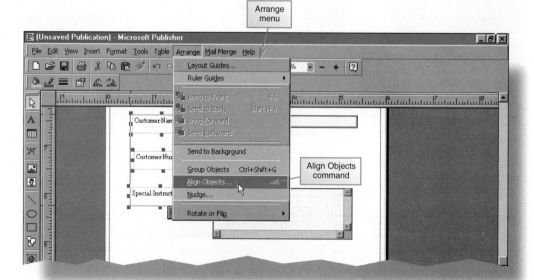

**FIGURE 5-69**

**3** Click Align Objects. When the Align Objects dialog box displays, click Left edges in the Left to right frame and then point to the OK button.

*The option buttons for left to right are grouped in a separate frame from the top to bottom option buttons (Figure 5-70).*

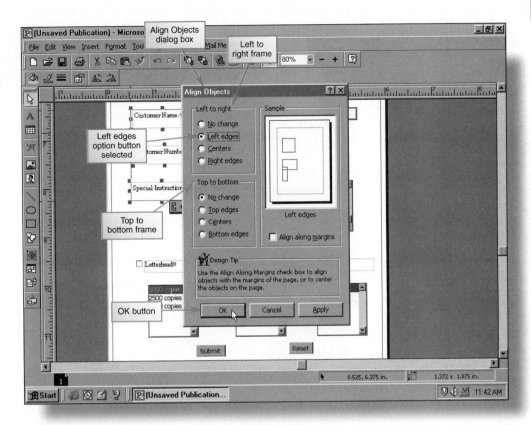

**FIGURE 5-70**

**4** Click the OK button. Repeat Steps 1 through 3 to align the three text box form controls.

*The three form controls align along their left edges (Figure 5-71).*

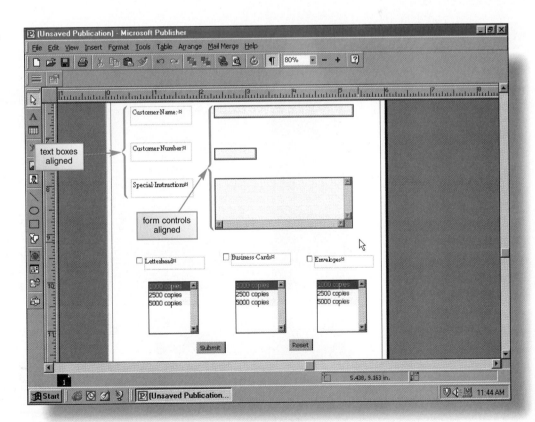

**FIGURE 5-71**

Microsoft **Publisher** 2000

**5** Use the Pointer Tool to drag a box around the letterhead check box and the list box directly below it.

*The two form controls display selected (Figure 5-72).*

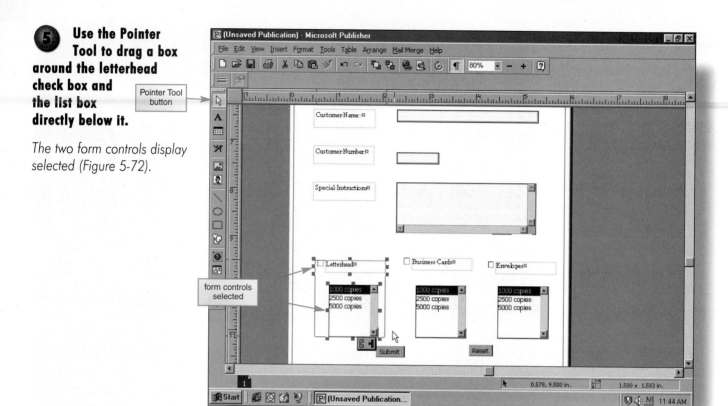

**FIGURE 5-72**

**6** Click Arrange on the menu bar and then click Align Objects. Click Centers in the Left to right frame and then point to the OK button.

*The Centers option button is selected (Figure 5-73).*

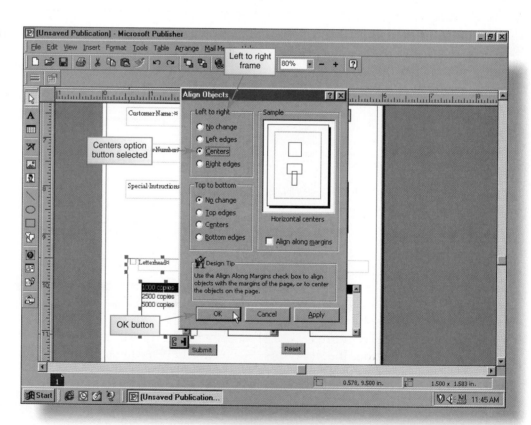

**FIGURE 5-73**

**7** Click the OK button. Repeat Steps 5 and 6 to align the Business Cards and Envelopes check boxes with their respective list boxes. Finally, align the top edges of the three check boxes and then align the top edges of the two command buttons.

*The electronic form controls display aligned (Figure 5-74).*

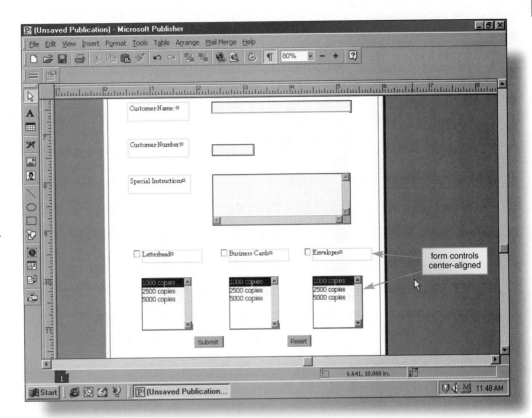

**FIGURE 5-74**

**Other Ways**

1. Select objects, right-click objects, click Align Objects on shortcut menu

# Checking and Saving the Publication

To complete the Web reorder form, you will run it through the Design Checker, save the Web files in a folder, and save the publication itself for future editing.

## Running the Design Checker

Recall that Publisher's Design Checker scans your publication for overlapping errors and large graphics that may prevent the page from loading quickly on the Web.

Perform the following steps to run the Design Checker. For a detailed explanation of running the Design Checker, refer to pages PUB 1.52 and PUB 1.53.

### TO RUN THE DESIGN CHECKER

**1** Click Tools on the menu bar and then click Design Checker. When the Design Checker dialog box displays, click the OK button.

**2** If a dialog box displays warning you of the logo frame overlapping the edge, click the Ignore button. If other errors occur, click the Explain button and then follow the instructions to fix the error. If necessary, click the Continue button.

**3** If a dialog box displays asking you to check your publication for its ability to download quickly, click the Yes button.

**4** After a few moments, Publisher's Design Checker indicates that the Design Check is complete. Click the OK button.

*The Design Checker terminates.*

**More About 2000**

## Tile Printing Options

When your publication page size is larger than a printed sheet of paper, as it is on some Web pages, banners, and posters, you can specify the overlap area for printing all segments or tiles of the publication. Additionally, you may print tiles individually from the ruler's origin.

## More About

### Web Page Backgrounds

Tiling also refers to a way to create a striking visual effect on your Web page without causing long download times. You can insert a small picture on the background and have Publisher repeat it several times to create a texture. The small picture can be downloaded quickly and tiled by the user's browser. Nearly all textures on the Web are created by tiling pictures. When working with a Web page, on the Format menu, click Color and Background Scheme. If you want to use a Publisher-supplied background, click the Standard tab and then, under Background, click Browse. If you choose a custom picture file, on the Custom tab, make sure it is 20 kilobytes or smaller. Large picture files will require people viewing your Web site to wait a long time for the graphic to download.

## More About

### Quick Reference

For a table that lists how to complete the tasks covered in this book using the mouse, menu, shortcut menu, and keyboard, visit the Shelly Cashman Series Office Web page (www.scsite.com/off2000/qr.htm), and then click Microsoft Publisher 2000.

## Saving the Web Files

Saving the Web reorder form involves creating a folder to hold the page and associated graphics for possible uploading to the Web. For a detailed explanation of the procedure summarized below, refer to pages PUBW 1.13 and PUBW 1.14 in the Web Feature project.

### TO SAVE THE WEB FILES

**1** Make sure you have a floppy disk with adequate free space in drive A. Click File on the menu bar and then click Save as Web Page.

**2** Click 3½ Floppy (A:) in the Look in list. Click the Create New Folder button.

**3** When the New Folder dialog box displays, type Web Reorder Form Files in the Name text box.

**4** Click the OK button in the New Folder dialog box, and then click the OK button in the Save as Web Page dialog box.

*The saved files are ready to post to the Web.*

You may preview your Web site with a browser by clicking the Web Page Preview button on the Standard toolbar.

Talk to your instructor about making this Web site available to others on your network, intranet, or the World Wide Web (see Appendix B). When you publish the site, do not forget to send all the files in your folder so the links and animation work correctly.

## Saving and Printing the Publication

You should save the publication itself for future editing. The Web folder contains HTML files, which are not directly accessible in Publisher. Follow these steps to save and print the publication.

### TO SAVE AND PRINT THE WEB REORDER FORM

**1** Insert a floppy disk into drive A.

**2** Click File on the menu bar and then click Save As.

**3** When the Save As dialog box displays, type CopyCat Web Reorder Form in the File name text box. Do not press the ENTER key.

**4** Click the Save in box arrow and then, if necessary, click 3½ Floppy (A:).

**5** Click the Save button in the Save As dialog box. If a dialog box displays asking you to resave the logo to the information set, click the No button.

**6** Click the Print button on the Standard toolbar.

*Publisher saves the publication on a floppy disk in drive A with the file name, CopyCat Web Reorder Form, then prints a copy on the printer. The completed Web reorder form is shown in Figure 5-1 on page PUB 5.5.*

The business forms for CopyCat Creations are complete.

## CASE PERSPECTIVE SUMMARY

Mr. Manderino received your e-mail with the attachment, CopyCat Work Schedule. After posting it in the workroom, he reminded you to save a backup copy as a template for future months. The CopyCat Invoice should automate the invoice process. Workers will load the file, fill it out, and print it for each order. And, speaking of automation, the whole staff loved your presentation of the Web reorder form with its masthead and form controls. Mr. Manderino directed you to upload the files and get them posted so customers can fill out their orders over the Web. Guess who gets to check the e-mail submissions every day?

# Project Summary

Project 5 introduced you to generating business forms. First, you created an invoice and a fax cover by copying objects from a wizard and pasting them on letterhead. Next, you created a table to display a work schedule. You learned how to edit by merging cells, filling cells, and creating a diagonal. Finally, you created an electronic form for Web ordering. You learned how to edit and align the various form controls and set their properties.

# What You Should Know

Having completed this project, you now should be able to perform the following tasks:

▶ Align Objects *(PUB 5.50)*
▶ Create a Table *(PUB 5.22)*
▶ Create an Invoice Template *(PUB 5.7)*
▶ Enter Data into a Table *(PUB 5.27)*
▶ Finish the Fax Cover *(PUB 5.21)*
▶ Format with a Drop Cap *(PUB 5.13)*
▶ Insert a Column *(PUB 5.31)*
▶ Insert a Design Gallery Web Masthead *(PUB 5.36)*
▶ Insert a Hot Spot *(PUB 5.40)*
▶ Insert a System Date *(PUB 5.17)*
▶ Insert a Tab Stop for the Date *(PUB 5.16)*
▶ Insert Command Buttons *(PUB 5.49)*
▶ Insert Form Controls *(PUB 5.42)*

▶ Insert the Logo and Instruction Text Frames *(PUB 5.38)*
▶ Merge Cells and Create a Cell Diagonal *(PUB 5.25)*
▶ Run the Design Checker *(PUB 5.53)*
▶ Save and Print the Invoice Template *(PUB 5.19)*
▶ Save and Print the Web Reorder Form *(PUB 5.54)*
▶ Save and Print the Work Schedule Table *(PUB 5.32)*
▶ Save the Web Files *(PUB 5.54)*
▶ Select Objects Using the Pointer Tool *(PUB 5.20)*
▶ Send a Publisher File via E-mail *(PUB 5.33)*
▶ Start Publisher *(PUB 5.6)*
▶ Use the Fill Command *(PUB 5.28)*
▶ Use the Nudge Command *(PUB 5.12)*

### More About 2000

### Microsoft Certification

The Microsoft Office User Specialist (MOUS) Certification program provides an opportunity for you to obtain a valuable industry credential — proof that you have the skills required by employers. For more information see Appendix D or visit the Shelly Cashman Series MOUS Web page (www.scsite.com/off2000/cert.htm).

# Apply Your Knowledge

➕ Project Reinforcement at www.scsite.com/off2000/reinforce.htm

## 1 Working with Form Controls

**Instructions:** Start Publisher. Open the publication, apply-5, on the Data Disk. See the inside back cover for instructions for downloading the Data Disk or see your instructor for information on accessing the files required in this book. The publication is a Web page order form for a tool company. You are to insert a masthead, a drop cap, graphics, hot spot, and form controls as described below to create an electronic form. You also need to edit the properties of the credit card information form controls. The completed form is shown in Figure 5-75.

Perform the following tasks:

1. Click the Design Gallery button on the Objects toolbar and insert the Capsules Masthead at the top of the publication. Triple-click each text frame in the masthead individually, and edit the text to match Figure 5-75.

2. Click the Got a question? text frame and then, on the Format menu, click Drop Cap. Choose a style from those available in your list.

3. Use the Clip Gallery Tool button on the Objects toolbar to insert two graphics. Place one graphic for questions to the left of the drop cap. Use the Nudge command to move it close to, but not touching, the text frame. Place another graphic for tools to the left of the customer information section.

4. Click the Hot Spot button on the Objects toolbar and make the questions graphic a hot spot to send e-mail to the tool company, at All_Things_Tools@taskmaster.com.

5. Use the Align Objects command on the Arrange menu to align the Zip code form control with the form control directly above it. Align any other controls that seem out of place.

6. Click the Credit Card # text box. Ungroup the label from the single-line text box form control. Double-click the form control. When the Properties dialog box displays, click to select the check box that hides sensitive text with asterisks. Do the same for the expiration date.

**FIGURE 5-75**

## Apply Your Knowledge

Project Reinforcement at www.scsite.com/off2000/reinforce.htm

7. Use the Form Control button on the Objects toolbar to insert a Submit button and a Reset button at the bottom of the page. Use the Align Objects command on the Arrange menu to align the two command buttons along their top edges.
8. Run the Design Checker.
9. If errors occur, click the Explain button and follow the instructions to fix the error. If a dialog box displays asking you to check your publication for its ability to download quickly, click the Yes button.
10. Make sure you have a floppy disk with adequate free space in drive A.
11. On the File menu, click Save as Web Page and select 3½ Floppy (A:) in the Look in list.
12. Click the Create New Folder button. When the New Folder dialog box displays, type Tool Order Form Files in the Name text box.
13. Click the OK button in the New Folder dialog box, and then click the OK button in the Save as Web Page dialog box.
14. On the File menu click Save As, and save the publication itself with the name, All Things Tools Order Form. Print the publication.

## In the Lab

# 1 Creating a Monthly Statement

**Problem:** Chris Zenakis owns and operates a lawn care service. He has asked you to create a monthly statement he can use to list services and payments. You decide to use a Monthly Statement Wizard and Chris's first customer as a sample (Figure 5-76 on the next page).

**Instructions:**
1. Start Publisher. From the Catalog, click Business Forms and then click Statement in the Business Forms list. Double-click the Borders Statement. Do not click the Finish button in the Business Form Wizard.
2. Click the Next button in the Business Form Wizard. When the Wizard asks you if you like to include a logo, click the No option button.
3. Click the Next button. When the Wizard asks you to choose a personal information set, click the Other Organization option button.
4. Click the Finish button. Hide the wizard.
5. Click the top text frame, press the F9 key, and then type Evergreen Lawn Care in the text box. Enter the address and telephone information as shown in Figure 5-76.
6. Insert an appropriate graphic using the Clip Gallery. Resize the graphic to fit above the Statement text frame. Use the Nudge command to place the graphic against the border.
7. Click the word Statement to select the text frame. Click Format on the menu bar and then click Drop Cap on the Format menu. Choose an appropriate style from the Available Drop Caps list. Enlarge the text frame if necessary.

*(continued)*

*In the Lab*

### Creating a Monthly Statement *(continued)*

8. Click the text frame for Statement #, Date, and Customer ID. Press CTRL+A to select the entire frame. Click the 1" mark on the Horizontal Ruler to set a tab. Enter the data from Figure 5-76 at the tab stop. Use your system date.

9. Click the Mailing Address text frame and type in your name and address.

10. Click the gray selector button above the word Type in the table. On the Table menu, click Delete Columns.

11. Enter the balance forward, three services, and one payment shown in Figure 5-76. Enter the total in the cell at the bottom of the right column.

12. Use the Align Right button on the Formatting toolbar to right-justify all amounts.

13. Save the publication with the file name, Lawn Care Statement, on your floppy disk. Print a copy.

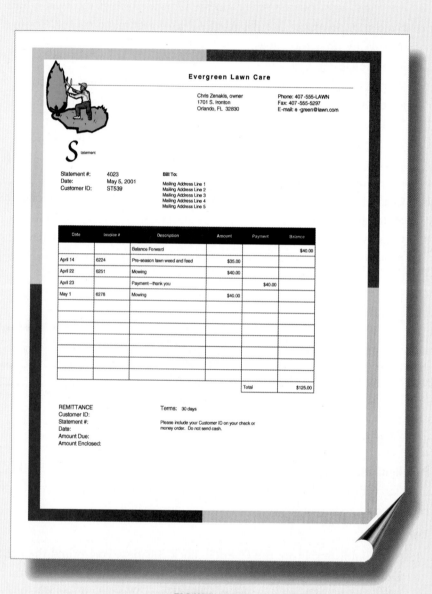

**FIGURE 5-76**

## 2 Creating an Origami Box

**Problem:** As head of the hospitality committee for your company's national project achievement dinner, you would like to place a commemorative coin at each place setting. The coins were shipped without presentation boxes, so you decide to try your hand at designing a do-it-yourself gift box. Printing on heavy card stock paper, you use the ancient art of Origami paper folding to create two boxes, one slightly larger than the other for a top and bottom box set.

# In the Lab

**Instructions:**

1. Start Publisher. From the Catalog, click Blank Publications and then double-click Full page. Hide the wizard. Increase the magnification to 66%.

2. Use the Table Frame Tool on the Objects toolbar to draw a table six-inches square. When the Create Table dialog box displays, create four rows and four columns, using the Default table format. Close the Create Table dialog box by clicking its OK button.

3. Click the gray corner selector box to select the entire table. On the Formatting toolbar, click the Line/Border Style button, and then click More Styles on the menu.

4. When the Border Style dialog box displays, click the Grid button in the Preset frame, and then click the OK button.

5. Click Table on the menu bar and then click Cell Diagonals. When the Cell Diagonals dialog box displays, click Divide up. Click the OK button in the Cell Diagonals dialog box. Click outside the table to remove the highlight.

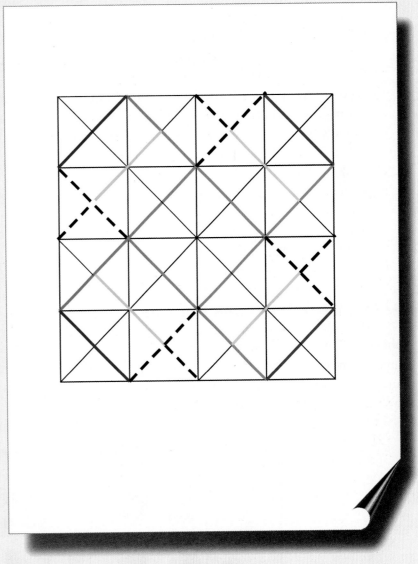

**FIGURE 5-77**

6. Using the Line Tool button on the Objects toolbar, draw seven lines to dissect the table cells the opposite way from the diagonals. Holding down the SHIFT key while drawing the line ensures a straight 45-degree line.

7. If desired you may draw colored and dotted lines over the other lines in the figure or simply use the figure as a reference for folding and trimming in Step 8 on the next page.
   a. To draw the colored lines, click the Line Tool button on the Objects toolbar and then click the Line Color button on the Formatting toolbar. Choose the appropriate color from the Line Color menu. Hold down the SHIFT key and draw the colored lines over the top of the black lines in the table as shown in Figure 5-77.

*(continued)*

*In the Lab*

**Creating an Origami Box** *(continued)*

    b. To draw the dotted lines, click the Line Tool button on the Objects toolbar and then click the Dash Style button on the Formatting toolbar. Choose an appropriate dotted line from the Dash Style menu. Hold down the SHIFT key and draw the dotted lines over the top of the black lines in the table as shown in Figure 5-77 on the previous page.

8. Save the publication as `Origami box` on your floppy disk. Print the publication, and then using Figure 5-77 as a guide, trim the printout and fold the bottom of the box set as follows:

    a. Cut around the edge of the table and on the dotted lines.

    b. Fold the orange lines first to form a box shell, keeping the tabs on the inside.

    c. Fold the blue lines inward.

    d. Fold the yellow lines third, working around from one corner of the box to the next.

9. On the Edit menu, click Select All. Click the Group Objects button and then SHIFT-drag a corner sizing handle until the box is approximately 1/4-inch larger. Print and assemble the top of the box set. (*Hint:* you may cheat and use a small piece of tape to hold down the "blue" fold if you like.)

## 3 Creating a Table with Graphics

**Problem:** As a physical education major, you are required to complete at least one summer internship for your degree program. You have accepted a position as Outside Activities Coordinator for a four-site day camp program for children and youths. Your supervisor has asked you to prepare a table for the spring mailing that shows camp facilities (Figure 5-78).

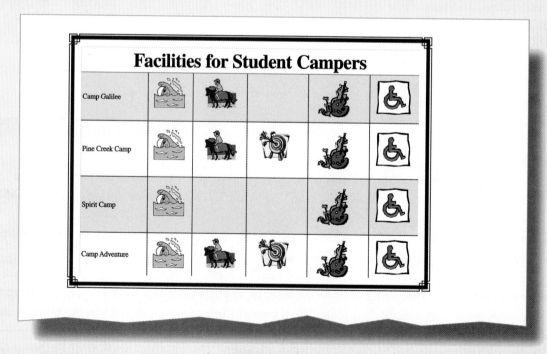

**FIGURE 5-78**

## In the Lab

**Instructions:** Perform the following tasks:

1. Start Publisher with a blank publication. Use the Page Setup command on the File menu to specify landscape orientation.

2. Use the Layout Guides command on the Arrange menu to change each of the margins to 0.5 inches.

3. Create a table beginning in the upper-left corner of the page, approximately seven-inches tall by nine-inches wide. Use five rows and six columns. Select the checkbook register format.

4. Click the Line/Border Style button, and then click More Styles. On the Border Art tab, choose a border similar to the Twisted Lines border shown in Figure 5-78. Use a Border Size of 24.

5. Enter the names of the camps in the first column, beginning with the second row. Drag through all four cells. On the Format menu, point to Align Text Vertically, and then click Center. Increase the font size to 14. In the gray selector bar above the table, drag the border between columns one and two to the right, approximately one-half inch, so that the camp names display on single lines.

6. Merge the cells across row one, and insert the heading shown in Figure 5-78. Center the heading and make it bold if necessary. Increase the font size to 36.

7. Drag the table to center it on the page if necessary. Click outside the table.

8. Locate a graphic of a swimmer. Position and size the graphic to fit in a single cell. Use the copy and paste technique to paste three copies of the swimmer. Position them as shown in Figure 5-78. SHIFT-click each of the four graphics and then, on the Arrange menu, click Align Objects. Choose to align their left edges.

9. Repeat Step 8 for graphics of horses, archery, arts, and handicap accessibility. When all graphics have been aligned on their corresponding left edges, align their top edges with the other graphics in each row.

10. Save the publication on your floppy disk with the file name, Camp Facilities Table. Print a copy.

## Cases and Places

The difficulty of these case studies varies:
▶ are the least difficult; ▶▶ are more difficult; and ▶▶▶ are the most difficult.

1 ▶ The owner of Plunge Plumbing, located at 807 State Street, Calumet City, IL, 60409, conducted an inventory and found himself short several items. Use the Bars Purchase Order Wizard to order materials from the We Supply All Corporation, whose logo is a picture of pipes. They are located at 1525 E. Huron, Chicago, IL, 60609. Plunge Plumbing needs five tubs of plumbing compound at $2.00 each, six elbow traps at $3.50 each, 10 rolls of soldering compound at $4.00 each, and 12 bags of rubber o-rings at $1.50 each. Fill in the Taxable column with Xs, as all the materials are taxable. Plunge Plumbing receives no discount and will pick up the order. The tax is 7.5%.

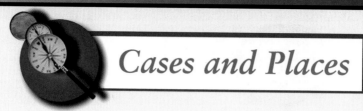

# Cases and Places

**2** ▶ You are a private investigator named Colonel Ketchup who needs an expense report for his client, Miss Pink. You include your daily charges of $200 for four days work, plus itemized expenses for a knife, a lead pipe, and a candlestick. Over dinner, you interviewed an expert witness named Professor Banana. Prepare an expense report using a Business Form Wizard. Itemize expenses and entertainment in the report. Include a logo of a magnifying glass.

**3** ▶▶ Research laboratories at major teaching hospitals usually are funded not only by their research grants, but also by providing services to the hospital and associated physicians. The Flow Cytometry Lab at University Hospital faxes results to pathologists and transplant surgeons at the hospital, and to blood banks all over the city. They need a standardized fax cover sheet for their multi-page lab reports. Using a wizard, create a fax cover template they will print on pre-printed Lab stationary. Leave two inches at the top of the page to accommodate their masthead and format the objects with the tools you learned in this project. Use a system date, a drop cap, and tab stops in each data entry field so the lab assistants can position text easily.

**4** ▶▶ Smitty's Garage needs a time card. He has just hired two extra mechanics and an office manager because business is booming. Using a Weekly Record Wizard, draw a box around the time card table, and then paste it into a blank publication. In the lower-left corner of the table, merge the gray cells in the penultimate row and insert the text, Name: and then merge the gray cells in the bottom row and insert the text, Date: to create room for the employees to sign and date the time card. Print multiple copies for Smitty's employees.

**5** ▶▶▶ As director of the outside sales force at a national retail company, you are responsible for providing each sales person with a company car. Each year you must submit a proposal to the president for approval. You would like some feedback from your sales associates all over the country and decide that a Web electronic form is the best way to reach them. Create a feedback form with check boxes, option buttons, list boxes, and text boxes. Collect information about makes of car, options, mileage, satisfaction ratings, and/or suggestions for improvement. Include a submit button linked to your e-mail address.

**6** ▶▶▶ Research four or five Internet Service Providers (ISPs) in your area. Ask friends and consult ISP advertisements. Use your school or work Internet provider as one of the examples. Look for information on monthly charges, type of Internet connection provided, rate of speed, and the e-mail handler programs they recommend or support. Create a table with a merged title cell and formatting to display your findings. Send the table publication to your instructor as an e-mail attachment.

**7** ▶▶▶ Microsoft Publisher is a popular solution to desktop publishing needs. However, other software is available for preparing everything from greeting cards to book publication film. Several products exist for desktop publishing such as QuarkXPress, Adobe Acrobat, and Print Shop; and products such as Microsoft Front Page and Macromedia Director create interactive kiosks and Web pages. *Surf the net* looking for pages that display a creation product logo. Compare Publisher's Web form controls to those of some other popular Web creation products and use Publisher to write a report about your findings. Include a table listing popular controls as columns, and products as rows.

Microsoft **Publisher 2000**

# Microsoft Publisher 2000

# Linking a Publisher Publication to an Excel Worksheet

**CASE PERSPECTIVE**

The director of human resources for West Assembly Division, Marcia Elana, sends out a statement to all employees in the retirement program showing the previous quarter's investment earnings. She currently uses Publisher to produce the investment statement that includes a table of the quarterly figures. The wording in the investment statement remains constant while the table of quarterly earnings changes each quarter.

Marcia recently heard of the Object Linking and Embedding (OLE) capabilities of Microsoft Office 2000. She wants to use it to create the basic investment statement using Publisher (Figure 1a on the next page), and then maintain the quarterly earnings on an Excel worksheet (Figure 1b on the next page). Each quarter, she envisions sending out the publication with the updated worksheet (Figure 1c on the next page). Once the link is established, she can update the worksheet each quarter, change the date in the investment statement, then print and distribute the report.

As Marcia's technical assistant, she has asked you to handle the details of linking the Excel quarterly summary to the Publisher investment statement.

# Introduction

With Microsoft 2000, you can incorporate parts of files or entire files called **objects** from one application into another application. In Project 2, you learned how to import a text file from Microsoft Word into Publisher. Now you will copy a worksheet created in Excel into a publication created in Publisher. In this case, the worksheet in Excel is called the **source publication** (copied from) and the publication in Publisher is called the **destination publication** (copied to). Copying specific objects between applications can be accomplished in three ways: (1) copy and paste; (2) copy and embed; and (3) copy and link.

All of the Microsoft Office applications allow you to use these three methods to copy objects between applications. The first method uses the Copy and Paste buttons. The latter two use the Paste Special command on the Edit menu with **Object Linking and Embedding** or **OLE**. Table 1 on the next page summarizes the differences between the three methods.

You would use copy and link over the other two methods when an object is likely to change and you want to make sure the object reflects the changes in the source publication, or if the object is large, such as a video clip or sound clip. Thus, if you link a portion or all of a worksheet to an investment statement and update the worksheet quarterly in Excel, any time you open the investment statement in Publisher, the latest updates of the worksheet will display as part of the investment statement.

Moving objects from Publisher into other applications deserves special consideration. Text frames paste, embed, and link in a similar manner as Microsoft Word documents; that is, as text. Other objects paste as pictures or link as icons. The embed option is not typically available when moving non-text objects from Publisher into another application.

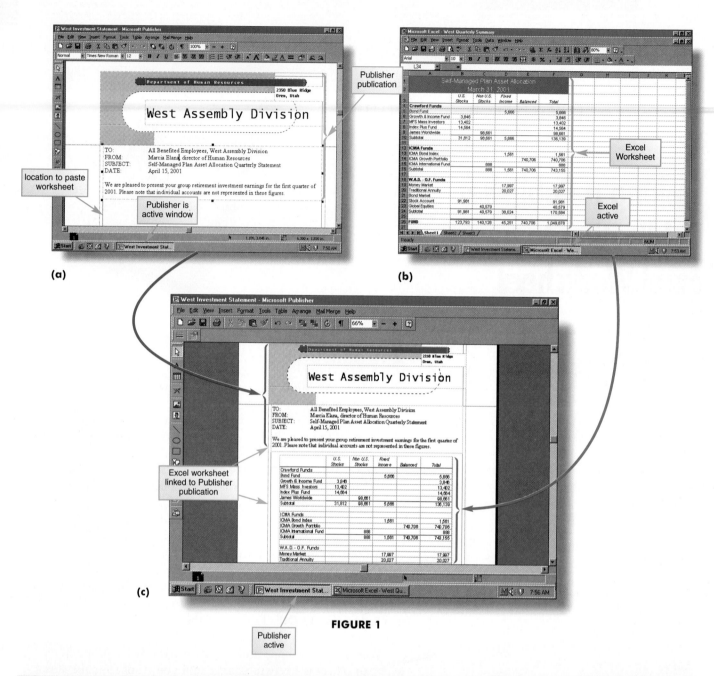

**FIGURE 1**

## Table 1   Copying Between Applications

| METHOD | CHARACTERISTICS |
|---|---|
| Copy and paste | Source publication becomes part of destination publication. Object may be edited, but the editing features are limited to those in the destination application. An Excel worksheet becomes a Publisher table. If changes are made to values in the Publisher table, any original Excel formulas are not recalculated. Publisher objects become pictures when pasted into Excel worksheets. |
| Copy and embed | Source publication becomes part of the destination publication. Object may be edited in destination application using source-editing features. Excel worksheet remains a worksheet in Publisher. If changes are made to values in the worksheet with Publisher active, Excel formulas will be recalculated, but the changes are not updated in the Excel worksheet in the workbook on disk. If you use Excel to change values in the worksheet, the changes will not show in the Publisher publication the next time you open it. |
| Copy and link | Source publication does not become part of destination publication even though it appears to be part of it. Rather, a link is established between the two publications so that when you open the Publisher publication, the worksheet displays as part of it. When you attempt to edit a linked worksheet in Publisher, the system activates Excel. If you change the worksheet in Excel, the changes will show in the Publisher publication the next time you open it. When copying from Publisher to Excel, a link becomes an icon in the worksheet. |

Most Office applications also provide a method for copying the entire file from one application to another. On the Insert menu, the Object command gives you the same linking or embedding options as discussed above, but extends the connection to a wider array of applications.

# Starting Word and Excel

Both the Publisher publication (West Investment Statement.pub) and the Excel workbook (West Quarterly Summary.xls) are on the Data Disk. If you do not have a copy of the Data Disk, see the inside back cover of this book. The first step in linking the Excel worksheet to the Publisher publication is to open both the publication in Publisher and the workbook in Excel as shown in the following steps.

<table>
<tr><td>**More About**</td></tr>
<tr><td>**Office 2000**</td></tr>
<tr><td>Because you can use OLE among Word, Excel, Access, PowerPoint, Publisher, and Outlook, Office 2000 can be viewed as one large integrated software package, rather than separate applications.</td></tr>
</table>

 **To Open a Publisher Publication and an Excel Workbook**

**1** **Insert the Data Disk in drive A. Click the Start button on the taskbar. Click Open Office Document on the Start menu. Click 3½ Floppy (A:) in the Look in list. Double-click the file name, West Investment Statement.**

*Publisher becomes active and the West Investment Statement displays in Whole Page View (Figure 2).*

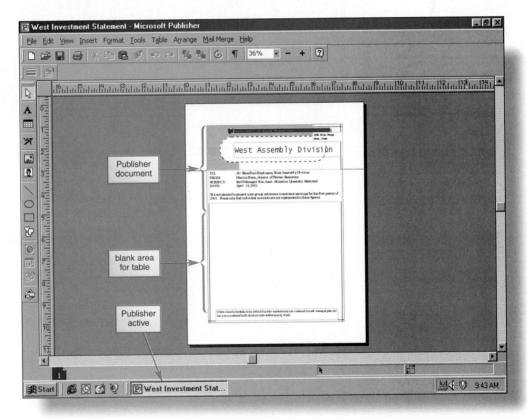

**FIGURE 2**

**②** **Click the Start button on the taskbar. Click Open Office Document on the Start menu. If necessary, click 3½ Floppy (A:) in the Look in list. Double-click the file name, West Quarterly Summary.**

*Excel becomes active and the West Quarterly Summary workbook displays (Figure 3). At this point, Publisher is inactive, but is still in main memory. Excel is the active window as shown on the taskbar.*

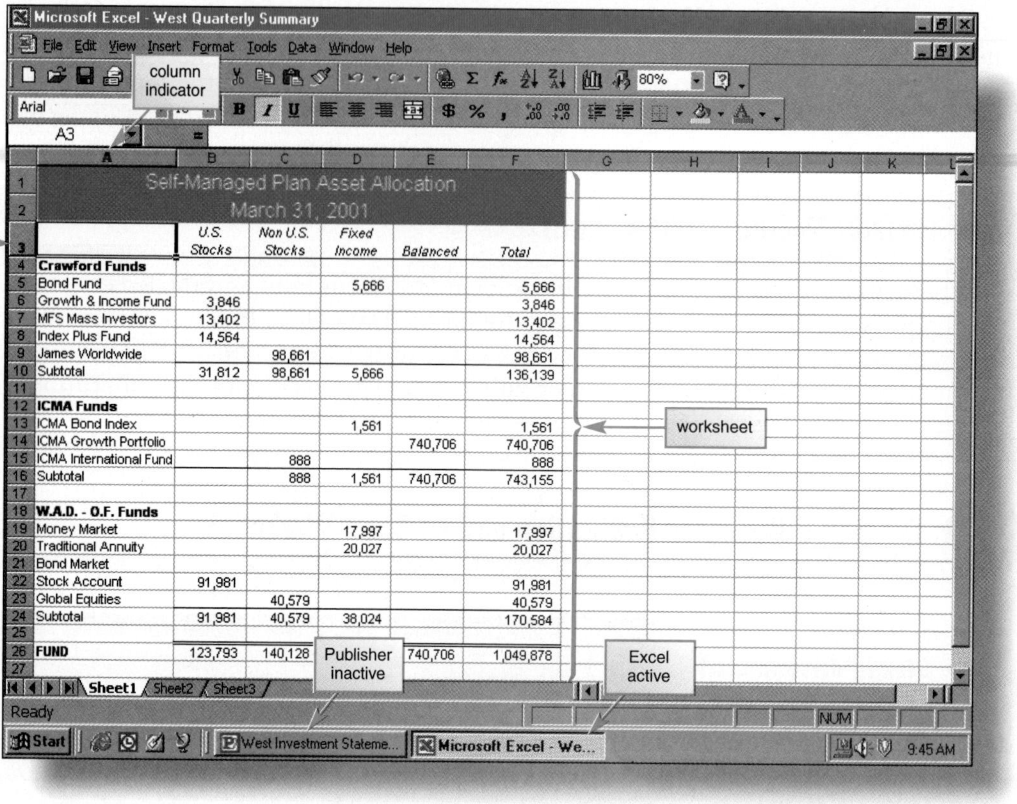

**FIGURE 3**

**More About 2000**

**OLE**

If you want to have more than one object at a time available for OLE, you can store objects to embed on the desktop, rather than using the Clipboard. When you use this technique, the objects are called **scrap**. To accomplish this task, part of the desktop must be visible behind the window of the source application. Next, right-drag the object from the source application onto the desktop. Once on the desktop, Windows displays the object as an icon. When the shortcut menu displays, click Create Scrap Here. Next, activate the destination document, drag the scrap from the desktop onto the destination publication, and drop it where you want it inserted. To delete a scrap from the desktop, right-click it and then click Delete on the shortcut menu.

With both Publisher and Excel in main memory, you can switch between the applications by clicking the appropriate button on the taskbar.

# Linking an Excel Worksheet to a Publisher Publication

With both applications running, the next step is to link the Excel worksheet to the Publisher publication. The Excel cell references in the following steps represent the intersection of the column (indicated by a capital letter) and the row (indicated by a number).

**Steps** To Link an Excel Worksheet to a Publisher Publication

**1** **With the Excel window active, drag through the range from cell A3 through cell F26. Click the Copy button to place the selected range on the Office Clipboard.**

*Excel displays a marquee around the range A3:F26 (Figure 4). You need not copy the heading because the Publisher publication text frames will explain the table.*

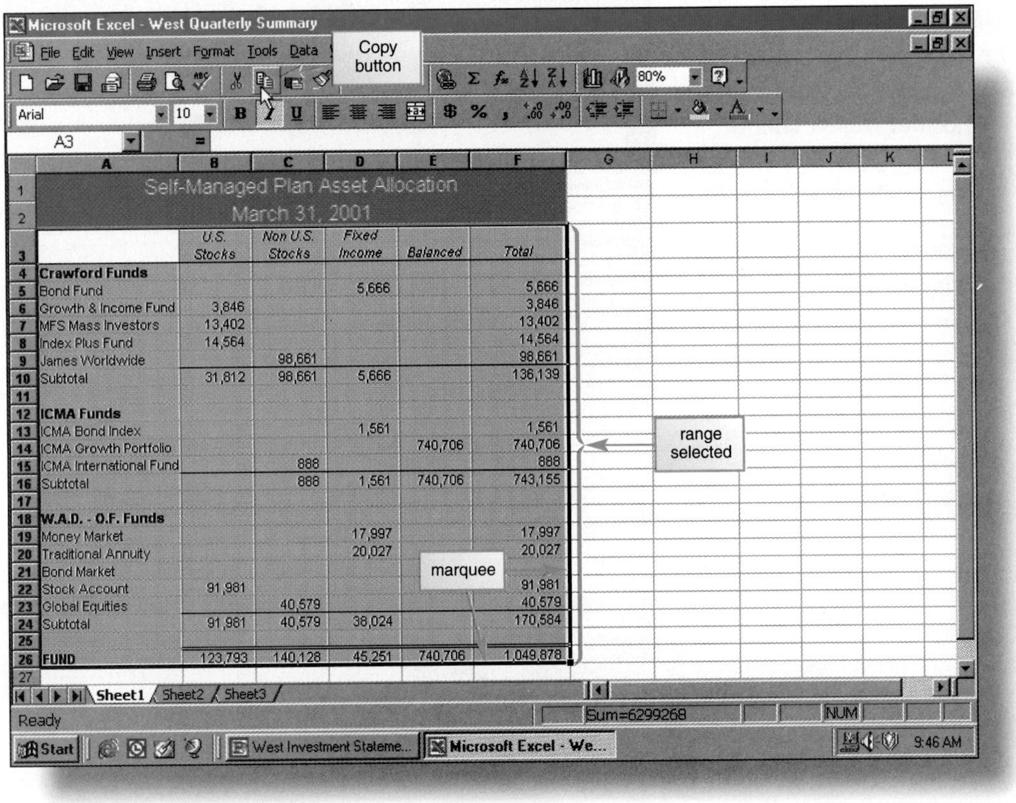

FIGURE 4

**2** **Click the West Investment Statement button on the taskbar to activate the Publisher window. Click Edit on the menu bar and then point to the Paste Special command.**

*The West Investment Statement publication and the Edit menu display on the screen (Figure 5).*

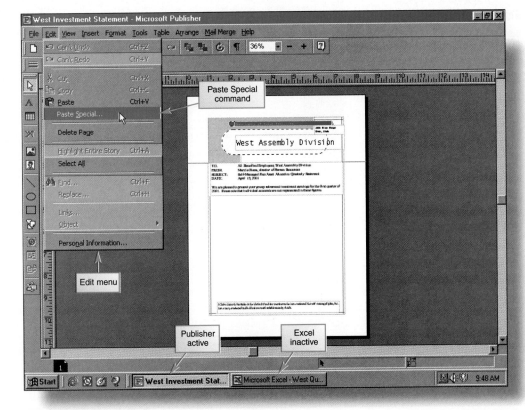

FIGURE 5

**3** **Click Paste Special on the Edit menu. When the Paste Special dialog box displays, click Paste Link. If necessary, click Microsoft Excel Worksheet Object Link in the As box. Point to the OK button.**

*The Paste Special dialog box displays (Figure 6).*

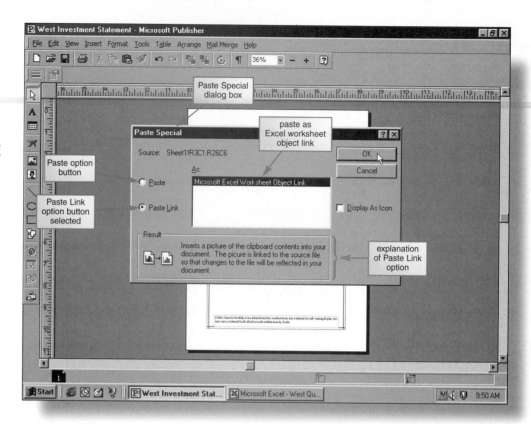

**FIGURE 6**

**4** **Click the OK button. When the table displays, drag it to the open space in the publication. Click the Zoom In button to increase the magnification.**

*The range A3:F26 of the worksheet displays in the Publisher publication (Figure 7).*

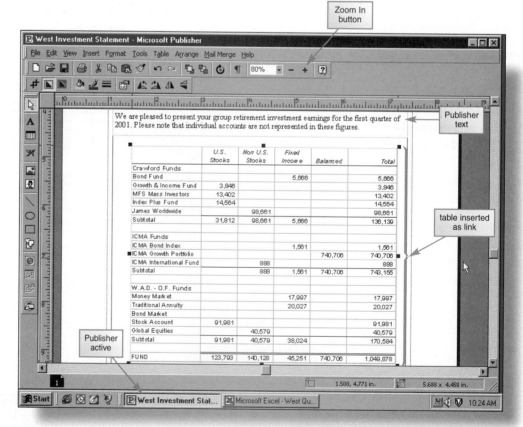

**FIGURE 7**

The Excel worksheet now is linked to the Publisher publication. If you save the Publisher publication and reopen it, the worksheet will display just as it does in Figure 7. If you want to delete the worksheet, select it and press the DELETE key. The next section shows how to print and save the publication with the linked worksheet.

# Printing and Saving the Publisher Publication with the Linked Worksheet

The following steps print and then save the Publisher publication with the linked worksheet.

 **To Print and Save the Publication with the Linked Worksheet**

**1** **With the Publisher window active, click the Print button on the Standard toolbar.**

*The statement and the worksheet print as one publication (Figure 8).*

**2** **With your floppy disk in drive A, click File on the menu bar and then click Save As. Type the file name** West Investment Statement Q1-2001 **in the File name box. Click the OK button.**

*Publisher saves the publication on your floppy disk with the file name, West Investment Statement Q1-2001.pub.*

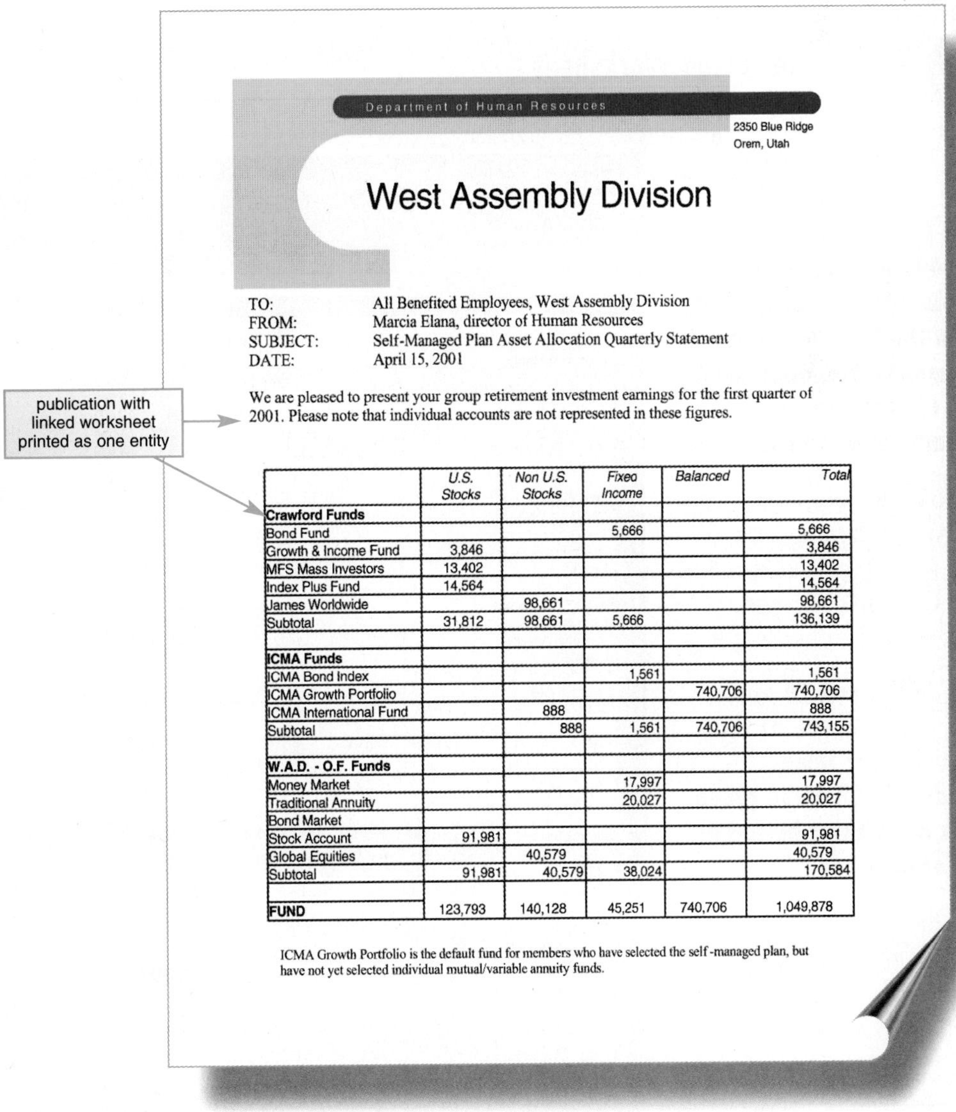

Department of Human Resources

2350 Blue Ridge
Orem, Utah

## West Assembly Division

publication with linked worksheet printed as one entity

TO:          All Benefited Employees, West Assembly Division
FROM:        Marcia Elana, director of Human Resources
SUBJECT:     Self-Managed Plan Asset Allocation Quarterly Statement
DATE:        April 15, 2001

We are pleased to present your group retirement investment earnings for the first quarter of 2001. Please note that individual accounts are not represented in these figures.

| | U.S. Stocks | Non U.S. Stocks | Fixed Income | Balanced | Total |
|---|---|---|---|---|---|
| **Crawford Funds** | | | | | |
| Bond Fund | | | 5,666 | | 5,666 |
| Growth & Income Fund | 3,846 | | | | 3,846 |
| MFS Mass Investors | 13,402 | | | | 13,402 |
| Index Plus Fund | 14,564 | | | | 14,564 |
| James Worldwide | | 98,661 | | | 98,661 |
| Subtotal | 31,812 | 98,661 | 5,666 | | 136,139 |
| | | | | | |
| **ICMA Funds** | | | | | |
| ICMA Bond Index | | 1,561 | | | 1,561 |
| ICMA Growth Portfolio | | | | 740,706 | 740,706 |
| ICMA International Fund | | 888 | | | 888 |
| Subtotal | | 888 | 1,561 | 740,706 | 743,155 |
| | | | | | |
| **W.A.D. - O.F. Funds** | | | | | |
| Money Market | | | 17,997 | | 17,997 |
| Traditional Annuity | | | 20,027 | | 20,027 |
| Bond Market | | | | | |
| Stock Account | 91,981 | | | | 91,981 |
| Global Equities | | 40,579 | | | 40,579 |
| Subtotal | 91,981 | 40,579 | 38,024 | | 170,584 |
| | | | | | |
| **FUND** | 123,793 | 140,128 | 45,251 | 740,706 | 1,049,878 |

ICMA Growth Portfolio is the default fund for members who have selected the self-managed plan, but have not yet selected individual mutual/variable annuity funds.

**FIGURE 8**

If you exit both applications and re-open West Investment Statement Q1-2001, the worksheet will display in the publication even though Excel is not running. Because Publisher supports Object Linking and Embedding (OLE), it can display the linked portion of the Excel workbook without Excel running.

The next section illustrates what happens when you attempt to edit the linked worksheet while Publisher is active.

# Editing the Linked Worksheet

You can edit any of the cells in the worksheet while it displays as part of the Publisher publication. To edit the worksheet, double-click it. If Excel is running in main memory, the system will switch to it and display the linked workbook. If Excel is not running, the system will start it automatically and display the linked workbook. The following steps show how to change the investment return for the James Worldwide fund (cell C9) from 98,661 to 99,500.

## To Edit the Linked Worksheet

**①** **With the Publisher window and the West Investment Statement Q1-2001 publication active, double-click the worksheet. When the Excel window becomes active, double-click the title bar to maximize the screen.**

*Windows switches from Publisher to Excel and displays the original workbook West Quarterly Summary.*

**②** **Click cell C9 and type** 99500 **as the new value for James Worldwide. Click the green check mark Enter button on the Formula bar.**

*Excel recalculates all formulas in the workbook (Figure 9).*

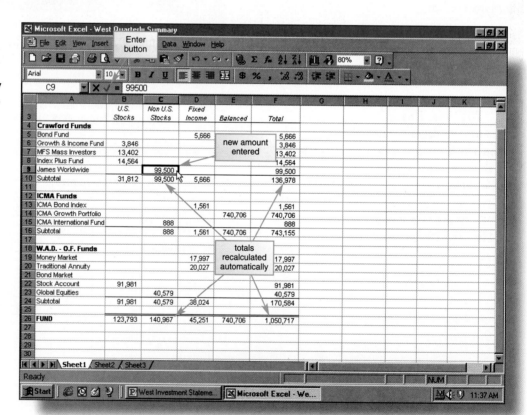

**FIGURE 9**

**3** **Click the West Investment Statement button on the taskbar.**

*The Publisher window becomes active. The amount for James Worldwide, which was 98,661 is now 99,500. New totals display for the Non U.S. Stocks subtotal, the Crawford Funds subtotals, and the grand totals (Figure 10).*

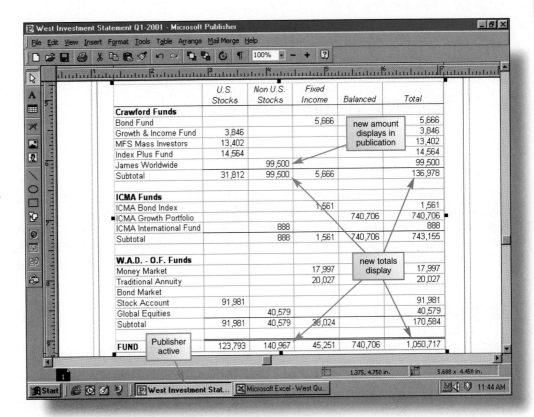

**FIGURE 10**

As you can see from the previous steps, you double-click a linked object when you want to edit it. Windows will activate the application and display the workbook or publication from which the object came. You then can edit the object and return to the destination application. Any changes made to the object will appear in the destination publication.

If you want the edited changes to the linked workbook to be permanent, you must save the West Quarterly Summary.xls file, before quitting Excel.

### More About 2000

### Embedding Graphics

When packing a publication that contains links to graphics, Publisher may make some conversions. For instance, if you link to a bitmap graphic, Publisher saves it in Tagged Image File (TIF) format. If you link to an EPS or vector-based graphic, Publisher saves it in Windows Metafile (WMF) format. Transparency is not preserved in bitmap images, except transparent GIFs, which are not converted.

CASE PERSPECTIVE SUMMARY

As the investment figures for the previous quarter come in, Marcia updates the Excel workbook. She then opens the Publisher investment statement from the previous quarter and modifies the date. After saving the Publisher publication, she prints it and distributes it to the appropriate employees.

# Integration Feature Summary

This Integration Feature introduced you to Object Linking and Embedding (OLE). OLE allows you to bring together data and information that has been created in different applications. When you link an object to a publication and save it, only a link to the object is saved with the publication. You edit a linked object by double-clicking it. The system activates the application and opens the file in which the object was created. If you change any part of the object and then return to the destination publication, the updated object will display.

# What You Should Know

Having completed this project, you now should be able to perform the following tasks:

▶ Open a Publisher Publication and an Excel Workbook *(PUBI 1.3)*
▶ Link an Excel Worksheet to a Publisher Publication *(PUBI 1.5)*
▶ Print and Save the Publication with the Linked Worksheet *(PUBI 1.7)*
▶ Edit the Linked Worksheet *(PUBI 1.8)*

**More About**

**Quick Reference**

For a table that lists how to complete the tasks covered in this book using the mouse, menu, shortcut menu, and keyboard, visit the Shelly Cashman Series Office Web page (www.scsite.com/off2000/qr.htm), and then click Microsoft Publisher 2000.

**More About**

**Microsoft Certification**

The Microsoft Office User Specialist (MOUS) Certification program provides an opportunity for you to obtain a valuable industry credential — proof that you have the skills required by employers. For more information see Appendix D or visit the Shelly Cashman Series MOUS Web page (www.scsite.com/off2000/cert.htm).

# In the Lab

## 1 Linking a Sales Worksheet to a Weekly Memo

**Problem:** LaKeisha James is Vice President of Sales for Corporate Intranets. Each week she sends out a memo (Figure 11a) to all district sales managers showing the previous week's daily sales by office. You have been asked to simplify her task by linking the sales worksheet (Figure 11b) to a weekly memo.

**Instructions:** Perform the following tasks.

1. One at a time, open the publication Weekly Memo and the workbook Weekly Sales Summary from the Data Disk.
2. Link the range A3:G25 to the bottom of the Weekly Memo publication.
3. Print and then save the publication as Sales Memo 04-09-01.
4. Double-click the worksheet and use the keyboard to increase each of the five San Diego amounts manually by $200. Activate the Publisher window and print it with the new values. Close the publication and workbook without saving them.

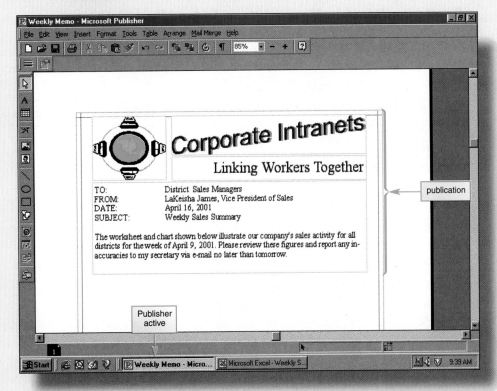

(a)

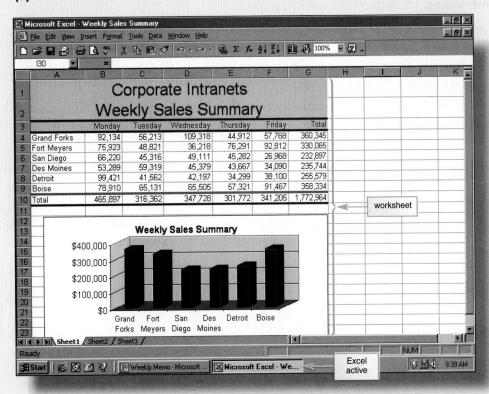

(b)

**FIGURE 11**

*In the Lab*

## 2 Pasting a Weekly Memo into a Sales Worksheet

**Problem:** LaKeisha James has asked you to paste the Publisher publication into the Excel workbook, rather than linking the Excel workbook to the Publisher publication, as was done in Exercise 1.

**Instructions:** Complete the following tasks.

1. One at a time, open the publication Weekly Memo and the workbook Weekly Sales Summary from the Data Disk.
2. With the Excel window active, drag through the row numbers 1 through 20 on the left border. Click Insert on the menu bar and then click Rows. Click cell A1.
3. Click the Publisher publication button on the taskbar. Click Select all on the Edit menu. Copy the selected objects.
4. Activate the Excel worksheet again and then click Paste Special on the Edit menu. Choose to paste the publication objects as Picture (Enhanced Metafile), at the top of the Weekly Sales Summary worksheet.
5. Save the workbook as Weekly Sales Summary with Memo 04-09-01 and print a copy. Quit Excel. Quit Publisher without saving the publication.

## 3 Viewing an Embedded Toolbar

**Problem:** LaKeisha James now has asked you to embed the Excel workbook, rather than linking it to the Publisher publication.

**Instructions:** Complete the following tasks.

1. One at a time, open the publication Weekly Memo and the workbook Weekly Sales Summary from the Data Disk.
2. With the Excel worksheet active, select the range A3:G25 in the worksheet. Click the Copy button on the Standard toolbar. Quit Excel.
3. With the Publisher publication active, click Paste Special on the Edit menu. When the Paste Special dialog box displays, click the Paste option button to embed the worksheet rather than link it. Click Microsoft Excel Worksheet Object in the As box and then click the OK button.
4. When the worksheet range displays as a table in the publication, double-click it. Notice that Excel is not linked or activated. Rather, row and column borders display around the table.
5. Look at the toolbars. The Standard toolbar now displays some buttons unique to Excel. Below the Standard toolbar is an Excel Formula bar. Point to each button on the toolbars and as their ScreenTips display, make a list of their names on a piece of paper. Turn the paper in to your instructor.

# APPENDIX A
# Microsoft Publisher 2000 Help System

## Using the Publisher Help System

At any time during a Publisher session, you can interact with its Help system and display information on any Publisher topic. It is a complete reference manual at your fingertips.

The two primary forms of Help are the Office Assistant and the Publisher Help window. The method you use depends on your preferences. As shown in Figure A-1, you access either form of Help by pressing the F1 key; clicking Microsoft Publisher Help on the Help menu; or clicking the Microsoft Publisher Help button on the Standard toolbar. Publisher responds in one of two ways:

1. If the Office Assistant is turned on, the Office Assistant displays with a balloon (lower-right side in Figure A-1).
2. If the Office Assistant is turned off, the Publisher Help window displays (lower-left side in Figure A-1).

Table A-1 on the next page summarizes the nine categories of Help available. Because of the way the Publisher Help system works, please review the rightmost column of Table A-1 if you have difficulties activating the desired category.

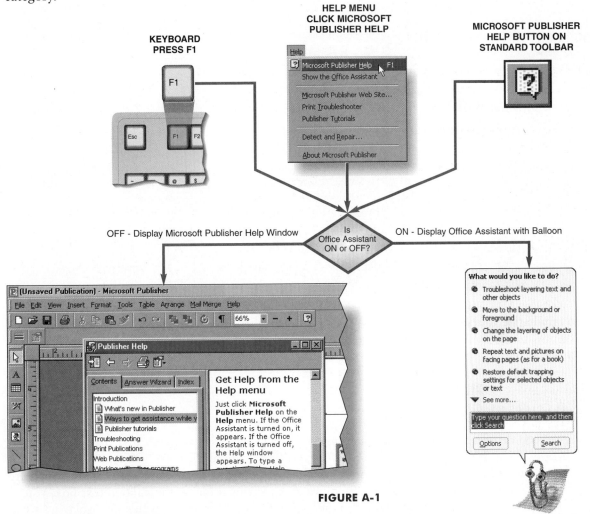

**FIGURE A-1**

**Table A-1    Publisher Help System**

| TYPE | DESCRIPTION | HOW TO ACTIVATE | TURNING THE OFFICE ASSISTANT ON AND OFF |
|---|---|---|---|
| Answer Wizard | Similar to the Office Assistant in that it answers questions that you type in your own words. It displays when the Office Assistant is turned off or when you click the Show button on the Publisher Help toolbar. | Click the Microsoft Publisher Help button on the Standard toolbar. If necessary, maximize the Help window by double-clicking its title bar. Click the Answer Wizard tab. | If the Office Assistant displays, right-click it, and then click Options. Click Use the Office Assistant to remove the check mark. Click the OK button. |
| Contents sheet | Groups Help topics by general categories. Use when you know only the general category of the topic in question. It displays when the Office Assistant is turned off or when you click the Show button on the Publisher Help toolbar. | Click the Microsoft Publisher Help button on the Standard toolbar. If necessary, maximize the Help window by double-clicking its title bar. Click the Contents tab. | If the Office Assistant displays, right-click it, and then click Options. Click Use the Office Assistant to remove the check mark. Click the OK button. |
| Detect and Repair | Automatically finds and fixes errors in the application. | Click Detect and Repair on the Help menu. | |
| Hardware and Software Information | Shows Product ID and allows access to system information and technical support information. | Click About Microsoft Publisher on the Help menu and then click the appropriate button. | |
| Index sheet | Similar to an index in a book; use when you know exactly what you want. It displays when the Office Assistant is turned off or when you click the Show button on the Publisher Help toolbar. | Click the Microsoft Publisher Help button on the Standard toolbar. If necessary, maximize the Help window by double-clicking its title bar. Click the Index tab. | If the Office Assistant displays, right-click it, and then click Options. Click Use the Office Assistant to remove the check mark. Click the OK button. |
| Microsoft Publisher Web Site | Used to access technical resources and download free product enhancements on the Web. | Click Microsoft Publisher Web Site on the Help menu. | |
| Object-specific Help | Used to access Help topics on manipulating specific objects. | Right-click the object and then click a Help link. | |
| Office Assistant | Answers questions that you type in your own words, offers tips, and provides Help for a variety of Publisher features. | Click the Microsoft Publisher Help button on the Standard toolbar or double-click the Office Assistant icon. Some dialog boxes also include the Microsoft Publisher Help button. | If the Office Assistant does not display, click Show the Office Assistant on the Help menu. |
| Question Mark button and What's This? button | Displays as a question mark (?) character or What's This? button. Used to identify unfamiliar items on the screen. | In a dialog box, click the Question Mark button and then click an item in the dialog box. Right-click an item and then click the What's This? button when it displays. | |

The best way to familiarize yourself with the Publisher Help system is to use it. The next several pages show different examples of how to use the Help system. Following the examples is a set of exercises titled Use Help that will sharpen your Publisher Help system skills.

# The Office Assistant

The **Office Assistant** is an icon that displays in the Publisher window (lower-right side of Figure A-1 on the previous page). It has dual functions. First, it will respond with a list of topics that relate to the entry you make in the text box at the bottom of the balloon. The entry can be in the form of a word, phrase, or question written as if you were talking to a human being. For example if you want to learn more about saving a file, in the balloon text box, you can type save, save a file, how do I save a file, or anything similar. The Office Assistant responds by displaying a list of topics (links) from which you can choose. Once you choose a topic, it displays the corresponding information.

Second, the Office Assistant monitors your work and accumulates tips during a session on how you might better accomplish your work. You can view the tips at any time. The accumulated tips display when you activate the Office Assistant balloon (Figure A-3 on the next page). Also, if at anytime you see a light bulb above the Office Assistant, click it to display the most recent tip.

You may or may not want the Office Assistant to display on the screen at all times. You can hide it, and then show it at a later time. You may prefer not to use the Office Assistant at all. In this case, you use the Publisher Help window (lower-left side of Figure A-1 on page PUB A.1). Thus, you need to know both how to show and hide the Office Assistant, and how to turn the Office Assistant on and off.

## Showing and Hiding the Office Assistant

When Publisher is first installed, the Office Assistant displays in the Publisher window. You can move it to any location on the screen. You can click it to display the Office Assistant balloon, which allows you to request Help. If the Office Assistant is displayed on the screen and you want to hide it, you click the **Hide the Office Assistant command** on the Help menu. You also can right-click the Office Assistant to display its shortcut menu and then click the **Hide command** to hide it. When the Office Assistant is hidden, then the **Show the Office Assistant command** replaces the Hide the Office Assistant command on the Help menu. Thus, you can show or hide the Office Assistant at any time.

## Turning the Office Assistant On and Off

The fact that the Office Assistant is hidden does not mean it is turned off. To turn the Office Assistant off, it must be displaying in the Publisher window. Right-click the Office Assistant to display its shortcut menu (left side of Figure A-2), and then click Options. Clicking the **Options command** causes the Office Assistant dialog box to display (right side of Figure A-2).

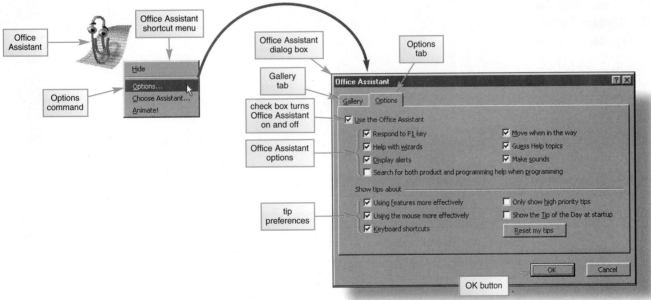

**FIGURE A-2**

The top check box in the Options sheet determines whether the Office Assistant is on or off. To turn the Office Assistant off, remove the check mark from the **Use the Office Assistant check box** and then click the OK button. As shown in Figure A-1 on page PUB A.1, if the Office Assistant is off when you invoke Help, then the Publisher Help window displays instead of the Office Assistant. To turn the Office Assistant on at a later time, click the Show the Office Assistant command on the Help menu.

Through the Options command on the Office Assistant shortcut menu, you can change the look and feel of the Office Assistant. For example, you can hide the Office Assistant, turn the Office Assistant off, change the way it works, choose a different Office Assistant icon, or view an animation of the current one. These options also are available by clicking the Options button that displays in the Office Assistant balloon (Figure A-3 on the next page).

The **Gallery sheet** (Figure A-2 on the previous page) in the Office Assistant dialog box allows you to change the appearance of the Office Assistant. The default is the paper clip (Clippit). You can change it to a bouncing red happy face (The Dot), a robot (F1), a professor (The Genius), the Microsoft Office logo (Office Logo), the earth (Mother Nature), a cat (Links), or a dog (Rocky).

## Using the Office Assistant

As indicated earlier, the **Office Assistant** allows you to enter a word, phrase, or question and responds by displaying a list of topics from which you may choose to display Help. The following steps show how to use the Office Assistant to obtain Help on sending an object to the background of a publication.

 **To Use the Office Assistant**

**1** If the Office Assistant is not turned on, click Help on the menu bar and then click Show the Office Assistant. Click the Office Assistant. When the Office Assistant balloon displays, **type** how do i send an object to the back **in** the text box immediately above the Options button. Point to the Search button.

*The Office Assistant balloon displays (Figure A-3). Your accumulated tips will vary.*

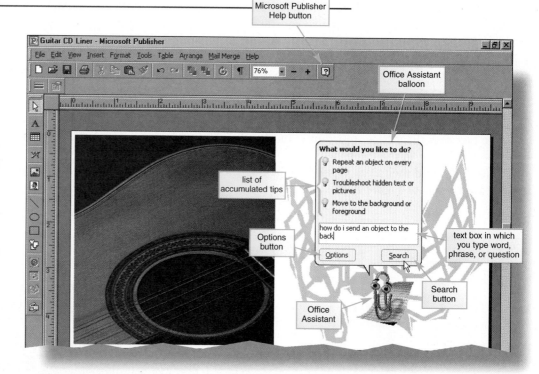

**FIGURE A-3**

**2** Click the Search button. When the Office Assistant balloon reappears, point to the topic, Change the layering of objects on the page (Figure A-4).

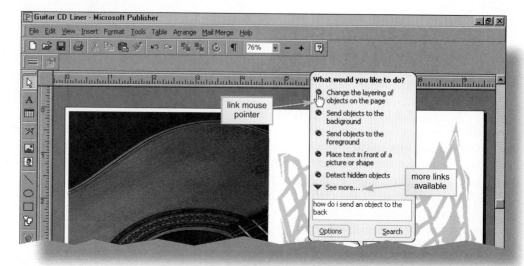

**FIGURE A-4**

**3** **Click the topic, Change the layering of objects on the page. If necessary, move or hide the Office Assistant so you can view all of the text in the Publisher Help window.**

*The Publisher Help window displays information on how to change the layering of objects (Figure A-5).*

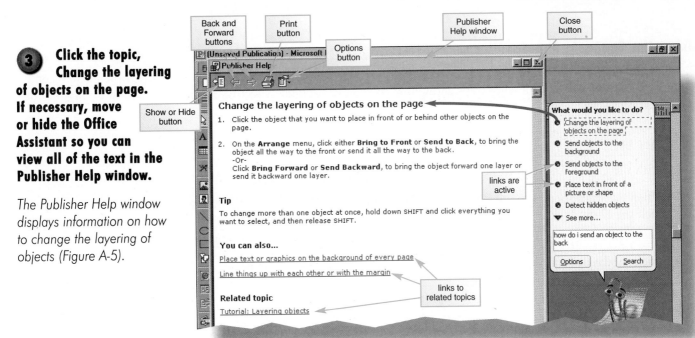

FIGURE A-5

When the Publisher Help window displays, you can read or print it. To print the information, click the Print button on the Publisher Help toolbar. Table A-2 lists the function of each button on the Publisher Help toolbar. To close the Publisher Help window shown in Figure A-5, click the Close button on its title bar.

# The Publisher Help Window

If the Office Assistant is turned off and you click the Microsoft Publisher Help button on the Standard toolbar, the **Publisher Help window** displays (Figure A-6 on the next page). This window contains three tabs on the left side: Contents, Answer Wizard, and Index. Each tab displays a sheet with powerful search capabilities. Use the Contents sheet as you would a table of contents at the front of a book to locate Help. The Answer Wizard sheet answers your queries the same as the Office Assistant. You use the Index sheet in the same fashion as an index in a book to look up Help topics.

Click the tabs to move from sheet to sheet. The five buttons on the toolbar — Show or Hide, Back, Forward, Print, and Options — are described in Table A-2.

Besides clicking the Microsoft Publisher Help button on the Standard toolbar, you also can click the Microsoft Publisher Help command on the Help menu or press the F1 key to display the Publisher Help window to gain access to the three sheets. To close the Publisher Help window, click the Close button in the upper-right corner on its title bar.

**Other Ways**

1. If Office Assistant is turned on, on Help menu click Microsoft Publisher Help, or click Microsoft Publisher Help button on Standard toolbar to display Office Assistant balloon

| Table A-2 Publisher Help Toolbar Buttons | | |
|---|---|---|
| BUTTON | NAME | FUNCTION |
| or | Show or Hide | Displays or hides the Contents, Answer Wizard, Index tabs |
| | Back | Displays the previous Help topic |
| | Forward | Displays the next Help topic |
| | Print | Prints the current Help topic |
| | Options | Displays a list of commands |

## Using the Contents Sheet

The **Contents sheet** is useful for displaying Help when you know the general category of the topic in question, but not the specifics. The following steps show how to use the Contents sheet to obtain information on laying out a publication.

### TO OBTAIN HELP USING THE CONTENTS SHEET

**1** With the Office Assistant turned off, click the Microsoft Publisher Help button on the Standard toolbar.

**2** When the Publisher Help window displays, double-click its title bar to maximize the window. If necessary, click the Show button to display the tabs.

**3** Click the Contents tab. Double-click the Print Publications book icon on the left side of the window.

**4** Click the Lay out a publication subtopic below the Print Publications book.

*Publisher displays Help on the subtopic, Lay out my publication (Figure A-6).*

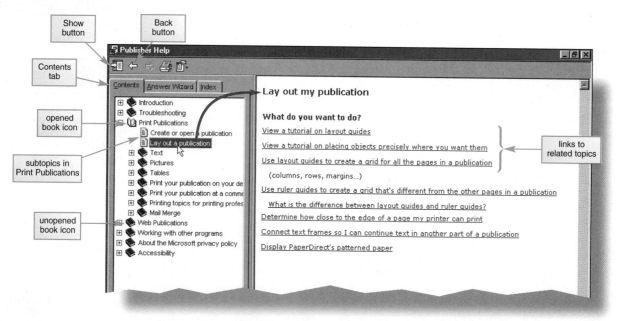

**FIGURE A-6**

Once the information on the subtopic displays, you can scroll through and read it or you can click the Print button on the Publisher Help toolbar to obtain a hard copy. If you decide to click another subtopic on the left or a link on the right, you can return to the Help page shown in Figure A-6 by clicking the Back button.

Each topic in the Contents list is preceded by a book icon or page icon. A **book icon** indicates subtopics are available. A **page icon** means information on the topic will display if you click the title. The book icon opens when you double-click the book (or its title) or when you click the plus sign (+) to the left of the book icon.

## Using the Answer Wizard Sheet

The **Answer Wizard sheet** operates like the Office Assistant in that you enter a word, phrase, or question and it responds with topics from which you can choose to display Help. The following steps show how to use the Answer Wizard sheet to obtain Help on editing tables.

## TO OBTAIN HELP USING THE ANSWER WIZARD SHEET

**1** With the Office Assistant turned off, click the Microsoft Publisher Help button on the Standard toolbar.

**2** When the Publisher Help window displays, double-click its title bar to maximize the window. If necessary, click the Show button to display the tabs.

**3** Click the Answer Wizard tab. Type how do i edit a table in the What would you like to do? text box on the left side of the window. Click the Search button.

**4** When a list of topics displays in the Select topic to display list box, click Select parts of a table.

*Publisher displays Help on how to select parts of a table (Figure A-7).*

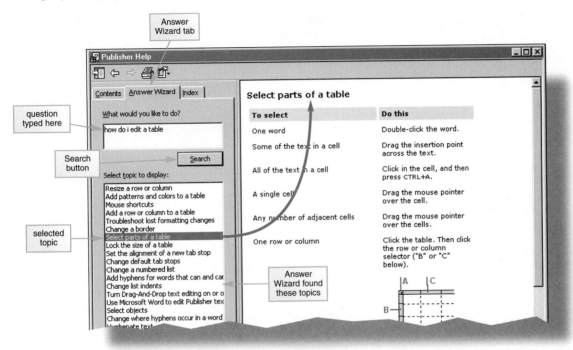

**FIGURE A-7**

If the topic, Select parts of a table, does not include the information you want, click another topic in the list. Continue to click topics until you find the desired information.

## Using the Index Sheet

The third sheet in the Publisher Help window is the Index sheet. Use the **Index sheet** when you know the key-word or the first few letters of the keyword for which you want Help. The following steps show how to use the Index sheet to obtain Help on posters.

## TO OBTAIN HELP USING THE INDEX SHEET

**1** With the Office Assistant turned off, click the Microsoft Publisher Help button on the Standard toolbar.

**2** When the Publisher Help window displays, double-click the title bar to maximize the window. If necessary, click the Show button to display the tabs.

**3** Click the Index tab. Type poster in the Type keywords text box on the left side of the window. Click the Search button.

**4** When a list of topics displays in the Choose a topic list box, click How will my poster look when I print it?

*Publisher displays Help about printing large publications (Figure A-8 on the next page).*

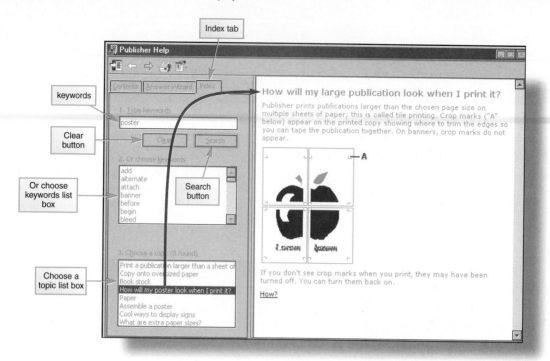

**FIGURE A-8**

An alternative to typing a keyword in the Type keywords text box is to scroll through the Or choose keywords list box (the middle list box on the left side of the window). When you locate the keyword you are searching for, double-click it to display Help on the related topic. The Or choose keywords list box also displays other topics that relate to the new keyword. As you begin typing a new keyword in the Type keywords text box, Publisher jumps to that point in the Or choose keywords list box. To begin a new search, click the Clear button.

# Question Mark Button and the What's This? Button

Use the Question Mark button or the What's This? button in a dialog box when you are not sure what an object on the screen is or what it does.

## Question Mark Button

In certain dialog boxes, a **Question Mark button** displays next to the Close button in the upper-right corner on the title bar (Figure A-9). You use the Question Mark button to display a detailed ScreenTip. For example, in Figure A-9, the Design Gallery dialog box displays on the screen. If you click the Question Mark button and then click a Mastheads preview, an explanation of the preview displays. You can print the ScreenTip by right-clicking it and then clicking Print Topic on the shortcut menu.

If a dialog box does not include a Question Mark button, press the SHIFT+F1 keys. This combination of keys displays the ScreenTip for the selected item. If no object is selected, the mouse pointer may change to an arrow with a question mark. You then can click any object in the dialog box to display the ScreenTip.

## What's This? Button

As with the Question Mark button, the What's This? button is used to display a detailed ScreenTip. To display the What's This? button, you simply right-click any object in a dialog box, then click the What's This? button to display the ScreenTip. For example, after you click the What's This? button in the Recolor Picture dialog box, a description of how to select a color displays (Figure A-10). You can print the ScreenTip by right-clicking it and then clicking Print Topic on the shortcut menu.

If an object does not have a ScreenTip, a message will display indicating no Help is available.

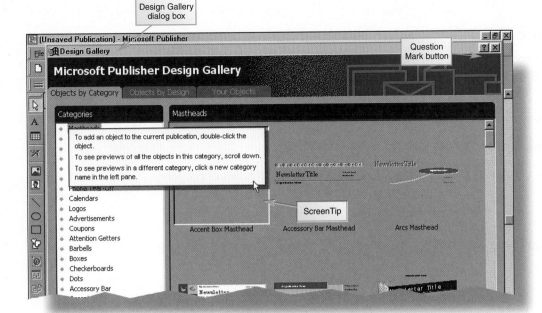

**FIGURE A-9**

# Microsoft Publisher Web Site Command

The **Microsoft Publisher Web Site command** on the Help menu displays a Microsoft Web page containing up-to-date information on a variety of Publisher-related topics. To use this command, you must be connected to the Internet. Once the page displays, you can click any of the articles about Publisher features and versions. The Web page contains several links, such as The Publisher Gallery and Office Update Web site.

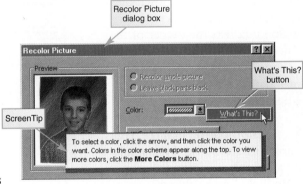

**FIGURE A-10**

# Other Help Commands

Four additional commands on the Help menu are the Print Troubleshooter, Publisher Tutorials, Detect and Repair, and About Microsoft Publisher commands.

## Print Troubleshooter Command

The **Print Troubleshooter command** on the Help menu offers assistance on printing publications. When clicked, a list of print Help topics displays. Shown in Figure A-11, the Publisher Print Troubleshooter tries to help you find a solution to your printing problems.

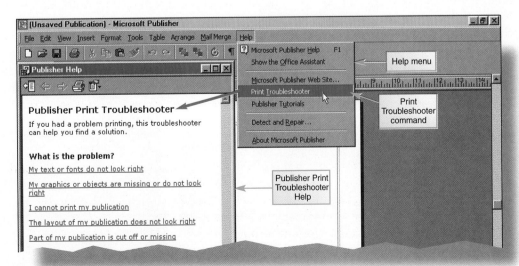

**FIGURE A-11**

## Publisher Tutorials Command

The **Publisher Tutorials command** on the Help menu displays a window containing a graphic that you can click to display a list of available tutorials (Figure A-12). The list contains links to several tutorial topics. You can right-click any tutorial screen to print, copy, or progress through the tutorial. Page navigation buttons also display in each tutorial screen so you can move forward and backward or jump to any page in the tutorial.

## Detect and Repair Command

Use the **Detect and Repair command** on the Help menu if Publisher is not running properly or if it is generating errors. When you invoke this command, the Detect and Repair dialog box shown on the left in Figure A-13 displays. Click the Start button in the dialog box to initiate the detect and repair process.

## About Microsoft Publisher Command

The **About Microsoft Publisher command** on the Help menu displays the About Microsoft Publisher dialog box shown on the right in Figure A-13. The dialog box lists the owner of the software and the product identification. You need to know the product identification if you call Microsoft for assistance.

Below the OK button are the System Info button and the Tech Support button. The **System Info button** displays system information, including hardware resources, components, software environment, and applications. The **Tech Support button** displays technical assistance information.

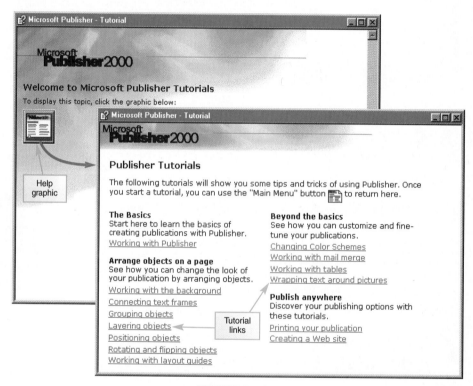

**FIGURE A-12**

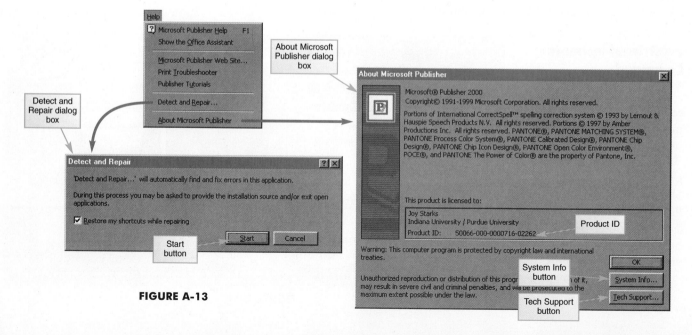

**FIGURE A-13**

# Use Help

## 1 Using the Office Assistant

**Instructions:** Perform the following tasks using the Publisher Help system.

1. If the Office Assistant is turned on, click it to display the Office Assistant balloon. If the Office Assistant is not turned on, click Help on the menu bar and then click Show the Office Assistant.
2. Right-click the Office Assistant and then click Options on the shortcut menu. Click the Gallery tab in the Office Assistant dialog box and then click the Next button to view all the Office Assistants. Click the Options tab in the Office Assistant dialog box and review the different options for the Office Assistant. Click the Question Mark button and display ScreenTips for the first two check boxes. Print the ScreenTips and hand them in to your instructor. Close the Office Assistant dialog box.
3. Click the Office Assistant and type how do i create a table in the text box at the bottom of the balloon. Click the Search button.
4. Click Create a table and type text into it in the Office Assistant balloon. If necessary, double-click the title bar to maximize the Publisher Help window. Read and print the information. One at a time, click the links to learn about copying text to adjacent cells and changing table size, columns, or rows. Print the information. Hand in the printouts to your instructor. Use the Back and Forward buttons to return to the original page.
5. Click the Close button in the Publisher Help window.
6. Click the Office Assistant. If it is not turned on, click Show the Office Assistant on the Help menu. Search for the topic, copyfitting text. Click the Get text to fit link. Read and print the information. Click the three listed links. Print the information on each link, then turn it in to your instructor. Close the Publisher Help window.

## 2 Expanding on the Publisher Help System Basics

**Instructions:** Use the Publisher Help system to understand the topics better and to answer the questions listed below. Answer the questions on your own paper, or hand in the printed Help information to your instructor.

1. Right-click the Office Assistant. If it is not turned on, click Show the Office Assistant on the Help menu. When the shortcut menu displays, click Options. Click Use the Office Assistant to remove the check mark and then click the OK button.
2. Click the Microsoft Publisher Help button on the Standard toolbar. Maximize the Publisher Help window. If the tabs are hidden on the left side, click the Show button. Click the Index tab. Type menu in the Type keywords text box. Click the Search button. Click Troubleshoot toolbars and menus. Print the information. Click the Hide and the Show buttons. One at a time, click the three links about setting toolbars and viewing all the commands. Read and print the information for each link. Close the Publisher Help window. Hand in the printouts to your instructor.
3. Press the F1 key. Click the Answer Wizard tab. Type help in the What would you like to do? text box, then click the Search button. Click Ways to get assistance while you work. Read through the information that displays. Print the information. One at a time, click the first two links. Read and print the information for both.
4. Click the Contents tab. Click the plus sign (+) to the left of the Accessibility book. One at a time, click the first three topics under the Accessibility book. Read and print each one. Close the Publisher Help window. Hand in the printouts to your instructor.

# APPENDIX B
## Publishing Office Web Pages to a Web Server

With a Microsoft Office 2000 program, such as Word, Excel, Access, PowerPoint, or Publisher, you use the Save as Web Page command on the File menu to save the Web page to a Web server using one of two techniques: Web folders or File Transfer Protocol. A **Web folder** is an Office 2000 shortcut to a Web server. **File Transfer Protocol (FTP)** is an Internet standard that allows computers to exchange files with other computers on the Internet.

You should contact your network system administrator or technical support staff at your ISP to determine if their Web server supports Web folders, FTP, or both, and to obtain necessary permissions to access the Web server. If you decide to publish Web pages using a Web folder, you must have the Office Server Extensions (OSE) installed on your computer. OSE comes with the Standard, Professional, and Premium editions of Office 2000.

### Using Web Folders to Publish Office Web Pages

If you are granted permission to create a Web folder (shortcut) on your computer, you must obtain the URL of the Web server, and a user name and possibly a password that allows you to access the Web server. You also must decide on a name for the Web folder. Table B-1 explains how to create a Web folder.

Office adds the name of the Web folder to the list of current Web folders. You can save to this folder, open files in the folder, rename the folder, or perform any operations you would to a folder on your hard disk. You can use your Office program or Windows Explorer to access this folder. Table B-2 explains how to save to a Web folder.

### Using FTP to Publish Office Web Pages

When publishing a Web page using FTP, you first add the FTP location to your computer and then you can save to it. An **FTP location**, also called an **FTP site**, is a collection of files that resides on an FTP server. In this case, the FTP server is the Web server.

To add an FTP location, you must obtain the name of the FTP site, which usually is the address (URL) of the FTP server, and a user name and a password that allows you to access the FTP server. You save and open the Web pages on the Web server using the name of the FTP site. Table B-3 explains how to add an FTP site.

Office adds the name of the FTP site to the FTP locations in the Save As and Open dialog boxes. You can open and save files on this FTP location. Table B-4 explains how to save using an FTP location.

**Table B-1   Creating a Web Folder**

1. Click File on the menu bar and then click Save As; or click File on the menu bar and then click Open.
2. When the Save As dialog box or the Open dialog box displays, click the Web Folders shortcut on the Places Bar along the left side of the dialog box.
3. Click the Create New Folder button.
4. When the first dialog box of the Add Web Folder wizard displays, type the URL of the Web server and then click the Next button.
5. When the Enter Network Password dialog box displays, type the user name and, if necessary, the password in the respective text boxes and then click the OK button.
6. When the last dialog box of the Add Web Folder wizard displays, type the name you would like to use for the Web folder. Click the Finish button.
7. Close the Save As or the Open dialog box.

**Table B-2   Saving to a Web Folder**

1. Click File on the menu bar and then click Save As.
2. When the Save As dialog box displays, type the Web page file name in the File name text box. Do not press the ENTER key.
3. Click Web Folders shortcut on the Places Bar along the left side of the dialog box.
4. Double-click the Web folder name in the Save in list.
5. When the Enter Network Password dialog box displays, type the user name and password in the respective text boxes and then click the OK button.
6. Click the Save button in the Save As dialog box.

**Table B-3   Adding an FTP Location**

1. Click File on the menu bar and then click Save As; or click File on the menu bar and then click Open.
2. In the Save As dialog box, click the Save in box arrow and then click Add/Modify FTP Locations in the Save in list; or in the Open dialog box, click the Look in box arrow and then click Add/Modify FTP Locations in the Look in list.
3. When the Add/Modify FTP Locations dialog box displays, type the name of the FTP site in the Name of FTP site text box. If the site allows anonymous logon, click Anonymous in the Log on as area; if you have a user name for the site, click User in the Log on as area and then enter the user name. Enter the password in the Password text box. Click the OK button.
4. Close the Save As or the Open dialog box.

**Table B-4   Saving to an FTP Location**

1. Click File on the menu bar and then click Save As.
2. When the Save As dialog box displays, type the Web page file name in the File name text box. Do not press the ENTER key.
3. Click the Save in box arrow and then click FTP Locations.
4. Double-click the name of the FTP site you want to save to.
5. When the FTP Log On dialog box displays, enter your user name and password and then click the OK button.
6. Click the Save button in the Save As dialog box.

# APPENDIX C

# Resetting the Publisher Menus and Wizards

When you first install Publisher 2000, menus display in a shortened form listing only the more frequently used commands. Wizards display step-by-step instructions when you begin publications, offer yellow balloon tips, and synchronize elements such as repeated tear-offs. As you use Publisher, it automatically personalizes the menus and wizards for you, based on how often you use specific commands. Options rise to the top of menus and less wizard assistance is offered. Each time you start Publisher, the menus and wizards display in the same settings as the last time you used the application.

To reset the menus and wizards to their installation settings, and so that they display exactly as shown in this book, perform the following steps.

 **To Reset Usage Data**

**1** **Click Tools on the menu bar and then point to Options on the Tools menu.**

*The Tools menu displays (Figure C-1).*

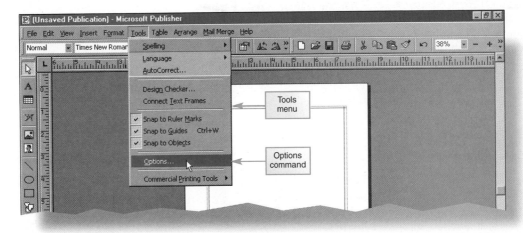

**FIGURE C-1**

**2** **Click Options. When the Options dialog box displays, if necessary, click the General tab and then click Menus show recently used commands first to select it. Point to the Reset Usage Data button.**

*The Options dialog box displays as shown in Figure C-2.*

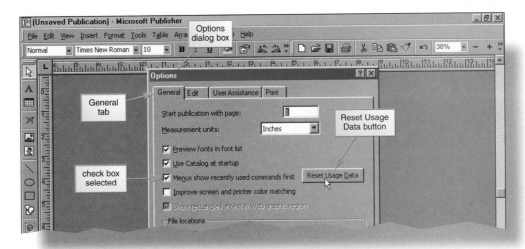

**FIGURE C-2**

**3** **Click the Reset Usage Data button.** When the Microsoft Publisher dialog box displays explaining the function of the Reset Usage Data button, click the Yes button. Click the User Assistance tab. If necessary, click Step through wizard questions to select it. To turn synchronization back on, click the Click to reset wizard synchronizing option button. Click the Reset Tips button to display the yellow tip balloons during editing. Point to the OK button.

*The User Assistance sheet displays in the Options dialog box (Figure C-3). Your check boxes may be checked already, if you are using Publisher for the first time.*

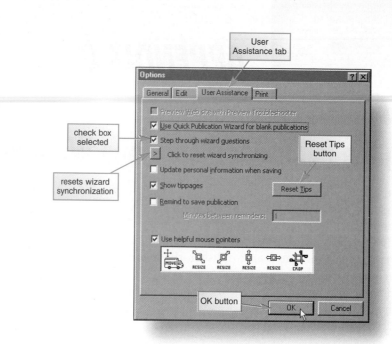

**FIGURE C-3**

**4** **Click the OK button.**

The wizard again will present step-by-step questions when you begin a new publication. Additionally, the wizard will synchronize repeated elements and display yellow tip balloons during editing. You do not need to save the publication to save the resetting choices you made.

# APPENDIX D

# Microsoft Office User Specialist Certification Program

The Microsoft Office User Specialist (MOUS) Certification Program provides a framework for measuring your proficiency with the Microsoft Office 2000 applications, such as Word 2000, Excel 2000, Access 2000, and PowerPoint 2000. Three levels of certification are available – Master, Expert, and Core. The three levels of certification are described in Table D-1.

| Table D-1 | Three Levels of MOUS Certification | | |
|-----------|-----------------------------------|--|--|
| LEVEL | DESCRIPTION | REQUIREMENTS | CREDENTIAL AWARDED |
| Master | Indicates that you have a comprehensive understanding of Microsoft Office 2000 | Pass all FIVE of the required exams: Microsoft Word 2000 Expert, Microsoft Excel 2000 Expert, Microsoft PowerPoint 2000 Core, Microsoft Access 2000 Core, Microsoft Outlook 2000 Core | Candidates will be awarded one certificate for passing all five of the required Microsoft Office 2000 exams: Microsoft Office User Specialist: Microsoft Office 2000 Master |
| Expert | Indicates that you have a comprehensive understanding of the advanced features in a specific Microsoft Office 2000 application | Pass any ONE of the Expert exams: Microsoft Word 2000 Expert, Microsoft Excel 2000 Expert | Candidates will be awarded one certificate for each of the Expert exams they have passed: Microsoft Office User Specialist: Microsoft Word 2000 Expert, Microsoft Office User Specialist: Microsoft Excel 2000 Expert |
| Core | Indicates that you have a comprehensive understanding of the core features in a specific Microsoft Office 2000 application | Pass any ONE of the Core exams: Microsoft Word 2000 Core, Microsoft Excel 2000 Core, Microsoft PowerPoint 2000 Core, Microsoft Access 2000 Core, Microsoft Outlook 2000 Core | Candidates will be awarded one certificate for each of the Core exams they have passed: Microsoft Office User Specialist: Microsoft Word 2000, Microsoft Office User Specialist: Microsoft Excel 2000, Microsoft Office User Specialist: Microsoft PowerPoint 2000, Microsoft Office User Specialist: Microsoft Access 2000, Microsoft Office User Specialist: Microsoft Outlook 2000 |

## Why Should You Get Certified?

Being a Microsoft Office User Specialist provides a valuable industry credential – proof that you have the Office 2000 applications skills required by employers. By passing one or more MOUS certification exams, you demonstrate your proficiency in a given Office application to employers. With nearly 80 million copies of Office in use around the world, Microsoft is targeting Office certification to a wide variety of companies. These companies include temporary employment agencies that want to prove the expertise of their workers, large corporations looking for a way to measure the skill set of employees, and training companies and educational institutions seeking Microsoft Office teachers with appropriate credentials.

## The MOUS Exams

You pay $50 to $100 each time you take an exam, whether you pass or fail. The fee varies among testing centers. The Expert exams, which you can take up to 60 minutes to complete, consist of between 40 and 60 tasks that you perform online. The tasks require you to use the application just as you would in doing your job. The Core exams contain fewer tasks, and you will have slightly less time to complete them. The tasks you will perform differ on the two types of exams.

# How Can You Prepare for the MOUS Exams?

The Shelly Cashman Series® offers several Microsoft-approved textbooks that cover the required objectives on the MOUS exams. For a listing of the textbooks, visit the Shelly Cashman Series MOUS Web page at www.scsite.com/off2000/cert.htm and click the Shelly Cashman Series Office 2000 Microsoft-Approved MOUS Textbooks link (Figure D-1). After using any of the books listed in an instructor-led course, you will be prepared to take the MOUS exam indicated.

# How to Find an Authorized Testing Center

You can locate a testing center by calling 1-800-933-4493 in North America or visiting the Shelly Cashman Series MOUS Web page at www.scsite.com/off2000/cert.htm and then clicking the Locate an Authorized Testing Center Near You link (Figure D-1). At this Web page, you can look for testing centers around the world.

# Shelly Cashman Series MOUS Web Page

The Shelly Cashman Series MOUS Web page (Figure D-1) has more than fifteen Web pages you can visit to obtain additional information on the MOUS Certification Program. The Web page (www.scsite.com/off2000/cert.htm) includes links to general information on certification, choosing an application for certification, preparing for the certification exam, and taking and passing the certification exam.

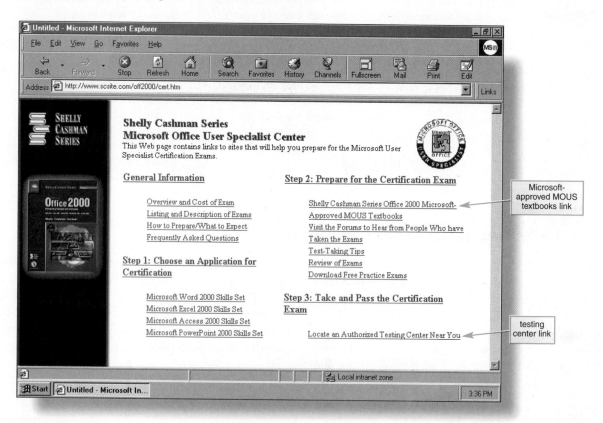

**FIGURE D-1**

# Index

About Microsoft Publisher command (Help menu), **PUB A.10**
Actual Size command (shortcut menu), PUB 1.22
Actual Size view, **PUB 2.20**
Additions, **PUB 1.45**
Address lists, PUB 4.45-49
Addresses, e-mail, PUB 4.20
Advertising flyer, with tear-offs, PUB 1.8-58
Align command (Arrange menu), **PUB 5.49**
Aligning objects, PUB 5.49-53
American National Standards Institute (ANSI), **PUB 3.29**
Animation objects, PUBW 1.9-10
ANSI (American National Standards Institute), **PUB 3.29**
Answer Wizard sheet (Publisher Help window), **PUB A.6-7**
Applications, copying between, PUBI 1.2
Archive attribute, file, **PUB 5.22**
Arrange menu
  Align command, PUB 5.49
  Nudge command, PUB 1.32, PUB 5.12
  Send to Back command, PUB 4.34
  Send to Background command, PUB 2.50
Arrows, lines with, PUB 2.41-43
Associate file, **PUB 4.30**
Associates, **PUB 4.30**
Attachment, **PUB 5.33**
Attention Getters, **PUB 1.46**
  editing, PUB 2.28-30
AutoCorrect feature, PUB 4.20
AutoFit Text, **PUB 1.19, PUB 3.25**
AutoFit Text command (Format menu), PUB 1.20, PUB 3.26
AutoFormat feature, PUB 2.40
Automatic kerning, **PUB 4.24**

Back button (Wizard), **PUB 1.12**
Background, **PUB 2.47**
  choosing not to display, PUB 2.52
  color, PUB 3.35-36
  letterhead, PUB 4.12-16
  text frame sent to, PUB 2.50
  Web page, PUB 5.54
BACKSPACE key, PUB 2.14
Best Fit, fitting text in text frame, **PUB 1.20, PUB 3.25**
Best Fit command (Change Text, AutoFit Text menu), **PUB 3.25**
Black-and-white printing, **PUB 3.49**
Blade coated paper, **PUB 3.48**
Blank publication page, PUB 4.6-9
Blank Publications tab (Catalog), **PUB 2.7, PUB 4.6**
Bleed, **PUB 3.42**
Book icon (Publisher Help window), **PUB A.6**

Border, flyer text frame, PUB 1.36-37
Border Art, **PUB 1.39**
Boundaries, **PUB 1.15**
  hiding, PUB 3.47
Brochure(s), **PUB 3.4, PUB 3.6**
  Web site conversion, PUBW 1.3-5
  tri-fold, PUB 3.4-58
Brochure Wizard, PUB 3.7-9
Bulleted list
  color and border for, PUB 1.36-37
  flyer, PUB 1.20-21
Bulletin board system, **PUB 3.19**
Bullets, **PUB 1.23**
Bullets button (Formatting toolbar), **PUB 1.23**
Business card, **PUB 4.30-38**
Business Card Wizard, **PUB 4.30**
Business forms, PUB 5.4-22
Buttons, hiding, PUB 4.7

Calendar, in brochures, PUB 3.39-46
Camera, digital, PUB 3.14
Camera ready publications, **PUB 1.6**
Catalog, PUB 1.10, **PUB 2.7**
  blank publication, PUB 4.6
Cell(s), **PUB 3.41, PUB 5.22**
  merging, PUB 5.24-25
Cell Diagonals command (Table menu), **PUB 5.24, PUB 5.25**
Central processing unit (CPU), **PUB 3.54**
Change Frame command (shortcut menu), PUB 1.38, PUB 2.28
Change Object command (shortcut menu), PUB 1.35
Change Text command (shortcut menu)
  default text, PUB 2.20
  font, PUB 1.20
Character(s)
  ANSI, PUB 3.29
  displaying special, PUB 5.19
  drop cap, PUB 5.13-14
  zooming, PUB 2.20
Character spacing, PUB 4.24-27
Character Spacing command (Format menu), PUB 4.27
Check box, **PUB 5.41**
Check Spelling feature, **PUB 2.52, PUB 3.12**
Chevrons, **PUB 4.52**
Clip art, **PUB 1.33**
  inserting, PUB 1.34
  inserting using keyword search, PUB 3.17-18
  Internet, PUB 2.31, PUB 3.17, PUB 3.19
  organizing, PUB 1.36
  sources, PUB 3.19
Clip Art pop-up menu, PUB 2.40
Clipboard, **PUB 3.27**

Clip Gallery, **PUB 1.33**
  adding pictures and keywords to, PUB 3.18
  keyword search, PUB 3.17
Close button (title bar), PUB 1.41
Close command (File menu), PUB 1.54
Closing publication, PUB 1.41, PUB 1.54
CMYK process colors, **PUB 3.49**
Code, field, PUB 4.50-53
Color
  background, PUB 3.35-36
  fill, *see* Fill color
  flyer text frame, PUB 1.36-37
  font, *see* Font color
  line, PUB 2.42
  overlapping, PUB 3.43
  palettes, PUB 4.16
  printing, PUB 3.47, PUB 3.49, PUB 5.32
Color-matching library, **PUB 3.49**
Color Printing command (Tools menu, Commercial Printing Tools submenu), **PUB 5.14**
Color scheme
  customizing, PUB 5.11
  flyer, PUB 1.13
  letterhead, PUB 4.15
  newsletter, PUB 2.30
Color Scheme command (Format menu), PUB 5.11
Columns, calendar, PUB 3.41
Columns, newsletter
  creating text in, PUB 2.21
  formatting, PUB 2.27
  within text frame, PUB 2.25-28
Columns, table, PUB 5.22
  inserting, PUB 5.30-32
  selecting, PUB 3.46
Command, dimmed, PUB 1.15
Command button(s), **PUBW 1.11, PUB 5.42-49**
Command Button Properties dialog box, **PUBW 1.11**
Commercial Printing Tools command (Tools menu), PUB 3.50, PUB 5.14
Components, personal information sets, **PUB 2.23-25, PUB 4.9-12**
Composite RGB, **PUB 3.49**
Connect across columns, PUB 2.47
Connect Frames toolbar, PUB 2.28
Connected text frames, PUB 2.21
Contents sheet (Publisher Help window), **PUB A.6**
Copy, mirrored, PUB 3.33-35
Copy button, **PUB 3.27**
  creating symbol text frame using, PUB 3.27-29
Copyfit, **PUB 2.47**
Copying
  between applications, PUBI 1.2

grouped objects, PUB 5.21
objects between publications,
    PUB 3.56-57
pull quote, PUB 2.38
symbol text frame, PUB 3.27-28
Copyrights, logo, PUB 3.20
Correcting errors, PUB 1.45-46
Coupons, **PUB 4.38-43**
Cover page, fax, PUB 5.4, PUB 5.19-22
Create Publisher Address List command
    (Mail Merge menu), PUB 4.46
Create Table command, **PUB 5.22**
Create Web Site from Current
    Publication command (File menu),
    PUB 1.51, PUBW 1.4
Cropping graphics, **PUB 4.27**
Custom Drop Cap tab (Drop Cap
    dialog box), **PUB 5.14**
Custom Shapes button (Objects
    toolbar), **PUB 3.20**
Customize button (New Address List
    dialog box), **PUB 4.49**

Data, **PUB 4.46**
Data labels, internal, PUB 5.41,
    **PUB 5.42**
Data source, **PUB 4.45**
Database, **PUB 4.45**
Date
  calendar, PUB 3.44-45
  inserting, PUB 2.51
  system, PUB 5.17
Date and Time command (Insert menu),
    PUB 5.17
Default, **PUB 2.11**
Default text, replacing, PUB 2.17-20
DELETE key, PUB 2.14
Delete Object command (Edit menu),
    PUB 2.31, PUB 2.35, PUB 3.14
Delete Object command (shortcut
    menu), PUB 1.50, PUB 2.32
Delete Page command (Edit menu),
    PUB 2.12
Delete Text command (shortcut menu),
    PUB 2.17
Deletions, **PUB 1.45**
  brochure objects, PUB 3.13-14
  DELETE key versus BACKSPACE key,
    PUB 2.14
  graphic, PUB 2.32
  logo, PUB 2.30-31
  newsletter pages, PUB 2.12
  object from flyer, PUB 1.49
  sidebar, PUB 2.32
Design Checker, **PUB 1.50,**
    **PUB 1.51-53, PUB 2.52, PUB 2.55**
  options, PUB 2.52
  Web page, PUB 5.53
Design Checker command (Tools menu),
    overlap, PUB 3.43
Design Checker dialog box, **PUB 2.56**
Design Gallery, **PUB 1.46**

adding graphics to, PUB 4.22
creating calendar using, PUB 3.39-46
Design Gallery Object, PUB 1.15
Design Gallery Object command (Insert
    menu), PUB 2.39, PUB 4.22
Design issues, PUB 2.7
  errors related to, PUB 2.52,
    PUB 2.55-56
  Web site, PUBW 1.3
Design set, **PUB 2.7**, PUB 2.11
Desktop publishing (DTP), **PUB 1.6,**
    PUB 1.14
Destination publication, **PUBI 1.1**
Detect and Repair command (Help
    menu), **PUB A.10**
Digital cameras, PUB 3.14
Digital printing, **PUB 3.49**
Digitizing, **PUB 3.14**
Dimmed commands, **PUB 1.15**
Displaying
  background, PUB 2.52
  special characters, PUB 5.19
  toolbars, PUB 1.15
Docked toolbars, **PUB 1.17**
Downloading, **PUB 1.52, PUB 2.17**
  time for, PUB 5.54
Drawing, inserting, PUB 3.14
Drawing programs, PUB 4.27
Drop cap, **PUB 5.13-14**
Drop Cap command (Format menu),
    PUB 5.13
Duplex printing, **PUB 2.57**

E-commerce, **PUB 5.35**, PUB 5.39
Edit menu
  Delete Object command, PUB 2.31,
    PUB 2.35, PUB 3.14
  Delete Page command, PUB 2.12
  Highlight Entire Story command,
    PUB 2.17
  Personal Information command,
    PUB 4.10
  Select All command, PUB 5.6,
    PUB 5.8
  Undo command, PUB 2.31
Edit Publisher Address List command
    (Mail Merge menu), **PUB 4.49**
Editing
  Attention Getter, PUB 2.28-30
  brochure front panel, PUB 3.33-36
  brochure text, PUB 3.9-13
  calendar in brochure, PUB 3.43-45
  flyer text, PUB 1.17-25
  graphic, PUB 1.33-36
  layout, PUB 4.31
  linked worksheet, PUBI 1.8-9
  masthead, PUB 2.13-17
  newsletter, PUB 2.14
  newsletter template, PUB 2.11-13
  personal information component,
    PUB 2.23-25
  personal information sets, PUB 4.9-12

reformatting text after, PUB 2.47
sidebar, PUB 2.39-40
sign-up form, PUB 3.37-38
tear-offs, PUB 1.23-25
techniques, PUB 2.14
Web objects, PUBW 1.6-12
Web properties, PUBW 1.5-6
Electronic commerce, **PUB 5.35,**
    PUB 5.39
Electronic forms, Web pages with,
    **PUB 5.35-36**
E-mail addresses, PUB 4.20
E-mail handlers, **PUB 5.33**
E-mail message, attaching publication
    to, PUB 5.33-35
Embedding, **PUB 3.51**
  fonts, PUB 4.29, PUB 5.14
  graphics, PUBI 1.9
Encapsulated PostScript (EPS),
    **PUB 3.54**
End-of-frame markers, **PUB 5.16**
Entry, address list, **PUB 4.45**
Envelopes, **PUB 4.42, PUB 4.43-44**
Envelopes layout, **PUB 4.42**
Errors
  checking publication for, PUB 2.52-56
  correcting, PUB 1.45-46
Eudora, **PUB 5.33**
Events, **PUB 5.39**
Excel worksheet, linking publication to,
    **PUBI 1.1-10**
Existing Files button (Catalog), **PUB 2.7**
Exit command (File menu), PUB 1.41
Expanded font, **PUB 3.27**
Expense report, **PUB 5.4**
Extensions, *see* File extensions
Extra Content (Design Gallery tab),
    **PUB 1.46, PUBW 1.8**

Facsimile, **PUB 5.19**
Fax, **PUB 5.19**
Fax cover, **PUB 5.4, PUB 5.19-22**
Field(s), **PUB 4.46**
Field code, **PUB 4.50-53**
File(s)
  associating, PUB 4.30
  downloading, PUB 1.52, PUB 2.17
  graphic, PUB 1.33, PUB 1.35
  importing, PUB 2.17-22
  inserting photograph from,
    PUB 3.15-16
  merged, PUB 4.55
  PostScript, PUB 3.54
  sending via e-mail, PUB 5.33-35
  uploading, PUB 1.51
File attributes, PUB 5.22
File extensions, PUB 1.50, **PUB 3.15**
File menu
  Close command, PUB 1.54
  Create Web Site from Current
    Publication command, PUB 1.51,
    PUBW 1.4

Exit command, PUB 1.41
New command, PUB 1.13
Open command, PUB 1.45
Pack and Go command, PUB 3.51
Page Setup command, custom size,
    PUB 4.39
Print command, PUB 1.40
Save As command, PostScript file,
    PUB 3.54
Save As Web Page command,
    PUB 1.53
Save command, PUB 1.28
Send command, PUB 5.33
Web Page Preview command,
    PUBW 1.13
Web Properties command, PUBW 1.5
File name, PUB 1.26, **PUB 1.27**
    saving existing publication with same,
        PUB 1.39
File Transfer Protocol, *see* FTP
Fill color
    business card, PUB 4.32
    calendar, PUB 3.46
    letterhead, PUB 4.13
    logo, PUB 3.22
    newsletter, PUB 2.29-30
    symbol, PUB 3.26
Fill Color button (Formatting toolbar),
    PUB 1.36
Fill Color command (Format menu),
    PUB 1.39, PUB 2.30, PUB 4.16
Fill Color feature, PUB 1.39
Fill command (Table menu),
    **PUB 5.27**-30
Fill effects, letterhead, PUB 4.14,
    PUB 4.16
Finding graphic, PUB 2.32-35
Finish button (Wizard), **PUB 1.12**
Flagged words, PUB 1.20, PUB 4.20
Floating toolbar, **PUB 1.17**
Flyer, with tear-offs, PUB 1.8-58
Flyer Wizard, PUB 1.10-14
Fold(s), brochure, PUB 3.7
Folder, **PUB 1.50**
    My Documents, PUB 1.54
    Web, PUBW 1.6, PUB B.1
    Web style, PUB 1.51, PUB 1.54
Followed, **PUBW 1.10**
Font(s)
    embedding, PUB 4.29, PUB 5.14
    expanded, PUB 3.27
    field codes, PUB 4.53
    flyer, PUB 1.18-19
    TrueType, PUB 4.28
    variegated, PUB 4.18
Font box arrow, PUB 1.18
Font color, brochure, PUB 3.35-36
Foreground, **PUB 2.52**
Form(s)
    brochure, PUB 3.37-38
    business, PUB 5.4-22
    electronic, PUB 5.35-36

Form control(s), **PUB 5.35,**
    **PUB 5.41-49**
Form Control command (Insert menu),
    PUB 5.48
Form letter, **PUB 4.45**
Format menu
    AutoFit Text command,
        PUB 1.20, PUB 3.26
    Character Spacing command,
        PUB 4.27
    Color Scheme command, PUB 5.11
    Drop Cap command, PUB 5.13
    Fill Color command, PUB 1.39,
        PUB 2.30, PUB 4.16
    Line/Border Style command, PUB 1.39
    Line Spacing command, PUB 3.13
    Size and Position command, PUB 1.31,
        PUB 1.32, PUB 3.32, **PUB 3.39,**
        PUB 3.40
    Text Frame Properties command,
        PUB 2.27
    Text Style command, PUB 4.29,
        PUB 4.35
Format Painter button (Standard
    toolbar), **PUB 3.27**
Formatting, **PUB 1.33**
    automatic, PUB 2.40
    automatic, after editing, PUB 2.47
    columns, PUB 2.27
    copied text frame, PUB 3.27
    flyer, PUB 1.36-39
    graphics options, PUB 4.27
    invoice template, PUB 5.11-19
    Measurements toolbar used in,
        PUB 4.24-27
    paragraph, PUB 5.15
    styles and, PUB 4.27-29
    table, PUB 3.43-46, PUB 5.22-24
    Web page, PUBW 1.7
Formatting toolbar, **PUB 1.16**
Four-color printing, **PUB 3.49**
Front page, **PUBW 1.1**
FTP (File Transfer Protocol),
    **PUBW 1.2, PUB B.1**
FTP location, **PUB B.1**
FTP site, **PUB B.1**
Full menu, **PUB 1.15**

Gallery sheet (Office Assistant dialog
    box), **PUB A.4**
.gif files, **PUBW 1.9**
Glossy paper, **PUB 3.48**
Go To Background command (View
    menu), PUB 2.51
Go to Page command (View menu),
    PUB 2.13
Gradient, **PUB 4.16**
Gradient fill effect, **PUB 4.16**
Grammar errors, PUB 2.52
Graphic(s), **PUB 1.31**
    adding to Design Gallery, PUB 4.22
    deleting, PUB 2.32

editing, PUB 1.33-36
embedding, PUBI 1.9
file extensions, PUB 1.50, PUB 3.15
finding, PUB 2.32-35
formatting options, PUB 4.27
moving and resizing, PUB 1.31-33
newsletter, PUB 2.13-17, PUB 2.31-46
on Web, PUB 1.33
portrait versus landscape orientation,
    PUB 2.35
proportions, PUB 2.36, PUB 3.33
replacing, PUB 2.40
spacing around, PUB 1.31
WordArt, *see* WordArt
Graphic files, PUB 1.33, PUB 1.35
Graphic region, **PUB 3.42**
Graphics Manager command (Tools
    menu, Commercial Printing Tools
    submenu), **PUB 5.14**
Group/Ungroup Objects button,
    **PUB 1.29, PUB 2.35**
Grouped heading, moving and resizing,
    PUB 1.30-31
Grouping/grouped objects,
    **PUB 1.29, PUB 2.35**
    copying, PUB 5.21
    logo, PUB 3.30-33
Grow to Fit Text command (Table
    menu), PUB 5.32
Guides, hiding, PUB 3.47

Hand off, **PUB 3.54**
Hanging indents, PUB 5.15
Hard copy, **PUB 1.40**
Heading
    mirrored copy of, PUB 3.33-35
    moving and resizing grouped,
        PUB 1.30-31
Height, page setup, PUB 4.39
Help menu, PUB 1.55
    About Microsoft Publisher command,
        PUB A.10
    Detect and Repair command,
        PUB A.10
    Hide the Office Assistant command,
        PUB A.3
    Microsoft Publisher Web Site
        command, PUB A.9
    Print Troubleshooter command,
        PUB A.9
    Publisher Tutorials command,
        PUB A.10
    Show the Office Assistant command,
        PUB A.3
Help system, PUB 1.55-57, PUB A.1-10
Hidden attribute, file, **PUB 5.22**
Hide Boundaries and Guides command
    (View menu), PUB 3.47
Hide the Office Assistant command
    (Help menu), **PUB A.3**
Hiding
    boundaries and guides, PUB 3.47

buttons and toolbars, PUB 4.7
Office Assistant, PUB A.3
Wizard, PUB 2.10
Highlight Entire Story command (Edit
menu), PUB 2.17
Home page, **PUBW 1.1**
Host, **PUBW 1.1**
Hot spot, **PUBW 1.10, PUB 5.39-41**
Hot Spot button (Objects toolbar),
**PUBW 1.11**
HTML, *see* Hypertext markup language
HTML code, PUBW 1.5
HTML file, saving Publisher publication
as, PUBW 1.1
Hyperlink, **PUBW 1.10**
hot spot, PUBW 1.10, PUB 5.39-41
inserting, PUBW 1.11-12
Hyperlink command (Insert menu),
PUBW 1.12
Hyperlink dialog box, **PUBW 1.11**
Hypertext markup language (HTML),
**PUB 1.50**
Web objects with, PUB 5.42

Illustration software, **PUB 3.17**
Images, **PUB 1.33**
brochure, PUB 3.14-19
Image setter, **PUB 3.49**
Import Clips button, **PUBW 1.10**
Importing, **PUB 2.17**
files, PUB 2.17-22
text for newsletter, PUB 2.17-22,
PUB 2.25-28
text styles, PUB 4.35-38
Imposition, PUB 5.6
Indentation, PUB 5.15, **PUB 5.17**
Index, **PUB 1.50**
Index.html, **PUBW 1.5**
Index sheet (Publisher Help window),
**PUB A.7**
In-house, PUB 3.6
Insert File button (Standard toolbar),
**PUB 5.35**
Insert Hyperlink button (Standard
toolbar), **PUBW 1.11**
Insert menu
Date and Time command, PUB 5.17
Design Gallery Object command,
PUB 2.39, PUB 4.22
Form Control command, PUB 5.48
Hyperlink command, PUBW 1.12
Page Numbers command, PUB 2.50
Personal Information command,
PUB 4.17
Picture command, clip art, PUB 1.35
Picture command, drawing, PUB 3.14
Picture command, photograph,
PUB 3.15
Symbol command, PUB 3.22,
PUB 3.29
Text File command, PUB 2.18,
PUB 2.26

Inserting
brochure images, PUB 3.14-19
calendar in brochure, PUB 3.39-41
clip art, PUB 1.34
clip art using keyword search,
PUB 3.17-18
command buttons, PUB 5.49
dates, PUB 2.51
drawing, PUB 3.14
extra content, PUBW 1.8-9
field codes, PUB 4.50-53
form controls, PUB 5.42-48
graphic in newsletter, PUB 2.32-34
hot spot, PUB 5.40-41
hyperlink, PUBW 1.11-12
object in flyer, PUB 1.47
page numbers in newsletter,
PUB 2.46-51
pages in newsletter, PUB 2.13
personal information components,
PUB 4.16-20
pull quote, PUB 2.36-37
system date, PUB 5.17
table columns, PUB 5.30-32
text from file to replace default text,
PUB 2.17-19
times, PUB 2.51
Web masthead, PUB 5.36-38
WordArt object, PUB 2.44-46
Insertion point, **PUB 2.27**
Instruction text frames, Web page logo,
PUB 5.38
IntelliSense™ technology, PUB 4.20
Internal data labels, PUB 5.41,
**PUB 5.42**
Internally create data source, **PUB 4.45**
Internet, clip art on, PUB 2.31,
PUB 3.17, PUB 3.19
Internet service provider (ISP),
**PUBW 1.1**
Intranet, **PUBW 1.1, PUB 5.33**
Inventory list, **PUB 5.4**
Invoice, **PUB 5.4, PUB 5.6-9**
Invoice template, **PUB 5.6-19**

Jump lines, **PUB 2.20**

Kern, **PUB 4.24**
Kerning, **PUB 4.24**
Keywords, **PUB 2.32**
Publisher Help search, PUB A.7-8
search engines and, PUBW 1.5
Keyword search, inserting clip art using,
PUB 3.17-18
Knocking out, **PUB 3.35**

Labels, **PUB 4.42**
Labels layout, **PUB 4.42**
Landscape, **PUB 2.35**
Laser printers, PUB 3.47
Layered objects, **PUB 1.29, PUB 3.30,**
PUB 4.35

Layout, object, PUB 4.31
Layout guides, **PUB 1.15, PUB 4.7**
setting, **PUB 4.7-9**
Letterhead, **PUB 4.12-23**
Libraries, **PUB 3.49**
Line(s), **PUB 2.41**
arrows and, PUB 2.41-43
sidebar, PUB 2.39
Line/Border Style button (Formatting
toolbar), PUB 2.41, **PUB 2.42**
Line/Border Style command (Format
menu), PUB 1.39
Line/Border Style feature, PUB 1.38,
PUB 1.39, PUB 2.41
Line break, **PUB 2.40**
Line spacing, text frame, PUB 3.13
Line Spacing command (Format menu),
PUB 3.13
Line Tool button (Objects toolbar),
PUB 2.41
Linen paper, **PUB 3.48**
Linking, Excel worksheet to publication,
PUBI 1.1-10
List box, **PUB 5.41**
Logo, **PUB 2.30, PUB 3.20, PUBW 1.5**
creating from scratch, PUB 3.20-33
deleting, PUB 2.30-31
Personal Information, PUB 4.20-22,
PUB 4.30
Web page, PUB 5.38
Lotus cc:Mail, **PUB 5.33**

Mail merge, PUB 4.45-55
Mail Merge menu
Create Publisher Address List
command, PUB 4.46
Edit Publisher Address List command,
PUB 4.49
Open Data Source command,
PUB 4.50
Mailing labels, **PUB 4.49**
Main publication, **PUB 4.45**
Manual kerning, **PUB 4.24**
Margins
around graphic, PUB 1.31
setting on ruler, PUB 5.15
setting using layout and ruler guides,
PUB 4.7
Markers, **PUB 5.15**
Masthead, **PUB 2.13**
editing newsletter, PUB 2.13-17
Web, PUB 5.36-38
Measurements toolbar, PUB 1.17,
PUB 3.32, **PUB 3.41, PUB 4.23-27**
Menu(s)
full, PUB 4.6
resetting, PUB C.1-2
short, PUB 4.6
shortcut, *see* Shortcut menus
Menu bar, **PUB 1.15**
Merge Cells command (Table menu),
**PUB 5.24, PUB 5.25**

Merging, **PUB 4.45**
  automating business forms by,
    PUB 5.11
  cells in table, PUB 5.24-25
Microsoft IntelliMouse®, zooming and,
    PUB 4.12
Microsoft Mail, **PUB 5.33**
Microsoft Office 2000, PUBI 1.3
Microsoft Office Suite, PUB 1.50
Microsoft Office User Specialist
    (MOUS) Certification, PUB 1.55,
    PUB D.1-2
Microsoft Outlook, **PUB 5.33**
Microsoft Publisher, *see* Publisher 2000
Microsoft Publisher Web Site command
    (Help menu), **PUB A.9**
Mirrored copy, of heading, PUB 3.33-35
Modifications, **PUB 1.45**
Motion clips, **PUBW 1.9**
Mouse over event, **PUB 5.39**
Mouse pointer shapes, PUB 5.30
Mover icon, **PUB 1.30**
Moving
  graphic, PUB 1.31-33
  grouped heading, PUB 1.30-31
Multiline text box, **PUB 5.42**, **PUB 5.45**
Multiple copies, printing, PUB 4.38
Multiple publications, PUB 3.54-57
Multitasking, **PUB 3.54**
My Documents folder, PUB 1.54

Navigation bar, **PUBW 1.6**
New button (Standard toolbar),
    PUB 1.13
New command (File menu), PUB 1.13
Newsletter, **PUB 2.4-59**
Newsletter Wizard, PUB 2.8-11
None, fitting text in text frame,
    **PUB 1.20**
Nonprinting tab characters, PUB 5.16
Normal layout, **PUB 4.42**
Nudge command (Arrange menu),
    PUB 1.32, **PUB 5.12**
Null symbol, **PUB 2.11**
Numbers, page, *see* Page numbers

Object(s), **PUB 1.15, PUBI 1.1**
  aligning, PUB 5.49-53
  animation, PUBW 1.9-10
  background, PUB 2.47-51
  copying between publications,
    PUB 3.56-57
  deleting brochure, PUB 3.13-14
  deleting from flyer, PUB 1.49
  Design Gallery of, PUB 1.46
  grouped, copying, PUB 5.21
  grouping, PUB 1.29, PUB 2.35
  imposition, PUB 5.6
  inserting in flyer, PUB 1.47
  layered, PUB 1.29, PUB 3.30,
    PUB 4.35
  layout, PUB 4.31

  overlapping, PUB 3.38, PUB 3.42-43
  positioning, PUB 3.30-33, PUB 5.12
  resolution, PUB 5.12
  selecting all, PUB 5.6
  selecting multiple, PUB 1.29
  sending from front to back,
    PUB 4.34-35
  table, PUB 3.41
  ungrouping, PUB 2.35
  Web, editing, PUBW 1.6-12
  WordArt, PUB 2.44-46
Object Linking and Embedding (OLE),
    **PUBI 1.1, PUBI 1.4**
Object-oriented terminology, PUB 5.39
Object Position box (status bar),
    **PUB 1.17**
Object Size, **PUB 1.17**
Objects by Category (Design Gallery
    tab), **PUB 1.46**
Objects by Design (Design Gallery tab),
    **PUB 1.46**
Objects toolbar, **PUB 1.16, PUB 1.29**
OCR (optical character recognition),
    **PUB 4.53**
Office 2000, certification program,
    PUB 1.55, PUB D.1-2
Office Assistant, **PUB 1.55-56,
    PUB A.2, PUB A.4**
Office Web pages, publishing to Web
    server, PUB B.1
OLE (Object Linking and Embedding),
    **PUBI 1.1, PUBI 1.4**
100% view, **PUB 2.18**
Open button (Standard toolbar),
    PUB 1.45
Open command (File menu), PUB 1.45
Open Data Source command (Mail
    Merge menu), PUB 4.50
Opening
  existing publication, PUB 1.42-45
  multiple publications, PUB 3.54
  multiple sessions of Publisher,
    PUB 3.55
Option button, **PUB 5.41**
Options command (shortcut menu),
    Office Assistant, **PUB A.3**
Options command (Tools menu),
    resetting usage data, PUB C.1-2
Options sheet (Office Assistant dialog
    box), PUB A.3
Order error, **PUB 3.30**
Order form, **PUB 3.37**
Outsourcing
  business cards, PUB 4.31
  printing, **PUB 3.46-54**
Overlapping objects, PUB 3.38,
    PUB 3.42-43

Pack and Go command (File menu),
    PUB 3.51
Pack and Go Wizard, **PUB 3.51-54**

Page(s)
  deleting in newsletter, PUB 2.12
  inserting in newsletter, PUB 2.13
  printing two-sided, PUB 2.57-58
Page icon (Publisher Help window),
    **PUB A.6**
Page layout, **PUB 1.14**
Page Navigation control (status bar),
    **PUB 1.17**
Page numbers, newsletter, PUB 2.46-51
Page Numbers command (Insert menu),
    PUB 2.50
Page Setup command (File menu),
    custom size, PUB 4.39
Page Setup dialog box, **PUB 4.42**
Page views, **PUB 1.23**
Page Width, **PUB 1.23**
Pagination, newsletter, PUB 2.11-13
Pamphlet, *see* Tri-fold brochure
Pantone, **PUB 3.49**
Paper
  brochures, PUB 3.6, PUB 3.7,
    PUB 3.47, PUB 3.48
  size of, PUB 3.7, PUB 4.7, PUB 4.38
  suppliers, PUB 4.12
Paragraph
  formatting, PUB 5.15
  line spacing before and after, PUB 3.13
Paragraph break, **PUB 2.40**
Paragraph marks, **PUB 5.16**
Paste button, **PUB 3.27**
Pasting
  pull quote, PUB 2.38
  symbol text frame, PUB 3.28
Patterns fill effect, **PUB 4.16**
Personal Information command (Edit
    menu), PUB 4.10
Personal Information command (Insert
    menu), PUB 4.17
Personal information component,
    **PUB 2.23-25, PUB 4.9-12**
Personal information management
    (PIM) software, **PUB 5.33**
Personal information sets, **PUB 2.23**
  editing, PUB 4.9-12
Photographs, brochure, PUB 3.14-16
Picture command (Insert menu)
  clip art, PUB 1.35
  drawing, PUB 3.14
  photograph, PUB 3.15
Picture Frame Properties button
    (Formatting toolbar), PUB 1.31
Picture Frame tool (Objects toolbar),
    PUB 1.35
Pixel, **PUB 5.12**
Placeholder text, selecting, PUB 3.9
Pointer Tool button (Objects toolbar),
    **PUB 1.29, PUB 5.19-20**
Portrait, **PUB 2.35**
Positioning
  calendar in brochure, PUB 3.39-41
  logo objects, PUB 3.30-33

Measurements toolbar and, PUB 4.23
objects, PUB 3.30-33, PUB 5.12
objects to prevent overlap,
  PUB 3.42-43
Posted, **PUBW 1.1**
PostScript, **PUB 3.54**
PostScript dumps, **PUB 3.54**
PostScript printer drivers, **PUB 3.54**
Preflight check, **PUB 3.54**
Prepress tasks, **PUB 3.54**
Previewing
  blank publication, PUB 4.6
  before printing, PUB 3.46-47
  Web page, PUBW 1.13
Previews pane (Catalog), **PUB 2.7**
Print button (Standard toolbar),
  PUB 1.40
Print command (File menu), PUB 1.40
Print Troubleshooter command (Help
  menu), **PUB A.9**
Printable region, **PUB 4.7**
Printer problems, PUB 4.7
Printer's marks, PUB 4.38
Printing
  area, PUB 4.7
  color and, PUB 3.47, PUB 3.49,
    PUB 5.32
  custom size publication, PUB 4.43
  duplex, PUB 2.57-58
  flyer, PUB 1.40
  multiple copies, PUB 1.40, PUB 4.38
  outside, PUB 3.46-54
  paper for, PUB 3.47, PUB 3.48
  tile, PUB 5.53
  two-sided page, PUB 2.57-58
Printing plates, **PUB 3.49**
Printout, **PUB 1.40**
Process-color printing, **PUB 3.49**
Proofing newsletter, PUB 2.52-55
Proofing Tools command (shortcut
  menu), PUB 2.55
Properties button, **PUB 5.42**
Property, **PUB 1.17**
Proportional, **PUB 2.36**
Proportions, graphic, PUB 2.36,
  PUB 3.33
.pub extension, **PUB 1.50**
Publication(s)
  advertising flyer with tear-offs,
    PUB 1.8-58
  attaching to e-mail message,
    PUB 5.33-35
  camera ready, PUB 1.6
  closing entire, PUB 1.54
  copying objects between, PUB 3.56-57
  creating Web site from, PUB 1.50-54
  custom size, PUB 4.38-42
  customizing with information sets,
    PUB 4.4-56
  design issues, PUB 2.7, PUB 2.52,
    PUB 2.55-56

formatting, *see* Formatting
linking Excel worksheet to,
  PUBI 1.1-10
modifying, PUB 1.45-50
multiple, PUB 3.54-57
newsletter, PUB 2.2-59
opening existing, PUB 1.42-45
printing, *see* Printing
proofing, PUB 2.52-55
saving as HTML file, PUBW 1.1
saving as Web page, PUB 1.53
saving existing, with same file name,
  PUB 1.39
saving intermediate copy of, PUB 2.22
saving new, PUB 1.26-29
tri-fold brochure, PUB 3.4-58
types of changes made to, PUB 1.45
Publication page, blank, PUB 4.6-9
Publications by Design tab (Catalog),
  **PUB 2.7**
Publications by Wizard tab (Catalog),
  **PUB 2.7**
Publish Web page, **PUBW 1.1**
Publisher 98, updates and, PUB 4.12
Publisher 2000, **PUB 1.6**
  opening multiple sessions of, PUB 3.55
  quitting, PUB 1.41
  starting, PUB 1.9-10, PUB 3.7
Publisher address list, **PUB 4.45-49**
Publisher Address List command,
  **PUB 4.49**
Publisher Help system, **PUB 1.55-57**,
  PUB A.2-10
Publisher Help window, **PUB A.5-8**
Publisher Tutorials command (Help
  menu), **PUB A.10**
Publisher window, **PUB 1.14-17**
Publisher-designed Publication,
  **PUB 2.11**
Pull quote, **PUB 2.31, PUB 2.36-39**
Purchase order, **PUB 5.4**
.puz extension, **PUB 3.54**

Question Mark button (dialog box),
  **PUB A.8**
Quitting Publisher, PUB 1.41

Readme file, **PUB 3.51**
Read-only attribute, file, **PUB 5.22**
Recoloring graphics, **PUB 4.27**
Rectangle, **PUB 1.29**
Rectangle Tool button (Objects toolbar),
  PUB 4.13
Redo button (Standard toolbar),
  **PUB 1.50**
Replacing
  placeholder text, PUB 3.9-10
  text, using imported file, PUB 2.17-20
Reset button, **PUBW 1.12**
Reset command button, **PUB 5.42**
Resetting menus and Wizards,
  PUB C.1-2

Resizer icon, **PUB 1.30**
Resizing, **PUB 1.31**
  graphic, PUB 1.31-33
  grouped heading, PUB 1.30-31
  imported images, PUB 3.17
Resolution, **PUB 5.12**
Response form, **PUB 3.37**
Rotation
  banner, PUB 3.34
  Measurements toolbar and, PUB 4.23,
    PUB 4.24
Rows, PUB 5.22
  calendar, PUB 3.41
  selecting, PUB 3.46
Ruler
  table and, PUB 5.27
  tools, PUB 5.15
Ruler guides, **PUB 4.7**
  setting, **PUB 4.7-9**
Rulers, **PUB 1.15**
Rulers command (View menu), PUB 4.7
Ruling lines, PUB 2.41

Save As command (File menu),
  PostScript file, PUB 3.54
Save As Web Page command (File
  menu), PUB 1.53
Save button (Standard toolbar),
  PUB 1.26
Save command (File menu), PUB 1.28
Save reminder feature, **PUB 1.26**
Saving
  existing publication with same file
    name, PUB 1.39
  intermediate copy of publication,
    PUB 2.22
  new publication, PUB 1.26-29
  publication as HTML file, PUBW 1.1
  publication as Web page, PUB 1.53
  Web site, PUBW 1.13-14
Scaling graphics, **PUB 4.24, PUB 4.27**
Scanned images, PUB 1.35, PUB 3.14
Scratch area, **PUB 3.22**
ScreenTip, **PUB 1.16**, PUB 1.18
  detailed, PUB A.8
Search engines, **PUBW 1.5**
Search keyword, inserting clip art using,
  PUB 3.17-18
Searching
  for graphic, PUB 2.32-35
  Publisher Help window and,
    PUB A.7-8
Select, **PUB 1.15**
Select All command (Edit menu),
  **PUB 5.6**, PUB 5.8
Selected, **PUB 1.12**
Selected Objects, **PUB 1.23**
Selecting
  all objects, PUB 5.6
  entire text, PUB 2.18
  large amounts of text, PUB 2.14
  multiple objects, PUB 1.29

placeholder text, PUB 3.9
table rows and columns, PUB 3.46
table, PUB 5.24, PUB 5.28
Selector buttons, **PUB 5.24**
Send command (File menu), **PUB 5.33**
Send to Back command (Arrange menu), PUB 4.34
Send to Background command (Arrange menu), PUB 2.50
Separated color, **PUB 3.49**
Sessions, **PUB 3.55**
Set up publication for printing, **PUB 3.48**
Shade fill effect, **PUB 4.16**
Shadow, table, **PUB 5.22**
Shapes
  logo, PUB 3.20-22
  WordArt, PUB 2.45-46
Short menu, **PUB 1.15**
Shortcut menu, PUB 1.20, **PUB 1.38**
Show Boundaries and Guides command (View menu), PUB 4.7
Show/Hide Wizard button (status bar), **PUB 1.14, PUB 1.17, PUB 3.9**
Show Special Characters button (Standard toolbar), PUB 5.15, PUB 5.16
Show the Office Assistant command (Help menu), **PUB A.3**
Shrink Text On Overflow, fitting text in text frame, **PUB 1.20**
Sidebar, **PUB 2.31, PUB 2.39**
  deleting, PUB 2.32
  editing, PUB 2.39-40
Sign-up form, **PUB 3.37**
  editing, PUB 3.37-38
Single-line text box, **PUB 5.42, PUB 5.43**
Size
  custom, PUB 4.38-42
  line, PUB 2.42
  paper, PUB 4.7, PUB 4.38
  toolbar, PUB 4.23
Size and Position command (Format menu), PUB 1.31, PUB 1.32, **PUB 3.32, PUB 3.39,** PUB 3.40
Sizing, Measurements toolbar and, PUB 4.23
Sizing handles, **PUB 1.15, PUB 1.18**
  corner, PUB 3.33
  middle, PUB 3.33
Smart object wizard, **PUB 1.46**
Snap to Guides command (Tools menu), **PUB 1.29,** PUB 2.47
Snap to Objects command (Tools menu), **PUB 1.29,** PUB 2.47
Snap to Ruler command (Tools menu), **PUB 1.29,** PUB 2.47
Snapping, **PUB 1.29**
Source publication, **PUBI 1.1**
Special Fold layout, **PUB 4.42**

Special Size layout, **PUB 4.42**
Spell checker, PUB 2.52-55, PUB 3.12
Spelling command (Tools menu), PUB 2.52, PUB 2.53, PUB 3.12
Spelling errors, PUB 2.52-55
Spot color, **PUB 3.49**
Spot-color printing, **PUB 3.49**
Standard for Web Offset Printing (SWOP), PUB 3.49
Standard toolbar, **PUB 1.16**
Starting Publisher 2000, PUB 1.9-10, PUB 3.7
Statement, **PUB 5.4**
Status bar, **PUB 1.17**
Story, continuing across text frames, PUB 2.20
Style, **PUB 4.27-29**
Style box (Formatting toolbar), PUB 4.28
Submit button, **PUBW 1.12, PUB 5.41**
Submit command button, **PUB 5.42**
Subsetting, **PUB 5.14**
SVGA, **PUB 5.12**
SWOP printing, PUB 3.49
Symbol command (Insert menu), **PUB 3.22,** PUB 3.29
Symbol text frame, PUB 3.22-26
Synchronization, text frames and, PUB 3.35, PUB 4.20
Synchronized, **PUB 1.24**
Synchronizing, **PUB 2.25**
System attribute, file, **PUB 5.22**
System date and time, **PUB 5.17**
System Info button (About Microsoft Publisher dialog box), **PUB A.10**

Tab, **PUB 5.15**
Tab stop, **PUB 5.15-16, PUB 5.17**
Tab stop marker, **PUB 5.16**
Table, **PUB 3.41**
  entering data in, PUB 5.26-27
  selecting, PUB 5.24, PUB 5.28
Table Frame Tool button (Objects toolbar), PUB 3.46, **PUB 5.22**
Table menu
  Cell Diagonals command, PUB 5.24, PUB 5.25
  Fill command, PUB 5.27-30
  Grow to Fit Text command, **PUB 5.32**
  Merge Cells command, PUB 5.24, PUB 5.25
Table selector, **PUB 3.46**
Tags, **PUBW 1.5**
Tear-offs, **PUB 1.23-25**
Tech Support button (About Microsoft Publisher dialog box), **PUB A.10**
Templates, **PUB 1.10**
  access to, PUB 2.7
  invoice, PUB 5.6-19
  newsletter, PUB 2.8-13
Templates button (Catalog), **PUB 2.7**

Text
  adding in text frame, PUB 1.22-23
  autofit, PUB 1.19, PUB 1.20, PUB 3.25
  best fit, PUB 1.19, PUB 3.25
  brochure, PUB 3.9-13
  creating in columns, PUB 2.21
  fitting in text frames, PUB 1.20, PUB 2.25
  importing for newsletter, PUB 2.17-22, PUB 2.25-28
  placeholder, selecting, PUB 3.9
  replacing using imported file, PUB 2.17-20
  selecting entire, PUB 2.18
  selecting large amounts of, PUB 2.14
  wrapping, PUB 1.19, PUB 2.17, PUB 3.13
Text boxes, PUB 5.42
Text File command (Insert menu), PUB 2.18, PUB 2.26
Text frame(s), **PUB 1.17, PUB 2.47**
  adding text in, PUB 1.22-23
  border, PUB 1.36-37
  brochure, PUB 3.9-13
  color, PUB 1.36-37
  columns within, PUB 2.25-28
  connected, PUB 2.21
  continuing story across, PUB 2.20
  fitting text in, PUB 1.20, PUB 2.25
  instruction, PUB 5.38
  letterhead, PUB 4.16
  line spacing, PUB 3.13
  newsletter masthead, PUB 2.13-14
  page numbers in, PUB 2.47
  sending to background, PUB 2.50
  symbol, PUB 3.22-26
  synchronization and, PUB 3.35, PUB 4.20
  transparent, PUB 2.52
  Web site, PUBW 1.6-7
Text Frame Properties command (Format menu), PUB 2.27
Text Frame Tool (Objects toolbar), PUB 1.17, PUB 2.48
Text in Overflow indicator, **PUB 2.26**
Text style, importing, PUB 4.35-38
Text Style command (Format menu), PUB 4.29, PUB 4.35
Thread, **PUB 3.55**
Threading, **PUB 3.55**
3-D effect, PUB 3.42
Tile printing, PUB 5.53
Tile windows, **PUB 3.57**
Time
  inserting, PUB 2.51
  system, PUB 5.17
Timecards, **PUB 5.4**
Tint fill effect, **PUB 4.16**
Toggle, **PUB 2.20**
Toolbars, **PUB 1.16**
  displaying, PUB 1.15
  docked, PUB 1.17

floating, PUB 1.17
hiding, PUB 4.7
size of, PUB 4.23
Toolbars command (View menu),
   PUB 1.16
Measurements, PUB 4.27
positioning calendar, **PUB 3.41**
size, PUB 4.23
Tools menu
Commercial Printing Tools command,
   PUB 3.50, PUB 5.14
Design Checker command, overlap,
   PUB 3.43
Options command, resetting usage
   data, PUB C.1-2
Options command, wizard step-by-
   step questioning, PUB 3.7
Snap to Guides command, PUB 1.29,
   PUB 2.47
Snap to Objects command, PUB 1.29,
   PUB 2.47
Snap to Ruler command, PUB 1.29,
   PUB 2.47
Spelling command, PUB 2.52,
   PUB 2.53, PUB 3.12
Tracking, **PUB 4.24**
Transparent text frame, **PUB 2.52**
Trapping, **PUB 3.43**
Trapping command (Tools menu,
   Commercial Printing Tools
   submenu), **PUB 5.14**
Tri-fold brochure, PUB 3.4-58
TrueType fonts, PUB 4.28
Tutorials, PUB 1.55-56
20 lb bond paper, **PUB 3.48**
Two-sided page, printing, PUB 2.57-58

Undo button (Standard toolbar),
   **PUB 1.50**
Undo command (Edit menu), PUB 2.31
Ungrouping objects, PUB 2.35
Unpack.exe, **PUB 3.51**
Up cap, **PUB 5.14**
Uploading, **PUB 1.51**
Usage data, resetting, PUB C.1-2
Use the Office Assistant check box
   (Options sheet of Office Assistant
   dialog box), **PUB A.3**

Variegated fonts, **PUB 4.18**
View(s)
page, PUB 1.23
toggling between, PUB 2.20
whole page, PUB 1.23, PUB 2.25

View menu
Go To Background command,
   PUB 2.51
Go to Page command, PUB 2.13
Hide Boundaries and Guides
   command, PUB 3.47
Rulers command, PUB 4.7
Show Boundaries and Guides
   command, PUB 4.7
Toolbars command, PUB 1.16
Toolbars command, Measurements,
   PUB 4.27
Toolbars command, positioning
   calendar, PUB 3.41
Toolbars command, size, PUB 4.23
Zoom command, PUB 1.22, PUB 1.23
Watermark, PUB 2.47
Web
coupons on, PUB 4.43
graphics on, PUB 1.33
newsletters on, PUB 2.5
Web folder, **PUB B.1**
Web masthead, PUB 5.36-38
Web objects, editing, PUBW 1.6-12
Web page
background, PUB 5.54
creating from scratch, PUB 5.36-39
formatting, PUBW 1.7
publishing to Web server, PUB B.1
saving publication as, PUB 1.53
with electronic forms, PUB 5.35-36
Web Page Preview button (Standard
   toolbar), PUBW 1.13
Web Page Preview command (File
   menu), PUBW 1.13
Web Page Wizard, **PUBW 1.1,**
   PUBW 1.3-4
Web properties, editing, PUBW 1.5-6
Web Properties command (File menu),
   PUBW 1.5
Web server, publishing Office Web pages
   to, PUB B.1
Web site, **PUBW 1.1**
address, PUBW 1.6
creating, PUBW 1.1-15, PUB 1.50-54
navigating, PUBW 1.6
saving, PUBW 1.13-14
viewing, PUBW 1.13
Web style folders, PUB 1.51, PUB 1.54
What's This? Button (dialog box),
   PUB A.8
Whole Page command (shortcut menu),
   PUB 1.49
Whole page view, **PUB 1.23**, PUB 2.25

Width, character, PUB 4.24
Window
Publisher, PUB 1.14-17
tile, PUB 3.57
Windows 98, PUB 1.50-51
Wizards, **PUB 1.10, PUB 2.7**
Answer, PUB A.6-7
brochure, PUB 3.7-9
Business Card, PUB 4.30
Business Forms, PUB 5.6
Envelope, PUB 4.43-44
Flyer, PUB 1.10-14
hiding, PUB 2.10
Label, PUB 4.49
newsletter, PUB 2.8-11
Pack and Go, PUB 3.51-54
panes, PUB 3.7
resetting, PUB C.1-2
smart object, PUB 1.46
turning off step-by-step questioning,
   PUB 3.7
Web Page, PUBW 1.1, PUBW 1.3-4
Word, importing styles from, PUB 4.35
WordArt, **PUB 2.44-46**
WordArt Frame Tool button (Objects
   toolbar), PUB 2.44
Words, flagged, PUB 1.20, PUB 4.20
Wordwrap, **PUB 1.19**
Worksheet, linked, PUBI 1.1-10
Workspace, **PUB 1.14**, PUB 3.22,
   PUB 4.7
Wrapping, **PUB 2.17**, PUB 3.13

Years, two-digit, PUB 5.17
Your Objects (Design Gallery tab),
   **PUB 1.46**

Zoom box (Standard toolbar),
   PUB 1.23
Zoom buttons, PUB 1.20-21, 20
Zoom command (View menu),
   PUB 1.22, **PUB 1.23**
Zoom In button, PUB 1.21, PUB 2.20
Zoom list, **PUB 1.23**
Zoom Out button, PUB 2.20
Zooming
editing and, PUB 4.31
IntelliMouse® and, PUB 4.12
Zoom box, PUB 1.23
Zoom buttons, PUB 1.20-21,
   PUB 2.20